Shigo, Alex L., 1930-
   A new tree biology: facts, photos, and philosophies on trees
and their problems and proper care / by Alex L. Shigo.
2nd ed.
   p. 636   cm. 23
   Bibliography: p. 601
   Includes index
   ISBN 0-943563-04-6:
   1. Trees.   2. Trees, Care of.   I. Title.
QK475.S44   1988
635.9'77 — dc19   88-30634
                                                        CIP

Seventh Printing, 1995
Second Edition, 1989
Copyright 1986 by Shigo and Trees, Associates.
Durham, New Hampshire 03824   USA

Printed in the United States of America
by Sherwin Dodge, Printer, Littleton, New Hampshire

DEDICATION

To Marilyn

The Author—Alex L. Shigo was born in Duquesne, Pennsylvania on May 8, 1930. He received his BS in Biology from Waynesburg College in 1956 and his MS and PhD in Plant Pathology from West Virginia University in 1958 and 1959, respectively. From 1959 to 1985 he was employed by the US Forest Service as chief scientist and Project Leader of a Pioneering Project on Discoloration and Decay in Forest Trees. He has dissected over 15,000 trees with a chainsaw. He has studied trees in many countries. His research yielded 270 publications and he has received many honors and awards. He believes that we must help trees by helping the people who work with trees by providing sound educational programs based on research.

A NEW TREE BIOLOGY

A New Tree Biology is a guide to a better understanding of trees and their problems and proper care.

Trees must be touched to be understood.

EDUCATION starts when you doubt something.

EDUCATION occurs when you resolve your doubts.

Figure 1.
A New Tree Biology is about the life, problems, and proper care of trees. *A New Tree Biology* can only be understood by touching trees.

Figure 2.

A New Tree Biology is a tree-touchers guide to the most massive, longest lived, and tallest organisms ever to inhabit earth. Trees support more communities of living things than any other organism on earth.

PREFACE

RESPECT is what I have always had for the people who work with trees. It is hard work to cut trees in the forest, and to care for trees in the cities, parks, orchards, nurseries, backyards, or wherever the trees grow.

TREE PEOPLE have shared their delights and problems with me for over 30 years. They have been a major force guiding my research. I have tried to gear my research to their needs.

CONVERSATIONS with tree people have been like a constant ribbon through my life. I have tried to organize this book as a continuation of our conversations; as if we are still talking.

THE NEW TREE BIOLOGY DICTIONARY should be used with this book.

The facts, photos, and philosophies in this book, and the dictionary, have come to me from many people and sources. My role has been primarily as a connector of the collections of all the material.

SPECIAL THANKS GO TO
MANY PEOPLE AND SOURCES:

THE UNITED STATES FOREST SERVICE for supporting my research for 26 years, and for use of most of the photographs.

Dr. H. L. Barnett, University of West Virginia, for giving me my background in mycology and pathology.

Prof. Dr. Josef Bauch, University of Hamburg, West Germany, for collaborative research that helped to expand the concepts of tree decay.

Prof. Dr. Aloys Bernatsky, Frankfurt, West Germany, for taking the messages of the new tree biology to many doubters in West Germany.

Dr. Robert Blanchette, University of Minnesota, for beautiful scanning electron micrographs (Figures 4-24, 4-25, 4-26, 4-27, 4-28, 4-29, 4-30, 4-31, 4-34).

Mr. and Mrs. Robert Bickelhaupt, Bickelhaupt Arboretum, Iowa for figure 10-13.

Dr. and Mrs. Stephen Botek for the petrified wood shown in figure 1-6.

Dr. Charles L. Bryner, Waynesburg, Pennsylvania, for giving me my background in botany.

Prof. Dr. Heinz Butin, Institute for Plant Protection, Braunsweig, West Germany, for information on cracks and on the fungi that infect dying branches.

Dr. Richard Campana, University of Maine (Retired), for help in obtaining the photographs on injected elms (figures 40-1, 2, and 3).

Mr. Francis De Jonghe, Arborist, France, for taking the concepts to France.

Mr. Philipp Dienst, Arborist, Mainz, West Germany, for organizing educational programs on the new tree biology in Europe.

Mr. Kenneth Dudzik, U.S. Forest Service, for taking many of the photographs and for printing most of them.

Mr. Robert Felix and the **National Arborist Association Inc.** for organizing educational programs on the new tree biology in the U.S.A. and for "taking me in."

Ms. Tess Feltes, Illustrator, Portsmouth, NH, for figures 12-2 and 12-5.

Mr. Pius Floris, Arborist, and **Jitze Kopinga**, Researcher, Holland, for taking the concepts to Holland.

Forestry Commission of New South Wales, Australia, for photographs of sections I cut in 1980; figures 2-22, 3-20, 3-42, 13-11, 17-5, 24-6, 24-7, 34-12.

Dr. Peter Garrett, U.S. Forest Service, for help on the genetics studies.

Mr. Denne Goldstein, Publisher, California, for giving me opportunities through Arbor Expo to reach the people who need the new information.

Dr. Richard Hammerschlag and **Dr. James Scherald** for making photographs in figures 1-32, 1-33, 1-34 possible.

Dr. George H. Hepting, U.S. Forest Service, Retired, for the photograph of the "old days," figure 2-1.

Drs. Martin Hubbes and **Vidar Nordin**, University of Toronto, for giving me 14 years of discussions with students and professors at the University of Toronto.

Mr. Niels Hvass, Copenhagen, Denmark, for photographs from Denmark and other countries (Figures 1-12, 10-14, 10-15, 35-17, 18, 19, & 21).

Mr. Robert Keller, Arborist, Frankfurt, West Germany, for samples that were photographed in Durham (Figures 2-24, 16-16, 39-9, 43-10 & 11).

Mr. Byron Kirby, Arborist, Exeter, New Hampshire, for many wood samples, especially of elms infected by the Dutch elm disease fungus.

Mr. Lee Lesh, Arborist, Saratoga, California, for the wood carving shown in figure 1-3.

Prof. Dr. Walter Liese, University of Hamburg, West Germany, for introducing me to tree scientists in Europe and for many helpful discussions on the new tree biology.

Mr. William Matthews, Arborist, England, for taking the new concepts to England, and other countries in Europe.

Dr. E. Alan McGinnes and **Nelson Rogers**, University of Missouri and U.S. Forest Service, respectively, for making it possible to study black walnut and for making many of the photographs of black walnut possible, and Figure 16-7.

Walter Money and **Charles Cissel**, Arborists, Bethesda, MD, for introducing me to the arborists.

Dr. John Mulhern, Physics Department, University of New Hampshire, for information and samples on electrophysiology (Figure 49-1).

H. Sharon Ossenbruggen, for the models shown in figures 2-35, 2-36, 34-40.

Richard Pratt, Arborist, Drakes Well, Pennsylvania, for samples and information on wounds made by climbing spikes.

Mr. William Rae and others, Arborists, Boston, Massachusetts, for providing wood samples with hardware.

Director Karl Roy, Bavaria State School for Violin Building, Mittenwald, West Germany for loan of the violins shown in Figure 1-4, and wood samples used for Figure 16-20.

Nicholas Rivett, Rivett Enterprises, Melbourne, Australia, for supporting 3 visits to Australia, and making it possible to learn about many trees in Australia, and to take many of the photos shown here of Australian trees.

Dr. Walter Shortle, my long-time colleague, for information on biochemistry.

Drs. Richard Skutt and **Ronald Lessard** for making the first pulsed electric current meter, the Shigometer, and to **Mr. Harold Wochholz** for making the first commercial model, and to **Robert Birtz** who later made the first digital model.

Dr. Joanna Tippett, Western Australia, for information on roots (Figures 31-5, 6, 7, & 8) and for photographs on kino veins in species of Eucalyptus (Figures 9-9, 9-10).

Dr. Tom van der Zwet, ARS, Kearneysville, West Virginia, for information and samples on fire blight.

Mr. Klaus Vollbrecht, Alnarp, Sweden, for photographs from Sweden (Figures 1-8, 11-1, 35-14, 15, & 16, 39-12, 13, 14, & 15).

Dr. Charles Wilson and **Dr. Michael Wisniewski**, ARS, Kearneysville, West Virginia for photographs on cells and mycoplasmas (Figures 4-33, 9-3).

Dr. George Yelenosky, ARS, Orlando, Florida, who helped me dissect many trees "in the beginning."

AND

My wonderful daughter, **Judy Ruth Smith**, who typed the entire manuscript from sheets with scribbles often almost (?) impossible to read!

My buddy, **Mr. Toby**, who saw to it that I spent a lot of time in the woods, touching trees, while the conversations went on and on.

Marilyn, who always understood.

Contents

A NEW TREE BIOLOGY

FACTS, PHOTOS, AND PHILOSOPHIES ON
TREES AND THEIR PROBLEMS AND
PROPER CARE

Chapter 1

Introduction

Figure 1-3

Early man recognized the value of trees. Trees were worshiped by some groups because the gods and spirits were thought to inhabit trees. This carving is an 18-inch long resin-soaked branch core wood from a pine in southwestern U.S.A.

Wood was used for a great variety of instruments. The spirits in the wood were released in melody and rhythm. Man and trees have developed close associations. The violins were made by the Bavarian State School for Violin Building in Mittenwald, West Germany.

Figure 1-4

Figure 1-5

Wood has always been used by man for a great number of products: timber for building, and for ships, paper and poles. Breakdown of wood products by microorganisms and insects has always been a problem. Wood contains cellulose, and cellulose is made up of glucose units, and glucose is used for energy by many organisms. The utility pole shown here was attacked by fungi and ants. Termites are major problems for wood products in warm climates.

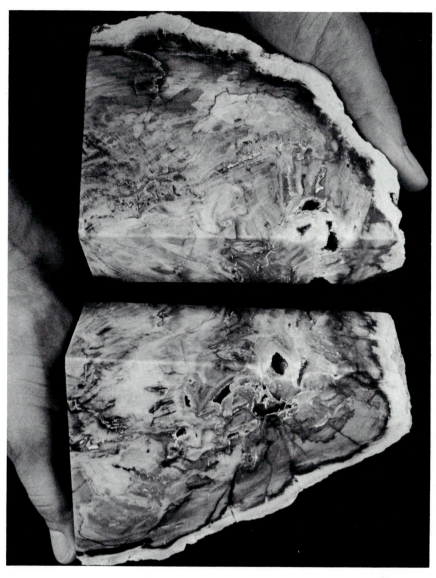

Figure 1-6

Breakdown of wood by many types of organisms has followed the evolution of trees. These sections of petrified wood from Brazil show hollows where the wood was decayed.

Trees as we know them today began to evolve over 200 million years ago. Some of the continents and islands that are present today may have been connected at that time. But, even if they were not, it appears that trees evolved about several basic themes. Many variations on the themes developed. For example, the seed cone from the banksia tree from Australia does resemble the cone from a pine from the U.S.A. Pines evolved in the northern hemisphere, and banksias and eucalypts evolved in Australia. Yes, pines and eucalypts are different in many ways, yet they are similar in their general makeup and function; the themes are the same.

Figure 1-7

Figure 1-8

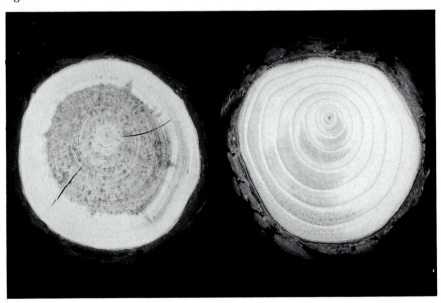

The above sections from 2 Scots pines reinforces the point about themes and variations. At left is a 150-year-old section from a pine near a bog in Lapland. At right is an 8-year-old section from a pine near a bog in Maine, U.S.A. Age and size are not related in trees. The themes of trees must have had high survival value, or, the factors that had high survival value became the themes.

A New Tree Biology

This sample of teak, which grows in many areas of southeast Asia, shows a trunk 10 years after 2 branches died and were shed. Insects infested the branch at left. Strong protection zones formed at the base of the branches. The zones resisted spread of micro-organisms into the trunk. Even the insects were confined to the branch core wood. Trees have evolved as highly compartmented plants that have many protection zones.

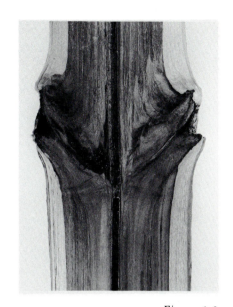

Figure 1-9

Figure 1-10

This Honduras mahogany, which grows in the tropics, had a branch at right that died and was effectively walled off. The branch at left was pruned. The pruning cut removed the natural protection zone at the branch base. Even though the wound closed, decay-causing microorganisms infected the trunk. Treatments that destroy natural protection zones cause trees serious injury.

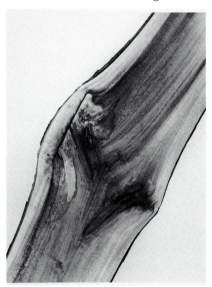

Figure 1-11

Pathogens can easily spread into trees when natural protection zones are destroyed. Pathogens caused a perennial canker on this acacia tree in Australia after the pruning cut removed the protection zone at the branch base. Just as trees developed themes for their construction — anatomy — and function — physiology — trees also developed themes for their protection and defense. Or it could be stated that the themes for protection and defense guided the themes for anatomy and physiology.

Figure 1-12

In Copenhagen, Denmark, people always cluster about this large, old, sycamore tree in winter and summer. Man has evolved along with trees as a friend and foe. Man had a "taking relationship" with trees, but this was no real problem because land that supported trees was so much greater than land that supported man. But, this situation has changed drastically during the last few centuries. Man and trees are now competing for space. Man can move. Trees can not move. Man still wants to continue the "taking relationship."

A New Tree Biology

New tools and machines have accelerated the taking of trees. Yes, trees are needed by man, and yes, trees should be cut. But, the taking process is more than the removal of trees.

Figure 1-13

Figure 1-14

Not only are trees being wounded during the taking processes, but forests are being wounded: soil compaction, disruption of water drainage patterns, disruption of soil temperatures, disruption of soil organisms.

Wood quality of residual trees is reduced as new machines and methods cause wounds higher on the trunk. This is the most valuable part of the tree for timber. *Figure 1-15*

Small wounds may start vertical cracks that cause serious economic damage. *Figure 1-16*

Machine-caused root and butt injuries may cause a slow death to young trees such as the black walnut shown here. *Figure 1-17*

This large old spruce may not die from the wound, but the fruit bodies of decay-causing fungi (arrows) indicate advanced decay in the valuable butt section. *Figure 1-18*

8

A New Tree Biology

Trees evolved in groups. The mixture of species in a group must have had some role in the survival of the few individuals that grew to maturity. Note the form of the black walnut trees (white bands) in a forest in southern Illinois, U.S.A. Some people call the other trees forest weeds. We know so little about the role of these "weeds" as they affect the trees we want and call valuable!

Figure 1-20

Figure 1-19
Figure 1-21

Of course each tree in a forest is an individual, but the collection of individuals of the same species makes up a species group. And, further, the species groups — now as an individual — make up the forest group. These black walnut trees grew from seeds planted on strip mine spoils 40 years before the photograph was taken. Almost all of the black walnut trees in this species group had very poor form, poor vitality, and many defects.

On the same site as described in Figure 20, a few black walnut trees grew rapidly, had good form, and few defects. Another triumph for genetic selection is the easy answer. The difficult question is what have we done to the gene pool in our forests after 2 centuries of high grading (cutting the best and leaving the worst)?

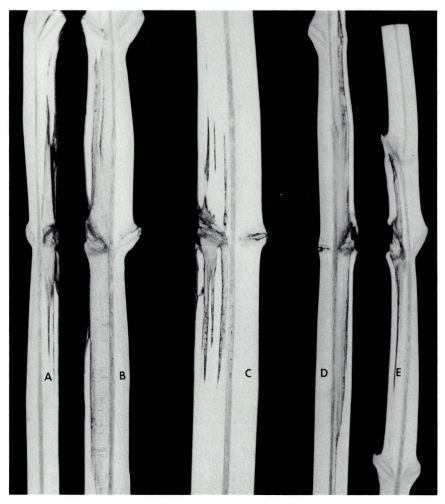

Figure 1-22

The power of genetic variability can not be over stressed. We know that some individual trees of a species are tougher, more defect resistant, and faster growing than other individuals. Attention in genetic selections in forestry has been primarily set for rapid growth. Yet, recent research shows that some clones of several tree species not only grow fast, but also resist the spread of defects caused by pathogens. Here is an example: All red maple stems above received a harsh flush cut (removal of the branch collar and the branch protection zone). One year after the wound, the stems were dissected. All stems in clones A and B developed cankers, but very little defect developed in stems from clone A. All stems in clones D and E did not develop cankers. Stems in clone D had large columns of discolored wood while stems in clone E had small columns of discolored wood. Stems in clone C not only resisted spread of pathogens, but the stems grew rapidly. All stems were 3 years old.

A New Tree Biology

High quality logs for valuable wood products are in high demand. The value of some high quality logs, such as a few of the black walnut logs shown here, may reach into the thousands of dollars. Even though some of the logs are free of defects, their small size limits their value. It is getting more difficult to get large, defect-free logs.

Figure 1-23

These black walnut cants are ready to be sliced for veneer. There is still a great amount of land available that can produce high value trees. The story is not all gloom and doom. But, it will be if some changes are not made soon.

Figure 1-24

An abundance of wood is available in many of the forests of the world. Much of the timber is still old growth from areas never cut.

Figure 1-25

Defects caused by decay are a major cause of low quality. Having an abundance of wood, and having an abundance of high quality wood are two different points.

Figure 1-26

Figure 1-27

The wood chipping industries have increased dramatically during the last 2 decades. Wood chips are used to heat factories or to generate power as shown here. Large chipping machines are moving into forests like hungry prehistoric monsters. They "eat" everything in their path. The chips are removed and reconstituted into a great variety of "wood" products. In many ways, this is good. The highly defective, low quality wood is used. And, there is an abundance of such wood in our forests. The sad part is that high quality trees in the chipping site often are also chipped (in some cases, there is a sorting process). The increase in the chipping industries attests to the fact that many forests contain low quality trees. Further, even chipping is not always the answer because products made from highly defective chips cause problems in manufacturing, and in the product.

Man wants forests also for recreation. Sad but true that man often causes trees near recreation sites serious injuries.

Figure 1-28

Figure 1-29

Stripping bark from birch trees can cause the ultimate injury — death. The bark is often taken as a souvenir of a great time in the north wood. Most people really do not think such bark stripping will hurt the tree. Education is the only answer.

Figure 1-30

Back home man still wants to continue the closeness with trees. This valley oak in southern California was dead 2 years after the photograph was taken.

Figure 1-31

This beech in North Carolina survived for one more year after this photograph was taken. The building, sidewalk, and road caused the tree serious injuries. Note the dead branches over the building. This is not a rare scene. Sadly it is too common. Again, people need to be made aware of the survival limits of trees.

Many trees are committed to an early death even before they are planted, or soon after they are planted. Many of these trees died. Root injuries due to improper digging, roots drying in the ball, planting in smooth-sided small holes, high amounts of fertilizer applied at planting time, and lack of water are common causes of early death. There is no excuse for these insults!

Figure 1-32

Figure 1-33

A fruit body of a decay-causing fungus was at the base of this tree 2 years after it was planted. The roots were injured during planting. The healthy, well-fertilized grass close to the tree base added to the tree's problems. Indeed, it is time to educate people about trees and their proper care.

Figure 1-34

Tree care to some people means covering wounds and improperly pruned branches with thick, dripping coats of wound dressing.

Figure 1-35

Thick bands of callus, as seen about this wound, are thought to indicate strong "wound healing." Trees do not heal wounds and thick callus is not associated with the development of decay. The old branch wound has been thickly-coated with wound dressing as was the most recently cut branch stub at right. The fruit bodies of the fungi associated with the decayed wood are at the bottom of the wound. The tree failed at the wound site in a storm a week after the photograph was taken. Hazard trees not only destroy property and power lines, but also people.

A New Tree Biology

Power lines, roads, driveways, houses, cars, and people are crowding trees. And the trees can not move away. They die!

Figure 1-36

Figure 1-37

Man always has a ready answer: Dutch elm disease, gypsy moth, acid rain, and an endless number of bugs and diseases. Yes, these are all agents that could cause problems and kill trees. But, it is time to recognize that man also plays a role in the many problems trees have worldwide. Man is a major part of the problem. Man can be a major part of the solution.

Trees dying in forests have been a common problem during the last decade. Chestnut blight all but eliminated a species. American chestnut trees are still abundant, but mostly as small trees. Birch dieback later took its toll. The beech bark disease killed American beech in New England. The dead trees in the foreground of this photograph are beech trees mostly. Higher on the slopes are dying red spruce trees (arrows). The photograph was taken near Hubbard Brook in the White Mountains National Forest of New Hampshire in 1960.   *Figure 1-38*

The aim of this guide is to help trees by helping the people who work with trees. The best way to help people who work with trees is to give them — you — clear, correct, and complete information on trees and their problems and proper care.

You can not separate the 3 points. Proper care depends on a clear understanding of the problem. An understanding of the problem depends on an understanding of the tree.

This introduction focuses on a few points: know the themes — how trees are built-up, how they defend themselves to stay built-up, and how they eventually breakdown — and what we can do to help trees wherever they grow.

What can be done? Education is the key to many people-tree-pathogen problems. This guide attempts to help solve some of these problems.

A New Tree Biology

Chapter 2

Emerging, A New Tree Biology

Figure 2-1

Trees are large, heavy plants that can kill you if they fall on you. To study trees, a keen mind is not enough. Hard physical work and skill in using many woodsman's tools are also needed for tree studies. A common trait of the early tree researchers was their eagerness to work hard in the field. This is a 1935 photograph of Harold Eno (left), Dr. George H. Hepting (center), and Dr. Perly Spaulding (right). They used axes and hand saws to cut and dissect trees. The early dissection work of Dr. Hepting set the stage for a new tree biology.

19

Figure 2-2

The lightweight, powerful chainsaw was the major tool that made it possible to dissect and study thousands of trees. From 1959 to 1985 the author (shown here in 1960) dissected over 15,000 trees with a chainsaw. Dissections made it possible to view longitudinal sections of entire trees. Early studies were mostly in birch, beech and maple that have bright, clear wood. All details could easily be seen in these trees.

Dissections showed that the central columns of discolored wood varied greatly in diameter and extent in trees of the same size, age, and species. The central colored column had many names: mineral stain, mineral streak, red heart, pink heart, heartwood, wound heartwood, pathological heartwood, precocious heartwood. Yellow birch trees 80 and 81 show the variations in central columns. Both trees had basal wounds. The color of the column in 80 was tan-pink, and did not appear moist. The column in 81 had bands of deep red with cream and black stripes. The colored wood was very moist.   *Figure 2-3*

Figure 2-4

The arrows show the wounds on paper birch 102. In many individual trees, the columns varied in size, color, and degree of moisture. Different portions of a column in the same tree could fit the names given to several types of internal colored wood; including heartwood. Dissections showed that the columns were associated with wounds.

A New Tree Biology

Columns of colored wood were also associated with old internal cores of branches. When several branches died at about the same time and position on the trunk, as shown here in a yellow birch, the diameter of the central column of discolored wood was the diameter of the tree at the time the branches died (black arrows). When hard zones formed at the base of the dead branches (white pointers) the wounds closed rapidly and the central colored wood did not appear to be altered, except for the color, which was usually a light shade of brown or pink-brown.

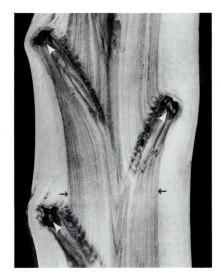

Figure 2-5

Figure 2-6

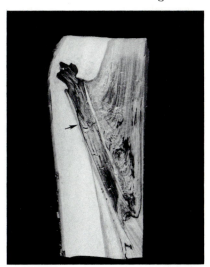

When branch stubs remained on the tree for long periods and when the hard zone at the branch base was breached by decay-causing fungi, the central core of altered wood was a deep red or pink in birch. But, the column was still confined to the wood present when the branch died (arrow).

Figure 2-7

Dissection at wounds also showed that the columns of infected wood were confined to the wood present at the time of wounding. When decay did develop, it did so within the column of discolored wood.

Figure 2-8

Dissection of red maple 103 shows the associations of branches and wounds with the internal columns. Before the chainsaw, it was very difficult to make long dissections. Concepts of discolored wood, decayed wood, and heartwood were developed from studies on cross sections. Longitudinal sections showed where the columns started — branch stubs, wounds, root injuries. As branches die, there will always be new openings into the trunk.

The old concepts of heartwood in beech, birch, and maple began to be questioned. How could it be explained that some individuals of a species had heartwood and others did not? The multitude of terms for colored wood in trees had to be addressed. This sugar maple was clear at the base but it had discolored wood above. The columns were associated with openings in the tree, and the columns were confined to wood present at the time the opening occurred.

Figure 2-9

Figure 2-10

The trunk of this sugar maple died and a branch became the new leader. The column of discolored and decayed wood was confined to the wood in the trunk at the time the top died. The new leader was free of defect. Note the cutting artifact in the base of the sections. Chainsaw dissections had to follow the curve of the pith center. This is why studies on trees cut in a saw mill give distorted views of internal columns. Straight cuts through curved cylinders will yield an artifact.

Figure 2-11

Dissection of this yellow birch shows a sound discolored core but a column of decayed wood along the outer portion of the central core (arrows). The decayed wood was associated with a large 50-year-old wound. The important point is that the decayed wood did not develop inward to the center of the tree. Why? The answer is that the central column of discolored wood was there from other wounds and branch stubs before the decay column associated with the large basal wound began to develop. An orderly pattern of defect column development began to emerge. Yet, the old concepts stated that the centers of trees were weakest, and that is why the centers were decayed first. More and more the old concepts began to be challenged on the basis of hundreds of longitudinal dissections.

A New Tree Biology

Figure 2-12

The hollow at the base of this beech (left sections) was associated with root rots. Note the clear wood surrounding the hollow. Most root and butt rot fungi do not grow upward into trunks. The wood is sound but discolored at the top of the sections at left. The diameter of the discolored wood is slightly increased because of the large branch wounds. The upper sections at right show a hollow associated with large old branches. A cross section at the base and at 10 or 12 feet above the base would both show a hollow. Longitudinal sections helped to clarify the causes of internal defects.

Emerging, A New Tree Biology

Figure 2-13

This 100-year-old paper birch had 2, 50-year-old basal wounds. The lower 8-foot-section (right) shows a hollow that was the diameter of the tree at the time the wounds were inflicted. The upper 8-foot-section (left) shows a column of discolored and decayed wood that was also the same size of the tree at the time of wounding. Hundreds of isolations for wood-inhabiting microorganisms were made from the clear and infected wood from the base of the upper sections to the tops of the sections. Over a period from 1959 to 1970, several hundred thousand isolations were made from the dissected trees. The isolations made it possible to map the position of different types of microorganisms throughout long sections of trunks.

Figure 2-14

Fungi that cause wood decay—Hymenomycetes mostly, and species in the Xylariaceae, mostly species of *Hypoxylon*—were isolated frequently from decaying wood. Under aseptic conditions, small pieces of wood were taken from the trunks and placed in a nutrient agar in Petri dishes as shown above. The microorganisms in the wood then grew out on the surface of the agar where they could be examined under a microscope and identified. The white, cottony growth from the wood is typical of many fungi that cause wood decay.

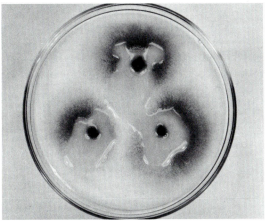

Figure 2-15

Bacteria and nondecay-causing fungi were also isolated frequently from discolored and decayed wood, and sometimes even from healthy-appearing wood. The bacteria were usually cream colored and jelly-like (clear, liquid material about the 3 dark spots in the Petri dish). The nondecay-causing fungi were greatly varied in color and growth characteristics. The black, thread-like growth in the Petri dish is an example of one of the common nondecay-causing fungi isolated from darkly colored wood in birch. The bacteria and non-decay causing fungi often grew well together in culture.

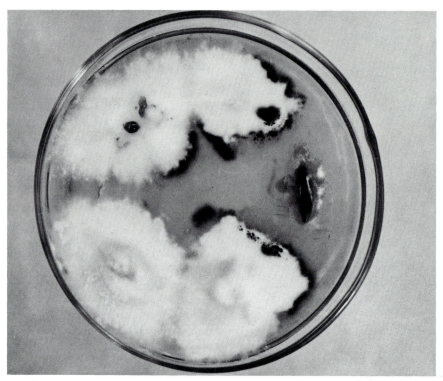

Figure 2-16

When the bacteria grew alone, they usually did not form dark pigments. The same when decay-causing fungi grew alone. But, when bacteria and decay-causing fungi grew close to each other, as shown here, dark pigments formed at the margins of the colonies. Note that only a few very small patches of white fungus growth were near the wood chip that yielded the bacteria. These early observations lead to new questions: were bacteria and nondecay-causing fungi a part of the infection process in wood, or were they just contaminates, as stated in the literature?

To this point in time most of the work was done on beech, birch and maple in northeastern U.S.A. Many questions about the development of defects in trees were awaiting answers. Questions about microorganisms and their interactions with the tree were also awaiting answers. There were great conflicts with the accepted concepts on tree decay and heartwood. It was time to expand the research to other tree species from other parts of the world.

A New Tree Biology

Figure 2-17

Dissections of black cherry showed that the decayed wood was confined to the wood present at the time of wounding (large white arrow). The decayed wood was surrounded by sound heartwood except where cracks began to form (small white arrow) and where other wounds lead to radial cracks (white pointer). The black pointer shows the bottom of the fruit body—conk, sporophore—of the decay-causing fungus associated with the decay. A monumental step forward was made when Robert Hartig in 1878 proved that the conk and the fungus causing the decay were the same organism. Before 1845 people believed that *decay caused fungi*. Hartig showed that *fungi caused decay*. The simple reversal of 2 words set the stage for new concepts in tree pathology. But, concepts are not static. Science advances as concepts are clarified further and expanded. An expanded concept of tree decay began to develop.

Figure 2-18

Studies on large, old Douglas fir trees in the Pacific Northwest, U.S.A., revealed patterns similar to those seen in beech, birch, and maple, and oak and cherry. Over 200 growth rings formed after this Douglas fir was wounded. The decay-causing fungi, and the ants, remained in the wood present at the time of wounding. Sound heartwood surrounds the central column of decayed wood. Question: If the fungi *are* heartwood-rotting fungi, why have they not grown radially into the heartwood surrounding the central column? Not enough time; 200 years?

A New Tree Biology

In many large, old trees studied in the Pacific Northwest, U.S.A, the centers were sound and decay was confined to the outer core, as in this true fir. Arrows show the size of the tree at the time of wounding. Decay developed to the arrows, but not beyond. Why? Why did the decay *not* develop rapidly into the center of the tree? The old simplistic concept that had decay developing rapidly into the central heartwood and causing hollows had to be reexamined. And, what about trees, such as birch and maple, that have no heartwood? How could you have heartwood decay, or heartrot in a tree that does not have heartwood?   *Figure 2-19*

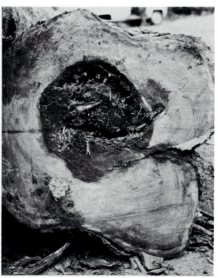

This Sitka spruce in the Pacific Northwest, U.S.A., did have a central column of advanced decayed wood. But, again the decayed wood was confined to the wood present at the time of wounding.   *Figure 2-20*

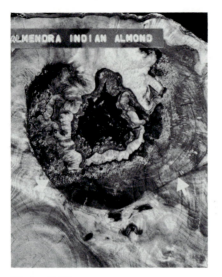

Dissections of 16 species of tropical trees growing in Puerto Rico showed patterns similar to those seen in trees in New Hampshire and the Pacific Northwest, U.S.A. Defects were confined by strong boundaries to wood present at the time of injury and infection (white arrows). *Decay did not develop freely in trees.*

Figure 2-21

Figure 2-22

Dissections of 15 species of *Eucalyptus* and related genera in Australia again showed typical patterns seen in other trees. The decayed wood in this eucalypt was confined to the sapwood present at the time of wounding. Many species of eucalypts have very durable heartwood due to chemicals — extractives — in the heartwood. Note the discolored heartwood along the radial cracks. *Heartwood does discolor.* The arrow shows a small radial crack that developed when the first callus tissues formed. The crack could break out later.

34

Figure 2-23

Dissections of many eastern white pine trees showed patterns of decay similar to other tree species. Advanced decay in the center of trees was surrounded by sound heartwood (arrows).

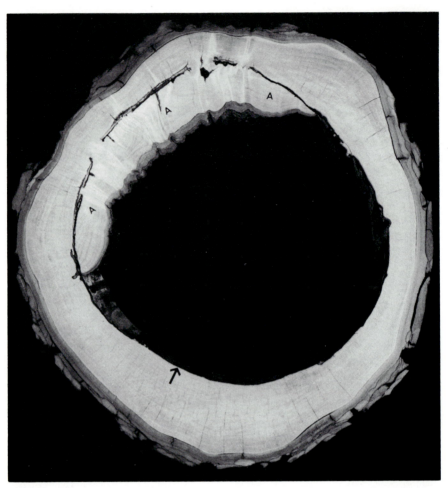

Figure 2-24

Trees in Europe were also studied. Samples, such as this maple from Frankfurt, again showed typical patterns for tree decay. The hollow was surrounded by a strong protection boundary (arrow). The callus in this sample inrolled into the top of the hollow (A).

The highly ordered patterns of discolored and decayed wood were confirmed in many species of trees from forests, orchards, and cities from many countries of the world.

Now we shall introduce some of the results from many experiments that help to clarify further the processes of discoloration and decay in trees.

A New Tree Biology

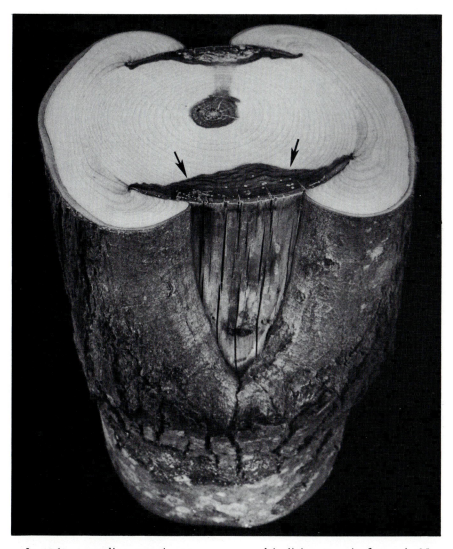

In 1962, wounding experiments were started in living trees in forests in New Hampshire. Many types of wounds were inflicted on hundreds of trees. Some wounds were inoculated with wood inhabiting microorganisms and some were not. Some wounds were treated with a great variety of materials. After one week to 17 years the trees were cut and the wounds were dissected. The results gave information on development of discolorations and decays and the infection patterns of microorganisms over time and space within the tree. This red maple is from one experiment that showed the strong boundaries (arrows) that resisted inward spread of pathogens. Callus growth was not associated with internal development of discolored wood. All 10 red maple trees in the experiment had similar patterns of callus formation and internal discoloration.   *Figure 2-25*

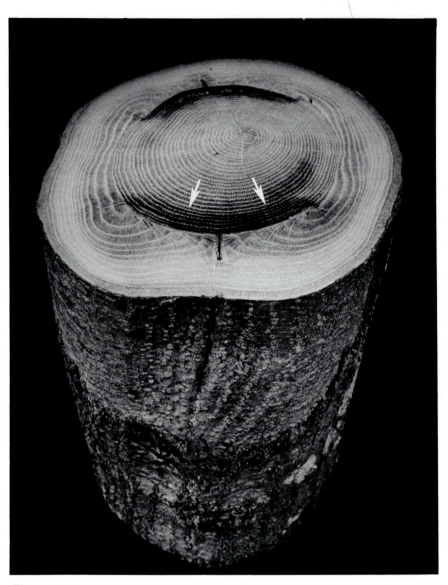

Figure 2-26

The 10 red oaks in the experiment all had closed wounds and small internal columns of discolored wood. The discolored wood was mostly the sapwood present at the time of wounding. Some internal tree mechanisms resisted inward spread of the pathogens (arrows). The pathogens did not spread rapidly into the heartwood.

A New Tree Biology

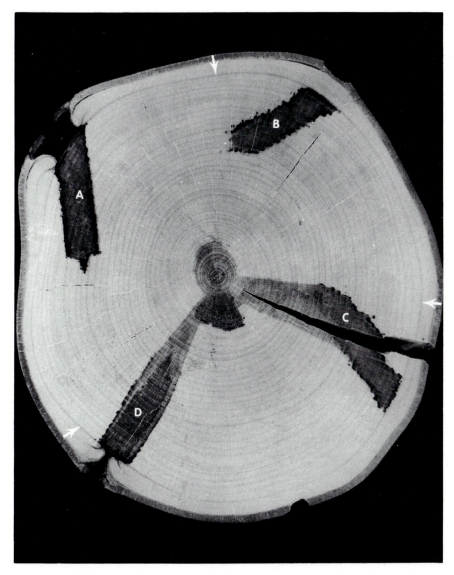

Wounds made by drill bits were used in many experiments because the wound could be replicated accurately many times. (Drill hole-type wounds are very common in nature; boring insects, bird wounds, ambrosia beetles, branch core wood (see Figure 28), and are made during many tree treatments; cable and bracing, injections, implants and increment borers.) The experiments began to shed light on the protection boundary (arrows) that formed after wounding. Wounds A and B were not close to the central core of discolored wood. Wounds C and D were close to the central core of discolored wood, and the wood between the central column and the drill wound died and discolored. *Figure 2-27*

Figure 2-28

Strong chemical protection boundaries separated decayed wood from sound wood (arrow) surrounding the dead branch core in this western hemlock from the Pacific Northwest, U.S.A. The step-like pattern of the chemical boundary from growth ring to growth ring is similar to the pattern of protective phenols produced along the margins of slanted drill holes in maple (see drill wounds B and C in Figure 27).

A New Tree Biology

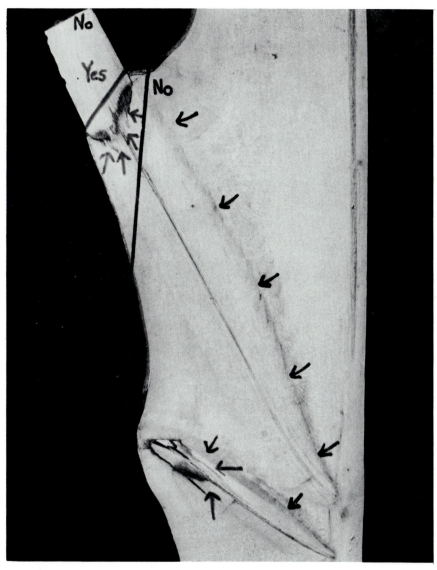

Figure 2-29

Experiments on branch development and pruning on 12 species of trees for 8 years showed that trees form strong protection boundaries at the base of dying branches. Pruning cuts that remove the boundaries lead to rapid trunk decay. The photograph shows the proper cut (YES line). The arrows at the branch base show the branch protection zone. The arrows along the branch core show the compacted xylem. The arrows below about the small branch show the results of boundaries that walled off the decayed stub.

Figure 2-30

More attention was focused on the protection boundary that formed after wounding, as shown by arrows in this western hemlock wounded by a black bear. The boundary was called a *barrier zone*. The barrier zone was characterized as a tissue that had a great amount of axial parenchyma, few conducting elements, low amounts of lignin, and in some species, suberin in the cells. Chemical boundaries within the wood present at the time of wounding resisted spread of the pathogens within the wood present at the time of wounding. This chemical boundary is called the *reaction zone*.

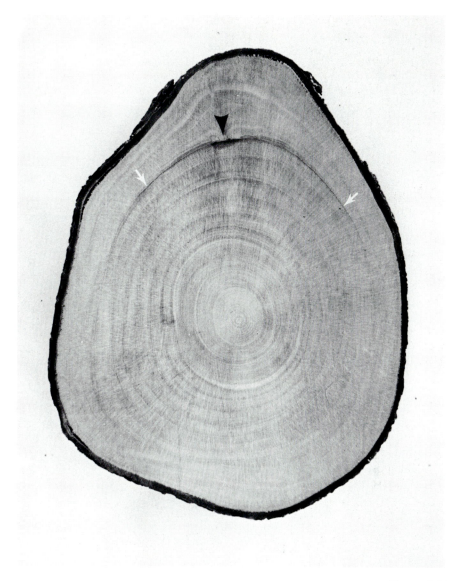

Figure 2-31

A barrier zone formed (white arrows) in this Honduras mahogany after it received a small wound (black pointer). Sometimes barrier zones will form far beyond some wounds, while in other cases the barrier zone will form only a very short distance beyond the wound. Note the slightly discolored wood behind the wound. The barrier zone does form in tropical species that do not have distinct growth rings.

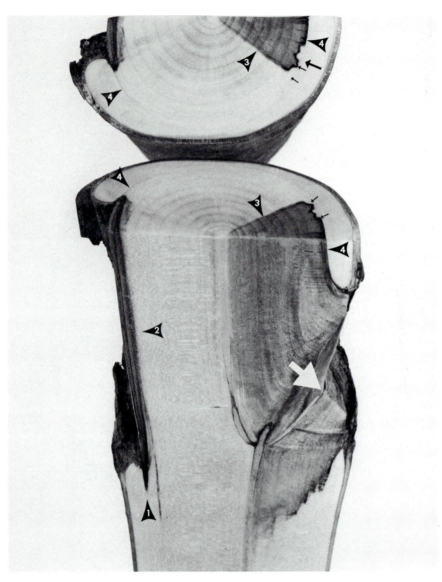

Figure 2-32

Here is a red maple sample that summarizes some points about pruning and also shows the 4 walls of CODIT. First, the pruning points.

Pruning cuts that remove the branch protection zone cause the tree serious injury. The wound at right did remove the protection zone (arrow). At left, a wound was inflicted that had the same area as the wound at right. After one year the wound at right had a large column of discolored wood while the wound of equal area at left had only a small band of discolored wood. Flush cut branches are not serious wounds because they are large but because they remove one of the major protection zones of the tree. These experiments were done on 15 trees, and the results were similar to the sample shown here.

Second, the CODIT walls. Pointer 1 shows wall 1 that resists vertical spread of pathogens. Pointer 2 shows wall 2 that resists inward spread of pathogens. There is no wall 2 in the wound at right because the discolored wood has developed inward to the pith. Walls do not stop pathogens, walls resist their spread. Pointer 3 shows wall 3 that resists lateral spread of pathogens. Walls 1, 2, and 3 make up Part I of CODIT. Wall 1 is the weakest and wall 3 is the strongest of Part I.

Pointer 4 shows wall 4, or the barrier zone. Wall 4 is the strongest protection wall of CODIT. Wall 4 is strong in a protection sense but weak in a structural sense. Wall 4 is a separating wall. It separates the inner infected wood from the healthy wood that continues to form after the barrier zone is completed.

The small arrows show the barrier zone within the growth ring. The barrier zone may form between growth rings or at any position within the growth ring depending on time of wounding.

Because the barrier zone is a structurally weak zone, cracks often start along the zone. The cracks may also develop outward in a radial path.

After 30 years of research on thousands of trees with the help and cooperation of many hard working and dedicated people, the pieces began to fall into place. Several themes became obvious: 1) Trees are highly compartmented plants. 2) Wood-inhabiting microorganisms survive by infecting wounds and dying branches and roots in succession. 3) Trees survive after injury and infection by strengthening natural protection boundaries and by forming new defense boundaries that resist spread of pathogens. 4) The effectiveness of protection and defense boundaries is under moderate to strong genetic control. (The ability of pathogens to spread beyond protection and defense boundaries may also be under moderate to strong genetic control.)

These themes have been included in an expanded concept of tree decay. To help clarify the themes and to use the information to help trees, a model of compartmentalization of decay in trees was developed. The model is called CODIT, an acronym for Compartmentalization Of Decay In Trees.

The CODIT model has 2 parts: I, walls 1, 2, and 3; II wall 4. Wall is a model term and should not be identified too closely with chemical and anatomical terms. Wall 1 resists *vertical* spread of pathogens; Wall 2 resists *inward* spread; and Wall 3 resists *lateral* spread. Walls 1, 2, and 3 are model representations of the *reaction* zone. The reaction zone is a continuous boundary about the developing column of infected wood. The walls help to identify the 3-D nature of the column. The reaction zone is the chemical strengthening of existing boundaries.

Part II is represented by Wall 4, which is the *barrier zone*. The barrier zone or Wall 4 forms after wounding. The cambium forms cells that differentiate to form the barrier zone.

Details on all of these points are given in later chapters.

Figure 2-33

This sample of a western hemlock from Washington, U.S.A. shows walls 2, 3, and 4 of CODIT. Wall 2 resisted inward spread and the center of the tree was sound. Walls 3 were also strong and the pathogens have not spread far beyond the lateral limits of the wound. Wall 4 did not form far beyond the wound. Note the thin dark boundaries along walls 3.

Figure 2-34   Page 30

Buck shot caused the wound in this red oak 9 years before the tree was cut. The wound closed after 4 years. Four growth rings of sound heartwood surround the wound. Walls 2 resisted inward spread and walls 3 resisted lateral spread. The tree had 5 growth rings of sapwood at the time of wounding. The decay causing fungi had spread into the heartwood present at the time of wounding. But, note the dark band of discolored heartwood surrounding the decayed wood. The discolored heartwood acts as a defense boundary. Protection boundaries are static and formed after injury and infection. Defense boundaries are dynamic and formed after injury and infection. Heartwood does compartmentalize.

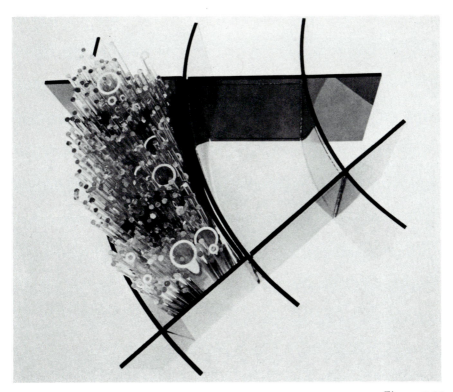

Figure 2-35

Models were constructed to show how trees are compartmented. The cell is the basic compartment. Each growth ring is divided into compartments as sheets of radial cells divide the rings like spokes in a wheel. The growth rings are then divided into compartments that "hold" the cells. The growth ring is also a compartment. Trees are highly compartmented plants.

Figure 2-36

A learning package was developed to help explain how trees are built-up—*compartmentation*—how trees defend themselves—*compartmentalization*—and how trees eventually break down—*disease and decay*. On the basis of this information many adjustments have been made in tree care treatments. Ms. H. Sharon Ossenbruggen is shown here with some of the models she constructed.

Pause

Helping Trees: Science, Art, and Common Sense

Science advances as old concepts are reexamined and adjustments are made. What about advancements in ways to help trees? How will they come?

Science is of no value if it does not change something for the better, even if the change is a better understanding of some process, and the new knowledge makes you feel better.

Science at its best is far from the complete answer for ways to help trees stay healthy, safe and attractive. Science does have its limitations when it comes to trees, especially when you consider trees in their natural habitats. Science, to advance, depends greatly on the scientific method. Experiments with controls must be done. Without a control there is no experiment.

Limitation of science increases as the number of variables increase. In mathematics and physics the variables can be easily controlled, so science works best there. When we move from chemistry to biology, the number of variables affecting living things increases greatly. There has never been an experiment with controls for a forest. Parts of the forest are studied or parts are taken into the laboratory where the variables can be controlled. The answers gained from such work are of limited value because the parts often have little reference to the whole system. The natural tree system is much bigger than the sum of its parts. The point is that science alone will not give us all the answers we need to help trees.

Science is knowing. Art is doing. Art implies skill. Helping trees is art as well as science. Art is doing the many tasks that are necessary to help trees grow and to help trees when they are in trouble. Art takes practice.

Art and science still leave the subject incomplete. There is still more. The remaining ingredient is *common sense*, the rarest ingredient in the world today.

Common sense is the innate ability to know what is best, or what is right, or how to do a task the best way, or to make the best decision. Common sense grows from experience and attention given to a subject or any living or nonliving thing. Common sense is a built in survival system. Common sense grows in a person as they send signals out, receive them back — feedback mechanism — and then rapidly made any correction or adjustment that is needed. Some people do this so fast that it appears as if the feedback and correction process never happened; but it did.

Helping trees depends greatly on common sense. The only way to get common sense about trees is to give them your attention, touch them, and watch them grow, wane and die. And, watch them when they do better after you have done something for them.

Common sense is also similar to what I call *constructive philosophy*; thinking in a way that results in a worthwhile answer or practical application and solution to a question or problem. Constructive philosophy can result in doing something that will help rather than hurt a person, an animal, or a tree. Common sense and constructive philosophy are entwined.

Why all this discussion on science, art, and common sense? Because the person who works with trees must have some of all of these ingredients.

The purpose of this book is to help trees by helping the people who work with trees. Education is the key to helping trees.

The introduction sets the tone and scope of the book. Indeed, trees are in trouble worldwide. But, just giving a statement on gloom and doom will not help trees. The introduction points out that every tree is different and the numbers of variations of problems are endless, or as many as there are trees. We must consider the themes. Once we learn the themes, it will be easy to recognize the variations and to know the course of action to help trees.

We have run too fast! Yes, we need all the modern tools and machines. But we also need to know what a tree is and how it defends itself and how it eventually dies and decays. It is time to go back and revisit the tree and the many living and nonliving agents that affect the life of the tree.

Everybody feels they know all they need to know about trees. On the other hand, our text books are overflowing with incorrect and incomplete statements: trees heal wounds, branches should be pruned flush to the trunk, frost starts frost cracks, large callus means rapid internal healing, heartwood is a dead, nonreactive tissue, fertilizers are tree food, and the list goes on and on. With incorrect information like this it is a wonder any progress has been made in tree care. It is mainly because so many working people have common sense that trees have been helped. Indeed, it is time to reexamine the tree.

The focus in the past has been more on *what* causes problems than on *how* a tree dies.

After several years of research on trees it became obvious to me that the missing ingredient to advances in tree care would come only after we had a better understanding of the tree.

Tree biology in the past meant anatomy and physiology mostly. If a healthy tree is defined as a plant without active infections, then there is no such plant as a healthy tree. Trees have hundreds, or even thousands, of active infections that are compartmentalized. Pathology must be added to tree biology.

The chapter on emerging new biology gives a brief outline of some of the work leading up to our present understanding of trees and their problems, and proper care. Proper tree care is not an easy task.

The remainder of the book gives many points about trees, and their problems, and proper care. The information is intended to help you become more aware of the tree and the many living and nonliving agents that affect trees. The information is not intended to give you the last word on insects, fungi, tree anatomy, pathology, and physiology, etc. Those interested in such details can find them in other books.

Again, and most important, I am trying to help the person who works on and with trees. The person who *touches* trees. People who do not touch trees will never understand this book. Help will come to trees when we bring together science, art, and common sense, and the greatest of these is common sense!

Figure 3-1

A New Tree Biology

Chapter 3

Trees and Insects and Mites

A Story of Many Interactions

Trees evolved in groups along with many other living things: other wood and nonwoody plants, insects, mites, birds, animals, nematodes, viruses, fungi, slime molds, algae, mosses, lichens, and later, man. The tree was like a social community center. It provided shelter, food, and reproductive sites for many other living things. Many of the living things established beneficial associations with trees. Even those that were pathogens were beneficial. Before insects, mites, and later, microorganisms, are discussed, it is essential to discuss the tree as an individual and as a group of individuals. What could be good for one could be bad for the other.

This *is not* a chapter on entomology! It is a chapter on tree-insect-mite interactions. The focus is on the tree.

Trees did evolve in groups. The individual trees of a species were connected either by grafted roots or by the mycelial strands of the fungi that are associated with fine, nonwoody roots, the mycorrhiza. You could think of the trees in a forest as the branches of a larger tree lying on its side. The group survives because most individual trees die soon after they begin to grow. Death of an individual is a survival factor for the group. Again, many individuals must die to perpetuate the group. The group is made up of individuals that were tougher than the others. Death is not good for the individual, of course. Another example; reproduction is essential for the group to survive. Sex or reproduction is not essential for an individual to survive. Pathogens are bad for the individual, but essential for the group that is made up of individuals that were able to survive the attacks of pathogens. My point is that we must view the tree as an individual and as a group at different times. When we take the tree out of its group habitat, then we must care for it in a way that it gets the benefits of the group.

Man wants trees for many reasons. Insects and mites also "want" trees for many reasons. We must be careful when we view the activities of insects and mites to be sure their activities are always harmful. They may be harmful to an individual when that is the only tree you have. They may also be beneficial to the group by keeping the weaklings to a minimum so that the group will survive. Again, the point, be careful when you make a judgement call about the activities of insects and mites.

55

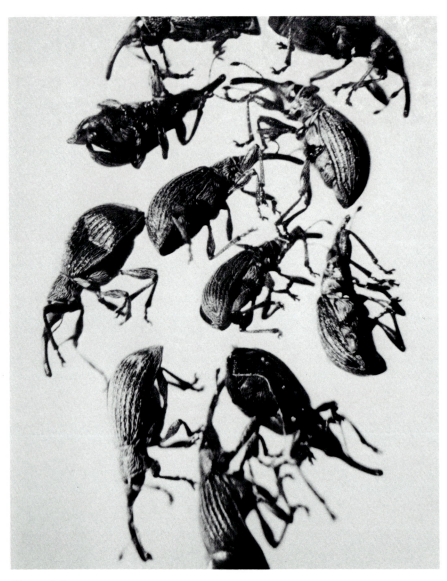

Figure 3-2
Thousands of insects living in, on, and about trees.

A New Tree Biology

There are several basic types of insects that live in, on, and about trees. They can best be described on the basis of their eating habits or the way they eat, the way they deposit eggs, protect themselves, and how the young ones start in life.

Insects chew, suck, rasp and suck, and bore nonwoody and woody parts of trees.

Some insects are aggressive in that they will attack a plant regardless of its health. Many insects are not so aggressive. They will attack weakened plants or trees, or weakened parts of trees. The insects on a tree may be a sign of other more basic problems. Killing the insects on such a weak tree may not help the tree.

The insects shown here are weevils. They can be easily distinguished by their long, thin head. These weevils eat birch seeds.

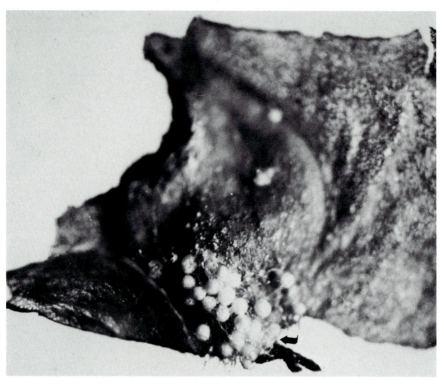

Figure 3-3

A birch seed that was attacked by a weevil. The weevils lay their eggs in the developing seed cones and the young insects eat the seeds. This pattern is common on many tree seeds. The black arrows show the microplye of the seed. This is where the germinating seedling will burst from the seed coat. This is a weak spot, an Achilles' heel, in a sense. This is where a fungus, a species of *Penicillium* (perfect stage shown here) infected the seed. Insects and fungi work together commonly in nature. It is important to know which one starts the problem when control attempts are made. Some insects carry their own fungus garden along with them. Special structures in some insects (mycangium) carry fungus spores or propagules (parts of an organism that can grow to produce the organism).

Figure 3-4

Insects that eat leaves not only reduce the energy trapping system, but they affect the appearance of the tree. Arborists must not only keep trees healthy and safe, but also attractive. Insects such as the gypsy moth, tussock moth, and spruce budworm have become household terms. Some trees die after they are infested; some trees recover. The condition of a tree at the time it is infested must play a major part in whether it lives or dies. Yet, when insect populations increase to high amounts, even healthy trees can be killed. Factors that affect the rise and fall of populations are not well understood. There is heated controversy on the merits of spraying insects in forests. Does spraying keep the populations at a high point? Insects have pathogens also. What does spraying do to the insect pathogens? The point here is to consider all sides of the subject before a decision is made to spray a forest. The lone tree in a backyard is another situation.

Figure 3-5

Many types of insects and mites cause galls on woody and nonwoody parts of trees. The insect or mite injures the plant during feeding or ovipositing (depositing eggs). The chemicals injected or infused into the plant by the insect or mite stimulate the plant to form great numbers of cells of normal size, or the cells grow to great proportions. Some of the cells take different shapes and it is difficult to believe that the gall is plant tissue. (Interested readers should read material on cecidiology, the formation of galls.) The galls on leaves usually do not harm the tree. Some people find some of the galls attractive while other people find them very unattractive. If galls are a problem, time sprays or injections to the attack time of the insect or mite involved.

Figure 3-6

The soft, cushion-like mounds on these American beech leaves were initiated by mites. Mites are not insects. Insects and mites are different in many ways, but the easiest way to tell them apart is that insects have 6 legs and mites and spiders — which are related — have 8 legs. A spray for an insect may not harm a mite. Know what your problem is before you attempt to control. Some mites look like small spiders, or ticks, which are also related to mites. One type of mite is cigar-shaped and very small. A hand lens is needed to see them. They are call eriophyid mites. Mites are very common on nonwoody and woody plant parts. We really do not know enough about their role in some tree diseases. They are a problem to the mycologists because they are often carried along with woody plant parts into fungus cultures. Fungi and mites do live closely together in nature. Mites are common in tree wounds. They may be important vectors of fungi and bacteria. The tree is alive with moving, small living things. The point here is to know that the unseen mite might be part of your tree problem.

Figure 3-7

Woody galls are common on many trees. These galls are on a red oak. Wasps commonly oviposit in leaves or soft twig tissue. The galls may be very numerous.

Figure 3-8

Witchesbrooms are bundles of twigs or small branches or even very large branches on some conifers in the West. The twigs or branches resemble a broom. The twigs and branches grow from a central point. In some cases only clusters of buds form and this condition is called a bud fasciation. The broom may form and die soon or it may last for many years. Mites initiate many types of witchesbrooms. Mites are the initiators of this broom on a highbush blueberry. Viruses may also be involved in formations that look like small brooms. Other organisms that stimulate brooms are mistletoes, dwarf mistletoes, rust fungi, mycoplasmas, insects, and underground "brooming" of roots(?) by nematodes (small roundworms, common in soil).

The brooms may act as protection to the organisms that stimulated the process. The point here is that trees and other woody plants evolved along with many other organisms. It appears that certain mechanisms through chemical means have evolved that serve to benefit these organisms that live in, on, and about trees. We know so little about these associations, yet some of our tree and forest management schemes destroy these other organisms, or just as bad, destroy their niche.

Figure 3-9   *Figure 3-10*

The large American beech in Figure 9 and the small beech in Figure 10 are covered with a white, cottony, soft-bodied scale insect called *Cryptococcus fagisuga*. The scale insect and fungi in the genus *Nectria* (*N. coccinea* var. *faginata* and *N. galligena*) cause a disease called beech bark disease.

The scale is parthenogenic; no males are known and reproduction takes place without fertilization. The eggs are deposited on the trunk. The young scale insects have legs, eyes, and antennae. As they mature a tube or stylet forms from their underside. The stylet is forced into the bark and the insect then loses through molting its eyes, legs, and antennae. The insect is attached to the bark by its stylet and the only food it gets is from the tree. The sap contains a high amount of carbohydrate and very little nitrogen containing compounds. The insect shunts the excess carbohydrate through a separate tube and forms a wax with it that covers its body, thus the white cottony appearance. The millions of puncture-type stylet wounds in the bark and the depletion of carbohydrate predispose the tree to infection by Nectria fungi. Some individual trees are highly resistant to the scale insect and the fungi.

Figure 3-11

The eruptions on the trunk of this American beech are associated with the infestation of another scale insect, *Xylococculus betulae*. This scale insect is found on birch also.

 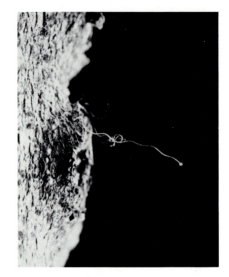

Figure 3-12   *Figure 3-13*

Here is an inside bark view of *Xylococculus betulae* in bark of a paper birch. The soft-bodied scale can grow to 6 mm. It is pink to bright red. The excess carbohydrate is used to form a "pearl cell" about the insect, and additional carbohydrate is expelled through a unique tube that protrudes from the insect. This scale does have males and fertilization does occur. Note the smaller scale next to the larger one. The scale insects often go into holes made in the bark by ambrosia beetles. Woodpeckers then dig out the scale insects for food. The digging wounds the tree, but also makes the bark rough and perfect for more scale insects to infest the tree. Connections in nature are wonderful. We must be careful not to break them.

Figure 3-13

The clear, long tube protrudes from *Xylococculus betulae*, a soft-bodies scale insect several millimeters deep in the bark of this American beech. The tube is made up of 9 rods of wax. Excess carbohydrate is shunted out the tube. Other insects, such as the aphids, also shunt excess carbohydrate in order to obtain a proper ratio of carbon to nitrogen in their diet. These insects only get what the tree gives them and the tree gives them a great amount of carbon and very little nitrogen. The insects have a gut system that shunts or sidetracks the excess carbohydrate so that the digestion process takes in the proper amounts of carbon and nitrogen. The "honeydew" from aphids is similar to the excess carbohydrate.

Other types of scale insects have a hard body covering. They are called armored scales. To control these scales it is necessary to spray when the insects are young and without their protective shield or they can be covered with thin oil when they are attached to the tree and have their hard covering. Be careful with oil sprays. Some types of oil can harm trees.

A New Tree Biology

Figure 3-14

Here is another 3 part system; a fungus, a scale insect, and a pine tree. The fungus is *Septobasidium pinicola* and the insect is a species of *Matsucoccus*. The tree is an eastern white pine. The fungus and scale usually attack weakened trees. They may appear at any position on the trunk, but most of the time they will be under dying or dead branches. When weakened trees begin to die, the fungus and scale will no longer attack the tree.

Figure 3-15

This flowering cherry tree in Seoul, South Korea was said to be dying from scale insects. Many branches were white from millions of insects. The trees had been topped for several years to reduce their size. The fungi quickly attacked the long, dying leader stubs. The trees were starving. The scale insects attacked a living but starving tree. The trees did compartmentalize the pathogens that entered the trunk through the topping wounds. In doing so, the space in the sapwood that normally stored starch was reduced greatly. Then the trees were fertilized heavily because they were obviously not healthy. The fertilizer stimulated the growth of large leaves and primary growth. The scale insects attacked, and indeed the trees were dying. The cause of death will be cited as scale injury. Insects and fungi are often cited as the cause of death of plants that have been greatly weakened by cultural practices. Know what starts a problem not what ends the life of a tree.

A New Tree Biology

Figure 3-16

Insects often deposit eggs in weakened spots on a tree. We need to learn more about this. How do they sense the low vitality spots? This pigeon tremex is ovipositing in bark on an American beech that was first infested by the beech scale and then infected by a species of Nectria. The bark was alive, but committed to an early death. The story does not end here. Soon after the pigeon tremex left the site, another insect, an ichneumon fly came to the bark and placed its eggs next to those of the pigeon tremex. The ichneumon fly has an ovipositor that can be several inches long. How it drills deep into wood with the hair-thin ovipositor is a marvel of nature. Again, the natural connections seem to be endless. The tree seems to be the mother organism of the world. Maybe it is! Maybe that's why when trees are in trouble, man will be in trouble.

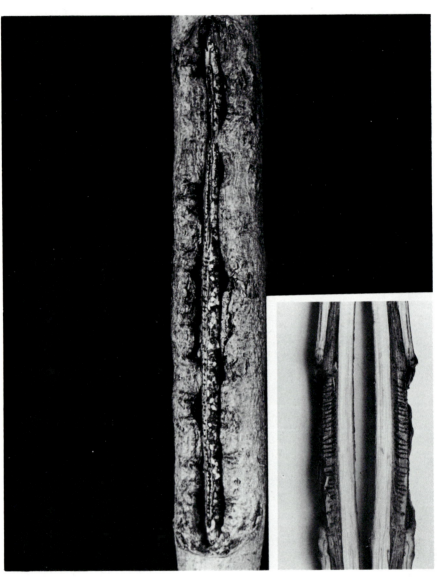

Figure 3-17

A New Tree Biology

Tree cricket ovipositing holes are common in many species of trees, especially in twigs that are growing rapidly. Trees near wet sites are usually the major targets because the tree crickets live in such sites. The photo of the small red maple stem shows the wound that resulted from the many puncture-type holes made during egg depositing. The dissected sample shows the slightly curved holes in the stem. Each hole contains one egg. Discolored and decayed wood is common in the wounded stems. The stems break easily in storms. Fungi that start perennial cankers may infect the wounds and as the tree grows, large cankers develop on the branches. Tree crickets and other insects oviposit in tree bark on trunks. And, the wounds are often infected by bacteria, yeasts, and wood-inhabiting fungi. Bleeding spots in the bark may form. When several injured spots are in close vertical alignment, large dead spots, inches to several feet, may form. The insects usually choose weakened spots on the trunk. Spots on trunks above dead or dying roots are commonly injured by ovipositing. Weakened spots on trunks below dead and dying branches are also selected by the insects.

It is often difficult to trace small trunk cankers to oviposition wounds. Sometimes the wound is made by the ovipositor but no egg was deposited. Or the egg may be attacked by bacteria or yeasts. The egg then serves as a nutrient source for the pathogen. By the time the canker or dead spot is noticed, it would be almost impossible to trace the cause back to the minute hole and the digested egg. Yeasts, mites, and even nematodes may inhabit the site.

Some wasps carry their own wood-inhabiting fungi along with them as they oviposit. This is common with some species of *Sirex*. The wood about the drilled hole for the egg then decays slightly.

The life of many insects is closely associated with trees. Their associations developed long before we began to evolve as a species. By understanding insect-tree associations better, we can made decisions that benefit all.

Figure 3-18

A New Tree Biology

Some small larvae of flies, especially *Phytobia pruinosa*, will mine the newly formed wood as it is formed by the cambium. The adult fly emerges from the soil early in the spring and deposits eggs in the cambial zone of branches and trunk at the top of the tree. The cambium is theoretically a single layer, but really it exists as a zone of tissues several layers thick. (This is a controversial point.) During dormancy the zone of cells that can divide to form new cells — phloem and xylem — is small, usually a few cell layers. As the tree begins to grow, the cambial zone increases in size. The cambial zone begins to produce wood (xylem) and inner bark (phloem) in a basipetal direction — top, downward. As the new wood cells are being formed on the inner side of the cambial zone, the larvae of the flies mine downward keeping pace with the development of the new wood. The cambium rarely "comes alive" throughout the tree all at the same time. The cambium "awakes" from the branches downward. This process may take several days to a few weeks before the cambial activity reaches the support roots. If this cambial process were not as described, the fly larva would be trapped in tough-walled wood cells before it mined to the bottom of the tree. The larvae mine into the woody roots and then exit into the soil where they complete their life cycle. The larvae start small and grow along the way. They may be 2 or more centimeters long at the end of their journey. When the flies find a tree they "like," they will continue to use it for their life. It often appears that young trees receive more mines. That may be so in some cases, but the number of mines usually stays fairly constant over the years. The tree diameter increases and the same number of mines in the small tree appear as fewer mines in a large diameter tree.

The arrows in the photograph show a darker band of wood in the paper birch disc. The center wood was brown-red, the ring about the center was cream, and the wood within the arrows was dark pink. These bands of colored wood are associated with wounds and death of branches.

Figure 3-19

A New Tree Biology

Wood defect caused by the cambium miner is called pith fleck. The mines cause very little injury to the tree, but the defects can cause a great amount of damage for the wood industry. Injury is a physiological problem for the tree. Damage is an economical problem for the person who seeks profit from the wood. The long dark streaks limit the wood for veneer and other high value products. The streaks are not so damaging when they are light in color, but when they are dark brown or black they cause serious damage. The dark mines result from infections by wood pathogens. The larvae are not always directly on their target and they do get too close to the cambium at times. When a small portion of the cambium is injured, pathogens can enter the tree.

It is also of interest to note that for some unknown reasons some larvae become very disoriented and will mine in greatly disordered paths. Usually the larvae keep their distance from other larvae.

There is no known way to determine the presence or intensity of mines in a tree from external signs. The first clue as to the intensity of the defect can be seen when the tree is cut. If a tree has many mines, especially dark mines, the log should not be sent for veneer or high quality products. If the mines are concentrated in the center of the tree, and the log is great enough in diameter, it may be used for veneer.

Birch in the southern part of its range appears to have more cambium miner than trees in the northern range.

Figure 3-20

A New Tree Biology

Cambium miner is also common in black cherry where gum often fills the mines and results in serious damage to the wood. The insect is found in maples, ash and many other hardwood species.

Many insects mine outer bark and stay in the outer bark. These insects cause no injury to the tree. Other insects mine the inner bark and kill the cambium. These insects cause injury. Here is an example in a species of *Eucalyptus* from Australia. Note also the small dark holes in the wood made by other insects. These insects are called pinhole borers.

Many insects live in and on trees and cause some injury or no injury to the tree. As some trees begin to wane and die, the insects will rush in and mine the bark and wood. If salvage operations move fast enough, damage to the wood can be held to a minimum.

The inner bark of trees is an energy rich tissue and many insects eat these tissues or deposit their eggs there so that food will be available for their young. But, it is not possible to have insect wounds without some infection. After trees are wounded it is impossible to hold back infection, this is why it is proper to say injury *and* infection. Many microorganisms grow in and about insect mines and galleries, especially those in the inner bark. Remember, insects require vitamins, just as we do, and they must have the help of microorganisms, like yeasts, to convert tree substances to essential vitamins.

Here is inner bark (left side) of a true fir from the Pacific Northwest, U.S.A. The insects not only mined the bark but also scored or injured the cambium and wood (right side). When thousands of these injuries occur over the trunk of a tree, the tree responds to each injury by strengthening natural boundaries and by forming new boundaries. These defense reactions take energy, lots of energy. And in doing this, the tree also walls off sapwood tissue that normally stores energy reserves. If no repeated insect attacks occur, the tree will build up its energy storing wood. Repeated attacks, even minor ones, can add up to starvation problems for the tree. Defense reaction will receive the priority for energy. But, this priority for energy may limit other tree processes. When this happens, the tree becomes weaker, and a better breeding place for more insects.

The repeated injuries also lead to boundaries that are weak structurally along the circumferential plane. Cracks may form along the plane of weakness. Pathogens on the inner side of the boundary — barrier zone, wall 4 CODIT — may then spread rapidly in the wood trapped behind the boundary.

The arrows show where an older insect wound closed (see pointer B, Figure 22).

A New Tree Biology

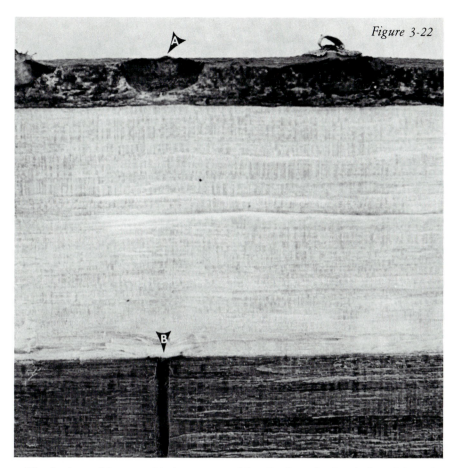

Figure 3-22

The bark on this paper birch was at position B when the beetle bored into the wood — hole beyond pointer B. The wound in the bark was still obvious after 20 years (pointer A). Note the dimple in the wood at point B. The dimple is similar to that shown in figure 21 by arrows. A column of discolored wood formed above and below the insect-bored hole. The length of the hole was the diameter of the column. The spindle-shaped columns may develop 10-20 centimeters above and below a hole.

In the sample shown here, the insect was not successful in its attempt to deposit eggs in the tree. The hole was bored, but the tree regains its vitality. The adult insect retreated from the tree leaving only a straight drill-type hole. Had the tree continued to wane, eggs would have been deposited, and the young insects would have mined a network of galleries in the wood as the tree died. So, the insects do not always "win." When many holes are bored, many barrier zones form and planes of weakness develop as described in figure 33.

Columns of discolored wood associated with the beetle holes are called by many names: flagworm streaks, T flags, mineral streaks, worm streaks.

Figure 3-23

Defect in paper birch caused by the ambrosia beetle, *Trypodendron* sp.

Figure 3-23A

Ambrosia beetles, *Trypodendron* sp. Ambrosia beetles receive their common name because of their close association with fungi (yeasts are also fungi). Many of the beetles have mycangia in their head — special internal body that holds spores or propagules of microorganisms. The beetles also are covered with hairs that make collection of propagules a certainty as they crawl through galleries lined with fungi, and through fungus fruit bodies. Many of the fungi associated with the beetle are called collectively the blue stain fungi. Many of the fungi do impart a blue stain to the infected wood, (conifers mostly) but not all. Many of the beetle-carried fungi belong to the genus *Ceratocystis*. This genus has some infamous members: *C. fagacearum*, oak wilt; *C. ulmi*, Dutch elm disease; *C. fimbriata*, plane tree canker stain; *C. coerulescens*, sapstreak of maple. Many of the "ambrosia fungi" have sticky spores. The fungi are usually warm temperate types.

A New Tree Biology

In paper birch that has been weakened, the ambrosia beetles bore into the lenticels (insects do "know" the easiest route into a tree). Trees are weakened when roots are injured after road building or during logging operations. Weakened trees are usually near old roads or trails where logs were skid out of the forest. The lenticels are soft, or spongy spots on the bark where the bark tissues are very close to the cambium and the active phloem (inactive phloem is older phloem that is crushed as new phloem forms every growth period). Gas exchange occurs through the lenticels. As trees get older, the lenticels become less efficient. This occurs in most trees when the strong, suberized, periderm, or outer bark forms.

Figure 3-24

Figure 3-25

When the bark was peeled from the sample shown in figure 24, and the outer layers of wood were shaved slightly, the pattern of discolored streaks above and below the holes could be seen. Note that the holes are all approximately the same diameter indicating that adults made the holes. When holes in wood change diameter, it indicates that a growing young insect made the holes. Trees with such holes as shown here do not yield high quality products.

The drill-hole type wound is one of the most common types in nature.

Figure 3-26

A large barrier zone formed (arrows) after this red maple received a serious wound 16 years before the tree was cut. The barrier zone separated to form a crack or ring shake entirely about the trunk. After 3 and 4 years, ambrosia beetles infested the tree (arrows). Slightly discolored wood is in the 6 growth rings that formed after the wound indicating another injury 6 years after the wounding period shown by arrows. It does not appear that growth rate was reduced, yet the beetles attacked the tree. A beetle gallery that did show the T-shaped position can be seen at the bottom of the sample near the wound (double arrows). This pattern indicates that eggs were deposited and the young began to mine outward.

The large barrier zone in this tree reduced the storage space for energy reserves. The discolored wood on the inner side of the barrier zone is dead wood, and dead wood does not store energy reserves. The healthy-appearing wood on the inner side of the barrier zone would have limited amounts of energy storage because barrier zones "break connections" between the wood on their inner sides and the new wood that continues to form after the barrier zone was completed.

This sample suggests that the beetles attacked while the tree's energy reserves were low or even depleted in spots. How insects can "sense" weak spots, or weak trees, is not well understood. Volatiles given off by the tree may be an answer, or part of the answer. Changes in electrical field near the weak spots, or, the weak tree, may be another possible answer. Trees do have constantly changing voltage patterns from positive to negative. Can it be that the bark is also an electrical insulator? And, when it is broken, electrical changes are emitted? We must keep an open mind.

Figure 3-27

Sapstreak is a disease of maples and a few other tree species including yellow poplar or tulip tree. The fungus *Ceratocystis coerulescens* is cited as the cause. Trees that have been injured or near logging sites seem to be infected more than other trees. But, infected trees have been found in fields and in areas where little or no man-caused disruptions have occurred. The cross-sections of infected trees have a star-burst pattern of brown-red discolored wood with edges or margins of green. A similar pattern occurs in maples infected with a fungus called *Verticillium*. As columns of discolored wood spread in a vertical direction from their main course in maples, the vertical margins separate to form thin streaks of discolored wood. The column of discolored wood at the source can be likened to the palm of a hand, and the streaks as the fingers. The point here is that the star-burst pattern can be explained. But, I have found ambrosia beetles associated with sapstreak maples in Michigan. The rough bark of the maples and the heavy coating of lichens made it extremely difficult to see the holes. But, longitudinal sections did show the holes.

Barrier zones are formed in the trees at the tips of the columns (arrows). The wood on the inner side of the barrier zone is a darker color than wood that forms after the zone is formed. The barrier zones and changes in wood color are impossible to see easily in a tree that has had repeated injuries, either from wounds, dying roots, dying branches, or insect attack.

This statement is not to say that ambrosia beetles are associated with *all* sapstreak maples. I know they are associated with some trees.

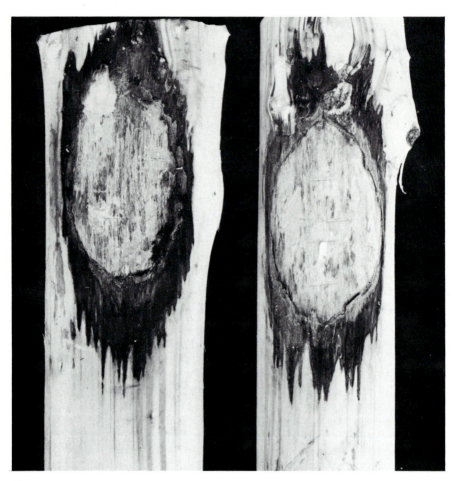

Figure 3-28

The bark was removed from these red maple trees one year after the wounds were inflicted in July. All 20 trees in this experiment were attacked by ambrosia beetles. The beetles bored into the bark above and below the wounds. Long streaks of discolored wood developed above and below the wounds. The wounds were part of experiments testing a great variety of wound dressings. The point here is that the beetles did not enter the wound surface but they did infect the bark above and below the wound. The pattern of streaking is similar to that shown in other samples from birch and maple in this book.

Insects were common in bark and wood near wounds in hundreds of trees used in the wound dressing experiments.

When viewing discolored streaks in trees it is absolutely essential to make more than cross-sections. Longitudinal sections must be viewed, and debarked sections must be studied. And, unless many trees are dissected and studied, there is no basis for comment.

A New Tree Biology

Figure 3-29

The 2 sections from a yellow birch are on the trunk section that shows the old basal wound. The section at right is 4 feet above the top of the wound, and the section at left is 16 feet above the wound. At 4 feet the discolored and decayed wood associated with the wound was well compartmentalized into a V-shaped column as viewed from the cross-section. Many insects infested the tree after it was wounded. The U-shaped discolored streaks indicate that the insects bored into the wood and back out. A strong-appearing barrier zone (arrows) separates wood present at the time of wounding from new wood that formed after the barrier zone was completed. It is highly unlikely that the wound at the base stimulated barrier zone formation completely about the trunk at 16 feet above the wound. A more likely explanation is that the insects attacked the trunk to 16 feet above after the tree was wounded. The thousands of insect holes coupled with the large basal wound set the stage for the extensive barrier zone. The man-caused logging wound, the insect wounds, and the tree response are all part of this story.

Figure 3-30

Insects that bore into wood not only cause defects in wood quality but their galleries also reduce the strength of the wood. (Again, this *is not* a chapter on entomology. The interested reader can find a wealth of information on boring insects in many fine entomology books.)

Insects boring into trees is an extremely complex subject because the variables are almost endless: time of attack, condition of tree, environmental conditions, time of insect in tree, type of wound, position of wound, insect enemies, large and small, organisms associated with the insect, etc. All of these variables exist as gradations, so gradations mixed with gradations is the usual story. But, there are some themes, and we will look at these.

When a tree is injured it will be infected. Microorganisms are a key part of the insect borer story. When the tree is injured and infected it will respond to form boundaries. The insects and microorganisms usually stay within the boundaries. Insects can bore through boundaries, so as long as the insect is in the tree, boundaries can be broken. Boundaries in Part I CODIT are easily broken. When part II CODIT, or the developing barrier zone is broken, the cambium is killed and the size or area of the wound is increased. Some insects bore into healthy wood, or wood not infected by microorganisms while other insects bore into wood altered by mechanical wounds. Some variations on these themes are given.

Figure 3-31

The sugar maple borer causes serious damage to maple trees. The beetle is *Glycobius speciosus*. It is a cerambysid, which means that it has long antennae and it also keeps its galleries free of frass—insect excreted wood. The beetle has a 2 year life cycle. Eggs are deposited in the fissures of the bark. The young grubs or larvae begin to mine into the inner bark. They mine in a diagonal pattern in an upward pathway. After mining in the inner bark and killing portions of the cambium, they mine into the wood, again in an upward spiral pattern about and into the trunk. The insect emerges after 2 years.

The photo shows the small diameter (arrow) of the gallery when the insect started. Note the increase in the diameter of the gallery as the insect grew. The grub can grow to over a centimeter in diameter.

Note the basal wound on the tree, also made by the insect. The small tree to the left, and the large tree in the left background also have sugar maple borer wounds.

Many insects start the journey from bark into wood, and out again. Few complete the route. A great graduation of injuries results: slight cambial injury to large holes in the tree. Many of the swollen "bumps" on sugar maple trees are aborted sugar maple borer galleries.

The initial path of the beetle kills cambium in a horizontal wound.

Trees and Insects and Mites

Figure 3-32

Figure 3-33

Figure 3-34

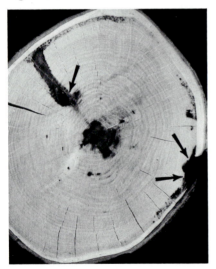

The tree in figure 32 had only a small portion of the wound open. The tree in figure 33 had a large open wound resulting from the borer attack. Other insects bored into the tree through the dead surface of the wound. Trees with large wounds may break during storms.

The wood present at the time of borer attack discolors slightly. The single arrow in figure 34 shows the borer gallery near the center of the tree. The two arrows show the entrance site. Note the clear wood that formed after the borer attack.

A New Tree Biology

Figure 3-35

The sugar maple at left had no sugar maple borers. The tree at right had many borers. Why? There are no sound answers, but the resistance of some trees is obvious and common.

Figure 3-36

This sugar maple tree had a large basal wound with a sporophore of *Fomes connatus* and a large old sugar maple borer wound above.

Figure 3-37

Dissection of the tree shows that the diameter of the tree at the time it received the basal wound was approximately the diameter of the tree when the sugar maple borer attacked. Most of the time, twisted grain and discolored wood are associated with borer wounds, but advanced decay can be present. The discolored wood associated with borer wounds is often called mineral streak. The discolored wood columns follow the palm and finger pattern.

A New Tree Biology

Some boring insects enter trees near dead branches. When branches die, the trunk tissues below the branch are weak spots (see chapter on branch attachment). Energy reserves may be greatly reduced in tissues below dying branches. Again, an Achilles' heel and a safe place for an insect to enter a tree. The branch crotch is also a place where many insects feed. As branches grow, the bark in the crotch wrinkles and inner bark tissues form near the surface. When a borer injures the trunk tissues in the branch crotch, the result is similar to a flush cut (see chapter on pruning). The point here is that insects seem to "know" the weak spots, or spots where small wounds lead to serious injury to the tree. The microorganisms also "help" the insect here, and the wound stays open.

Figure 3-38

Figure 3-39

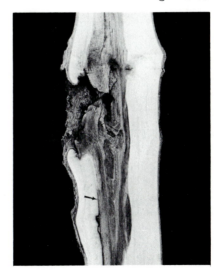

A dissected maple, 3 years after a borer, *Xylotrechus acerus*, entered the young stem near a dead branch. The discolored wood associated with the wood was compartmentalized within the wood present at the time the beetle wounded the trunk (arrow).

Some boring insects move so fast that the microorganisms trail behind in the wood about the gallery. Other boring insects move slower, and the microorganisms are infecting the wood in front of them. Some borers stimulate the tree to produce gums—cherry, peach—and resins—pines—that keep the wounds open. Birds in search of borers also enlarge wounds. The birds may also take propagules of microorganisms with them over great distances. You can not talk only about insects and trees.

Trees and Insects and Mites

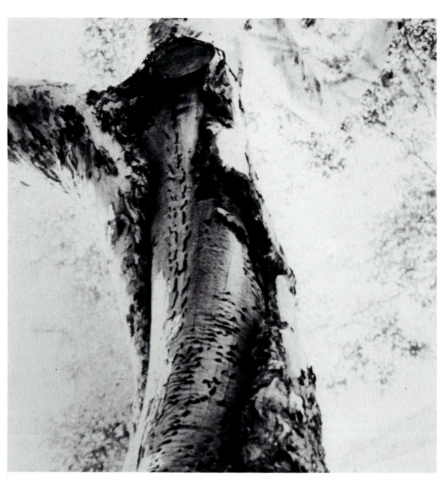

Figure 3-40

In figure 38, branches and improper pruning were mentioned. Here is an example of this pruning-insect problem on a eucalypt in Australia. Several large branches were cut very close to the trunk and the branch protection zones were removed. Worst yet, the pruned branches were in vertical alignment. Because branches do have a conduction connection only below the branch on the trunk, the pruning cuts greatly weakened the trunk tissues below the branches. The borers took immediate advantage of the situation and hundreds of insects infested the tissues of the trunk below the cut branches. The same situation can occur when roots are injured, except the injured roots are not seen but the borer wounds are. Death of roots after planting or transplanting trees is a common starting point for borer attack into the tree base.

Root injuries due to machinery, and improper pruning cuts are major starting points for insect attack in orchard trees. The point again, give insects a weak spot and they take it and move rapidly.

Figure 3-41

In the tropics, once a weak spot or wound occurs on a tree the insects attack rapidly. But some insects, as shown here in a teak sample, follow the microorganisms. The insects followed the CODIT patterns because the microorganisms followed the pattern. In such cases the insects may eventually cause the spread of microorganisms to decrease, and thus also slow the progress of the insects. This occurs when the cavities are so open that high amounts of oxygen enter them. There is also a drying effect that stalls the spread of microorganisms. Many tropical trees have very durable wood because of extractives that resist spread of microorganisms. If these built in controls were not operating in a warm, wet climate, the trees would be digested before they reached their first year.

Figure 3-42

Termites are major causes of tree and wood product damage in the tropics and subtropics. Termites, or white ants as they are often called, are different in many ways from ants. Ants may live in trees and eat someplace else. Termites may live some place else and eat in trees or wood products.

This eucalypt from Australia was attacked by small boring insects when the tree was young. The central cavity in the tree was infested by termites. The other hollow to the right was infested by termites. Note the sound wood that separates the 2 hollows. Termites follow the microorganisms and the microorganisms follow the CODIT patterns. Wood infected by microorganisms in a living tree will be the first wood infested by termites when a product is made from the tree.

Termites are blind. They build mud-like galleries from their nests to the trees. The galleries guide them plus maintain the proper oxygen and humidity necessary for their living processes. Termites are known to build nests in line with the electromagnetic fields. Termites may also be able to communicate by electrical signals.

A New Tree Biology

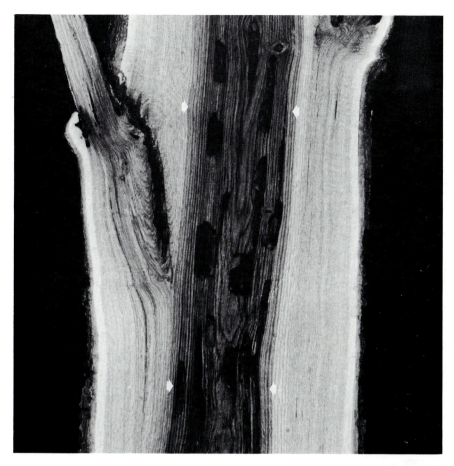

Figure 3-43

The white arrows show a column of discolored heartwood in a red oak that is infested by ants. The discolored heartwood is compartmentalized within the heartwood, and the ants are following the microorganisms, which follow the CODIT patterns. Note the large, clean cavities made by the ants. The ants have had over 50 years to mine in a radial direction, but they have not done it.

The close linking of many organisms in natural stems gives the systems their unique strength. It is difficult to disrupt a system that has so many complex interacting parts, and all help others in yet unknown ways. But, when one part of the system is disrupted, several to many other parts of the system will also suffer. It is almost impossible to understand how only one part could be disrupted.

The same philosophy follows for studying natural systems. You can not take each part out too long for study or it no longer is the same as it was when in the system. When a part of the system is removed too long it becomes an artifact. Sad, but true, how many studies on artifacts have been done! (Because the light was better and it was more comfortable.)

Figure 3-44   *Figure 3-45*

Figure 44 shows a large wound in a red oak. Most of the ant galleries are above the wound. Again, the ants did not mine into the wood that formed after the wound (arrows). Note how abruptly the decay column ends. It appears that the ants may regulate the spread of the column by keeping the galleries clean and dry.

Figure 45 shows a large cavitiy behind a wound on an American beech. The cavity was inhabited by ants. Note the abrupt ending to the column. If ants had no regulatory means for controlling spread of the microorganisms, the microorganisms would soon eat the ants out of their home.

Figure 3-46

Ant galleries in a large Douglas fir utility pole. The pole was a transmission pole—
carries power over long distances. The pole had to be replaced after 14 years because
of rot and ants. The rot and the ants did not spread into the center or into the
outer core of wood. Why? This pattern of defect is called in between rot for obvious reasons: between the inner and outer core of wood. The rot and ants follow
wood altered after branch death (see chapter on branches). The preservative in the
outer layers of wood had *nothing* to do with the pattern. The pattern is common
in Douglas fir and the group of southern hard pines that are used for utility poles.

Figure 3-47

The rot and ants were in the center of this cedar pole. The letter G shows the ground line. The lower section is at left and the upper section at right. Again, the wood preservative had nothing to do with the patterns. The pole was defective before it was put in the ground. The center rot was associated with large dead branch stubs. The rot developed in the center and the ants followed. In this case a few ants did spread beyond the center boundary (center section). Natural systems are never absolute.

When utility poles fail because of rot and insects before 75 years of service, this is a serious economic problem for industry, and for you and me because we pay the bills in the end.

Too much low quality wood from low quality trees is moving into products that affect our lives in many ways. Poles and trees full of rot not only injure property but kill people. There is no excuse for this, especially when we know the indicators for internal defects, and we have new electrical methods for detecting rot.

I have dissected many poles that were full of ants and I have seen the hardwood poles in Australia that are full of termites. These insects follow the microorganisms, and the microorganisms follow the wounds, dead branches, and dead roots. These defects don't just happen. And more powerful preservatives are not the answer. It is time for wood products industries to recognize these trees and know that defective trees make defective products.

Insects are not going to go away. We may be able to control many of them on our 90 day food crops. But, on our 90 year or 900 year tree crops, there must be other answers. The best answer is education. The more we can learn about these systems the more we can do about them. Or, we will know what parts we can alter and what parts we can not, and for how long.

Man is a major part of the complex system. We must start making decisions from our *real* role within the system and not as some other ultimate force outside of the system.

Chapter 4

Trees and Microorganisms

Trees and microorganisms evolved in close harmony over a 200 million year period. Microorganisms that inhabited trees survived so long as they digested trees. Trees survived so long as they were not digested by microorganisms. A paradox? No! Compartmentalization resolved the apparent paradox. Trees could not move away from destructive forces, so they evolved while standing their ground. Trees evolved as highly compartmented plants. Compartmentation means the subdivision of unit space. Compartmentation also means that there are "doors" between the "rooms" and "communication lines" connecting the "rooms." Compartmentalization means the "doors" are closed and the "communication lines" are broken. More details will be given on this later. But now we need to know that trees do "wall off" injured and infected tissues, and the microorganisms in the walled off compartments may digest the tissues within the compartment.

If a healthy tree is defined as one without active infections, then there is no such thing as a healthy tree. Trees have hundreds, or even thousands of active infections. The infections are within the walled off compartments. Every little insect wound, every little dead twig or root will be infected. But, seldom do the microorganisms spread freely in trees. The point here is that trees and microorganisms have resolved the paradox.

A few other points before we look at some microorganisms. The individual versus the group trees must be considered again. The pathogen can be the ultimate problem for the individual if the tree dies. Yet, many trees die before only the few strong live to form the group. The pathogen exerts a pressure against the individuals, and only those that survive become a member of the group with the "privilege" to reproduce.

The concept of individual and group is fine when you consider the open natural forest, but not so fine when you must consider the one tree in your front yard. Yet, trees *did* evolve under the individual-group plan. And, when we bring them into our world, we must be *aware* of the natural pressures that are on that tree. This is why pruning, watering, spraying, fertilizing, etc. become necessary for the individual tree in our life, but not so for the natural group.

Trees, insects, fungi, man, wildlife, and other living things make up a fabric with many different threads. As indicated before, you cannot pull one thread out and keep it out of the fabric too long or it loses its identity as a part of the fabric. My point again; beware of the study of artifacts. I will tease out a few threads gently here keeping in mind the danger of artifacts or telling you things you really do not need to know.

This chapter, like the one on insects, is not meant to give you the last word on microorganisms. It is not a crash course in microbiology. I will try to introduce a few concepts of interactions between trees and microorganisms. And, like insects, the microorganisms will not go away. We must learn to live with them.

101

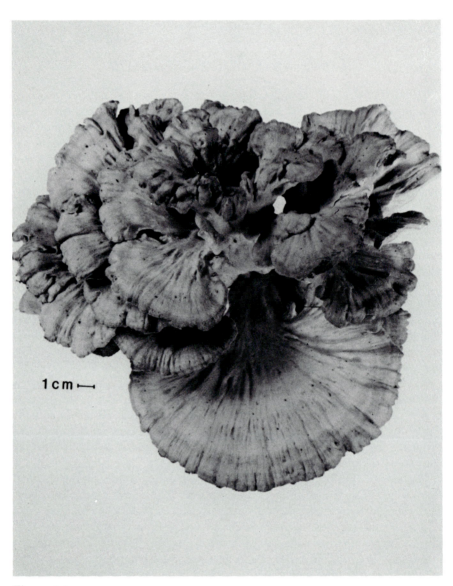

1 cm ⊢——⊣

Figure 4-1

A New Tree Biology

Some microorganisms are not so micro. The reproductive parts of some tree-inhabiting fungi—conks, sporophores, mushrooms—weigh over 25 pounds and can persist for 50 or more years. When we say microorganism we usually mean the microscopic bacteria, yeasts, and vegetative parts of fungi. The single cells of bacteria can be as small as a few microns, and a micron is a thousandth of a millimeter, and a millimeter is a thousandth of a meter which is about 39 inches. The bacteria are small. If you take a bacterium that was 3 microns long and enlarged it to the height of a 6-foot person and then enlarged the person by the same amount, the person would be *700 miles* tall!

We commonly see fungus conks, or sporophores on trees similar to the one shown here. It is a sporophore of *Polyporus sulphureus*. The sporophore is bright orange to yellow and easy to identify. It does signal advanced rot in the tree—brown rot. Brown rot means the fungi are digesting the cellulose mostly and only altering the lignin in the wood.

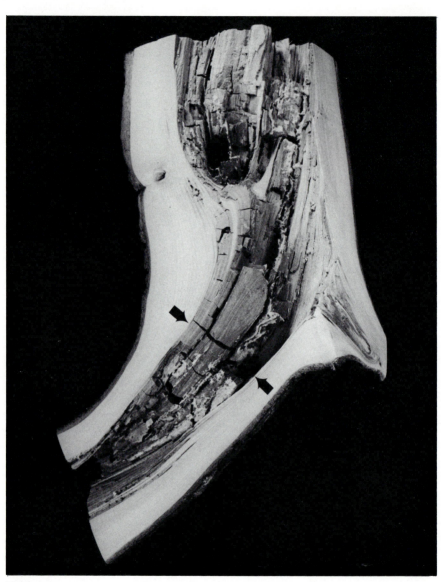

Figure 4-2

A New Tree Biology

Wood that is infected by fungi that cause brown rot has a dry, cubical appearance as shown here in a root of balsam fir. Brown rot is more common in conifers than deciduous hardwoods. Brown rot is common in species of eucalypts, which are hardwoods. The rot in the root shown here was confined by a barrier zone (arrows). Roots also compartmentalize infections.

Brown rot usually ends abruptly, but the sound-appearing wood beyond the rot in a vertical direction is usually weakened greatly.

Brown rot is often called dry rot. Of course some moisture is required by the fungi to rot the wood. The fungi can survive for long periods in a dormant state. When water does come, the fungi grow rapidly and also alter the wood beyond them in such a way that moisture is stored. There is moisture in the air, and enough moisture can come from the air to keep the fungi alive and growing.

Figure 4-3

A New Tree Biology

Brown rot is common in utility poles and other wood products. The brown rot-causing fungi follow the CODIT patterns in the tree and in poles and wood products. The center of the utility pole was altered when it was a tree. The diameter of the rot column was the diameter of the tree when large branches died. The tree is a southern yellow pine (a group of about 5 species are all called southern yellow pines by the industry). Southern yellow pines are hard pines. They have a central core of durable heartwood. The central wood in this tree was infected, or altered, before it formed heartwood. Altered meaning that the normal aging pattern of the wood has been changed as a result of branch or root death or by mechanical wounds. Altered wood is usually infected but the infection may be by organisms other than decay-causing fungi. Industry recognizes *only* visibly decayed wood. Wood altered in the living tree will be the first wood to rot in a product. It will be the first wood infested by ants and termites.

Figure 4-4

A New Tree Biology

White rot is another type of rot where the fungi digest the cellulose and lignin at about the same rates. There are many variations on the theme of white rots. Some white-rot causing fungi digest small pockets of wood, and the rotted wood is called "pocket rot." Some fungi rot the wood in such a way that the wood becomes string like and the rots are called "stringy rots."

The fruit body on this American beech is *Fomes connatus*. (I have decided to use old, familiar scientific names here. The name changes are so fast and mixed now that the tree person need not get involved in the process.) The fungus is easily identified because it usually has green moss and algae growing on it. The fungus causes a typical white rot. The rot columns digest most of the wood leaving a hollow in the tree. The rot columns caused by the fungus end abruptly and seldom develop into the butt and roots.

Blue green algae grow on the sporophore and also up into the pores that produce the spores. Blue green algae are as small as bacteria. The fascinating fact about the blue green algae is that some species can fix nitrogen. The question here is whether the blue green algae *may* play a role in making nitrogen available to the tree. We suspect that trees get nitrogen from other sources than the soil and the nitrogen fixing organisms in the soil.

Note also the black spots on the trunk. This is another fungus called *Ascodichaena*. It penetrates the outer bark and the hyphae—vegetative tubes of a fungus—grow along the phellogen—bark cambium. Is it possible that we have a "mycorrhizae-type" system within the bark of trees? Many microorganisms inhabit the outer bark of trees, and as indicated here, some grow very close to living cells in the bark.

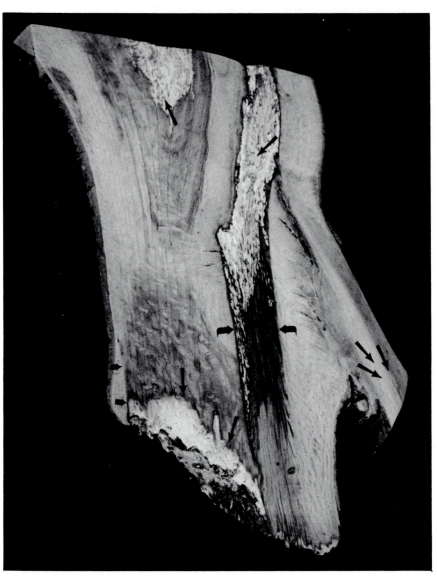

Figure 4-5

A New Tree Biology

The long arrows show 3 columns of white rot in a beech root. The 2 arrows with the curved tails show that the column is well compartmentalized. The large root was cut off in root-wounding experiments. Note that after 3 years, very little rot spread into the root. Discolored wood was beyond the decayed wood in all 3 columns. The small arrows show the root barrier zone. The arrows indicate also the size of the root when it was cut off. Roots are very strong compartmentalizers. Note the small root that "branches off" the larger root at right (triple arrows). Branching roots have connections to larger roots similar to branches on trunks (see chapter on branch attachment) but the opposite direction.

When roots are injured during construction, make certain that the dying roots are removed by making cuts that do not tear the wood. A sharp cut will help the tree to compartmentalize the infection. Roots on small trees that are injured should also be cut "clean" before the tree is planted. There is no need for any wound dressing.

Figure 4-6

White rots are also common in utility poles and wood products. A recent survey showed white rots more common than brown rots in utility poles. The white rot in this pole was confined to wood infected in the living tree. Branch stubs are highly suspect again as the starting points for the central column of infected wood in the tree. The central column in the tree was probably sound-appearing. The Shigometer method detects these sound appearing columns of wood in trees and "young poles." The Shigometer method is said to "call" sound wood as decayed wood. The problem again is that industry only recognizes the problem after it is too late. Yet, industry wants an early detection system. This is a real paradox! The early detection system is available but it won't be accepted because the wood often "appears sound." And, the problem goes round and round. Research by several independent researchers in several countries showed that wood goes to a high state of ionization before it decays. The Shigometer method is very sensitive to the wood that is highly ionized — the resistance to a pulsed current decreases in such wood. It is extremely difficult for people to understand the early stages of wood decay.

Figure 4-7

A New Tree Biology

The fruit bodies (arrow) on this beech wound indicate infection by a species of *Hypoxylon*. These fungi belong to a family called Xylariaceae. Fungi in this family also cause white rots, but the fungi are not the typical rot-type fungi. The typical rot fungi are called Hymenomycetes. They belong to a larger group called Basidiomycetes. This means that the fungi produce spores on a structure called a basidium, which is like a peg or a golf tee. The Hymenomycetes have a fertile layer, a hymenium, that produces these spores. The Hymenomycetes produce the spores in bodies that have pores or gills. Meanwhile, species of *Hypoxylon* and *Xylaria* do not produce spores the way the Hymenomycetes do. *Hypoxylon* and *Xylaria* belong to a group called the Ascomycetes. They produce their spores in an ascus, which means a sac. The fruit bodies are usually small. The hard, round fruit bodies of the *Hypoxylon* on the beech here are called stromata. The stroma (singular) is a tissue that holds the asci (plural) or sacs of spores.

The spores in the fruit bodies of the Hymenomycetes — conks, mushrooms — and the Xylarias are the result of a sexual process. Two cells have come together to unite their genetic material. When we speak of sexual phases in nature, it means that the 2 contributing members are morphologically different — the male looks and is different from the female. But, in the fungi this is not the case (this is so in other organisms also). Both contributing members look the same. Now we speak of compatibility groups; a + meets a − , and a "sexual union" occurs. This is what happens in the conks and mushrooms, and in the ascus.

But, some fungi don't do this. They produce spores without going through the contributing process. These fungi are called — justly so — Imperfect fungi. Some fungi like species of *Hypoxylon* have a perfect stage — the ascus in the stromata — and an imperfect stage — spores produced on structures called conidiophores. The spores are often called conidia (conidium, singular).

Figure 4-8

The imperfect fungi or Fungi Imperfecti, are the ones commonly associated with discolored wood. They are also some of the first fungi to infect wood after wounding or the death of roots and branches. They are sometimes called the discoloring fungi. This is not a good term, because the Hymenomycetes and species of *Xylaria* and *Hypoxylon* are also associated with discolored wood. We will call them imperfect fungi here.

The imperfect fungi not only infect wounds rapidly, but they also infect the exposed surfaces of cut logs. They infect the dying cells first because this is where the energy storage material is in the trees; in the parenchyma cells. Wood does contain living cells — parenchyma — in the sapwood. The parenchyma are cells that have a slightly thinner cell wall than the other wood cells. Parenchyma cells may stay alive for over 150 years in some tree species such as sugar maple. But, when a tree is cut, these cells with living contents and energy storage materials — starch, oils — are the first target for the imperfect fungi, and the Hymenomycetes also.

Some of the imperfect fungi are called the sugar fungi. They may not grow deep into wounded wood, but they will grow rapidly on the sap that covers a fresh wound. They will also grow on the sap that covers the cut end of a log. The sugar fungi grow very rapidly and take over or colonize the wound surface quickly. Some of the common members of the group are species of *Penicillium*, *Gliocladium*, *Alternaria*, and *Mucor*. There are many, many more!

Many of the first fungi to "arrive" at a wound or on the cut surface of a log have sticky spores. The insects quickly bring the fungi to the targets. Yeasts, which are fungi, are also early invaders. They often form a "skin" over the sugary sap and ferment the sap. The product is ethyl alcohol. Many insects and animals from bees to birds to bears get their "spring tonic" this way.

The section shown here shows black patches where the insect-carried fungi infected. Note the white patches forming over the black patches. The white patches are fungi parasitic on the black fungi. We call these fungi mycoparasites. So, the chain of energy transfer continues. The fungi also have their problems; from other fungi. Energy and space to exist are factors that are high on the survival chart. Those who do not compete effectively for an energy source and space to exist, die.

Figure 4-9

A beech tree was cut into logs each 4 feet long on July 26 in the White Mountains of New Hampshire. On August 31 each log was cut into 3 bolts. The ends of those exposed to the air in July are at the bottom left of each pile. The surface of the second bolt is bottom right, and the surface of the third bolt is at the top of each pile.

The dark fungi grew rapidly over the ends of the bolts and deep into the bolts. Midsummer is the time these fungi flourish, especially with their insect friends. The surfaces of the bolts not only contained fungi, but insects, mites, nematodes, bacteria, mycoparasites (white spots) and small animals like snails. The new space to grow and the new energy source started a new world of life. (Watching the ends of logs can be an exciting project for all ages.)

Trees cut in midsummer should be processed quickly or discolored wood will develop rapidly. Many organisms may colonize the cut surfaces but only a few organisms grow into the bolts. The invading fungi follow the bands of dying parenchyma cells. In conifers, the stain is called blue stain because the wood often has a blue color. The blue streaks look like spokes of a wheel because the ray parenchyma have a pattern like spokes of a wheel. In summer, trees have mostly sugars in the living cells and in the transport cells. This makes it easy for the bacteria and fungi to spread rapidly on an easy diet.

A New Tree Biology

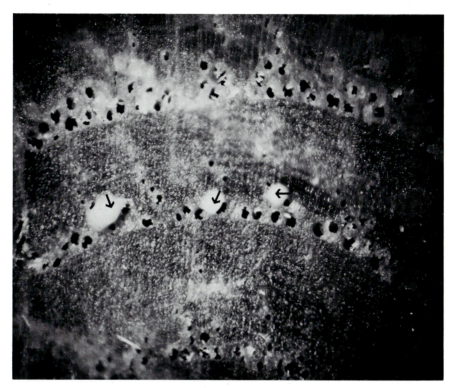

Figure 4-10

Bacteria also abound in wood exposed by wounds. The arrows show pustules of bacteria oozing from large spring vessels in a red oak. The pustules formed immediately after the section was cut. The bacteria were associated with darkly discolored heartwood that was in the path of wood boring insects. Again, the interaction of several organisms. The bacterium is *Clostridium quercinum*. It was the first species of *Cloistridium* to be found in trees. Species of *Cloistridium* grow where free oxygen is very low to lacking. We call such bacteria anaerobes (an, without; aerobe, air). Bacteria and fungi that require oxygen are called aerobes. Some bacteria are essentially aerobes but they can exist as anaerobes; these forms are called facultative anaerobes. Other forms go the other way; facultative aerobes. They are anaerobes that can exist as aerobes.

The faculative state gives an organism a distinct survival advantage because they can continue to live as the microenvironment about them changes. Many of the bacteria in wood called wetwood are facultative forms.

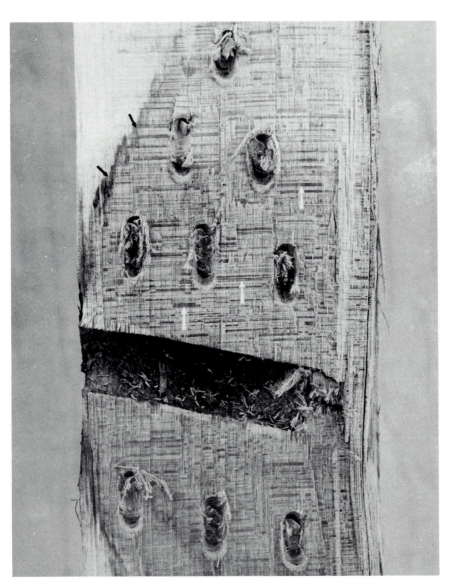

Figure 4-11

A New Tree Biology

What grows on the surface of a wound or a recently cut log is different from what grows in the wood. It is one thing for the organisms to compete among themselves on the wood surface, but another thing to compete or interact with the tree as some organisms grow into the wood. The first organisms to grow into the wood against the defense system of the tree are called pioneers. The pioneer must be a successful colonizer of the wound surface and a successful invader against the chemical and anatomical barriers of the tree.

After a tree is wounded, some cells are killed, some are injured and begin to die, and others deeper in are not injured. As cells are injured and die, their cell contents come in contact with the air. Chemicals in the cells react with the oxygen and these new compounds are usually antimicrobial—inhibitors—and they can not be broken down by the invading organisms. Yet, some pioneers can grow into the tree against the antimicrobial compounds. Some pioneers have developed unique ways to digest the defense compounds. Other organisms fight "fire with fire"; that is they alter the tree's compounds in such a way that makes the compounds not harmful. Some pioneers can tan (as in tanning) the tree compounds. The interactions between pioneers and trees are intense to say the least. The genetics of the pathogens and the tree play an important role in the struggle. A strong pioneer against a weak tree system puts the odds in favor of the pathogen. A strong tree system against a weak pioneer puts the odds in favor of the tree. The tree has the first opportunity to respond, but remember, the wound does injure the tree also.

Pioneers and other organisms that grow in trees are pathogens because pathogenesis is described on the whole organism basis, not on its parts. If an organism rots the tree, and it falls over and dies, the rotting organism is indeed a pathogen. We must talk trees, not parts of trees, or worse yet, "dead wood."

The photo shows a drill-type wound after 4 months in a red maple. A new growth ring has yet to form so there is no barrier zone. The 3-D margin of the column is the reaction zone (black arrows). Note the darker color of the margin of the column above the wound. Note also the shape of the column. The discolored column is actually a composite of many columns. Each column is within each growth sheath (growth ring if you wish). The living response power of the tree is greater in the younger growth rings. There are more parenchyma cells with living contents in the younger growth rings near the bark.

The white arrows show the sheets of radial parenchyma. The invading pioneers attack the dying parenchyma first.

The small cavities in the wood were formed when chips were cut out with a gouge. The chips were placed in a nutrient agar medium to determine the organisms growing in the wood.

Figure 4-12

A New Tree Biology

Here are a few details on how organisms are isolated from wood in trees. Blocks or billets of wood containing infected wood are cut from the tree. The billets are cut larger than needed. In the laboratory, or in a special room, the billet is cut to a smaller size. The bark is removed. The billet is taken to another room; a clean room. No air currents should be in the room. Keep air circulation to a minimum. On a block of well sterilized wood, the billet is partially split open with a flame-sterilized ax. The billet is then pulled apart. It is best not to pass the ax head or a knife entirely through the billet, especially where isolation chips are to be taken. Do not add alcohol to the freshly split surface. Do not add alcohol to the gouge. If the surface that is to yield the chips is suspect for contamination, pass the surface lightly over an open flame. Take chips of uniform size from the desired places with the flame-sterilized gouge. Use a set pattern for the chips, or remember your pattern and mark the positions after the chips are taken. With a sterlizied forceps, take the chips from the sample and place them into a Petri dish that contains an agar medium. Place the chips in a vertical position in the agar making certain that one of the pointed ends of the chip touches the bottom of the Petri dish.

Examine the cavities where the chips were taken in figure 11. Note they are all about equal size and depth. Make your first cut with the gouge in a vertical position. The tip of the gouge should be at a right angle to the billet. Push the gouge into the wood to depth of 4 millimeters. Take the gouge out, and make your second cut 10 millimeters away from your first cut in a longitudinal direction. With a twisting motion that starts with the gouge at a right angle to the billet, continue to decrease the angle as the tip of the gouge meets the first cut. If you do this properly, the chip will "pop" out of the sample and "sit" in the cavity. The chip can be easily taken from the cavity with the forceps. With some practice, the method can assure uniform chips for isolating organisms.

If the sample surface requires intense flaming, then take a chip, throw it out, and take a second chip within the cavity. This will take you deeper into the wood, and decrease the chances for surface contamination.

Mark your dishes *before* you start. If you are using a set pattern for taking chips, mark the bottom of the Petri dish with a line. Then go clockwise or counterwise with your chips from the line on the bottom. This will avoid the need to make many marks on the Petri dish. Always date the dishes.

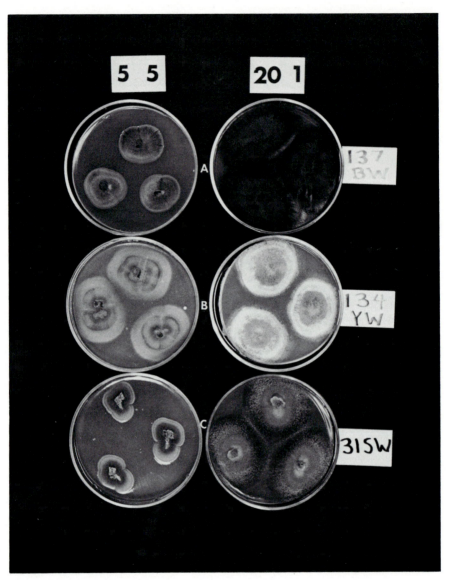

Figure 4-13

Some say, you are what you eat. This is very true for the fungi and bacteria. Fungi can appear very different in culture depending on the growth medium. The photo shows an example of different growth patterns associated with one medium that contained 5 grams glucose and 5 grams yeast extract in 1 liter of water with 20 grams agar (called 5-5 here, vertical line at left). Another medium was similar except it had 20 grams glucose and 1 gram yeast extract (called 20-1, vertical line at right). Note the differences in the 3 fungi; 137 bw, 134 yw, and 31 sw, on the 2 media.

Agar is a fine granular material made from red seaweed. When dissolved in water, heated, and cooled, the agar remains in a semi solid state at room temperature. The fungi grow on and into the agar, and the cultures can be easily examined.

When spores are wanted in culture, and this is the usual case for identifications, the carbon source, or sugar in the medium, should be low. When the carbon source is high, vegetative growth will take place, and few spores will develop. Yeast extract is often used to supply amino acids — for proteins, nitrogen source —, vitamins, and essential elements.

Over the years, I have used many different media depending on the aim of the experiment. But, for making isolations from wood, I have used 10-2 (10 grams malt extract, 2 grams yeast extract) more than any other medium. This medium supports rapid growth of most wood-inhabiting bacteria and fungi. In older media, yeast extract was not used, and Hymenomycetes grew well, but the imperfect fungi and bacteria did not grow well. It is also very important to place the chips as described. Many bacteria grow only on the bottom of the dish. Some fungi grow only on the top of the chip and not "down" on the agar.

The media and methods used for isolating organisms play a major role in what you isolate.

If you are looking for specific organisms it is best to use a medium selective for their growth. Many selective media are known. If you want Hymenomycetes the best medium is the wood itself. Cut the billet in half and place it back together. Leave it for ten days in a cool dark room, and the fungi will grow between the 2 sections. (A class project demonstrating this point can be of interest. Take a small tree trunk that has rot. Cut the trunk into discs and put them back in order. Leave it for a few days. The growth of the fungi will "glue" the discs together.)

Figure 4-14

Fungi and bacteria are also grown in liquid culture. Liquid culture makes it possible to accurately define the contents of the medium. Knowing the exact contents of the medium is essential for many studies.

The 4 flasks all contain the same ingredients—5 grams glucose, 1 gram yeast extract per liter of water—except for added microelements. The fungus is the same in all flasks; *Daldinia concentrica* (member of the Xylariaceae). In the flask at left 1 milligram (one thousandth of a gram) of calcium was added, next; 1 milligram of zinc; next to the right, 1 milligram of iron; and last at right, 1 milligram of manganese. The fungus grew best when zinc (Zn) was added. It was dark green and the liquid medium was green indicating the pigments were moving from the fungus out to the liquid medium. When iron was added, the fungus culture was green, but the filtrate, or the liquid medium was colorless. The fungus and the filtrate were colorless when manganese was added. This experiment showed that minute amounts of microelements could make the difference between poor and strong growth, and pigmentation. These essential elements should *never* be called "minor" elements. Indeed they are not minor.

Consider this experiment as we look at the tree and the fungi that grow in trees or the fungi that grow on fine, absorbing (please, not feeder roots!) roots of trees, the mycorrhizae. Small or extremely minute changes in soil element content or element availability could have profound effects on the soil microorganisms and the tree.

Fertilizers provide essential elements; microelements in many cases as well as the elements that are required in much higher amounts. (Calcium is not always considered a microelement, but an element required in higher amounts along with potassium, phosphorus and nitrogen.) The elements do not provide energy. The elements are not *nutrients*. Nutrients provide energy. Energy comes from the sun. Tree food is sugar. Add elements to an energy source and you have nutrients.

Figure 4-15

Fungi are also grown on wood blocks. Wood blocks are placed in soil or on agar media, stabilized, and then inoculated with fungi. When wood blocks are placed on soil, you really never know what elements in the soil move into the block of wood. The same can be said for agar. A better way to conduct experiments with wood blocks is to hang them over water. The water maintains the moisture in the jars. The wood does not absorb other ingredients from the soil or agar. In the experiment shown here, wood dowels were cut from a column of discolored and decayed wood longitudinally from most advanced decayed wood, left, to clear wood beyond the column, right. The dowels were cut at 10 centimeter intervals. The dowels were heat sterilized in an autoclave and inoculated with a decay-causing fungus. Note that the dowel that was most decayed in the tree—dowel in first jar at left—was the dowel that supported the most rapid growth of the fungus in culture. The dowel in the jar at far right was sound in the tree. It did not support growth of the fungus in culture.

Back to utility poles, and wood product decay. Wood that is sound in the living tree resists decay when made into a product. Wood that was decayed or near decay in the living tree will decay rapidly when made into a product and when conditions for decay are proper. It is very difficult or impossible to "see" the early stages of decay. But, once the triggers are set in the living tree, they will "fire" easily in the product.

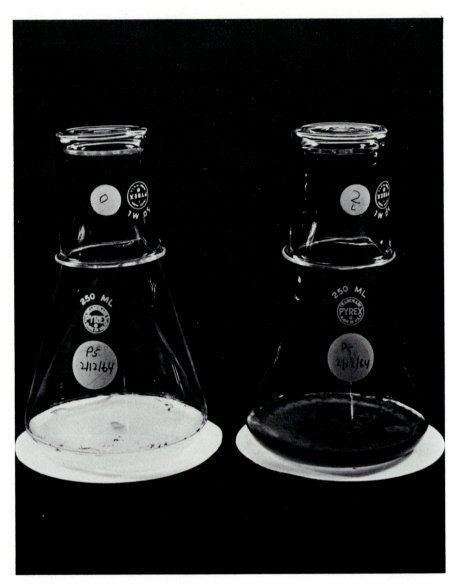

Figure 4-16

A New Tree Biology

Phialophora melinii and other species of *Phialophora* and related species are some of the most aggressive pioneers in trees. These fungi have some unique abilities: utilize nitrate nitrogen, digest or alter antimicrobial phenol-based defense substances, and grow in high amounts of microelements. They also have a reproductive structure (see figure 22) that enables them to produce spores in confined spaces, like inside vessels.

The flasks show *Phialophora melinii* in 2 different media: left, 5 grams glucose and 1 gram yeast extract in 1 liter water; right, same as at left except 2 milligrams of manganese as manganese sulfate was added to the medium. Without the amendment the fungus grew fairly well but did not produce any pigment. In the amended medium at right, the fungus grew very well and provided dark pigments in the mycelium—collective term for the hyphae or the vegetative part of a fungus. Little pigment diffused into the medium at right.

The point here, again, is that a little can go a long way when the ingredient is essential for life.

Phialophora melinii was the most frequently isolated fungus from discolored wood in beech, birch, and maple.

I believe fungi in this genus and related genera, *Trichicladium canadense*, for example, cause a type of soft rot in living trees. The fungi are closely associated with bacteria, and a more correct statement would be that these fungi *and* their associates cause a type of soft rot in living trees. The soft rot is a digestion of the middle layer of the secondary wall of the wood cell. The middle layer, or the S_2 layer is very thick (in comparison to the other layers) and contains most of the energy containing materials.

Microorganisms are not altruistic, they do not give up their lives so others can survive. When microorganisms gain "control" of some space to exist and some energy, they hold on to it for as long as they can.

Once a pathogen spreads into a tree it must "fight" 2 battles all the time to maintain its space and energy source. The pathogen must survive against the pressures of the tree to compartmentalize it and to limit its space for expansion and limit its energy source. The pathogen must "push" against the reaction zone, or walls 1, 2, 3 of CODIT. Also, the pathogen must protect itself from other microorganisms that are competing for the new space and energy. So, the pathogen has 2 battle fronts at least. And, pathogens get sick, too. Viruses do infect fungi. Other fungi and bacteria exert "survival pressures" on the pioneer. Knowing about these pressures gives us opportunities to give the advantage to the tree, or to organisms that can maintain their niche in the tree but not spread rapidly and cause the tree problems.

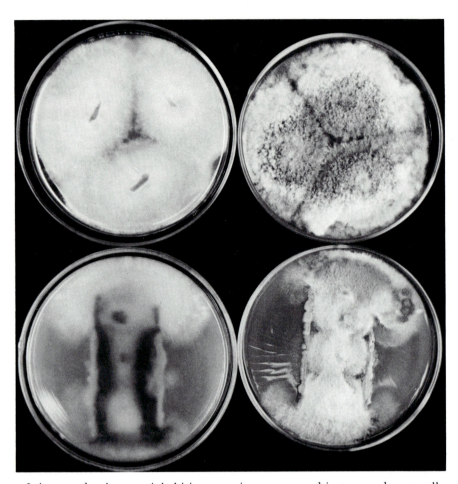

It is a wonder that tree-inhabiting organisms can spread in trees and eventually break down the wood. The organism must constantly "win" all types of battles, including the change of temperatures. Some organisms use temperature changes as their time to spread. These organisms that must grow — or else — in summer must compete with many others. So, the populations change in the tree just as the flowers change in a field over the year. Interactions with other organisms coming into "bloom" and then going out must be constant and each time the risks for the ones going out must be great. Will they be able to remain? Will there be a hollow next year where there is wood this year?

Fungi and bacteria are closely associated in trees. The cultures here show a decay-causing fungus in the upper Petri dishes — right, top of culture; left, bottom of culture. A bacterium isolated close to the fungus in the wood was inoculated near the fungus: right, top of culture of fungus and bacterium; left, bottom of culture. Note the dark pigments where the bacteria and fungus touched.

Pigment formation is important because colored wood may be a valuable product, or it could be a defect. The point; interactions caused varied results. *Figure 4-17*

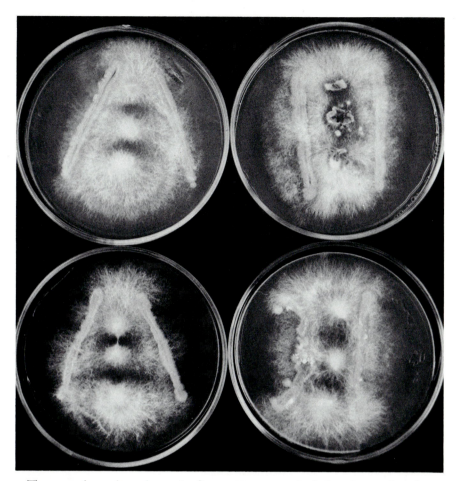

The same bacterium shown in figure 17 was streaked close to another decay-causing fungus. The bacterium and the fungus were compatible; no growth loss of the fungus, and no pigmentation.

The expanded concept of tree decay includes concepts of compartmentalization *and* microbial succession. Succession means that many organisms are involved in the process that may result in discolored and decayed wood. All wounds do not lead to decay. All wounds do not lead to large columns of defects. Compartmentalization and succession are at work. Nature is not made up of a system of absolutes. Natural systems resonate or vibrate over time. Most of the flowers in a field return the next year, but not all, and the scene is not always the same. The changing environment is a great factor in regulating successions and repeats of previous patterns. The advancing microorganisms in the tree by their advancement are also constantly changing the micro-environment. The point is that natural systems are always changing. The more we know about the rhythms of change the more we can do to alter the patterns or predict the patterns.   *Figure 4-18*

Trees and Microorganisms

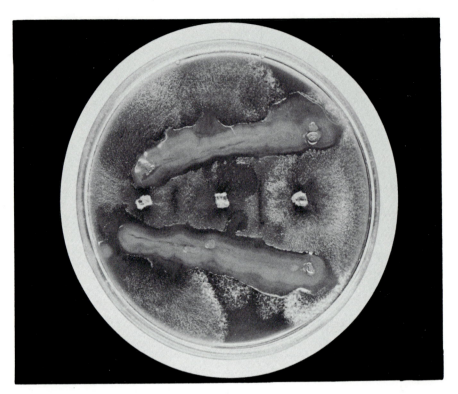

Figure 4-19

Bacteria and nondecay-causing fungi—*Cytospora decipiens* shown here—often grow together in discolored wood. The discolored wood is then caused by the tree *and* the microorganisms. The color of the wood may be in part due to the colors of the microorganisms. Yet, we know that the colors of the microorganisms is strongly affected by the substrate it is growing in. So, interactions are the rule more than the exception in nature.

The bacteria and fungus shown here were isolated from the same discolored wood chip. They are growing well together in culture. How each organism benefits the other is not well known. We do know that many close "partnerships" do occur, and if they are taken apart for study, then an artifact results.

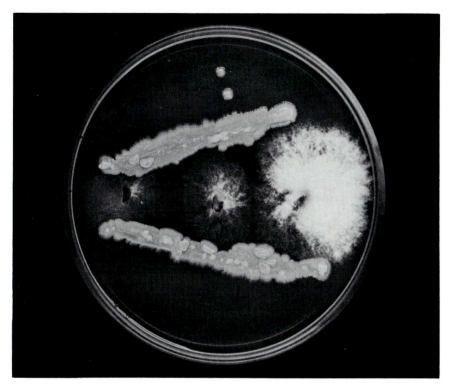

Figure 4-20

The bacterium isolated from discolored wood that bordered a column of decayed wood in a living tree was streaked alongside of the fungus isolated from the decayed wood. Here we see that the bacterium and fungus are not compatible in culture. The closer the bacteria is to the fungus, the slower the fungus grows. Yet, in the living tree the bacterium may still be beneficial to the decay-causing fungus, because the bacterium may stall or prevent other fungi from growing into the wood occupied by the decay fungus. Great care must be taken when extrapolating information gained from laboratory results to the living tree. What may appear one way in culture may be another way in the living tree.

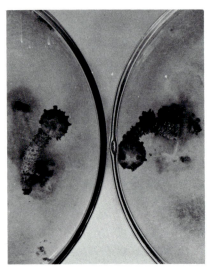

The nondecay-causing fungi usually produce spores in culture. It is necessary to use a microscope to see them. Some decay-causing fungi produce fruiting bodies, or sporophores, in culture as shown here for a species of *Pholiota*. Many decay-causing fungi produce sporophores on trees. Some sporophores persist for many years—conks—while others last for only a few days or weeks. Because sporophores are not on wounds does not mean that decay is not present inside. Removal of the sporophores will not stop the spread of decay inside the tree.

Figure 4-21

Figure 4-22

Some fungi produce spores inside the tree. The bacteria may form "resting spores" or they may be covered with materials that keep them in a "dormant" period for long times. The fungus shown here is *Phialophora melinii*. It is producing spores from structures called phiallides (arrows) in a vessel in a living red maple. The phiallides are bottle-like structures that are uniquely suited for producing spores in confided spaces. Other fungi, such as those that cause wilt diseases, may also produce spores within vessels. Some fungi produce yeast-like spores in confined spaces.

A New Tree Biology

Here is a sporophore of *Coriolus (Polyporus) versicolor* on a root wound on a yellow birch. The fungus is a common one that infects injured sapwood in a great number of tree species. *C. versicolor* is one of the first decay-causing fungi to spread into wounds. It is often replaced by other fungi.

Figure 4-23

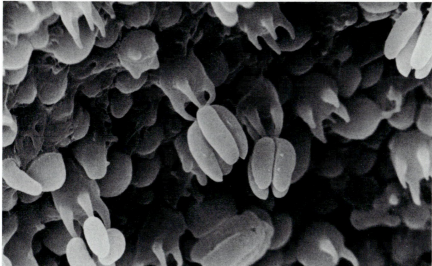

This photo was taken with a scanning electron microscope. It shows the spores—basidiospores—being produced within the pores of the sporophore of *Coriolus versicolor*. Note the 4 minute pegs that "hold" the spores. The spores are carried by wind, insects, or water to new wounds. A sporophore may produce billions of spores in a few days. People who try to protect wounds with sealants and other materials need to understand the ways of the micro world. A crack on a wound smaller than the eye could see would be a gigantic cavern for these spores. Many fungi produce spores for long periods, and they continue to do so for many years. The micro world is very patient. Man-made wound dressings protect the fungi after they get into a wound.

Figure 4-24

Figure 4-25

The micro world is a world full of beauty and wonder. These "flowers" are really crystals of calcium oxalate along the hyphae of the decay-causing fungus *Hirschioporus (Polyporus) abientinus.* It was growing in a white pine. The crystals are called druse crystals and the structures that hold them are called cystidia. The photo was taken with a scanning electron microscope. The crystals formed by some fungi aid in their identification. The crystals are the results of fungus processes that "tie up" materials that accumulate as the wood is decayed. Whether it is a fungus or a human, waste products can cause problems as they accumulate. The organisms in the micro world have developed many ways to deal with waste products. A better understanding of their methods could help us with similar problems. Indeed, we can learn much from nature if we take the time.

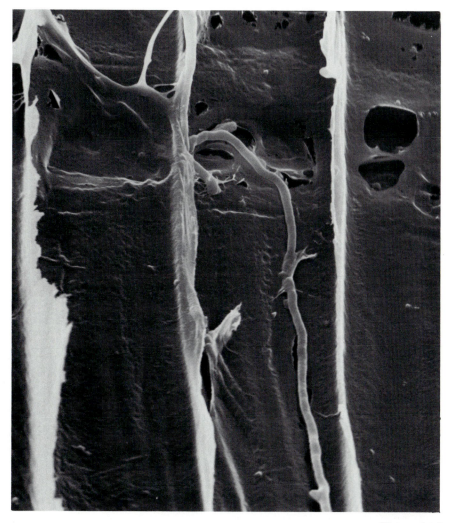

Figure 4-26

This section of a western white pine was in the early stages of decay (white rot). Note the eroded wall of the tracheid under the hypha of the fungus. The photo also gives a clear view of the inside of a tracheid. The vegetative part of a fungus is called a hypha (hyphae, plural). Another term for the fungus "tube" is mycelium (mycelia, many strands; plural). Some hyphae digest cell walls only in direct contact with them. Other fungi produce enzymes that spread beyond the hypha. In a sense, the wood may be predigested in this way. The enzymes of the fungi are able to break the glucose bonds in cellulose and then get their energy from the glucose. The white rot fungi (shown here) break down cellulose and lignin at about equal rates. Hollows in trees result when white rot fungi attack.

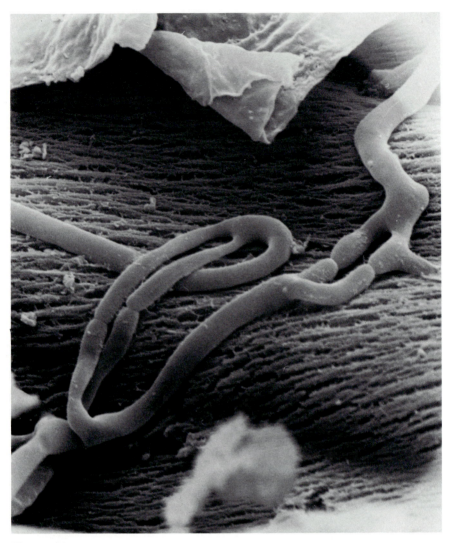

Figure 4-27

The fungus hypha shown here is also in a western white pine. The fungus is *Poria placenta*, and it causes a brown rot. The brown rot fungi may "send" enzymes far beyond the hypha. The enzymes break down cellulose, but only alter the lignin slightly. The decayed wood often has a dried appearance, and the wood has cracks that form cubic patterns. In wood products, the brown rot is often called "dry rot". The brown rotted wood will absorb water rapidly. The fungi grow rapidly when conditions are proper, and when conditions are not proper, the fungi wait. The fungi are very patient.

A New Tree Biology

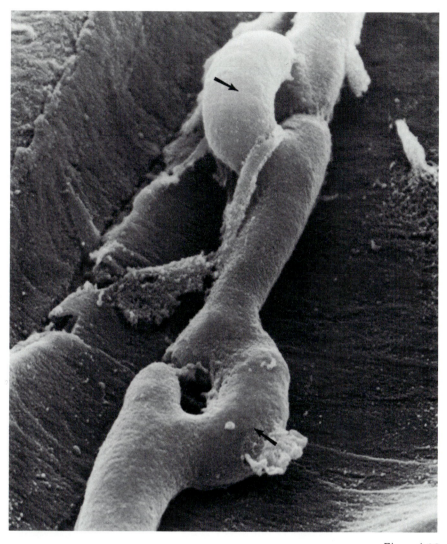

Figure 4-28

The arrow shows structures called clamp connections. Many fungi that decay wood *(Basidiomycetes)* have these structures. The clamp connections are the sites where nuclei from the hyphae meet and join. The fungi have developed many ways to unite nuclei. One very prominent mycologist once described the sexual ways of the fungi as, "how do I love thee; let me count the ways" (Dr. Kenneth Raper, in his president's address to the Mycological Society of America). ("Sexual ways" is used loosely here, because sex usually means morphological distinctions between opposite partners. Compatibility is a better word with the fungi because the genetic material that is combined is different but the contributing partners are not morphologically distinct.)

Trees and Microorganisms

Figure 4-29

Bacteria and *Coriolus (Polyporus) versicolor* in a tracheid. Note the eroded cell walls. Fungi and bacteria often are associated closely in decaying wood. The 3 inserts show single bacteria. Note the "tails" or flagellae that propel them. The bacteria can "swim" rapidly through the microscopic films of water that cover the insides of cells. The fungi must grow from place to place. The bacteria can move on their own power.

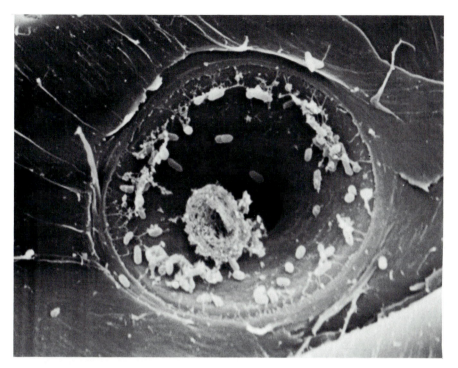

Figure 4-30

The openings between wood cells are called pits. The pits are unique "valves" that regulate movement of materials. There are 3 major types of pit pairs between cells: simple pits with no borders, between 2 living parenchyma cells; bordered pit between 2 dead cells; and half bordered pits between a living and dead cell. Bordered pits are between tracheids in conifers. Bacteria may digest the cells in the pits, and the "valve action" is destroyed. Pit digestion may occur in living trees and in wood products, or timber. The bacterial infections are most common when the trunks are ponded or floated in rivers. Pit digestion is one of the 5 ways microorganisms alter wood (also, white rot, brown rot, discolored wood, and soft rot).

When wood ages, or after injury, the pits close, or aspirate. When closed pits are attacked by bacteria, the result is wood with many openings. Spruce wood with many open pits may be the best wood for the tops, or bellies, of wood instruments. The old masters worked with wood that was floated down rivers or ponded for long periods. Pits can also be opened in sections of cut wood by applying cellulases, or enzymes that will digest the pit membranes. This has been done. The sapwood will have wood with open pits.

Thus, there are 3 ways to have wood sections (especially spruce for instruments) with open pits: 1, wood from sapwood with living parenchyma cells and connected with the tracheids; 2, wood that has had the pits attacked by bacteria (ponding, floating in rivers); and 3, chemical breakdown of pits using enzymes — cellulases.

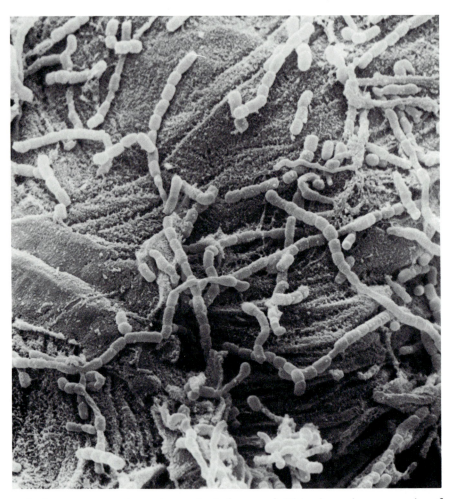

Actinomycetes, as shown here, also infect wood. This photo shows a species of *Streptomycetes* in the phloem of a cut section from a Douglas fir. The Actinomycetes are common in soils. The so-called "good earth" odor is usually given by the Actinomycetes. They are usually grouped closer to the fungi than the bacteria. The cells are connected to form long strands or chains as shown here. The Actinomycetes are "famous" for the many beneficial antibiotics they produce for human diseases. The Actinomycetes also form nodules on roots of some woody plants *(Alnus* spp.) and the microorganisms fix nitrogen (nitrates) that greatly benefit many plants.

The soil contains many organisms that are essential for growth of trees. Other woody plants that are often called weeds may also have associations with the microorganisms that help to fix nitrogen. When man destroys the forest woods and damages the soil so badly that beneficial organisms die, then the trees that are wanted for man's benefits will also die. It is happening now. Nature comes in large packages, not simple units only for the benefit of man. *Figure 4-31*

Myxomycetes are strange organisms. They are sometimes called slime molds. They are strange because they have characteristics of plants and animals. The body of the organism is called a plasmodium. The contents in the plasmodium are in constant flowing motion. The plasmodium can move. The spore-bearing structures may be a variety of bright colors, or black as shown here.

Myxomycetes also are among the many organisms that inhabit wood. When they are isolated from wood onto agar, cells that are similar to protozoa form. They have flagellae and are very motile. Resting spores are formed in culture. Indeed, many organisms are associated with the alteration and eventual breakdown of wood in trees and products.

Other organisms that inhabit wood and soils are nematodes and amoebae. One group of amoebae has the appearance of bats when viewed under the microscope. This group is called the vampiridae. The amoebae digest bacteria and other small organisms.

The nematodes are minute roundworms that not only inhabit soils but they may inhabit columns of decayed wood in trees. Some nematodes attack fine roots with a needle-like sucking mouth part. In doing so, they may also transmit viruses to the tree. A recently discovered tree disease has nematodes and fungi and insects all associated. The nematode is called the pine wilt nematode. Again, the point is not to give details on nematodes, amoebae, myxomycetes, etc., but to make you aware of the many organisms that are interacting among themselves and with the tree. It is a natural web of connections. *Figure 4-32*

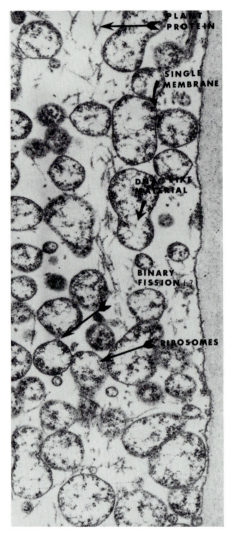

Figure 4-33

Viruses and mycoplasmas must also be added to the list of wood inhabitants. It is often difficult to place these bodies in discrete categories. A virus may exist as a crystal form and then "come alive again" within a living cell where it may "take over" the functions of the cell. Viruses appear like small rods or match sticks when viewed under the electron microscope. They are common in many trees.

Mycoplasmas are shown here. The arrows point out some features of the bodies. The mycoplasmas are associated with a group of diseases called "yellows" and with witchesbrooms. They have been found within the inner bark of several species of trees. They are associated with the spike disease of the sandlewood tree. (The sandlewood tree, for its weight, is the most valuable tree in the world. The pernambuca of Brazil could be ahead of sandlewood when pernambuca contains high quality wood for instrument bows.)

Figure 4-34

Fuel or energy that powers the life processes of all the organisms that inhabit wood come ultimately from the sun. The energy of the sun is trapped in a molecule of carbon dioxide and water and we call the substance sugar. The sugar, or more correctly here, glucose, makes up the cellulose of wood. The organisms break down the cellulose — shown here in a western white pine — to glucose and unlock the energy of the sun that was held in the chemical bonds. The chemical bonds once unlocked and energy released then "give back" carbon dioxide and water. The energy of the sun is passed on as stated in the laws of thermodynamics. When time is extended, and when conditions for life are proper, all living matter will break down. By understanding these processes we can often extend the periods when wood can be useful to us and wildlife. The breakdown processes start when organisms infect wounds, and dying branches and roots. Prevention of wounds, proper pruning, and proper cultural practices that prevent death of branches and roots can extend greatly the life of trees.

Trees and Microorganisms   145

Figure 4-35

Organisms that get their energy from wood also break down wood products. To complete the list of 5 basic ways that organisms alter wood, it is necessary to say a few words about soft rot (more on wood product decay is in the chapter on utility poles). Soft rot is the erosion or digestion of the S_2 layer of the secondary wall of wood cells. Wood cell walls are made up of a primary and a secondary wall. The primary wall is thin. The secondary wall is thick, and is divided into 3 layers called S_1, S_2, and S_3. The middle layer, S_2, is the thickest layer. It contains the greatest amount of cellulose. Bacteria and nondecay-causing fungi may grow in this layer. The infected wood appears like brown rot, or as if the wood were burned as shown here. A type of soft rot can also occur in trees as fungi such as *Phialophora* and closely related genera also digest the S_2 layers. Soft rot is a problem in hardwood utility poles (especially in Australia), and in softwood poles in the U.S.A. (Note the ant entrance and exit hole; arrow.)

Figure 4-36

A soft rot-type of problem is found in softwood utility poles as shown here. The wood appears water soaked. The affected portions of the wood may extend to the surface of the pole. The electrical resistance of the infected wood is very low; 19 k ohms shown here. Noninfected wood is over 500 k ohms.

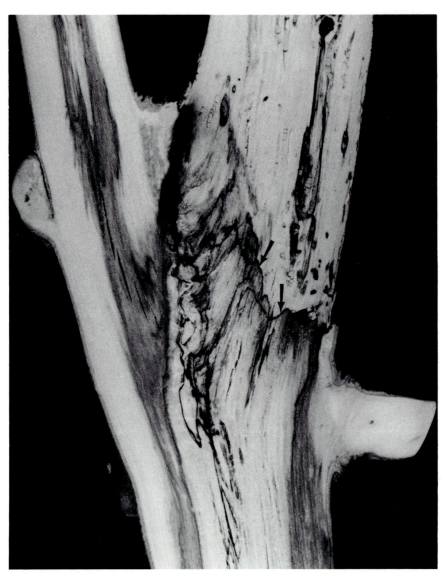

Figure 4-37

A New Tree Biology

Tree, organisms, interactions, and the web of life have been the subject repeated many times in this chapter. It deserves all the repeating that pages will allow. Nature does not come in discrete little boxes. A tree that lives to maturity must interact with thousands of organisms during its life. The apparent paradox is that wood-inhabiting organisms survive so long as they digest trees. Trees survive so long as they are not digested by organisms. Over hundreds of millions of years some "deals" had to be worked out. The compartmented tree with boundaries was the answer to survival for all and the resolving of the apparent paradox.

The oak section shown here is a good example of the point of boundaries and survival. Trees form boundaries as defense chemicals form to strengthen natural boundaries after injury and infection. The strengthening of the natural boundaries results in the reaction zone or Part I of CODIT. More boundaries form as tree and organisms interact. Each contribute to the boundary that protests both the tree from rapid spread of the pathogen and the pathogen from other pathogens that could grow into the newly colonized space. So, boundaries resulting from the interaction of tree and organisms are mutually beneficial. Then, after the wood has been occupied by the pathogen, the pathogen forms boundaries—zone lines—that continue to protect it from other pathogens. Thus, there are 3 types of boundaries: 1, tree alone, 2, tree and organisms interacting; and 3, organisms against organisms.

The arrows show the zone lines. The decay is spreading downward through the discolored heartwood. The dark boundary between the decayed wood and the sound heartwood is a boundary formed by the interaction of the tree and the decay-causing pathogen. The boundary formed by the tree alone at the base of the large dead branch has been breached by the pathogen. Boundaries are not absolute. They do not stop a force; instead they resist.

Trees are generating systems. As boundaries fall and as parts are shed or compartmentalized, new parts are formed in new positions. This is the unique feature of the tree's survival system. The more we know about it, the more we can do to help the survival system. And, if we cannot help it, we should not inflict treatments on the tree that destroy its natural survival system.

Figure 5-1

A New Tree Biology

CHAPTER 5

Trees and Animals

Trees support the lives of many large organisms. Trees are used for food, shelter, and sites for reproduction. Many animals also use trees for resting, nesting and for places from which to hunt or capture prey.

The major characteristics of a tree that benefits wildlife is *size*. A good tree for wildlife must be a big tree. Small, decaying trees may support wildlife, but only small animals for a short time. The large healthy tree that has a few wounds, and a few cavities will have long term benefits for many small and large organisms. Some large animals can only use large trees for shelter. The point here is that even when we talk about wildlife and cavities we still must talk about healthy trees. A healthy long-lived tree will be a better wildlife tree.

As forests are cut repeatedly, the number of large, old, healthy trees decreases. The best way to force an organism into extinction is not to attack the organism but to attack its niche; the place where it lives and reproduces. To try to protect an organism on one side, and to destroy its niche on the other side is a folly we see done worldwide. This is why so many animals are becoming extinct, or have entered the list of endangered species.

Animals, like the microorganisms, require their territories to be so large. When the boundaries of the territories begin to shrink, the niche loses one of its major requirements: space to live and reproduce. And niches in the forest have boundaries just as the niches within trees have boundaries. Streams, ledges, soil type change, and other natural formations set the natural boundaries. Man has added some new boundaries as roads, dams, and all types of construction have changed water drainage patterns and have made some territories smaller. Trees and organisms that live in, on, and about trees can still adapt to some of these changes. But, when the changes repeat faster than adaptation can occur, trouble will result for trees and its community of associated organisms.

This chapter expands on this theme. Again, this is not a quick course in wildlife management or wildlife biology. It is a chapter on trees and some of their larger associates.

The photo at left shows an eastern hemlock with many holes made by the yellow-bellied sapsucker. Examine the site carefully. This area was recently logged. There is not much left for wildlife.

Figure 5-2

When yellow-bellied sapsuckers inflict many wounds in a tree such as the hemlock shown in figure 1, many barrier zones form. The barrier zones form as cambial xylem cells differentiate to form a tissue that is very strong in a defense way but very weak in a structural way. As the wood ages, circumferential separations may occur along the barrier zones as shown in this eastern hemlock sample. The defect is called ring shake. Ring shake is a serious defect because the boards cut from a log with the defect will fall apart. The "shake" may continue far beyond the wound site. Think of a shake line as a small tear in a piece of strong cloth such as canvas. A pull on a piece of canvas will seldom result in a tear, but if the pull is on the canvas with the small tear, the cloth will separate. The same patterns occur in trees that have weak spots in the wood.

The yellow-bellied sapsucker pecks into several hundred species of trees. The birds eat insects mostly, but they often mix the insects with sap and inner bark and feed this to their young. The birds migrate in winter. The males often return before the females in spring. The birds may eat sap and inner bark in spring before insects, especially ants, become plentiful.

Sapsuckers pecked this paper birch at one location on the trunk. A swollen black band formed. On some trees such as maples and oaks, the birds may peck several holes in a horizontal line. Sap flowing from the holes is often inhabited by yeasts. The fermentation process produces ethyl alcohol. The sap may also be a food source for fungi that have black mycelium. The bark on the trees will become black. Black bark on maples is a sign of sapsucker injury.

Figure 5-3

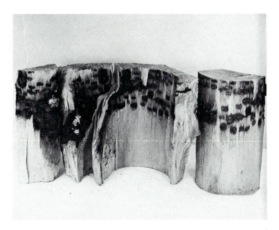

Figure 5-4

Dissection of the black band shown in Figure 3 reveals the shake zone. When sapsuckers peck birch to form the black band, the peck injury usually occurs at one time period and is not repeated. On some trees the birds continue to peck until the trunk is girdled, and the portions of the tree above the girdle die. When the dead tops break and fall to the ground, their presence indicates a sapsucker territory. The tops have many peck holes and are easy to identify.

Figure 5-5

Bridges of dead bark may remain over large wounds made by the sapsucker. When all the bark bridges fall off, it may be difficult to identify the wound as a sapsucker wound. Bark bridges on the forest floor are indicators of a sapsucker territory. Sapsuckers establish their territories about their nesting sites. Trees within the territory will be pecked. Once a bird selects a favorite tree, in the forest or in the back yard, it will continue to peck on it. There are no known humane ways to discourage the birds from pecking in a selected tree. For some unknown reason, the birds will often select exotic trees, or trees planted on sites where they do not usually grow.

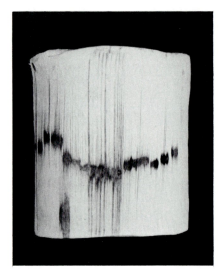

Figure 5-6

The bark has been peeled from this yellow birch to show the defects associated with 1-year-old sapsucker wounds. It is a rare panel wall that does not have a few of these streaks. When logs with these defects are used for rotary-cut veneer, the streaks and dark spots from the wounds will be present in the veneer. You can not grow trees free of sapsucker injuries when nesting sites are nearby; usually within 300 to 400 feet.

Figure 5-7   *(Page 155, left)*

Yellow-bellied sapsuckers are very particular in the trees they select for nesting. A favorite tree is the aspen, especially when the tree has a central core of firm decay that is about 4 to 6 inches in diameter. The red-cockaded woodpecker in the South selects pines

A New Tree Biology

| Figure 5-7 | Figure 5-8 |

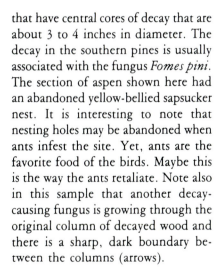

that have central cores of decay that are about 3 to 4 inches in diameter. The decay in the southern pines is usually associated with the fungus *Fomes pini*. The section of aspen shown here had an abandoned yellow-bellied sapsucker nest. It is interesting to note that nesting holes may be abandoned when ants infest the site. Yet, ants are the favorite food of the birds. Maybe this is the way the ants retaliate. Note also in this sample that another decay-causing fungus is growing through the original column of decayed wood and there is a sharp, dark boundary between the columns (arrows).

Figure 5-8

Many other birds and small animals use cavities in living and dead trees for shelter and nesting (arrow). Large trees are best but small cavities in small

trunks are also essential for many small animals. The tree, fungi, insects, and animals are all associated in this story. Many animals and insects take the fungi to new sites. The fungi rot the wood and cavities start. In living trees, the cavities have boundaries that remain even after the trunk dies. The animals also take tree seeds long distances, and new forests can start. The insects are not all bad. Many are beneficial: pollination, destroy weak seeds and seedlings, help to break down forest litter, etc. Insects are also food for the animals. And, the circle continues. We must be careful when we target one group as bad or destructive. There will always be parts of the circle that appear destructive, but somehow the system has functioned very well without the help of man for hundreds of millions of years. Man is now a part of the circle, and when we make decisions, they should be made from the view within the circle rather than from a position far outside the circle.

Trees and Animals

Figure 5-9

The basal wound on the western hemlock in Washington was made by a black bear. The bear tears the bark from several species of conifers in the spring. The sap flows from the trees and yeasts grow on the sap. Bears have been observed tearing at the bark of trees while foam flows from their mouths. Could it be that the bears get some of the products of the yeasts, and then they go on a bark biting spree "thinking" that every new bite will produce more? The fact remains that black bears do cause serious damage to young trees in the Pacific Northwest. They usually bite the most vital trees.

Figure 5-10

Woodpeckers often peck through sound wood to get ants, termites, borers and other insects that may be deep in the trunk. Insect borers were in this white pine (arrow). The woodpecker had to work very hard to reach an insect. The oblong-shaped feeding hole is different from the nesting holes that are usually round. Note the resin-soaked wood above the hole and the discolored heartwood. The wounds start new columns of decay that attract more insects that later become more bird food.

A New Tree Biology

Squirrels bite the bark of twigs and young trunks of many species of trees. Maples and birches are favorites, but oak and beech are commonly wounded by squirrels. The squirrels bite the sunny side of smooth-barked maples early in the spring when the sap is beginning to flow (arrow). A typical bite pattern shows one wound where the top teeth anchor into the bark and 3 to 5 wounds opposite these as the bottom teeth move upward to meet the front teeth (examine arrow area closely). The sap flows from the wounds and frequently yeast begins to grow in the sugary liquid. (Sap in maples can be as high as 4% sugar — sucrose — in the spring.) The sap may concentrate in the sun below the wound. When the squirrels return, it is not known how much maple syrup or sugar they get and how much of the product of fermentation supplied by the yeasts. Like the black bears, squirrels have been observed in spring moving rapidly from tree to tree biting small twigs and trunks along the way.

Figure 5-11

Figure 5-12

The arrow shows a wound in a black birch branch inflicted by a red squirrel. The branches often break at the wound site during high winds, or after a heavy snow. The wounds are usually infected by microorganisms.

Serious injury results on small trees when many squirrel wounds are inflicted and infections start, as shown on these young maple trunks. The young stems break easily at the canker sites.

Figure 5-13

Figure 5-14

The single arrow shows the wound made by the top teeth of a red squirrel. The double arrows show the multiple wounds made by the bottom teeth. The sample at right shows the infected wood associated with a squirrel wound on a young red maple. The dark streaks are often part of the defects called mineral streaks. Mineral streaks start from dying branches and wounds made by insects—sugar maple borer—, animals—yellow-bellied sapsucker, squirrels—, and machines.

Figure 5-15   *Figure 5-16*

Many large plants also live in and on trees. The epiphytes are the first ones to come to mind, and the orchids head the list. In the moist tropics, plants grow in layers from the soil upward. Space to exist is a major factor affecting their survival because moisture is abundant in the rain forests and temperatures vary very little. Trees parasitic on other trees are more common in warm climates. The most famous parasitic tree is the sandlewood. The wood is valuable because of its pleasant aroma. The largest flower in the world — *Rafflesia arnoldii* — is a parasite on roots of a vine — *Tetrastigma lanceolarum* — that grows on trees in Indonesia, Malaysia, Brunei, Thailand, and the Philippines. The flower may grow over 3 feet in diameter. Insects pollinate the flower and small animals are thought to disseminate the seeds. The circle of organisms associated with this flower is one of nature's many marvels. But, two species of *Rafflesia* are thought to have become extinct in the last few decades. The niches that support the flower have suffered greatly from the wars of man. Sad. Big trees, big vines, and big flowers require big spaces. When big spaces are reduced, the big inhabitants die. So simple. So difficult to have understood.

The figures above — 15 and 16 — show that vines can also cause trees serious problems. Nature vibrates. We must be careful what we call good or bad or beneficial or destructive. Maybe we should look more at the large picture rather than its parts. I am always reminded that the systems have survived and that means something.

Figure 6-1

A New Tree Biology

CHAPTER 6

Survival

Some Philosophy

Survival means to remain alive under conditions that have the potential to kill.

Trees, as we know them today have been evolving on this earth for over 200 million years. They have survived the killing forces of countless pathogens and the ravages of environmental extremes. Somehow, some trees have remained alive under all types of conditions that had the potential to kill. But, trees did not accomplish this by acting as individuals. Trees connected or interacted with a great number of other living things, and together they survived. The power of interactions and connections kept many living things alive. Indeed, trees evolved in groups. They had group protection and group defense. They were protected and defended by their neighbors and associates, and trees protected and defended them. A tight circle or web of connections was the way the individuals within the group survived.

Now the connections are being broken. The heart of the survival system is being threatened. The most deadly words to the survival system are "suddenly and repeated." Given enough time most members of the large circle adapted to adverse conditions. But, when adverse conditions repeat faster than adaptation can occur, then the entire system is threatened.

Trees never knew a stump until axes and saws came into the forest. Trees never knew complete removal of trunks, machine compaction of soils, sudden changes in water drainage patterns due to roads, pollution, and disruption of niches for soil organisms. The list goes on. These actions have come *suddenly*. They are being *repeated*.

Man has also taken the trees out of the group and planted them as individuals. This is a new condition for trees. A tree planted as an individual requires special attention. It must be pruned, watered, fertilized, and attended to in a way that gives it the protection and defense of the group.

We have run too fast with trees in forests and cities. It is time to hold for a moment, and to go back and reexamine the tree *and* its circle of associates. There is hope. We can mend the torn pieces of the web if we start now. This is the theme of this chapter.

Figure 6-2

A New Tree Biology

Trees trap the energy of the sun in a molecule we call sugar. Sugar is tree food. Of all the energy from the sun that reaches earth, only 0.1% is trapped. Trees trap 50% of that energy. Trees are our major energy trapping system. Trees also hold the soil to prevent erosion. And, trees may even affect the weather. The warming and cooling patterns over trees contribute to cloud formations. When trees are removed and the soil gets hot, as in the tropics, clouds may not form. The result is drought. It has happened in our time. My point is that we can not discount the importance of trees as a force affecting many living *and* nonliving systems on this earth.

Indeed, the tree does seem to be the "mother earth living center." Maybe this is why so many ancient cultures worshiped the sun *and* the trees. The sun was the sender and the tree was the major receiver.

When we say tree, we usually think of the above ground parts. No doubt those parts are important, but more activities for the tree and its associates go on under the ground, unseen. The parts above ground need the parts below ground, and *vice versa*. When too many of the above ground parts are destroyed, the parts below ground will also suffer. Not only the tree roots, but the many organisms that are associated with the tree roots.

The point here is that you can not attack one — above ground parts — without attacking the other — below ground parts. But this is still not all bad. Yes, we must harvest mature trees. And, when the "suddenly" is not "repeated" the system will adjust. But, when the "suddenly" is "repeated," faster than adaptation, trouble will start not only for the tree but for the tree associates. Trees may be planted back on the site and all looks well above ground, but the world below the ground may still be in a period of shock. This is a difficult point to make understood because we gauge so much from what we see; and we see the above ground parts.

Survival depends on vibrations of constant adjustments among all members of the system. When one part *zigs* the other part *zigs*. The system then vibrates on the *zig* motif. When changes occur and parts of the system go to a *zag* state, then in time the entire system vibrates about the *zag* motif. Trouble starts when some parts of the system switch to *zag* while other parts are still in the *zig* position.

Trees, like all organisms, die 3 basic ways: 1, mechanical disruption; 2, dysfunction; and 3, infection and energy loss (starvation). In the last few centuries man has caused tree problems in all 3 categories. New tools and machines have caused new kinds of wounds. Mechanical disruption is a common way many trees die. Dysfunction is primarily a problem of genetics. Some vital part fails — dysfunction. We really do not know how the gene pool has been disrupted by our practices. Yet, when you consider that less than 1% of the trees that start life in the forest ever reach the age where they reproduce, and that we plant trees in cities that come from seed lots where we expect 80 to 90% success in growing trees, it must mean that we are planting many trees in plantations and in cities that would never grow in the forest. The natural system would eliminate them very quickly. We protect them at a high cost. Man has also aided many virulent pathogens by moving trees out of their natural habitats. The point here is that we have made it very difficult for trees to zig and zig, or zag and zag. And, when one part of the system is zigging and the other part is zagging, trouble will follow. We want too much too fast.

Figure 6-3

A New Tree Biology

Trees in the virgin forests grew to massive sizes and some grew for thousands of years. The Pacific coastal redwoods are massive trees with diameters of over 25 feet at the base and some over 345 feet tall. The *Eucalyptus regnans* in Tasmania were even taller than the redwoods only a few decades ago. The really big ones are gone now. The trees in the virgin forests had insect and disease problems, pollution — especially sulfur — from volcanos, and storms and environmental extremes. Yet, some trees still grew for many years and to massive sizes. Now, trees in our forests seem to be dying at younger ages and smaller sizes. My point is that I do not think we should blame the insects, diseases, environmental extremes, or pollution for these problems. Yes, all play a part in the general problems we are seeing worldwide, but I believe the major problem is that man has violated the natural system by acting too suddenly and by repeating the injuries to the system. Once the zig or zag motif moves to zig and zag, the entire system begins to weaken. Then any number of other agents can easily move in. But, even all of this will not eliminate or destroy the natural system based on the tree community, because the system still has another survival tactic. The tactic is to make the parts smaller and to decrease the amplitude of the zig-zig, or zag-zag vibration motif. This is what the American chestnut tree did. It is still abundant throughout its old range, but now it is a small tree, or even a bush or shrub. Many stems grew long enough to reproduce. The tree is *not* extinct. It has changed to a smaller organism and it is now adjusting the reproduction cycle to a shorter time — it is going from the *zig-zig*, through the zig-zag, and to a new zag-zag motif. The American elm is starting the same procedure. Elms have all but gone from most cities, but they are abundant in many areas along the new wet spots along new highways. We have created a new favorable niche for the elm. The niche is similar to its original habitat. The trees along the roads still get infected. I believe they will follow the path of the American chestnut and survive as a smaller tree with an earlier reproductive cycle.

Man with all his and her brains is still not smart enough to destroy the inner circle of trees and associates. Long before this could happen, the man-induced injuries to the tree system willl have harsh effects on man, and this will cause a readjustment in man's system long before the trees are hurt. For these reasons it is essential to learn more about the tree and its associates.

When trees are in trouble, man is in trouble.

Survival of all living things depends on 8 major factors: 1, energy; 2, space to exist; 3, water; 4, essential elements (16); 5, concentrations of factors; 6, time; 7, temperature; 8, genetic code.

Animals move, and they seek out the survival factors, usually each as a unit. They find their food, go to the drinking area, move to a warmer or colder area, etc. They even move to regulate the genetic code as only the strongest male individual wins the privilege to reproduce.

Trees cannot move. They either "like" where they are growing, adapt to unfavorable conditions, or die. All the survival factors are linked for plants. When one factor is affected, the others are also affected.

The survival factors are finite. Only so much energy from the sun reaches the earth. The earth is only so big. Only so much water and elements exist. It is as if we live in a large Petri dish! Yet, we seem to see the number of living things increasing on earth. Just as the Petri dish with its agar nutrient medium has its limitations for growth, so does the earth. The only major difference between the earth system and the Petri dish is that energy keeps coming into our system. This encourages life to proliferate. But, still the other factors are finite. As life proliferates in the earth system, 2 major alternatives arise: 1, larger numbers of organisms will die as smaller pathogens infect and utilize the stored energy of the infected organisms, or 2, organisms will evolve to be smaller with a shorter reproductive cycle. As mentioned already, this is the survival tactic of the American chestnut.

We do not know how many times in the past the large circle of connected organisms went through these processes. Could it be that in the past life did begin to approach the limits of the survival factors? The situation would be like the collapse of a giant star as the entire system had a gigantic implosion. And, the organisms at the end of the food chain would be most affected. Those that were able to survive would be smaller with shorter reproductive cycles. If such an event happened or would happen, I still see the trees as the best suited for survival because of their inability to move, and because of their obligatory associations with the other living things in, on, and about them. Movement away from problems or adverse conditions is always a short term solution. Holding your ground in the face of difficulties is a long term solution. This is why I believe trees are so tough. They cannot move away from problems. And, when really disastrous problems occur, and there is no room for those who run normally, to run, then they will be the first to perish.

Lack of movement on one hand appears to be a problem for trees, but over the long term it has been their best survival tactic.

Pain "tells" an animal to move. Trees could not move, so the pain response had no survival value. Trees evolved as highly compartmented plants and their survival systems were centered about standing their ground and forming boundaries about their enemies. Yet, what we call the enemies, were really not enemies to the group. They were enemies to the weak individuals. The pathogens killed the weak individuals, thus maintaining only the strongest for the group. We often "trip" over our words because we think—justly so—like humans. But we should be careful not to inflict trees with our human remedies. We must also be careful where we plant trees because the planted tree still has only 3 choices: 1, grow; 2, adapt; 3, die. Many trees are committed to an early death at the time they are planted. They may be individuals that would never have survived in the forest. Death is the rule for the individuals in the forest. Life is a rare reward for those that can stand their ground against problems. Those that live become a part of the group. The point here is that what may be bad or destructive for the individual is good or beneficial for the group. We view trees primarily from the individual. And our orchards, plantations and city trees are individuals. By protecting the individuals that are weak, we may be weakening the group. What does all of this mean? It means that we need healthy trees—individuals—in our orchards, plantations, and cities, and they will come 2 ways: 1, selections from a large gene pool in the natural group, or 2, genetic selections and improvements through new technology. In the first case, we must be careful not to destroy the natural gene pool. A tree that does not produce the best timber may have genes to survive after others are infected. With the second point, we must start selecting and breeding trees that can survive in new environments like orchards, plantations, and in cities.

Indeed, survival is a difficult subject to discuss. Philosophy still leaves much that demands better answers. Yet, it is *nice* to know these things and to ponder what may have happened to the dinosaurs, but when forests are dying *now*, orchards have a new problem called "short life," and Mrs. Jones has a sick tree in her yard that she wants "healed" fast, then we must do something now. We must do the best we can. But, we should always work on at least 2 levels: 1, do what we can to help the tree or trees now; and 2, try to develop programs that will prevent the situation from happening again.

The New Tree Biology demands that you understand trees, and to make decisions based on tree biology. The New Tree Biology means long-term programs for our forests, orchards, plantations and city trees. The problems we have today have taken hundreds of years to develop and they will still not be solved by miracle medicines and magic in a short time. Again, we must do the best we can for the sick trees now, and then begin to develop long term programs. If we do not, it will not only be bad for the trees, but for us. We are at the end of the food chain!

But, what about the "balance of nature?" Is not this balance the answer to survival problems? Let us examine this myth. A balance is a static state — no change. When any part of the natural system does not change, it dies, or it becomes an easy target, and will die soon. Nature does not seek a "balance." Natural systems do vibrate about some mean or central point. The vibration is the zig-zig that we have discussed. Nature always "seeks to compensate" but usually goes beyond the desired point. This motion is what keeps the system alive or dynamic or everchanging. Because it is always changing it has the built-in ability to change again when impacted.

One of the major problems we have as humans is that it is very difficult to conceive of long term processes. We may be able to understand a century, or even hold onto the events of a thousand years. But, 10,000 years? A million years? The thread breaks. The numbers become just numbers and not meaningful measurements of events over time. Yet, to understand the zigs and zags of trees and the large circle of tree associates millions of years of events must be understood. Again, why do you need to know this stuff? Because a century or two of changes are sudden changes to the system. Three or even four centuries may be the generation time of many trees. So the impacts have only begun to affect the system. So--- what can be done? A better understanding of trees is the first step. It is not so much what we must start doing as what we must stop doing. We must make decisions on trees from a basis of tree biology, not human biology!

Let us now discuss how the tree traps energy and how the tree system functions.

Figure 7-1

A New Tree Biology

CHAPTER 7

Leaves

Trees are highly compartmented, woody perennial, shedding plants, that usually have a single stem and are massive and long-lived. Trees are highly compartmented because the basic compartment, the cell, has a tough wall made up of cellulose mostly with lignin as a "glue." Cellulose is a compound made up of glucose units. Lignin is a complex polymer that binds the cellulose units. Some cellulose units are very orderly and they are called crystalline units while other units are not so orderly and they are called amorphous units. Regardless, the cell wall of trees is tough. Animals have a thin weak membrane about their cells. Animals are compartmented, but very weakly compartmented. A thin splinter of wood cells will stand upright, but a similar group of muscle cells, even from a tough body-builder, will not stand upright if taken out of the bundle of cells in a muscle. Each tree cell and the group of wood cells are self supporting. A tree has built-in strong mechanical support. Animals need a skin to hold the cells together and a framework of bones to hold the cells and the skin and the organs upright. Hardly a comparison to the structure of trees. But we can move; for reasons that are good or bad. Heavy compartmentation negates movement. Animals move to avoid destructive agents. Trees meet them head on. Only the tough trees stay alive.

Trees are shedding organisms. Many of their parts are "used" and then shed. Shed does not mean cast off. Shed means that some type of partition, or better yet, boundary, forms to separate the "used" part from the rest of the tree. Trees are compartmented. Trees are made up of many strong boundaries. The boundaries separate the "used" parts form the remaining healthy or still functional parts. The boundaries also separate aged, injured, and infected parts from the healthy parts.

Trees normally shed their nonwoody parts—the parts that do not have secondary growth. Primary growth is more like the cell types that make up annual plants. Primary growth lacks lignification. Primary growth is the result of cells that are formed and differentiate, but do not have additional cells growing or forming over them. The leaves, needles, reproductive parts, absorbing roots, and outer bark are examples of primary growth. Secondary growth occurs where new cells form over the older cells. Secondary growth means lignification of the aging cells. Secondary growth means layers of cells over time.

Trees usually set boundaries between their nonwoody parts and the woody parts that will be a part of the secondary growth. A tree grows as a cone over a cone over a cone, etc. In this system a tree is both an annual and a perennial plant. Some parts are similar to annuals, and some parts may be similar to biennials—2 and 3 year needles.

Shedding is also a way that a tree "regulates" mass. As parts are shed the living mass or dynamic mass of the tree is reduced. Trees "keep" wood and inner bark, and sometimes outer bark and shed the other parts. And, as wood cells age, the tree sets boundaries and forms chemical zones that separate the aged cells from the newly forming cells. Trees are compartmented and generating systems. New cells are always being formed in new locations.

The figure shows some of the tree parts that are normally shed. Energy is required to form the parts and energy is required to set boundaries to wall off the parts. As the themes of trees are developed here you will see the constant role of energy in all of the tree functions.

My methods of discussing these points is to give some basic information, and then, give more details as the story is told. I constantly repeat and roll the story like one rolls a snow ball. If you roll a snow ball too far in one direction it will either collapse or become a snow roll, not a ball. The direction of roll must constantly change. Some parts always fall away as direction is changed. But, if the method is strictly followed, a nice round ball will result. This is what I am trying to do.

Figure 7-2

Some trees not only shed nonwoody parts but also wood parts such as twigs, woody roots, and even branches. Oaks, hemlocks, and aspens shed twigs. Some trees shed large branches such as the Brachychyton tree from Australia (Fig. 2). Branches that form from epicormic buds—adventitious buds or dormant buds; adventitious where they form anew in the cambium; dormant where they are carried along in the cambium—may be "pinched off" by the trunk collar that surrounds the base of the branch. This type of branch shedding can cause serious damage to property and people. Tree treatments that stimulate the formation and growth of such branches, such as topping, should not be done, especially on trees that form heavy horizontal branches. This problem also occurs on fruit trees, and especially in warm climates, where large, heavy branches will form in a short time. On some species of Eucalyptus the problem is compounded because the epicormic branches grow horizontal first and then new branches grow vertical from the tip, thus causing the weak union at the trunk to break.

The technical term for branch and twig shedding is *cladoptosis.*

Figure 7-2

Figure 7-3

Figure 7-4

Needles and leaves (Figs. 3 and 4) are major energy trapping organs of a tree. Trees have 3 organs: 1, roots; 2, stems or trunks; 3, leaves. Reproductive parts are adaptations of the needles and leaves. Chlorophyll in the leaves (meaning needles also, henceforth) captures the energy of the sun. The center of the chlorophyll molecule is magnesium. The center of hemoglobin in blood is iron.

As sun light strikes the chlorophyll it is not only trapped in a chemical reaction of carbon dioxide and water, but the chlorophyll is also broken down. The tree must continue to renew the chlorophyll. This takes a constant supply of energy. The energy of the sun—heat energy—is "held" in the chemical bonds that hold the carbon dioxide and water together. The molecule is glucose. The molecule is soluble in water and can move out of the leaf or other green part of the plant that has chlorophyll. Chlorophyll can be in young stems and branches and in the young central tissues called pith.

The tree food moves out of the leaves in the phloem. Just exactly how materials move downward in the phloem is not clearly understood. Some pumping action of the cells is suspected as the driving force. The place where the tree food is made is called the source. When the material or substance moves to another place and is changed chemically so it cannot move further then we speak of this place as the sink. When the energy-containing material is used we say that it moved from a source to a sink. The leaves are "loaded" as they form sugar. The leaves are "unloaded" as the sugar moves out. Leaves usually move sugar

A New Tree Biology

only out of their tissue, they load and unload. If certain growth regulators are added to leaf tissue, the leaves may reverse their flow and reload from their own sugar source. This can be done when cytokinins—growth regulator—are added to the tissue. Knowing this is important because we look at the day when we can really "feed" trees. Feeding trees means giving trees food—sugar, energy releasing materials—not essential elements. The elements in fertilizers are essential and we need to fertilize some trees, but tree fertilizers do not give the tree an energy source, thus fertilizers are not tree food. When essential elements are added to an energy source, then we have a nutrient. Trees do not get food or nutrients from the soil.

Buds begin to form in the axles of leaves (Fig. 5) as soon as the leaf begins to develop. The trees take no chances. If the leaves are destroyed, the new buds break and form more leaves. And, as these new leaves form new buds are also forming. Consider some of the leaf problems trees have early in the spring. If it were not for the reflushing of the buds, the tree would

Figure 7-5

die. Many insects and fungi attack the newly formed leaves.

The buds may contain only flower parts, only leaf parts, or a combination of flower and leaf parts. Of course, the leaf parts extend to form stem tissues, especially when the bud is at the tip of the twig. On most trees the leader bud, or dominant bud grows fastest and usually forms tissues that extend the branch or growing tip of the tree. But, in some trees such as the beech, lateral buds, or side buds, may also grow rapidly to form long extensions of lower branches. The beech may grow for long periods by extensions of lateral branches. When the top bud or leader does get space in the upper canopy, the shape of the tree changes rapidly. Then the large lower branches die and may start trunk defects 1 to 4 meters above ground.

Leaves

Figure 7-6

Leaves are attacked by a great number of insects, mites, and microorganisms (Fig. 6). These organisms do affect the energy-trapping system directly. The infected areas are usually walled off. Many types of fungus infections are called leaf spots because they have limited margins. Mites may form galls on the leaves, but the galls do not reduce greatly the energy-trapping ability of the leaf. The insects that eat the leaves do cause problems. When the leaves are destroyed — gypsy moths, spruce budworms, etc. — the tree usually forms new leaves. To form new leaves, the tree must use stored energy from the previous year. When energy reserves are low, the reflush of leaves may take so much of the reserves that other tree processes begin to weaken, especially the defense process. If other pathogens attack at this time — root-infecting organisms — they may be able to spread rapidly in the tree. The root-infecting fungi may be the first to attack weakened trees because it also takes energy to form root periderms, or corky, or suberin boundaries at the base of nonwoody roots. If the root protection boundaries do not form, or if they are weak, the fungi may spread from the nonwoody roots into the woody roots.

Figure 7-7

When some buds open, the number of leaves and the length of the new twig extends only so far as predetermined within the bud. The growth is said to be determinate. On some trees the growth continues until late in the season; nondeterminate growth. Another condition occurs in some trees. Some buds begin to burst midway through the growth period. This type of growth has many names tied to religious events that also occur at about this time.

The eastern hemlock (Fig. 7) shows the recent opening of some buds. American elm will also have this type of extended twig growth.

Just as some buds "get the message" to burst, later in the season some needles are shed long before others. On hemlock and other trees, some twigs always die every year. The dead twigs appear to be at random. When so many twigs are shed on hemlock — cladoptosis — the entire branch will die. How the tree regulates these aging processes is now well known. Of interest also, is that young hemlock seedlings seldom grow where hemlock needles are on the soil. This phenomenon occurs with other species of trees also. Trees do have many systems that we understand very little.

CHAPTER 8

Fruit

Figure 8-1

Figure 8-2

Reproductive parts are modified leaves. The cone is on an eastern white pine (Fig. 1), and the fruits below are on a witchhazel (Fig. 2). A fruit is a ripened ovary and all of its adnate parts. A seed is a ripened ovule. There are many variations on the theme of fruits: nuts, samara, cones, pomes, etc. A great amount of energy is stored in seeds. Some trees form seeds early in the growth period—elms, maples, aspen—while others form them late in the season—oaks, walnuts. Many trees are cyclic in producing seeds; they do not have heavy seed crops every year. Other trees, such as elms, birch, and aspen usually have a heavy seed crop every year. The American elm produces mature seeds before the leaves are fully developed. This is a high energy drain on the tree. American elm stores starch all year while other trees store starch mostly in the dormant period.

The resin on pine cones is normal. Insects may infest the cones and the frass of the insects gets into the resin.

Some trees have flowers with male and female parts together—elms—other trees have male flowers and female flowers on the same tree—oaks—and other trees have male flowers on one tree and female flowers on other trees—ash, holly.

Cones containing seeds from a yellow birch above (Fig. 3), and male cones below (Fig. 4). The male cones start to develop in the fall. The female cones are very small in the fall. The male cones grow rapidly in the spring and shower female cones with pollen. Many insects and fungi attack reproductive parts. The male and female cones shown here are infested and infected.

Of the billions of seeds produced by trees in the forest, few ever germinate. The few that germinate start a difficult life that is constantly threatened by many insects and fungi. The seeds and seedlings provide for these organisms. If even a fraction of the seeds grow, space to survive would be a critical factor that would affect their development. Yet, there are always a few that survive and eventually make up the group.

Figure 8-3

Figure 8-4

Fruit

Figure 9-1

A New Tree Biology

CHAPTER 9

The Cambium and Bark

The cambium is the cell generator. The cambium is made up of living cells that divide to increase the number of cells in the wood and bark. In the process of cell division, the cambium increases its number of cells also.

When the word cambium is used, it is usually the vascular cambium that is meant. The vascular cambium divides to produce wood or xylem on its inner side toward the center of the tree, and phloem or inner bark on its outer side. All cells produced by the cambium are alive at the time they are separated from the cambial mother cell. As the cambium divides, the newly formed cells accumulate to form a zone of living cells. This zone of living cells that circles the tree is called the cambial zone. The cells in the cambial zone look, and act, like cambial cells, because that's what they are. Whether a single layer of cambium really exists is a point of controversy. The cells in the cambial zone have not differentiated to form wood cells or phloem cells.

The cambium is made up of cells oriented in the axial direction of the tree, and cells oriented in the radial direction. When the cambial cells that are axial begin to age and differentiate to form wood, they form vessels, fibers, and axial parenchyma in deciduous hardwoods, and tracheids, fiber tracheids, and axial parenchyma in conifers. The axial transport cells — vessels and tracheids — and the fibers enlarge rapidly, and the small amount of protoplasm in the cells, breaks away from the cell walls. The cell ages, enlarges, and dies. The time from "birth" of the cell until death may be several days to several months. In some trees, fibers may contain living contents for several years.

The axial parenchyma and radial parenchyma may contain living contents in some tree species for over a hundred years. Reports of living cells, 150 years old are given for sugar maple. The parenchyma cells are relatively thin-walled cells that do contain a great amount of protoplasm.

The parenchyma cells that are in wood and bark are extensions of the cambium. But, unlike the cambium, they do not divide to form new cells. The best possible reason for this is that the parenchyma in wood are "locked" in place by other cells. There is no room for their divided progeny to grow.

The parenchyma cells are connected by thin strands of living material called plasmadesmata. The connections make up the symplast. The dead portions of cells and empty space surrounding the symplast is called the apoplast. The symplast makes up the living network within a tree, and the network is connected to the cell generator, the vascular cambium. The symplast in the phloem continues outward to form the bark cambium, or the phellogen. In the photo at left (Fig. 1), the large arrow shows the cambial zone made up of 5 to 8 cells. The smaller arrow shows the radial parenchyma cells in the phloem. The pointer shows radial parenchyma in wood. In figure 2, the arrow shows the bark cambium, or phellogen. It also forms a cambial zone made up of several to many cells. The phellogen zone produces cells that differentiate to form bark or phellem on the outer side and phelloderm on the inner side. As the circumference of the tree increases the vascular cambium produces cells that increase the circumference of the cambial zone. This same process occurs in some trees — birch, beech — for the phellogen, but in other species, the phellogen ruptures as the circumference of the tree increases. (More on this is given in the chapter on bark.)

The important points to know are that the vascular cambium is really a zone of cells. The wood and phloem are alive when produced by the cambium. Some cells, the axial and radial parenchyma, may remain alive for many years. The living network or "webwork" in trees is the symplast. The symplast is the "message carrier" in trees.

The vascular cambium is like a queen bee, ant, or termite. It is trapped in place. It must rely on others for food. It only produces cells. The outcome of the cells, or into what forms they differentiate, are not directly controlled by the cambium.

The bark cambium (arrow), or phellogen, phellem, or outer bark, and the phelloderm are often called the periderm (Fig. 2). The rough, hard, corky phellem may also be called the rhytoderm.

It is important to think of the living cells as a network that reaches outward to the corky bark and inward to several or many growth rings. Parenchyma cells do die. As the tree grows older, the oldest parenchyma cells of the margins of the network are dying. The parenchyma within the wood die in place because there is no place to move. This may not be the case with cells in the inner bark — phloem — and outer bark — periderm. The inner and outer bark cells are always on the move because the tree is expanding in circumference. Boundaries formed in the bark will also always be on the move. This means that most protective or defensive boundaries in the bark may be broken every growth period, not by pathogens, but by the natural processes of bark expansion. This is why many pathogens spread rapidly in bark. There are times when the tree defense system is not very effective because of the expansion of the bark.

Time for some "constructive philosophy" on this point. A tree is a very strong organism. But, it does have some very weak points that occur at set times. The timing of natural living processes in plants is called phenology. When bark cells are expanding, the tree has a temporary "Achilles' heel." The weak spot is there only for a short time, but if a pathogen attacks at that time, it will have the advantage over the tree. Once the time period for the weak spot is over, the tree regains its defense system. This is one reason why boundary-setting or compartmentaliza-

Figure 9-2

tion is not *always* successful. Few natural processes are absolute in that they function perfectly all the time.

The point here is that boundaries in the bark are not the same as boundaries in the wood. Boundaries in the wood may hold for many years, while bark boundaries hold for a year. This means that an aggressive bark pathogen has a new opportunity to spread in the bark every year. This is exactly what many bark pathogens do and they cause perennial cankers, canker rots and root rots.

The Cambium and Bark   181

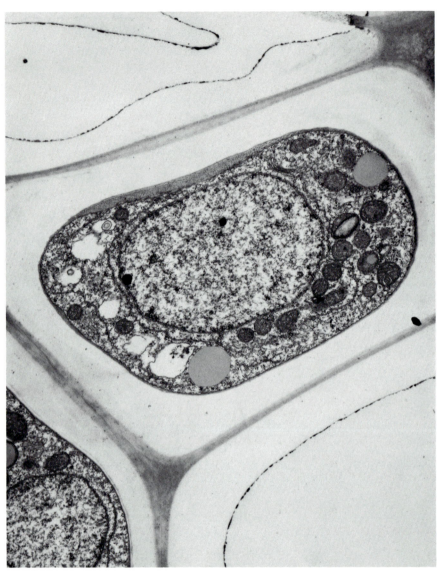

Figure 9-3

The photo at left (Fig. 3) shows a living cell in wood. The living contents are called protoplasm. Many bodies with boundaries exist within the living cell. This is also a type of compartmentation. The concept of compartmentation can begin with the cell and build upward or it can still start with the cell and work downward into the cell. The nucleus is the body that contains the genetic matter of the cell. Some of the other bodies are mitochondria, Golgi bodies, and lysosomes. The lysosomes are bodies that contain substances that lyse, or digest, the cell contents after injury and infection. The chemical substances are kept within their bodies by boundaries. Energy storing materials—oils, starch—are kept within the protoplasm of living cells. The living cell is a center of many types of dynamic and potential activity.

The cell locked within the wood requires a constant supply line for food, water, and essential elements. The cells must also have ways to exhaust waste and gases. The movement of materials into and out of cells is powered by energy trapped in the process called photosynthesis. It is important to know that the living cells deep in the wood of trunks and support roots are dependent on the leaves for their energy and on the absorbing roots for their water and essential elements. Even when the tree is not growing or when the leaves are trapping energy, the living cells still require a constant supply of food, water and elements. As trunk sections and support roots get larger, the demands for energy by the living cells in the wood increases. The energy costs of keeping cells alive is high. This must be kept in mind when pruning, topping, and when roots are destroyed. Living cells do protect themselves from starvation by storing oils, starch, and other materials. But there are limits to the amount of energy that can be stored. When trees are topped or pruned harshly, the stored energy in the living cells must not only maintain the living processes, but the energy must be used to produce new leaves and absorbing roots.

When energy reserves are low and there is not enough time to reload the reserves, the tree is in danger. If no injuries or infection occur at this time, most trees can rapidly replenish their reserves. But, if injuries or infection occur at this time, the tree could be in for trouble.

Trees begin to store energy after the leaves have matured. The soluble sugar is changed to insoluble oils and starch near the end of the growth period. The current growth ring does not store energy reserves until the end of the growth period. As the treee goes into dormancy, the energy reserves are at their highest point. Some trees can still trap energy in twigs and trunks where there is chlorophyll during the dormant period. This is common with conifers, and evergreen hardwoods. In spring when new growth starts, the energy reserves are usually at their lowest point at the time leaves are forming. This is a very dangerous time for trees. The period may last only a few days, or even a shorter time. But, if infections or injuries occur at the time the reserves are at their lowest point, the tree may not be able to mount a strong defense system. Chemicals for boundaries and for antimicrobial compounds must start from reserve materials mostly. When reserves are low, the defense system is also low.

Learn the energy flow patterns of the trees you work with. Be very careful with any treatment during the energy low period and the period when soluble food — sugars — are being converted to insoluble energy reserves. This latter period is when leaves are falling. Be careful when leaves are forming and when leaves are falling.

Results of wounding experiments showed that the symplast can regulate the activities of the vascular cambium. Holes were drilled almost through the trunk of maple and birch trees (Fig. 4a). Care was taken not to touch the cambium with the drill bit. Samples that had cracks from the tip of the drill bit outward were discarded. The photo of one of the samples (Fig. 4b) shows the dark outline of the tip of the drill bit. Eleven healthy growth rings were between the drill bit tip and the vascular cambium at the time of the wounding. The sample was prepared 2 years after wounding. The arrow shows the barrier zone that formed after wounding. Note the wide growth rings distal to the arrow tip. Note also the change in the radial parenchyma within the growth ring that formed after wounding. This response was replicated in other samples on other trees, suggesting that the cambium need not be touched to respond. The barrier zone attenuated in a circumferential direction to both sides of the arrow indicating that the wound response was greatest directly distal to the tip of the drill bit.

The significance of these results is that they show the cambium as tissue that can receive "messages" from the symplast. Such a process has great survival value. If the tree is in trouble because of low energy reserves or infection, which may also result in low energy reserves, the cambium would respond to the problem even though the problem was not directly associated with the cambium.

We do not know the nature of the "message sender." It could be a chemical response or an electrical response. Regardless, the response of the cambium to injuries to the symplast is real. This may help to explain why barrier zones may form far in advance of injured wood.   *Figure 9-4*

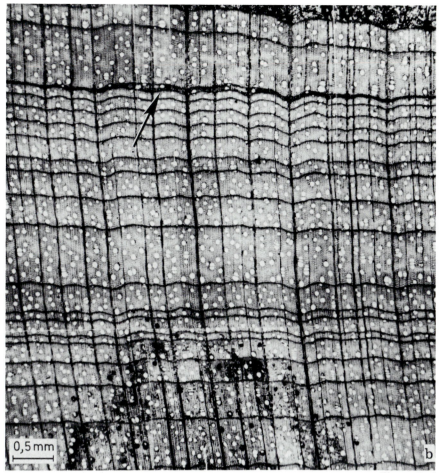

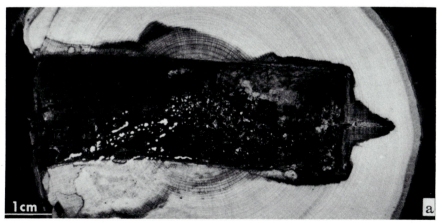

Figure 9-4

The Cambium and Bark

Figure 9-5

A shallow 1-year-old bark wound was on this *Quercus robur* from Holland (Fig. 5). The wounded area was from the crack at left to the crack at right. The wounded area at right was so shallow that new wood continued to grow. The old rough bark was removed when wounded and new bark formed. The new bark was generated, not regenerated because the new bark is in a new spatial position from the old bark. Trees do not *re*generate cells, which means forming a new cell in the same spatial position of an older cell. Note the small mounds of new wood and bark on the white dry face of the wound at left. When wounds kill cambium, but not the extending radial parenchyma cells, the parenchyma cells may divide to form new wood and bark. This shows that the ray parenchyma are really the extension of the vascular cambium. But, the ray parenchyma cannot normally divide because they are locked in place by other wood cells. When the ray cells have room to divide, they will as shown here. When shallow wounds are covered with black plastic and kept moist, the cells formed by the ray parenchyma may differentiate to form roots.

A New Tree Biology

Figure 9-6   Figure 9-7

The bark on the 2 American beech trees (Fig. 6) is smooth and tight. The bark cambium on these, just as on the paper birch in the background at right, divides in 2 directions: anticlinal, to increase width of wood and phloem; and periclinal, to increase circumference of the cambium. In such a way, the phellogen remains intact and the outer bark also remains intact.

This photo shows some other points of interest. In the forest, few large, low, horizontal branches ever develop. Trees shed the lower branches when they are small. Trees evolved in groups and branch shedding was a normal process.

Note also the irregular white lines on the beech trees. The lines are caused by slugs that eat the algae on the bark. Indeed, the tree is a community center for many organisms. Of course, smaller organisms within the slugs make it possible for them to digest the algae.

In contrast to the smooth bark on the beech trees, the bark on this large, old Douglas fir (Fig. 7) is very thick, corky, and rough. The bark plates form as the bark cambium splits. The nature of the cambial splits determines the outer bark patterns. Bark is the first line of protection for trees. Bark contains long fatty acids called suberin, and waxes. The suberin gives bark its "corky" characteristic. Very few organisms produce enzymes that can break down cork. (Could it be that the corky bark is also a very good electrical insulator?)

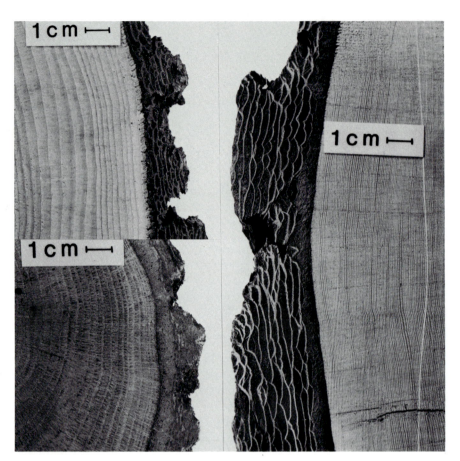

Figure 9-8

Here are some cross-section views of bark: white pine, above left; red oak, lower left; Douglas fir, right (Fig. 8). Note the crushed phloem or inner bark, and the plates of outer bark. As the bark cambium breaks in the bark, or forms fissures, the crushed phloem or inner bark comes to the surface. No matter how thick the outer bark is on a tree, the phloem will be at the inner surface of the fissures.

When the needle electrodes are used with the Shigometer to measure the electrical resistance of the cambial zone, the needles should always be in a verticle position and pushed into a fissure. The needle will then go easily into the inner bark and through the vascular cambium. The needles should be pushed inward until they begin to penetrate wood.

A New Tree Biology

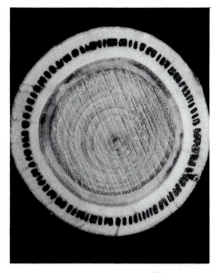
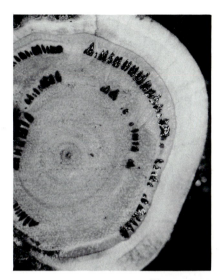

Figure 9-9   Figure 9-10

The eucalypts have several bark patterns. The so-called stringy-bark eucalypts have outer bark that is like a thick, tough fiber mat. Trees with this type of bark are highly resistant to fire. Other bark patterns are similar to the corky bark plates on oaks. The smooth-barked eucalypts have a thick, moist bark, and the outer shell of bark is shed. On large trees, the large sections of bark could cause serious injury if they fell on a person.

When some eucalypts are wounded, the cambial zone responds to form a defense zone of ducts called kino veins. Kino is a polyphenol, and is called an extractive. The kino can be dark red to blood red. In figures 9 and 10 the trees were wounded in experiments designed to study the position of kino veins. In *E. wandoo* (Fig. 9) the kino veins formed on the outer side of the cambial zone and appear here as isolated ducts in the bark. In figure 10 the kino veins formed on the under side of the cambial zone and were "locked" within the wood of this *E. camaldulensis*.

The kino veins or bands are a type of barrier zone that forms as a result of injury. It is of great interest to see that they may form on opposite sides of the cambium in trees that receive similar types of wounds. It may be that in some tree species, the outer cells of the cambial zone are stimulated to form cells that differentiate into kino veins, while in other tree species, the inner cells of the cambial zone may form the cells that differentiate to form kino veins. The point here is that different trees do different variations on the theme of defense boundaries.

The bark on some trees may become thick and swollen. Corky bark is a term given for this condition. The spindle-shaped swollen trunk area is common on sugar maple and yellow birch as shown here (Fig. 11). The cause of the corky bark is not known.

The dissection of the tree shown in figure 11 shows the thick corky bark (Fig. 12). The thick bark is associated with radial streaks that give the cambial area the appearance of a condition called stem pitting. The internal defects associated with the swollen area seldom develop beyond the corky bark.

Figure 9-11

Figure 9-12

A New Tree Biology

Figure 9-13   Figure 9-14

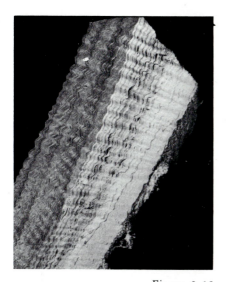

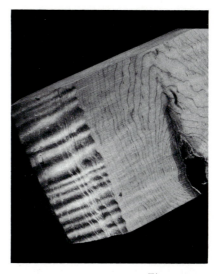

Figure 9-15   Figure 9-16

Here are sections showing different wood conditions associated with thick corky bark. Corky bark may be the visible sign of several different problems. Figures 13 and 14 show a pattern that has been seen in maples, birch, and black cherry. The sections show cambial miner injury also. Figures 15 and 16 show wavy wood patterns associated with thick corky bark. We know very little about problems of the inner, and outer bark. It does appear that the corky bark "syndrome" is also associated with the vascular cambium, or the wood would not be affected.

Figure 9-17

The white patches on the bark of these American beech trees (Fig. 17) are caused by the presence of millions of scale insects; the beech scale, *Cryptococcus fagisuga*. The insects suck liquids from the tree. Two species of fungi in the genus *Nectria*; *N. gallegena*, *N. coccinea* var. *faginata*, are known to attack the weakened trees. Yet, some trees are highly resistant to the scale insect and the fungi. Thicker bark and rapidly formed defense materials in the bark are some of the factors affecting resistance.

Some fungi grow into bark and even grow along the phellogen. What role these fungi play in beneficial or destructive processes is poorly understood. Could it be that some bark-fungi associations are similar to the root-fungi (mycorrhizae) associations? We do not know the answers, but we know the fungi are there. We also know that algae cover the bark of many trees. Are some of the algae members of the blue-green group? Algae in this group can fix atmospheric nitrogen. If they did this in lenticels, the nitrogen could be available to the tree. My point here is that we know some parts of many stories, but very few complete stories about bark and its inhabitants.

A New Tree Biology

It seems that the more beautiful the bark is, the greater the temptation by vandals and thoughtless people to disfigure and hurt the tree. Because beech bark does not shed, it is a favorite bark for recording all types of occasions (Fig. 18), from first loves to where a bear was killed. In too many cases, the tree suffers from the treatment.

Another favorite tree for bark injuries is the paper birch (Fig. 19). The tourist *must* go home with just a small piece of bark, and it is thought that such a small piece from such a large healthy tree will not hurt. Many birch trees are killed every year along the most scenic areas because of bark stripping. It is a pity when people will travel so far to see the wonders of nature, and then disfigure, or even kill, the very things they come to admire.

Education and awareness programs are badly needed in this area. It is your responsibility and mine to do all we can to get the messages out to people. The vandal has never been stopped throughout history, but some of the tree injuries are done by people who really do not think they are hurting the trees. We can't stop all the injuries, but we can reduce them greatly. This is our job!

Figure 9-18

Figure 9-19

CHAPTER 10

Roots

Roots support the tree, store energy reserves, absorb water, and with the help of root-associated fungi, absorb elements that are essential for life (Fig. 1). There are woody roots and nonwoody roots. The woody roots are large support roots and smaller fine roots. The nonwoody roots are nonmycorrhizal or mycorrhizal — associated with fungi.

The anatomy of roots is basically the same as trunks. The roots have a vascular cambium, bark and wood. There is no pith in the center of roots. The roots usually have more parenchyma cells and fewer fibers. The distinction between growth rings is not as clear in roots as it is in trunks. Roots do not have a normal, colored, core of heartwood. The anatomical changes from trunk to root occur in a transition zone at the base of the tree. There is seldom an abrupt anatomical change from trunk to root. If there is a pith center, the section is trunk and not root.

Roots, like branches and twigs, also age and die. As roots die, boundaries form that resist the inward spread of pathogens. When nonwoody roots die, a corky periderm — boundary — forms that separates the nonwoody infected root from the healthy woody root.

Roots, like trunks, are dependent on the leaves for their food. Roots also have a higher proportion of living cells to dead cells than trunks. And, energy is required to keep the living cells in a healthy condition. Roots — nonwoody, mycorrhizal — do supply the tree with water and essential elements. But, roots do not supply the tree with energy releasing materials. Roots do not make food.

When trees are fertilized or when essential elements are added to the soil, the tree *is not being fed*. Trees do not get food from the soil. Fertilizers are essential, but fertilizers are not tree food. The nonwoody roots should not be called "feeder roots." What are they feeding on?

Roots have protection features — bark, high amount of living cells, low nitrogen content of wood — just like trunks. When roots die, boundaries form. When roots are injured and infected, boundaries form.

Many aggressive pathogens infect roots when soil conditions or root health conditions weaken the protection features and the defense systems. When soil is compacted, oxygen for normal metabolism of the living root cells is hampered. When methane gas fills the open spaces in the soil, oxygen is forced out of the soil, and the results are the same as compaction. When water fills the pore spaces in the soil, again there is no oxygen. Oxygen is required for respiration. Respiration is the process that "burns" energy materials — sugar — to release power to "run" the cell processes. Respiration is an energy-releasing process that requires oxygen. Photosynthesis is an energy capturing process that releases oxygen.

When normal cell processes are interrupted, or energy becomes limiting, the roots become stressed. Stress is a reversible process. Stress is a condition resulting from some disruption, breakage, drain, or shunt of energy. When the condition

Figure 10-1

of stress continues, then the tissues become strained. Strain is an irreversible condition resulting from excessive stress. When roots become stressed and strained, boundaries that would normally form do not form, or they are very weak boundaries. The pathogens then spread rapidly from nonwoody roots into woody roots. Or if it is the time of year—phenology—when bark boundaries are normally weak, then the pathogens have a double advantage for rapid spread. When the tree does regain its energy reserves (if it does) or when normal bark boundaries begin to form, the pathogens may be walled off. But, by this time some vascular cambium has been killed. The walling off of the root-infecting pathogens may take place, but at a high price to the tree. In walling off the pathogens, large portions of the root wood are also walled off. The walling off of wood decreases greatly the volume of living cells that normally store energy reserves. So, the "fuel tanks" become smaller. This is not so injurious if no new infection occurs within the current growth period or the next growth period. The tree will produce new wood to store more energy reserves. But, when pathogens repeat the attack before the tree can generate (not regenerate) enough new tissue to store enough energy reserves to maintain the root, the infected parts go from stress to strain. The tree must then set new boundaries at another position to resist further spread of the pathogens. If the tree is successful in this second attempt to resist the spread of the pathogens, the pathogens may still continue their spread within the root wood present at the time of infection. A seesaw action begins. How many other roots become strained will then determine whether the tree lives or dies.

Figure 10-2

Woody roots are attached to larger woody roots the same way as branches are attached to trunks (Fig. 2). Most tree branches grow upward while most secondary or "branch" roots grow downward. There is a ridge of root bark that forms at the junction of the smaller and larger root. The bark ridge is similar to the branch bark ridge (see chapter on branches). In branches, the junction of branch and trunk is a potential infection site for many pathogens that cause cankers. The same potential may also exist for the root crotch.

A New Tree Biology

Figure 10-3

Here is a dissected tap root of a white oak (Fig. 3). The colored core of heart-wood attenuates rapidly in the downward direction. Note the clear wood in the lateral roots. The pointers show the barrier zone associated with the pocket of rot.

Very few species of trees have deep tap root systems. Exceptions are some of the pines that grow in very arid areas and most notable, the jarrah eucalypt that is native to southwestern Australia. The pine roots in some areas of Texas may grow over 3 meters downward. The jarrah has a shallow root system and a deep root system that may grow beyond 10 meters downward. How the deep roots get oxygen is not well understood. Most trees have almost all of their roots within a meter below the surface. Many trees, such as the maples, have many roots just below the surface of the soil.

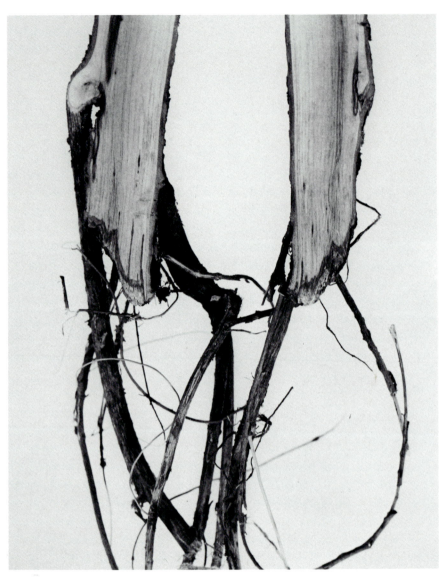

Figure 10-4

A New Tree Biology

Wounding experiments on roots of several tree species showed that severed roots form boundaries rapidly, as shown in this white oak sample (Fig. 4). The sample was prepared 1 year after wounding. Note the small edge of decayed wood at the cut surface and the boundary of discolored wood behind the decayed wood. When cells discolor and die, as shown here, the discolored wood is more protective than nondiscolored clear wood. This type of discolored wood is the result of a hypersensitive reaction. The cells change their living contents into antimicrobial materials, and in doing so they commit "suicide." (When cells die — or starve — and discolor, another type of condition exists.) The decay-causing fungi must then digest the discolored wood in order to spread deeper into the wood. Some microorganisms may also inhabit the discolored wood. But microorganisms are not altruistic, they do not kill themselves so others can live. Microorganisms "hold onto" a niche as long as they can. In time, their niche is changed and other microorganisms do occupy the niche. This takes time. So long as the tree has time to generate enough new tissues in new locations, the better the chances are for survival of the trees, and also the microorganism in the niche. When pathogens or wood-inhabiting microorganisms spread too rapidly, this could be to their disadvantage. They will occupy the niche only for a short time.

The section of white oak shows that while the injured root and the microorganisms were interacting, new woody roots formed. New roots were generated in new locations.

When roots are injured during construction or planting, it is best to make straight cuts through the roots to remove injured and crushed tissues. Such treatment will help the tree to set firm internal boundaries as shown here, and to generate new roots.

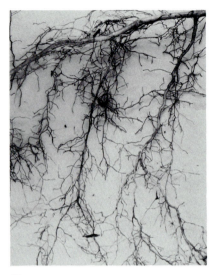

Figure 10-5

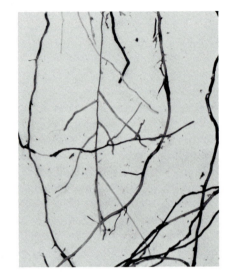

Figure 10-6

Figure 10-7

Figure 10-8

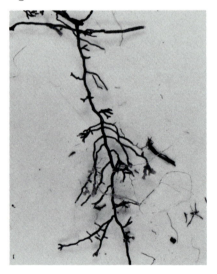

A New Tree Biology

Figures 5, 6, 7, and 8 show examples of fine, absorbing nonwoody roots that are associated with fungi. The root-fungus association is called a mycorrhiza (mycor, fungus; rhiza, root). Figures 5 and 6 show mycorrhiza on a hardwood; red maple. The fungi that are associated with most hardwood roots belong to a group called the Phycomycetes. The fungi grow intimately within the root cells and produce swollen, balloon-like roots (Fig.6).

The fungi that are associated with conifer roots may either grow tightly around the nonwoody root, into the root, or around and into the root. Most mycorrhizae on conifers have a branched appearance (Fig.7). The branches usually form at right angles to tree roots. When branches of some trees are covered with leaves and forest litter, roots and mycorrhizae may form on them as shown on the balsam fir branch (Fig. 8).

The root-fungus association is one of mutual benefit. The tree supplies energy for the fungus and the fungus "helps" the root to absorb elements, especially phosphorous.

Some trees are obligatory for the mycorrhizae — oaks, beech, pines — while other trees may live with only some mycorrhizae — maples, birch, aspen. Most trees start life without the mycorrhizae, but the obligatory species must make the associations soon or they do not grow.

There usually is no problem in the forest for these associations because the soils abound with a variety of fungi that are associated with tree roots. But, it must be kept in mind that the associations of roots and fungi are mutualistic, and necessary for both. If the trees are removed from a site, and if a fungus is dependent on that tree for its life, the fungus may begin to die. If the tree is planted back on site at a later time, the fungus necessary for the growth of the tree may not be present. The strict nature of the associations is not well known. But, we do know the associations do exist, and that disruptions to the soil can disrupt the fungi.

When trees are heavily fertilized at regular intervals, the root-fungus associations may diminish. So long as the trees are fertilized regularly, the trees will grow well. If fertilizers are stopped suddenly, the tree may begin to be stressed.

The mycorrhizae may also act as "insulators" against aggressive root pathogens. When soil conditions change and disrupt the fungi on or in the roots, the advantage may go to an available pathogen. If such a condition occurs when the tree is approaching a normally weak period for boundary setting, the pathogen may have a double advantage.

The micro world in the soil is poorly understood. A major reason for this is that it takes hard physical work to dig roots. The answers will not come from washed roots, or from roots dug by machines. To understand roots, they must be dug carefully. We have a very long way to go on this subject!

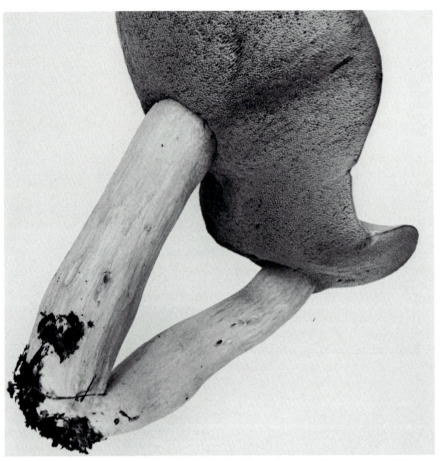

The fungi associated with tree roots, especially those fungi associated with conifers, produce fruit bodies that are called mushrooms. (Toadstool is a very loose term meaning a fruit body that is poisonous.) The root-associated mushrooms may form from early spring until late fall. Most of the forms produce mushrooms during late summer. A notable early fungus fruit body that is associated with tree roots is the morel—*Morchella* spp. It belongs to a class of fungi called Ascomycetes because it produces its spores in small asci, or sacs. Most of the myocorrhizal fungi belong to the class of fungi called Hymenomycetes because the spores are produced on pegs that line a hymenium or a fertile layer of tissue. The spore-producing pegs (see chapter on microorganisms) may be along a variety of gills and pores, and surfaces that range from smooth to wrinkled, to those that look like long teeth.

The fungus shown here is a *Boletus* (Fig. 9). Many of the mushrooms are edible. Some are not! It is not wise to eat mushrooms that you are not certain of their safety. When you think you do have a safe one, but some small doubts still linger, eat only a small portion and wait to see how you feel. Be very careful with wild mushrooms.   *Figure 10-9*

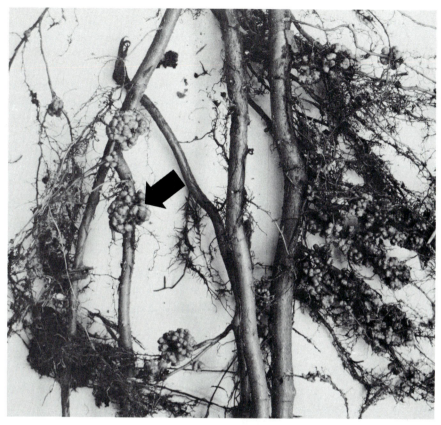

Other microorganisms are also associated with some species of trees—bacteria, actinomycetes. The nodules shown by the arrow on this alder root is associated with actinomycetes (Fig. 10). The actinomycetes aid in nitrogen fixation—atmospheric nitrogen is changed to nitrate, which can be taken up by the roots. When the nitrate goes into the tree it is changed to other nitrogen compounds including amino acids. The nitrogen seldom moves in trees as nitrates. The amino acids form proteins and proteins are major parts of the living substances, especially protoplasm.

When trees absorb nitrate it really does not matter whether it comes from a chemical fertilizer or from an organic compound that was broken down. Organic sources provide soil conditioning by aerating the soil, usually in their application. So this is how organic sources have some advantages over chemical sources. But, nitrate is nitrate when it moves into a root regardless of the source. Organic fertilizers may also contain essential elements not in the chemical fertilizer.

Alder is often called a forest weed. Yet, it helps to provide nitrogen for other trees such as Douglas fir. When we decide what is a weed, and remove it, the close associations that took millions of years to develop may be abruptly destroyed. Indeed, we must consider the whole system, not only parts that we think are beneficial to us.   *Figure 10-10*

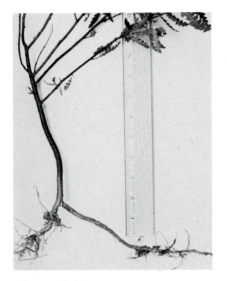

Figure 10-11

Other woody plants in the forest also contribute to the welfare of trees. This sweetfern *Camptonia* sp., is a common plant found in poor soils (Fig. 11). The plant forms nodules on the roots and they fix nitrogen. The poor soils are made better by such plants. Are they weeds? Should we destroy them because they are not trees? Nonsense! Yet, when many of these plants and others that are also a part of the whole system are destroyed, the very plants we want, the trees, will eventually suffer.

Figure 10-12

Here is another common plant in the forest, Indian pipes, or ghost flower, *Monotropa uniflora* (Fig. 12). This flower has no chlorophyll. It must get energy some way. This plant is associated with tree roots and fungi. The many associations in the forest are awesome and wonderful. My fear is we may learn about some of them after it is too late.

A New Tree Biology

Figure 10-13

This silver maple in Iowa had several low, large branches pruned, and the cuts were covered with moss held in place by black plastic (Fig. 13). After one year the plastic was removed, and a large network of roots had developed from an epicormic bud at the 39 inch position on the rule.

Every bud, or cell, has the genetic code to be root, stem, or leaves, the three organs of a tree. The environmental conditions of the cells at the time differentiation is occurring will determine the outcome of the cells. Moss over wounds is an old technique for developing new plant shoots.

Figure 10-14

Figure 10-15

When trees are grown in containers, problems that seldom occur in the natural forest begin to develop (Fig. 14). The twisted, girdling roots shown here are from a tree grown in a small container. Once the roots begin to entwine the trunk, the pattern will continue. On young trees, the girdling roots should be removed.

On older trees as shown in figure 15, it is best to leave the girdling roots alone. More harm than good may be done in attempts to remove large girdling roots.

Girdling roots are a man-made problem. Growing trees in containers and wire baskets causes new problems. This is a perfect example of new tree problems brought on by new (?) technology. Before containers and baskets trees were dug out by hand and transplanted mostly by bare roots. Many trees were balled and burlapped also, and held together by reverse nail pinning. New problems also have come with machine dug trees, and machine dug holes for trees. When the sides of the machine dug holes are slick and smooth and compacted—especially clay soils—the tree is planted back in a pot. And, girdling roots will start.

When planting, the planting site more than the hole must be considered. The native soil should be loosened far beyond the tree. Grass should be kept away. The soil should receive only small amounts of amendments, unless there is little or no soil. This can occur in city plantings. There are few general rules that hold for all sites. Fertilizers should be applied after the tree is established. No moat for catching water should be made. The tree will be back in a pot again. The

A New Tree Biology

tree should be braced, but not so tight that it cannot move. Wire through a rubber tube or hose, will still injure bark. The pressure of the wire diameter will still be the same hose or not. Strapping is good; still the tree must move.

Why trees are wrapped with burlap and cloth and other products is a mystery to me. Studies show that these materials do little except hide wounds, cankers, and cracks that were on the tree when it left the nursery. The coverings also make excellent homes for insects. Never accept a tree that is wrapped! You never know what is under the wrapping.

I am still not convinced that painting trees, especially fruit trees, with white paint is beneficial. The paint is supposed to reflect sunlight and reduce bark injuries. My dissections of injured fruit trees — peach — showed dead roots and wounds inflicted at planting time as the cause of basal cracks. The cracking process is a 2-part process. The tissues must be preset by a wound or dead branch or root *and* then the pressure of the heat or cold may cause the present weakend spot to crack outward.

Another cause of basal cracks is graft incompatibility. A portion of the graft union may not "take" and the result is the same as a wound. A barrier zone forms, and weak radial tissues form. When some other pressure is exerted such as sudden heat or cold, the preset weak radial tissues will crack outward. Graft incompatibility seems to be on the increase as more work is done to produce new varieties of trees. Graft incompatibility may also cause some trees to "pull out of their socket" 10 or even 15 years after grafting. I have seen this in maples that were 6 inches in diameter.

My point here is that as technology and industry change, new problems will arise: wire baskets, machine dug holes, new grafted varieties, etc. When some part of the system goes from zig to a zag, we must also go from zig to zag. If we keep zigging while other parts are zagging, the tree will suffer. This is a major problem where traditions have guided the way trees are treated. Larger roads, more cars, more buildings, changes in water drainage patterns, pollution, etc. have caused many zigs to go to zags. It is not that old methods were wrong, that is *not* the point. The point is that other parts of the system have changed. The tree cannot move. We must keep pace with changes that we cannot control.

Problems with roots are usually not recognized until it is too late. Yet root problems are some of the most serious problems trees have today. If we know all there was to know about the above ground parts of a tree, we would still know only a half of the whole story.

CHAPTER 11

Prelude to the Branch

Tree ferns and palms have one growing point. There are always a few exceptions, but for the most part the statement is true. The palm may be thought of as one large branch. When some ancient woody plants began to form more than one branch, this had to be a monumental moment in the development of trees as we know them today. If one growing point was killed, the other growing points would continue to grow. It was a redundant system that gave the tree better opportunities to survive for longer periods, even under conditions that were not always proper for growth. The single-branched trees — palms — never "migrated" far beyond the temperate zones that had freezing periods.

In the 3-tree concept, the branch is considered tree 1. When a tree is young it is primarily a collection of branches. The trunk makes up a small portion of the young tree. As the tree grows, the trunk and woody roots increase in size, and some branches begin to die. The collection of branches on a well-defined trunk now lives as a tree 2. In tree 1 each branch produces energy for itself and some for the developing trunk and roots. As tree 2 begins to form, the ratio of energy demands between branches — tree 1 — and trunks and roots, begins to change. The trunks and roots require more energy because they are larger. As some branches are not able to meet "the demands" of the enlarging trunk and roots and still have enough energy for themselves, they shed portions of themselves to survive. When the "demands" of the trunk and roots continue to increase while the branch is getting smaller, the energy source is so reduced that eventually the branch dies and is set off from the trunk by an elaborate boundary-forming process.

As many tree 2s grow, they are connected in their natural environment by root grafts or by the fungi that are associated with the many nonwoody roots; the mycorrhizae. The collections of tree 2s then gives us tree 3. Tree 3 is the community tree and each tree 2 is like a branch on tree 3.

A branch is a subdivision of a unit. A tree without branches is not a tree. A tree is a collection of branches. In a sense, each branch "repeats" or reiterates the tree. The trunk forms as portions of the branches come together. But how are these tree branches attached to the trunk? From an engineering vein, it is impossible to cantilever a horizontal beam from a vertical beam and have the horizontal beam stay on. It cannot be done. Yet the tree does it; over, and over, and over again. How?

The answer to how branches are attached to tree trunks has been the most exciting natural puzzle I have ever tried to solve. I still do not have all the answers, but enough of the pieces have been put in place to see the theme of branch attachment. There are many variations that await more study.

Indeed, the branch was a major jump forward for the evolving tree. The branch increased the number of growing points. But, nothing — that I know of — in nature comes in singles. There is always another side of the subject. The other side deals with all the things that could go wrong as the branch develops, and all the things

208

Figure 11-1

that could go wrong after the branch dies. Both situations could make conditions proper for organisms that inhabit wood. Both situations pose a potential Achilles' heel—a weak spot—that is the sitution many times.

As you learn more about trees and natural systems you will see that the weak spots are always there. The weak spots are often time situations. The weak condition may last only a few minutes or a few days. The longer the weak condition lasts, the better the chances for aggressive organisms to attack. Once we have a better understanding of these potential weak spots or Achilles' heels, the more we can do to select trees that have stronger systems, or we may be able to do things that help the tree to pass through the weak period or vulnerable time much faster.

The New Tree Biology demands more than your muscles; the New Tree Biology demands your mind. It demands that you understand the zig-zig, and the zag-zag and the way natural processes go. Then *you* will be the best one to make decisions on how to best help trees. It is my strong belief that this is the best way—only way— to go. You know your business much better than I will ever know it. If you can add more knowledge to your training, skills, and common sense, trees will benefit; I'm sure!

Figure 12-1

A New Tree Biology

CHAPTER 12

Branches

Trees do not go from a dormant state, or from a state of slow grow, to a sudden state of rapid growth entirely over the trees. Trees go toward a dormant state part by part and when they resume rapid growth they also do so part by part. Even trees in the tropics have periods of slow growth and periods of rapid growth. In temperate zones, the growth processes start with the "awakening" of the fine roots, or the absorbing roots. The snow may still be on the ground when this activity starts. The absorbing roots and their fungi associates begin very early to absorb water and elements. Activity then goes next to the tips of the twigs. The buds begin to swell. The water and elements essential for their growth come from the transport system—vessels, tracheids—from the previous year. Within the buds are the partially preformed parts that will become leaves, needles, or reproductive parts—male flowers, female flowers, mixed flowers of male and female parts, or leaves. All variations do occur. The important part is that the bud is next in line—usually, not always—after the awakening of the absorbing roots. Stored energy in the buds and twigs act as a battery to "start the engines." The buds open and new parts begin to develop. The vascular cambium begins to develop next. Stored energy and small amounts of energy trapped by the newly-formed green—chlorophyll—tissues help to fuel the living process. But, most of the fuel must come from energy stored the previous growth period. As soon as new leaves begin to form new buds also begin to form. If problems—diseases—of the leaves occur or insect problems occur, the buds will be ready to form new parts. Trees have many redundancy systems.

The vascular cambium begins to function from the tips of the twigs inward, or down the branches. Such a downward development is called basipetal. The basipetal functions of the vascular cambium result in new phloem and xylem—wood—in a downward wave. The branch is developing—usually—before the trunk. The cambial activity "moves" to the trunk and further downward to the support roots. And, finally to the formation of new nonwoody roots. The old nonwoody roots begin to shed, and new roots, absorbing, and new associations with the "good" fungi start again.

This is the usual theme of tree activities. The tree then begins to use the current year's transport system for new growth and for trapping new energy to be stored for the next cycle of growth. Why do you need to know this for branches?

It is important to know that branch tissues usually form before trunk tissues. As the newly forming wood and bark tissues approach the base of the branch, they turn abruptly (arrow, Figure 1) and *do not* go onto the trunk. Instead, they form a collar about the base of the branch. Here they do rest on the trunk. The collar of the base of the branch formed by the tissues is called the branch collar. Later, water and elements will move upward through these tissues, but not when they are still immature. Transport is still with the cells formed the previous season. Food produced by the leaves will also follow the same pathway downward in the phloem, after the new transport system becomes functional.

The surprising solution to the branch attachment puzzle was that the branch is really not connected in a structural way to the trunk! This sounds impossible. The diagrams in figure 2 help to explain how the branch stays on the trunk. The branch not only stays on the trunk, but it stays on with such strength that high winds and great pressure seldom (not always) separate branch from trunk. It *is* because the branch is not directly connected to the trunk that the branch does have such staying power.

Diagrams 1 and 2 show 2 views of tissue arrangement at the branch base. The dark lines show the branch tissues. The tissues turn abruptly at the branch base. As the tissues develop downward below the branch, they do mix with the trunk tissues. But, such an arrangement below the branch can hardly be called a strong connection or attachment. It is important to note that the branch tissues do not grow onto the trunk except directly below the branch. If this were the only attachment to the trunk, the branch would never support itself. Diagrams 1 and 2 are taken from figure 1. The bark was peeled from an oak sample when the leaves had just completed their expansion.

Diagrams 3 and 4 help to solve the puzzle. After branch tissues slow their growth rate, the trunk tissues begin to grow faster. The trunk tissues grow over the branch collar. The trunk tissues form a collar over the branch collar. By the time the trunk collar starts its growth the latewood in the branch tissues is nearing completion. Diagram 4 shows how the trunk collar circles the branch collar (arrows). The trunk collar may not always meet below the branch at the position shown by the arrows. A trunk collar gap will result in a sunken spot below the branch. On some individual trees of a species, almost every branch on young trees will have a trunk collar gap. We suspect that this feature may be under moderate to strong genetic control. When branches with a gap are pruned properly, there still may be a dead spot under the branch. On large old branches, the gap is more common. If the dead spot does form, wait one more growing season and carefully remove the bark. Do not cut into the wood. Do not enlarge the wound. Do not try to anticipate where the dead spot will be before it happens. Do not accept young trees that have many sunken spots below branches.

212   *A New Tree Biology*

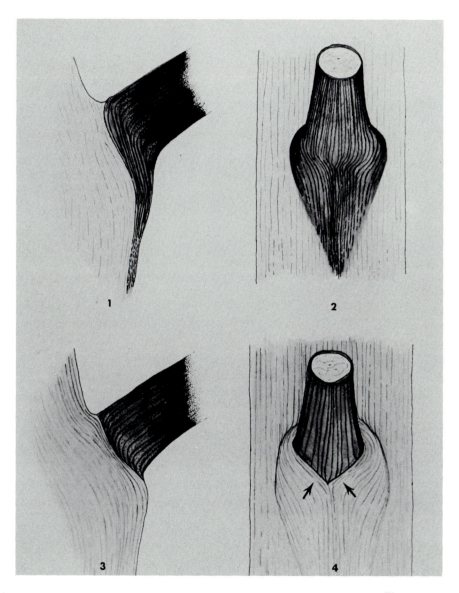

Figure 12-2

Compare this oak section peeled in midsummer after leaves were matured (Fig. 3) with the oak section peeled in spring when the leaves had just expanded (Fig. 1). This section shows the branch collar enveloped by the trunk collar. The arrows show a small trunk collar gap. The vessels transport water and elements upward. The vessels transporting water and elements to the branch are under those that are transporting water and elements around the branch and upward on the trunk. The downward path of substances in the phloem are similar — the branch phloem turns abruptly around the base of the branch and then goes downward. An extremely important point is that there is no direct local conduction from trunk tissues above a branch into the branch. All the old diagrams in textbooks show such a conductive pathway. The branch and the trunk shown here are the same age. The trunk collar slowly restricts the flow of materials into the branch, and in this way slowly slows the growth rate of the branch.   *Figure 12-3*

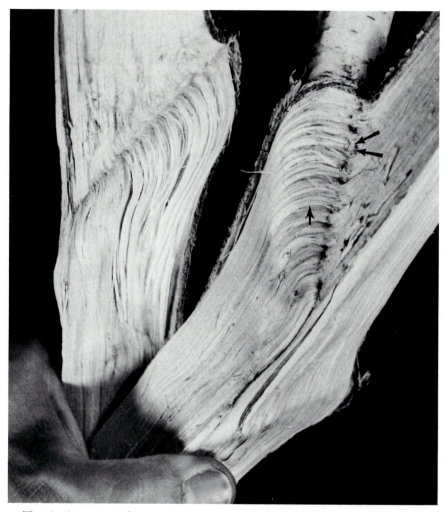

The single arrow in figure 4 shows the trunk collars that form around the branch collars. The trunk collars circle the branch collars in a ball and socket union. The collars are entwined like the wire in an armature of an electric motor. With such an arrangement the branch and trunk are together yet separate—except for the small strip of tissues below the branch. The double arrows show the point where the tissues make an abrupt turn. When a straight longitudinal cut is made through this zone, it appears that the trunk tissues from above the branch do connect with the branch; but, they do not. *Figure 12-4*

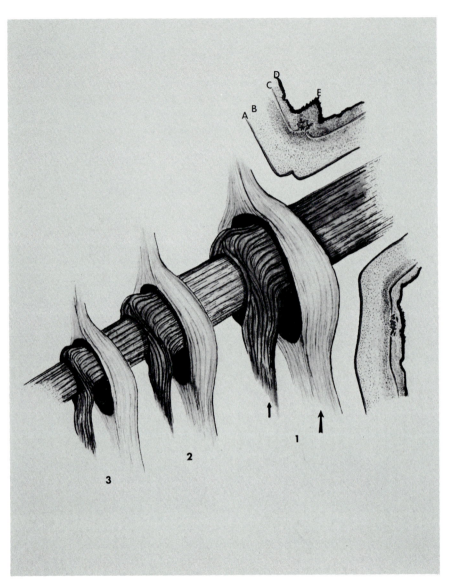

Figure 12-5

This diagram (Fig. 5) shows a summary of the points discussed. The drawing shows 3 growth rings pulled apart (shown as 1, 2, and 3). The small arrow in growth ring 1 shows the branch tissues. The tissues do not end abruptly as drawn, but they mesh with the trunk tissues below the branch. The large arrow in growth ring 1 shows the trunk collar that envelops the branch collar. When the growth rings are intact or pulled back into their normal position, each trunk collar locks over a branch collar, and each branch collar seats or fits into a trunk collar, and on it goes. This interlocking system of collars is the most wondrous natural phenomenon I have ever seen. The system gives the branch extraordinary strength and resiliency, and yet the branch is really not attached to the trunk in a structural way. The small "tail" of branch tissues beneath the branch would hardly support even the smallest branch.

This diagram shows some other features that will be discussed in more detail later. The vascular cambium is A, the phloem is B, the phellogen or bark cambium is C, and the outer bark or suberized phellem is D. The mounding of tissues in the branch crotch is shown at E. Below E, the mounding of the phellogen is shown. When the branch tissues grow first and then the trunk tissues grow — asynchronous — the phellogen has time to develop without disruption within the crotch because there is room to spread. But, when branch and trunk do grow at the same time — synchronous — the phellogen may rupture and living cells may be at or near the surface for short periods. Suberization of the newly formed phellem would not have time to occur, and the stage would be set for easy infection by any pathogen available in the crotch. The phellogen in the branch crotch is an Achilles' heel. Most canker-causing organisms spread into bark at this point.

We know very little about cultural practices that might synchronize branch and trunk growth. Later we will see that this situation in the crotch may lead to the inward turning of the vascular cambium. When this happens, included bark will form. Included bark starts a weak union between branch and trunk.

Figure 12-6

A New Tree Biology

The microscope section in figure 6 is made up of 56 individual photographs. (Made by Kenneth Dudzik.) The photo shows a longitudinal section of an American elm branch at right and the joining trunk. Longitudinal cuts through the vessels show them as long white canals. But, the vessels in the crotch area appear as white circles (single arrows). This is because the long vessels change their orientation 90° as they turn to form the trunk collar. The radial parenchyma sweep upward in the crotch and all the tissues appear as they would on a cross section or transverse section.

Note also the central pith in the branch. The double arrows show where the branch pith meets the trunk pith. A sheath about the trunk pith separates the trunk pith from the branch pith. Also, at the base of the branch pith the cells appear more compact. This zone is called the pith protection zone. The cells have thicker walls in this zone, and the cells contain a higher amount of phenols. The branch pith and the trunk pith are not connected in a conducting way.

The pith protection zone is the first protection zone that forms in young trees. If pathogens do infect the young branch, the pathogens would have difficulty spreading from branch into trunk. Indeed, trees have many boundaries that resist spread of pathogens.

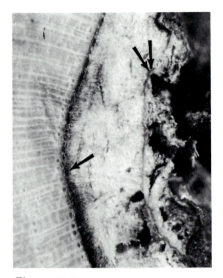

Figure 12-7

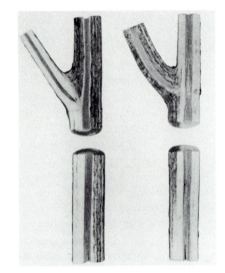

Figure 12-8

Figure 12-9

Figure 12-10

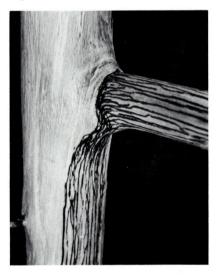

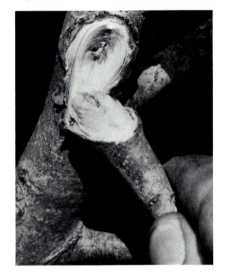

Figures 7, 8, 9, and 10 summarize some of the points discussed and they show some important additional details. Figure 7 is a longitudinal section through a branch crotch of an American elm. The section has all the characteristics of a transverse section — circular cuts through vessels, radial sheets of parenchyma. The single arrow shows the vascular cambium, or better to say cambial zone. The double arrows show the bark cambium or phellogen. Note how close it is to the surface. Any aggressive organism would have an easy time for infection at this micro niche. The young phellem is beyond the phellogen and the soft tissues between the vascular cambium (single arrow) and the phellogen (double arrow) is phloem.

Figure 8 shows some sections of red maple that were used in experiments to study dye patterns in branches and trunks. When dye was infiltrated into the trunk from above, the dye moved downward in the trunk tissues, but it did not spread into the branch (left section). When dye — toulidine O — was infiltrated into the branch (right section) the dye did not spread into trunk tissues above the branch. The same patterns were seen when the dyes were "pulled" upward by vacuum in the upper ends of the sections. Pathogens that attack trees — fire blight bacterium, *Erwinia amylovora*; and the Dutch elm disease fungus, *Ceratocystis ulmi*, followed the same pattern as the dyes. Pathogens did not spread freely in trees. Pathogens in trunks did not spread to branches below them.

Figure 9 shows an oak that was peeled at the time the leaves had expanded in the spring. The vessels are marked with ink. The sample shows that branch tissues *do not* continue on to trunk tissues; except directly below the branch. Note the old trunk collar surrounding the branch.

Figure 10 shows a branch being pulled out of an aspen. The many trunk collars or rings can be seen. When a branch is pulled slowly out of its ball and socket position, the interlocking collars can be felt slipping one over the other.

Figure 12-11

A New Tree Biology

The swollen collars at the base of young oak branches are shown in figure 11. The young stem at right shows 1-year-old branches with circular callus (arrows). There is an abrupt change in diameter from the base of the young branch to the "doughnut" collar. The collar is trunk tissue. The point is that callus is circular the first year.

The stem at left is 2 years old. The expanding stem has caused the circular collar to widen and to begin the formation of a branch bark ridge (arrow left, upper), and another bark ridge below the branch (arrow left, lower). The points of the double arrows show where the branch tissues turn abruptly downward.

The trunk tissues circle the branch tissues. When pruning young trees great care must be taken so as to not injure the trunk tissues. The collars at the branch base are branch collars and trunk collars, but for ease of identification they are called branch collars. Once you begin to recognize the collars it is difficult *not to* see where branch and trunk meet (double arrows, left). Pruning cuts that injure or remove the collars will cause the tree serious injury. Some species of trees form very large collars. The temptation is to remove them, but the collars are the natural protection features of young trees.

Many problems that continue on for many years may start when the young collars are removed; frost and sun injuries, cankers, insect infestations. Nature often "exaggerates" protection features on young trees. Many tree problems start in the nursery when the protection features are destroyed. On some species of trees—*Tilia, Ulmus*—early removal of the collars will lead to sprouts. When the sprouts are removed, twice the number of sprouts will grow. And when they are removed, again they will be replaced with twice the number. It is like a pollard of a side stem. On species of *Tilia* and *Ulmus* the "pollarded" trunk will form large swollen spots not so different from the terminal branch pollards.

Figure 12-12

A New Tree Biology

What are often called branches are really not branches but codominant stems. The pear, *Pyrus communis*, sample in figure 12 has many codominant stems but only one branch (arrow, left). Each codominant stem is connected to 50% of the trunk below it. The tissue arrangements are also different from branches. Because each codominant stem has equal rank, there is no branch collar or trunk collar. A bark ridge does form where the stems come together (upper arrow in crotch). A raised bark ridge forms where the first circle of raised bark formed. The lower arrows show the lower bark ridges. When a codominant stem is removed, the cuts should go from the right side of the upper arrow to the lower arrow at right for the removal of the right stem. For the removal of the left stem, start at the left side of the upper arrow and cut to the point of the lower arrow at left. The *stem bark ridge* in the crotch is the key to proper pruning of codominant stems. The bottom raised bark ridges show where the cuts should end.

Branches have built in protection zones at their base, but codominant stems do not have such zones because they are really extensions of the stem. The problem that comes with a tree with many codominant stems is that any pathogen can spread downward, or upward, with little natural resistance. These points are very important for fire blight — *Erwinia amylovora* — and Dutch elm disease — *Ceratocystis ulmi*. Once these pathogens infect codominant stems, they can spread rapidly. Some varieties of pear have many codominant stems and few branches. These trees are killed rapidly when infected by *E. amylovora*. The same can be said with elms that have the vase-shape form that is made up of many codominant stems.

Once a tree begins forming codominant stems, its crown will begin to form. In the forest this could be the beginning of the end for young trees that require high amounts of sunlight. Once a tree does grow to the height of the canopy and codominant stems begin to form, further height growth is greatly diminished. The "tree" that forms from the codominant stem reiterates the form of the entire tree. The multiple tree, or tree 2, becomes fully developed when many codominant stems form.

Early pruning could either reduce or enhance the formation of codominant stems. In this way the height of the tree could be controlled. But, you can not come back after a tree is mature and try to do this. Early pruning is the best way to assure tree health, size, and safety.

Figure 12-13   *Figure 12-14*

Figure 13 shows a bark-peeled oak that has had codominant stems. Figure 14 shows an oak with a large branch. Note the arrangement of the wood tissues in figure 13. The tissues from each codominant stem come together but they do not turn to form a collar. Figure 14 shows the normal abrupt turn of the branch collar (arrows). The trunk is still in "command" here. The codominant stems have equal rank.

Figure 13 also shows the large sheets of radial parenchyma (arrows).

Here is a dissected sample of American elm showing 2 pairs of codominant stems (Fig. 15). The arrows show where the buds formed that produced the stems. Note that the pith is not continuous from one stem to the other. Many beetles, including those that are vectors for *Ceratocystis ulmi*, chew the bark within branch crotches and codominant stem crotches as shown here. Once the beetle breaks into the wood, spores or propagules of a pathogen can spread upward or downward in both codominant stems and the trunk below. Where there are branches, the beetle destroys the first protection zone and gives the pathogen "one free open gate."

The codominant stem at right was killed (Fig. 16) and the trunk below shows the closure on this elm. When codominant stems die, a large dead spot may develop under the stem. Do not increase the size of the dead spot. Take away the dead bark and try to remove the dead stem without injuring the other stem or the trunk. This is a very difficult procedure.

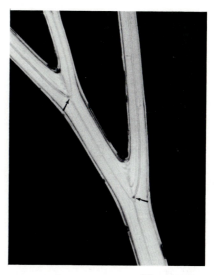

Figure 12-15

Figure 12-16

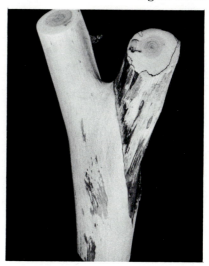

Figure 12-17

A New Tree Biology

The many low codominant stems of these black walnut trees greatly reduces their value for wood production (Fig. 17). The trees were grown from seed. Once a tree begins forking—codominant stems—it usually keeps doing so. This could be a valuable feature for a city tree, but not for a forest tree that is being grown for high value wood products. Spacing is an important environmental factor affecting forking. Yet, wide spacing is often wanted so as to increase growth rate. If you start with wide spacing, and then begin early pruning, you should be able to grow high quality trees very fast. This was the rationale in Europe over a century ago. The problem was that the pruning cuts removed the branch collars and they got fast growing trees with larger defects. Hardly the answer. This is also the time when wound dressing research (?) took a great step forward. Everybody had the magic answer to reducing decay. The foresters *knew* they were right because the close harsh pruning cut did result in large callus—"good healing." All that was needed now was a good medicine to stop rot. Sad, but true, the medicine has still not come. But, there is a way to go back to the original aim to grow trees faster with wide spacing and to still have few defects. The answer is in knowing the difference between branches and codominant stems, and knowing how to prune them properly.

The basic thread of this book, or conversation with you, is an understanding of the tree. I believe that once you have a better understanding of the tree, you will come up with the best answers for doing what you want to do with trees. The example here is knowing the difference between branches and codominant stems, knowing that branches have collars, knowing that callus is not directly associated with the decay process, knowing that many of these features are under strong genetic control, and the list goes on. And, the list will be discussed as we go on to other subjects.

It is time to start with the tree and work toward solutions, not with some supposed magic cure, medicine, or machine, and see what it will do! We have gone too far in that direction. It won't be easy to change directions, but for the future of our trees, it must be done.

Figure 13-1

A New Tree Biology

CHAPTER 13

Branch Shedding

Trees are highly compartmented, woody, perennial, shedding plants that are usually, but not always, tall and single-stemmed. The focus here is on branch shedding (Fig. 1). Trees also shed leaves, needles, absorbing roots, reproductive parts, and outer bark. When twigs, roots, and branches die, they are also shed. Shed is different from cast off. Trees do not cast off parts. What trees do is to form boundaries between the dead or dying part and the still living part. Trees shed roots, but they surely do not cast them off.

Trees have built in boundaries that facilitate shedding of parts. As the part begins to die, the boundary usually begins to form. Trees have 8 natural boundaries: 1, abcission zones (nonwoody parts); 2, root periderm zone; 3, pith protection zone; 4, twig abcission zone (cladoptosis); 5, bark protection zones (there are 2 zones that are similar in function to the zones in wood, reaction zone and barrier zone); 6, branch protection zone; 7, reaction zone; 8, barrier zone. If the 2 bark zones are separated, then 9 natural protection zones exist.

They are all natural boundaries because the position for them is preset in the tree. But, the boundaries are altered, or changed, or strengthened after aging processes have gone to a certain point or after injury and infection processes have started. Except for the reaction zone and its equivalent in bark, the zones have a set position. The reaction zones in wood and bark do move under the pressure of aggressive pathogens.

Another feature of all the zones except the reaction zones is that they are very strong in a protective way, but very weak in a structural way. This has survival value because the aged and dead parts can be physically separated from the healthy parts. The reaction zones should be more accurately defined as defense zones rather than protective zones. Protection means a static condition. Some changes have built a wall that protects against invasion. The best way to protect yourselves from an enemy is to separate yourself from him (her?). The reaction zones are in tissues present at the time of infection. The reaction zones are forming in response to repeated attacks by the pathogens.

The branch was a giant step forward for the developing woody plant we later called a tree. It gave the plant redundancies for meristems—the growing points. But, nothing in nature comes all good all the time. As already mentioned, an Achilles' heel or weak spot may form in branch crotches. And now to address another problem: what should the tree do when the branch dies and is infected? The dead branch would give pathogens easy entrance into the trunk. Some protection zone had to develop or the "idea" of a branch would not have survival value. So, along with the branch came the branch protection zone at the branch base.

I hope you can appreciate the many intricate details that "mother nature" had to deal with. This is mainly because nothing came all good all the time. The only possible answer to such a dilemma was to keep the good parts as long as possible and when the seesaw swings to bad, get rid of the bad parts as fast as possible. This is what happened with branches. They are "tied on" the trunk in a unique way that gives them extraordinary strength and resiliency. Yet, when the branch is infected and begins to die, the tree begins to form a basal protection zone that quickly sheds the branch. The fungi play an active role in the process as they digest the wood of the branch at the base; but on the branch side of the protection zone.

But, again, all protection and defense zones and processes do not function properly all the time. Things do go wrong. And, it is not so different for the zones in trees. The zone may be weak or the pathogen may be strong. When a weak zone and a strong pathogen come together, the zone will be breached. The tree must then form new zones, which it does. Now we go from protection to defense. If all else fails, the tree is still a generating system so it can continue to form new cells in new positions while it is fighting another battle internally to resist the infection of older cells that are locked in position. And, all of these processes take fuel, energy. The tree and the pathogen play a time game. If the pathogen goes too fast, it "eats away" its home. We are then back to compartmentalization, where both parties can optimize the time they survive. (The snow ball keeps rolling.)

Branch shedding in the forest is a continuous process. Small branches are constantly dying. The large branches may provide small animals with temporary home sites, or the insects in the dying branches provide birds and other animals with food. In the tropics, termites quickly infest dying branches, and the wood may never reach the forest floor. The dead wood is cellulose mostly and this means sugar to the microorganisms that can cleave the cellulose molecule into smaller pieces until the glucose is released.

Shedding is the trees' way of "keeping clean." Shedding rids the tree of organisms that could attack the trunk and roots. The tree can always grow new branches and branch roots, but the tree cannot grow another trunk or main support roots.

The arrows in figure 2 show two branches that have decayed and fallen from the trees. The falling branches do present hazards for people in the forest. Falling branches are major causes of damage to power lines, property and people. The conditions of branches should be constantly checked on trees that are growing near power lines, valuable property, and especially where people sit, walk, or travel in vehicles. Special attention should be given to the architecture of the branches. Even sound branches can present problems. Be on the alert for trees that were released because of road construction, picnic area construction, or for any other reason. Trees that are part of a group regulate each other's growth patterns and also protect each other from wind. When the neighboring trees are cut leaving only a few trees, the trees remaining will quickly grow into the new space. Branches will either grow upward or outward into horizontal positions. The tops may be growing faster than

Figure 13-2

the roots. When a horizontal branch begins to die, the internal shedding system goes into action. But, this is a "new" condition for a released tree. The shedding process may proceed rapidly ending with the fall of the branch.

The branch shedding process must be understood by people who are responsible for trees in parks, cities, or any place where falling branches could cause damage to power lines, property, or people. As man gets closer to trees, this problem will increase.

Figure 13-3

Figure 13-4

Figure 13-5

Figure 13-6

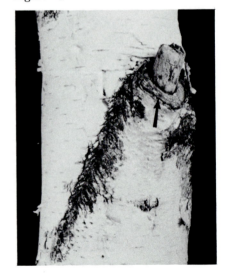

A New Tree Biology

When branches begin to wane, a sharper distinction between branch and branch collar begins to form (arrow on birch branch, Fig. 3). Care must be taken with this indicator because on some trees, especially some tropical trees, there is a natural sharp distinction between branch and branch collar even on very healthy branches. The arrow on the birch trunk (Fig. 3) shows the branch bark ridge (BBR). An upward turned BBR indicates a strong trunk-branch union. Note the slightly sunken area below the branch. As most branches wane, the sunken spot increases because either the trunk collar does not circle the branch collar, or the branch tissues that lie on the trunk below the branch have slowed their growth rate. The more you study branches, the more these subtle features will mean to you for your trees.

Figure 4 shows the callus collar (arrow) that encircled the small dead stub. The callus collar is different from the trunk collar. The callus collar starts to form after the branch dies. It is a variation of the trunk collar. The callus collars are usually circular whereas the trunk collars are more oval shaped and meet above and below the branch.

When shedding proceeds properly, the branch falls away and the callus collar closes the opening as shown in figure 5.

Figure 6 shows another round callus collar on a paper birch (arrow). Callus collars should never be injured or removed when pruning a tree. Dead stubs and branches should be removed because they are an energy source for the tree-inhabiting organism.

Callus collars also form around large dead branches (Fig. 7, arrow). The great temptation on such trees is to remove the large swollen branch collars and callus collar. The swollen branch collars may grow outward to several feet on large old dying and dead branches. The question is even more important then. The answer is still the same for the health of the tree. If the large collars are removed, the trunk will be infected rapidly. If people feel that the large swollen collars are unsightly, then they can be removed at the expense of causing the tree serious injury.

When trees are pruned, the dead wood should be removed first, then the dying or infected wood, and last the living wood. The process should not be reversed! Dead wood removal is good for the health of the tree. The dead wood removal also removes the food source for the fungi that could spread beyond the boundaries and into the trunk. Boundaries resist not stop the spread of pathogens. When you give the pathogens the advantage, they will usually take it. Dead wood removal can be done any time. Winter is a good time to remove dead wood, and for pruning of living branches also.

Figure 13-7

A New Tree Biology

Figure 13-8   *Figure 13-9*

Branch shedding processes are the same in forest trees and amenity trees. A major difference between the 2 types of trees is that amenity trees will have larger, lower, horizontal branches than most forest trees. It is rare to see a forest tree with low, large, horizontal branches. The lower branches on forest trees usually die at an earlier age than those on amenity trees.

Figure 8 shows a decayed stub on red oak in a forest. A well-formed callus collar surrounds the stub. Figure 9 shows the dissection of the trunk. The decay was advanced on the stub but the decay did not spread into the trunk. The wood remaining in the stub was heartwood at the time the branch died. When branches die and when heartwood-forming trees are wounded, the sapwood decays first.

The black arrows show the size of the tree when the branch died. The wood at the position of the arrows was sapwood at the time of branch death and the vascular cambium was also at the position of the arrow points. The heartwood was discolored on the inner side of the arrows. The discolored wood associated with the stub spread downward not upward because there is no conduction connection between the branch and trunk above the branch.

The open arrows show a discolored column associated with infected branches that were on the young tree. Note that the columns of infected heartwood are interspersed with sound heartwood. Note that the callus collar is clear wood. Removal of the swollen branch collar would remove the tree's very effective protection zone.

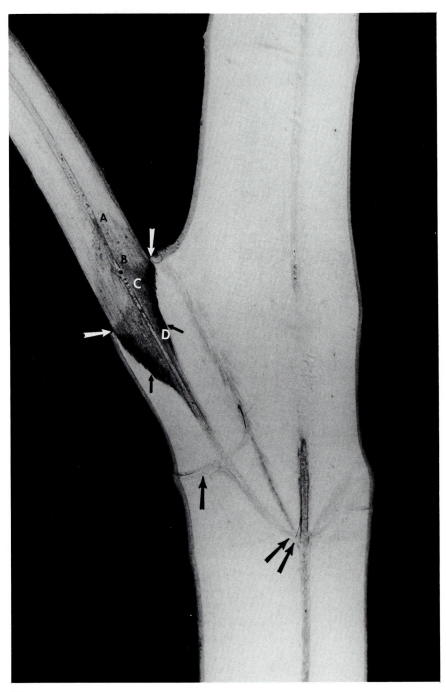

Figure 13-10

This red maple sample (Fig. 10) shows several important parts of the branch protection zone. The dissection was made one year after the branch was cut with a 12-inch stub. In experiments of branches, over 1200 trees of 12 species were treated in a variety of ways. All trees were cut and dissected after different time periods so as to follow the progress of the trees' response. Many branches that died naturally were also studied. Of course there were many variations on the theme of shedding. Conifers were different in some ways from hardwoods. Details of the theme and variations will be given in this chapter.

As a branch dies or after it is abruptly cut off, the tree begins to convert energy reserves into antimicrobial substances. In heartwood, more phenol is produced, and the phenol is combined with oxygen to produce materials that may not only kill or repel microorganisms, but the materials may also kill tree cells. In conifers the antimicrobial substances have a terpene base.

As branches die, the first chemical boundary may form out in the branch base, the position shown here by A. That position or boundary may be so strong that decay-causing organisms do not spread beyond that point. The branch is weakened at that point and may break leaving a long stub. In some trees, such as the oaks, the first position of the boundary may be far out in the branch and long stubs result.

In the section shown here (Fig. 10), a second boundary at B was obvious. A third boundary was at C, and the boundary present at the time of dissection was at D. Each growth sheath (or ring) has its own column of phenol-based antimicrobial materials. The D boundary is more like an inverted cone in 3 dimensions. The small black arrows show the extent of the last-formed boundary. The white arrows show where the trunk collar surrounded the branch. A proper pruning cut would be from white arrow point to white arrow point.

Some other features on this section are the epicormic bud trace—a dormant bud—at the position of the large arrow, and pith protection zone at the points of the double arrows. The pith of the branch does not connect directly with the pith of the trunk. A sheath of hard, strong tissues surrounds the pith of the trunk and the pith of the branch. The pith protection zone has cells that are thicker walled than normal pith cells, and the cells have a higher amount of phenol-based materials.

For the extra keen eye, note the other dormant bud trace that is opposite the one shown by the large black arrow. The bud trace grew into the developing branch and caused a small pocket of included bark. The upward sweeping cells that separate branch from trunk on the inside are called compacted xylem.

Figure 13-11

Figure 13-12

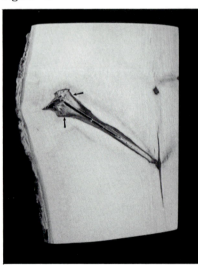

Dissections of *Eucalyptus* and *Angophora* trees in Australia showed similar branch protection zones associated with dead stubs. The arrows show the zone in an *Angophora* (closely related to the *Eucalpytus*). Note how abruptly the decayed wood stopped on the outer side of the zone (Fig. 11).

Figure 12 shows how effective the branch protection zone can be. The tree is a yellow birch, and the branch died 18 years before the tree was cut and dissected. The arrows show the strong chemical boundaries that walled off the decayed wood. The form of the decayed pocket indicates that the branch was "pinched off" and the sharp top remained. When a branch breaks close to the trunk, a very small callus collar forms. The all important point here is that the tree does have a process to resist spread of pathogens into a tree.

The word pathogen has been used repeatedly here for a wide variety of wood-inhabiting organisms. Pathogenesis is a condition of the whole organism, the whole tree, not only its parts. Any organism that threatens the life of another organism is a pathogen. Trees die 3 ways: 1, mechanical disruption; 2, dysfunction; and 3, infection or starvation (both disruption of energy). Mechanical disruption means the organism is broken in such a way that life is threatened (I often call it the "Humpty Dumpty effect"; you can't put it back together again). When organisms rot wood, and the branch or entire tree breaks, the organisms involved are indeed pathogens.

The branch protection zones do not always function perfectly. When the zone is weak or when the pathogens are very strong, the zone may be breached (Fig. 13). The first position of the zone is called the A position. In figure 12 the A position held back the spread of pathogens. When the A position is breached the pathogens may spread into the branch core wood. The tree still sets boundaries to resist further spread. The corewood position is B. When position B is breached, the pathogens spread into the trunk, but they still stay within tissues present at the time of branch death. This is position C (see black arrows in figure 9). The pathogens have advanced to position C in this yellow birch. As many position Cs occur in a tree, the central columns of discolored wood coalesce to form a continuous column. This colored wood should not be confused with the central colored wood that forms normally in some trees as the cells age and die — heartwood.

Figure 14 shows a dissected dead branch and trunk of an aspen, *Populus tremuloides*. Most individual trees in this species have very weak branch protection zones, or no zone as shown here. When twigs die, the pathogens spread rapidly into the branches. When branches fill up with dead spots, then die, and the pathogens spread into the trunk. The trunk may still wall off the pathogens to the wood present at the time of branch death, but in doing so, the volume of wood in the trunk that can store energy reserves is decreased. As the many columns of discolored wood coalesce, a trunk with many columns of discolored wood results.

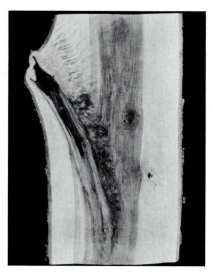

Figure 13-13

Figure 13-14

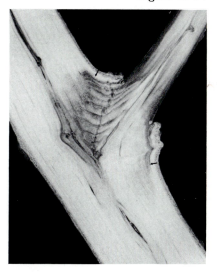

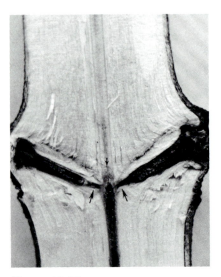

Figure 13-15

This close view of a small maple trunk (Fig. 15) shows that the struggle for survival starts early in the life of trees. The branch protection zones are there and also the pith protection zone. One-year-old branches are shown here. The pith is very large in young branches. A pathogen has an easy path down the branch pith—until it meets the pith protection zone (lower arrows). A similar pith protection zone is shown by the upper arrow for the trunk pith. Note the discolored pith in the trunk below the arrows. The tree is indeed *highly compartmentalized*, and the tree has many "gates" that stop, stall, or resist entrance. The system repeats and repeats, and that is why its survival record is better than any other organism on earth.

Figure 16 shows some variations on the theme of young branches, protection zones, and spread of pathogens. Trunk A has two B-type branch cores. Trunk B has a C-type infection, below left. Trunk C has an A type branch core at above right. Trunk D has two B-type branch cores. Note the pith protection zones in all samples.

Figure 13-16

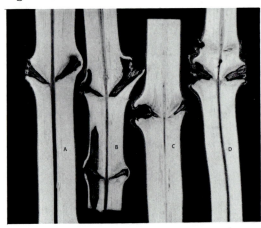

Conifers have a variation on the theme of branch protection zone. When the conifer branches are alive, resin is being impregnated into the core wood of the branches, and in some branches a core of resin also forms outward in the branch. As the branch begins to wane and die, the tree "seals off" the small amount of still living wood that surrounds the base of the branch. The small white arrows in figure 17 show this area in an eastern hemlock. The black arrows show the size of the tree when the branch died. Note the larger growth rings above the dead branch. This growth process results in a cylindrical trunk as branches continue to die in an upward direction on the trunk. A close look at the branch base will still reveal a dark band of concentrated resins. This would be the A position (large black arrows). The resin core may develop far out into branches, and when the branch dies, it breaks where the resin core ends. This is bad for forest products because long dead stubs remain on the tree. Evidence of the resin-soaked corewood can be seen by observing an old decayed conifer on the forest floor. The wood will be decayed away, but the resin-soaked branch cores will still be sound. One extra note; the large white arrow shows the compacted xylem.   *Figure 13-17*

Branch Shedding   243

Figure 14-1

A New Tree Biology

CHAPTER 14

Epicormic Branches and Limb Drop

Epicormic means upon the trunk. There are two types of epicormic branches: 1, from dormant buds that are carried along through the wood and eventually may develop to form a branch; 2, adventitious buds that form anew, *de novo*, (from the beginning), within the cambium, usually after some injury. The dissection on a red oak in figure 1 shows the bud trace of a dormant bud and its eventual sprouting to form a branch (open arrows). The wound inflicted 10 cm above the bud in some way stimulated the bud to develop into the branch. The sample was cut one year after the wound was inflicted in wounding experiments. The black arrows show the barrier zone that formed after the wound was inflicted. The large arrows show the crack associated with the wound.

When the dormant bud formed the branch, some of the old bark remained behind the branch, and new bark formed around the branch. A branch collar does form when dormant buds sprout, and a trunk collar also starts to form. But, the trunk collar may circle the base of the branch. If growth of the trunk collar is rapid, it may actually squeeze out the new branch. This is not so likely to happen when the branch is at a sharp angle upward, but it could happen when the branch is horizontal. Many epicormic branches do get pinched off, or their growth is stalled by the trunk collar. Trouble starts when the epicormic branch starts to grow in a horizontal direction, and then new shoots on the branch begin to grow upright. This happens with such species as *Eucalyptus*. The decay at the base of the branch and the added weight of the branch may suddenly end in the failure of the branch. Another situation of this type starts when trees are topped — the main leader is cut off. New shoots, epicormic, but usually adventitious shoots, begin to form at the cambial zone. The branches may grow in a horizontal direction while decay is spreading downward in the old leader stem. The leader stem is getting weaker and the branch is getting heavier. The same problem occurs on fruit trees that get added weight when the fruit matures.

This type of limb or branch drop is more common in warmer climates where the newly formed epicormic branches grow very fast. Harsh topping cuts are major starting points for this type of limb drop. In cooler climates the epicormic branches do not grow so rapidly, and many of them wane, or die, before they become a hazard risk.

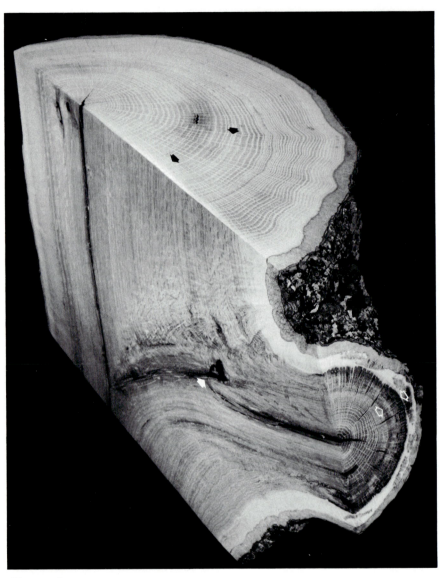

Figure 14-2

The large branch on this red oak may not qualify as an epicormic branch but it was from a late forming bud on the primary branch that died (white arrow). The primary branch was shed and the wound closed quickly. The new branch may have been from a dormant bud.

Injuries on the branch caused a ring of infected, discolored wood (open white arrows). The black arrows show the very prominent large rays common to most oaks.

Living limbs drop from trees 4 basic ways: 1, fracture several inches to several feet out from the base of the branch; 2, fracture at the base of the branch; 3, pull out of the socket around an epicormic branch; 4, the trunk fails and the branch pulls out with a large section of the trunk.

The first type of fracture is common where branches have grown out into new space provided by new roads, recreation areas, or construction. The branch can actually grow itself to death, to mechanical disruption. This situation is made worse where old internal cracks are in the branch base. The cracks or radial and circumferential shakes (not visible cracks, but weakened zones) could have been started by wounds, or improperly cut branches. As the branch grows into the new space, the ends get heavier. The internal cracks begin to spread. When the cracks cause the trunk to separate as 2 beams, then trouble is on the way. When one beam, the top beam, or top portion of the trunk, begins to slide over the bottom portion, the cracks propagate all the faster and further. The sliding action of the top beam over the bottom causes compression on the bottom and tension on the top. In a sense, the pressures load the 2 beams until the opposing forces reach a point that can no longer hold the weight of the branch. The branch "explodes" downward. The fracture is caused by a shearing resulting from one portion of the branch sliding over the other.

Be on the alert for edge trees. Trees that had competition taken away. Trees that have new space. Be on the alert for wide, spreading heavy branches that have thick foliage. Look for vertical cracks at the base of suspect branches and trunks. Branches with many old open stubs are highly suspect. Suspect branches should be removed or braced.

The second type of fracture occurs when branches were pruned improperly close to the base of the suspect branch. Wounds near the base of the branch may also start the weakening process. On some trees, such as species of *Eucalyptus*, brown rot will develop at the base of branches that had wounds, or old branch stubs. It is very difficult to recognize brown rot because the rot may appear as sound wood. The rot ends very abruptly but the wood will be weakened far in advance of the rot. Be on the alert for branches that have wounds near their base. Be on alert for large stubs on the suspect branch. Be on the alert for cracks at the base of branches.

The third type of limb drop starts with topping cuts or large wounds that stimulate epicormic branches to develop. Learn to recognize epicormic branches. They will usually have a large swollen ring of tissues about their base. They will be near old top cuts and near old large wounds. Be especially careful with epicormics that go from a horizontal position to many vertical branches at their tips.

The fourth type of limb drop is really a type of trunk failure. The trunk may have large columns of decayed wood. Here again, the branch could grow itself to death if suddenly released. Be on the alert for large branches on trees with obvious trunk decay.

Branches do not just suddenly fall from trees without a cause. There are always at least 2 or 3 factors or more happening at the same time. The branch or trunk must be weakened and some increasing force must move the wood to a point of failure.

Many observers state that branches usually drop during calm, hot weather, and in late afternoon. These conditions may affect not only the weight of the branch but the propagation of internal shake zones. There are 2 basic ways you can fracture a branch: 1, add weight to the end; 2, weaken the base. I have examined many branches that failed in the United States and Australia. I always found cracks or decay at the base. We may be looking at the wrong end for the causes of limb drop. The heat may be more of a factor at the base than at the tips. If it were the overloading of the tips of the branches, then every branch should fail on any tree late in the afternoon. It does not happen. It is the same story with so-called frost cracks. If frost caused frost cracks, every tree in any one area should have them. They don't. But, when trees are present with internal cracks, and then the wood is suddenly cooled, the cracks spread outward. There must be two parts to the problem. The one possible exception is where edge trees suddenly get new space and the branch may grow itself to mechanical disruption.

Limb drop is rare in forests. Limb drop may be similar to girdling roots; a man made problem.

Figure 15-1

Echinodontium tinctorium (Et) is a fungus that is associated with a white rot of true fir, *Abies concolor* in the Pacific Northwest. Some comments on the disease seem to fit here because it brings together many of the points discussed so far.

The sporophore is found below dead branch stubs (Fig. 1). The columns of decay in the trees are usually — not always — in the wood present when the branches died. The white arrow in figure 1 shows the crack in the trunk wood and the hard wood covering of the branch. At this point, the last growth ring in the trunk can be traced into the branch. Yet, there is discolored wood, and some early decayed wood beyond this point. How can this be explained?

A New Tree Biology

CHAPTER 15

E.t. and the Tree

Here is the same sample (Fig. 2) as it appeared immediately after it was cut. The large central column of decayed wood was surrounded by discolored wood. The dark spots at the arrow tips help to explain the extension of the defect beyond the diameter of the wood at the time of branch death.　　　*Figure 15-2*

Figure 15-3

Figure 15-4

When the sample was split (Fig. 3) along a tangential plane, the significance of the many dark spots became clear. The spots were caused by insects that had infested the inner bark and wood when the tree was the diameter of the dark spots (arrow). The thousands of small wounds sets up a new column of greater diameter.

Compare this finished sample (Fig. 4) with the sample after it was cut (Fig. 2). The large white arrow shows the crack associated with the death of many branches. The black arrow shows the radial crack associated with the branch that supports the sporophore. The small white arrows show insect wounds. There are 60 growth rings after the insect infestation. The 60 rings were approximately 3 centimeters wide.

An important point shown by this story is that what you first see may not be the complete story. More than one agent may be a part of the story. Samples must be prepared properly or you will be studying artifacts.

This fungus infects very small twigs on branches. The fungus may grow in the small branches or remain in a dormant state until the branch dies. The fungus may then grow into the trunk tissues present at the time of branch death. Other branch stubs, and other wounds may expand the diameter of the rot column. Organisms do not grow freely in trees. There are several reasons for all processes.

Figure 15-5

Another tree defect that needs clarification is the pencil rot problem in cedars (loose common name for several related species) (Fig. 5). The fungus associated with the disease in western cedars is *Polyporus armarus*. The fungus causes a brown rot. Brown rots usually end abruptly, but the sound-appearing wood beyond the rot may be greatly weakened.

The problem of brown rot pockets resulted from many branch infections. The fungus infects the branch base and the small strip of branch tissue that forms downward as a tail (see pull-apart branch diagram in chapter on branches). The fungus stays within the branch tissues as they lie on the trunk.

The important point here is that you must understand the tissue arrangements of the branch-trunk union. If the branch-trunk tissues are not understood, this defect will not be understood. Again, I state that my interest in this conversation with you is not to present a one-sided problem view of trees. Too much of that has already been done. I believe that if you understand the tree, the problems and proper care will come clear. To study only problems and care without an understanding of tree biology is not only a waste of time, but adds more confusion to the literature.

CHAPTER 16
Wood and Boundaries

What is wood? Wood is an orderly arrangement of cells that have walls of cellulose and lignin mostly, in all stages of aging. When the cambium divides to form the cambial zone, and when the cells of the cambial zone begin to differentiate, they are all alive. All wood cells start as living cells. The living cells are oriented in an axial or radial direction. Once the cells begin to differentiate, they can no longer be called a part of the cambial zone. It is possible for the axial and radial parenchyma to divide, but they are locked in place by other cells, thus making division impossible (unless wounds release the locked condition).

The all important ingredient of wood is cellulose. Cellulose is the most abundant natural material in the world. That is often considered the good news. The bad news is that the second most abundant natural material is lignin. Cellulose is made up of glucose units. The energy of the sun is held within the chemical bonds of the glucose. Cellulose holds the promise for so many beneficial processes for man and all other living things. Then there is lignin. We really do not know what to do with it. It is closely associated with cellulose, and that is our major problem. The lignin must be removed before we can get to the cellulose. This is not an easy task. Especially when we really know so little about lignin. Yes, much has been written, but that does not mean much is known. How much you know about something can best be measured by how well you can regulate the factor. We pulp wood to rid it of lignin. The lignin and the materials used for pulping contaminate our streams. It is a real problem. Of course, some microorganisms — bacteria and fungi — can alter, and in some cases, even digest the lignin. The white rot fungi do this. Indeed, the microbes hold the best promise for dealing with the "natural glue."

Yet, trees would not have their most important feature without lignin. Nothing comes all bad in nature; or all good either. The cellulose and lignin construction gives trees extremely strong mechanical support. The mechanical support of trees is the one feature that sets trees apart from all other organisms. Every part of the wood can support itself. The smallest splinter will stand upright. Try that with an equal "splinter" of animal muscle. It won't work.

Strong mechanical support gave trees the ability to stand taller and longer than all other plants. This feature gave trees an opportunity to optimize limited space and to optimize the trapping of the sun's energy. The feature—strong mechanical support—then became strongly linked to survival factors. So, from this view, lignin is not so bad!

Now, again, the other part of the story. Microorganisms had enzyme systems that could release energy in wood. Wood gave trees their survival advantage on earth, and here are the organisms—the microbes—that are waiting to take it away. A real problem was developing. Trees were surviving because they had wood, and so long as the wood was not broken down, the trees would survive as massive, long-lived organisms. On the other hand, the wood inhabiting organisms survived because they could gain energy from wood by breaking it down. Somewhere, somehow, some "survival deals" were made. Trees developed as highly compartmented organisms. (Animals are weakly compartmented.) Wood-inhabiting organisms survived by digesting the wood within compartments. Such an arrangement gave both a chance to survive.

From the side of the tree, mechanical support provided by wood is still the major survival feature of trees. The tree has priorities, and the first is to protect and defend its major survival feature—wood. Let us take a closer look at wood and discuss how trees protect it and defend it.

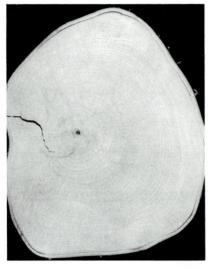

Figure 16-1

When most people are asked to draw the inside of a tree, they will start by drawing a circle. Most studies on wood and tree structure have come from cross sections (Fig. 1). This is easy to understand why. It is very difficult to cut longitudinal sections, and when such sections were viewed they were really artifacts, because a straight cut through a collection of cones or cylinders of unequal shape will result in an artifact. It was much easier, and more accurate to study the cross section. This is why we call the growth increments, rings. They appear as rings on the cross section, but not as rings on a longitudinal section.

The vascular cambium does produce a new layer of wood on its inner side and a layer of bark or phloem on its outer side. The wood is formed and the cells are locked in place. Wood cells do not move. The vascular cambium and the bark cambium — phellogen — are always on the move. They are always in a new spatial position every growth period. The phloem is made up of loosely packed cells, and these cells are also on the move. This is why boundaries can "hold" for long periods in wood, but only for short periods in bark. The natural movement prevents bark boundaries from "holding" for long periods.

The teak tree starts life as a square-stemmed plant, but other trees do start as cylinders, or as cones; one over the other every growth period. This cone over cone structure has many advantages for strength, but there are also some built-in problems with the design. Sudden shrinkage or expansion of the wood could result in internal cracks. The radial elements in the wood trunk do minimize these problems. But, remember, nature does not come in absolutes. Things can, and do, go wrong. A weak link in the wood design is the ever-present risk of radial separations. In figure 1 of a birch, small radial checks from the drying, and shrinkage, of the wood can be seen. The large crack at left occurred at felling.

The important points here are the cone on cone design of trunks and roots, wood does not move, bark moves, and there are always some weak spots in all natural systems.

Figure 16-2

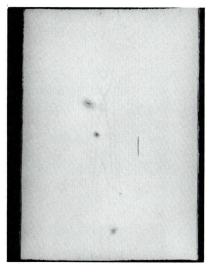

I wonder what people would have called each growth layer if they saw only longitudinal sections first; growth stripes? Here is a longitudinal view of a spruce. The birch in figure 1, and this spruce (Fig. 2) have no color change in the older wood cells near the center of the tree. Does this mean that these wood cells have not aged? Of course not! Aging and dying of cells starts immediately after they are "born" from the vascular cambium. Many species of trees do not have changes in color of wood cells associated with aging. This is not to say that these trees do not have columns of discolored wood. That is another matter to be discussed in detail as we go on.

The center of this sample helps to make the point about an artifact. The saw cut was straight and flat with the surface but strange patterns are seen. What is seen is definitely not what the internal structure of wood really is like. This is an example of a cutting artifact. As we go on, some other artifacts will be pointed out. To study an artifact and think it is the real thing can lead to disaster! It has been done.

The width of each growth increment indicates the growth rate that occurred each year. The thick-walled cells that form late in the annual growth period help to mark each growth increment. This tree had rapid growth when it started. The growth rate decreased slowly over the first 20 years. Then there were 10 years of slow growth followed by 9 years of faster growth, but not as fast as the young growth. The wood that forms early in the life of a tree is called juvenile wood. The early-formed wood usually does not have the strength properties of the wood that forms later. The center wood, or juvenile wood, is formed when the tree is primarily tree 1, or made up of living branches. The trunk is then the coalescence of the branches. As the branches begin to die upward on the trunk, tree 2 begins to emerge. The wood in tree 2 or the trunk wood not directly connected to living branches is different from the juvenile wood; it is usually stronger. Juvenile wood is not so common in forest trees, because most forest trees do not start life with rapid growth. The notable exceptions are those trees that grow rapidly in suddenly exposed areas that occur after fire or blow down. Conifers grown in plantations head the list for juvenile wood. But, even forest trees start life as tree 1, or mostly branches. The point here is to recognize the changes that take place as trees go from mostly branches, to mostly trunk.

Figure 16-3

Figure 16-4

Figure 16-5

Figure 16-6

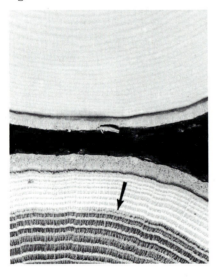

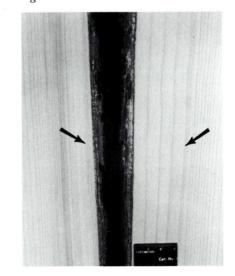

The theme is wood produced in an orderly way every growth period. The variations are almost endless, or as varied as there are tree species. In figure 3 a section of Douglas fir is shown. The arrow points to the vascular cambium. (Douglas fir is really not a fir tree.) The wood cells that form late in the growing season have thicker walls, thus giving a distinct ring appearance when viewed on the cross-section surface. Note that the thin check lines start in the late wood.

In figure 4 the balsam fir section at the bottom has a faint ring pattern when compared to the red pine above. The latewood of the pine is very distinct. The fir has thin bark, while the pine has thick bark.

In figure 5 a red maple, above, is compared with a red oak, below. The maple has clear, bright wood, and no central column of colored heartwood. The red oak has a sapwood in the sample of 7 growth increments and the arrow shows where the heartwood starts. The "growth" rings are very distinct in the oak sample because the latewood cells have thicker walls and also the earlywood vessels are very large. Note that there is little thick outer bark in the samples.

Figure 6 shows 2 longitudinal sections of Norway spruce, *Picea abies*. The arrow in the sample at left shows 4 growth rings. The arrow in the sample at right also shows 4 growth rings. The tree at left grew the 4 growth rings to a width of 3 centimeters.

The points of the sections is that there are many variations on the theme of wood and growth increments. Indeed, different trees have different patterns of growth.

A point here is that we often think that fast growth is healthy. Growth rate is not a measure of health. Health is the ability to resist strain. Strain is an injurious irreversible condition resulting from energy blockage, disruption, drain, or shunt. Too often when we grow trees in cities we want them to grow rapidly the first few years, then to grow slowly. If they get too big, too fast, then the tops are cut off. This is a sad way to treat trees. Most city trees should grow slowly. Topping of fast growing trees has come to be a common practice.

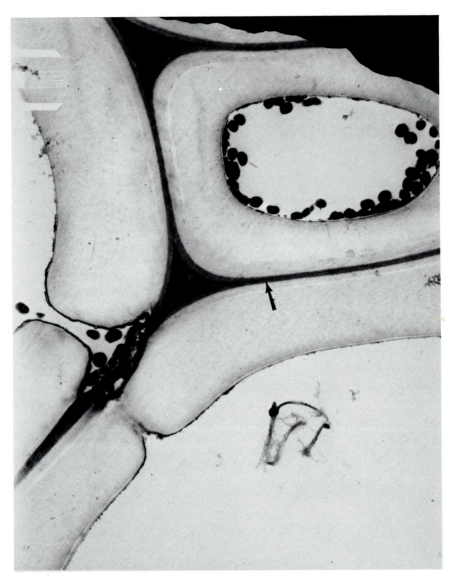

Figure 16-7

A New Tree Biology

The cell is the basic unit of all organisms (Fig. 7). The most simple-in-form (not simple in function) organisms have one cell. As organisms with multiple cell make-up developed, some of the cells "performed" special functions. A group of cells of similar make-up performing a special function is called a tissue. A group of tissues performing a special function is called an organ. Trees have 3 organs: roots, stems, and leaves. Trees have cells that are basically nonwoody — leaves, needles, reproductive parts, absorbing roots, phloem — and those that are woody. The trees "keep" most of the woody parts and the inner bark — phloem — and shed the nonwoody parts.

Cells in wood transport materials, support the tree, and maintain the living processes. They all have a role in protection and defense. Sapwood has cells that transport, support, store energy reserves, and protect and defend the tree. Heartwood has cells that maintain mechanical support, and still play a role in protection and defense. Heartwood cells do not contain living materials and they are not involved in active transport for the tree. Heartwood cells may still contain some residual granules of starch. More on heartwood in another chapter.

The cells in wood have 2 major walls: 1, a primary wall; and 2, a secondary wall. The secondary wall is thick and subdivided into 3 parts: S_1, S_2, and S_3. The S_2 or middle layer of the secondary wall is very thick.

The arrow in figure 7 shows the middle lammela. It is the layer between the cells and it is rich in pectin. Enzymes called pectinases are required to breakdown pectin. (The letters "ase" or "ases" usually indicate an enzyme that acts on a specific material, or in better terms the substrate.)

The uniqueness of the tree wood cell is the combination of cellulose and lignin. Of course there are other substances present such as hemicellulose, but the other substances are greatly overshadowed by cellulose and lignin. The inner lining of the cells may also contain other substances that have a sugar base. These substances are called oligosaccharins. These materials may have strong regulating powers on the cells. The oligosaccharins are classed as part of the group of plant growth regulators (auxin, gibberellin, ethylene, cytokinen, abscisic acid, and oligosaccharin). Hormones are for animals, growth regulators for plants. The oligosaccharins may be important in defense reactions. Indeed, we have a long way to go.

The section in figure 7 is from a ring shake zone in black walnut. The dark bodies in the cells are thought to be bacteria. The wood is magnified 18,360X under an electron microscope.

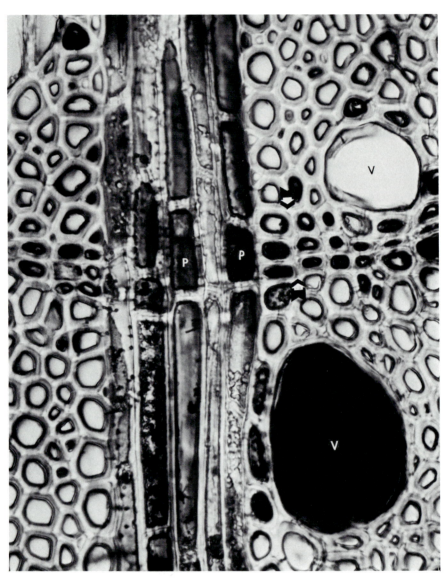

Figure 16-8

Here is a cross-section of red maple magnified 1000X under a light microscope (Fig. 8). Thin sections for study are cut on a microtome, which is a machine that holds the wood block as a long sharp knife is pulled over the block. It is a refinement of a shaving machine. Wood sections from 5 to 20 microns are usually cut. It is difficult to cut sections thinner than 10 microns, but it can be done by a skilled operator. Some sections are viewed immediately after they are cut while others are placed in various materials to fix the materials in place and then to add stains that

A New Tree Biology

enhance features of the cell. Some stains are specific for certain compounds, and the stains help to identify materials and their concentrations. Histology is the study of prepared sections and histochemistry means that specific stains are being used to identify chemical compounds. Histology and histochemistry combine art and science. A great amount of skill is required to prepare sections for study. Yet, a person skilled with a razor blade and having the basic understanding of a light microscope can prepare sections that will show many of the basic features of wood and bark. My point is that you can learn a great deal about wood and bark without going to the microtome and the electron microscope.

The red maple section shows some basic cell features of diffuse porous wood. Diffuse porous means that the vessels are approximately the same size throughout the growth increment, and the vessels are equally arranged in the growth increment. In ring porous hardwoods, to be shown later, the vessels formed early in the growth period are much larger than those formed later. As always in nature, there are all gradations within the extremes.

The dark V above shows an open vessel while the light V below shows a closed vessel. Vessels may be blocked or closed several ways: gums or granular materials, a varnish-like "skin" that forms in vessels, blockage of the openings between vessels, air pockets or embolisms, masses of microorganisms, pit closure. Balloon-shaped structures called tyloses are more common in the ring porous species. Some tyloses have suberin in their walls. Vessels can be blocked in many ways, and this must be kept in mind when compartmentalization is discussed later.

The letter P shows radial parenchyma cells. The cells are shorter and in a band of parenchyma, shown between white arrows, that formed at the end of the growth period. The band of parenchyma is called marginal or terminal parenchyma. Some trees produce a thick band or multilayer of cells while others, such as American elm, produces a thin layer, or even no marginal parenchyma. The marginal parenchyma is often lacking in growth increments in the roots. This is why some people believe that organisms can spread radially once they get into the roots. I do not believe this, and there is more evidence to show that it is not so than there is to show that it is so.

Some radial parenchyma cells may expand and actually be in 2 growth increments. It is possible. The thick-walled cells throughout the section are fibers.

Note the granular or coagulated cell contents in the ray parenchyma cells. The cells are aging and dying from the time they are formed by the cambium. They seem to die in a scattered pattern in maple, meaning that all the parenchyma in the rays are not dying at the same time. Some ray parenchyma cells in sugar maple have been shown by histochemical tests to be alive after 150 years!

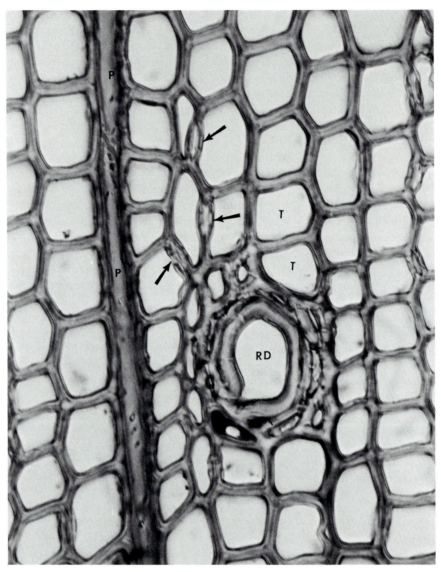

Figure 16-9

This thin cross section from a red spruce (Fig. 9) is the same magnification as the red maple section in figure 8, 1000X. Conifer wood is different from hardwood in that conifer wood is made up mostly of cells called tracheids (T). The tracheid acts as both a transport cell and a cell that provides mechanical support. Sometimes the tracheids are called fiber tracheids when walls are thicker. The walls of the tracheids do thicken in cells produced at the end of the growth period. Some conifers have a thick band of thick-walled latewood cells—southern yellow pines— while other conifers have only a slight difference in the wall thickness of the latewood cells—most species of spruce.

The letter P shows a parenchyma cell in the ray system. Most conifers have only single sheets of parenchyma in their rays. The rays may have many cells in the longitudinal or axial plane. As with all trees, there are always exceptions, and some conifers may have thicker sheets of ray cells.

A resin duct is shown by the letters RD. Resin ducts are not special types of cells, but cell arrangements. The ducts develop 2 ways: 1, living parenchyma cells clump together and form an arrangement that produces high amounts of resin; or 2, some living cells break down, or lyse, to form a duct that produces resin. Regardless how they form, they do start from living parenchyma cells that either clump together, or enlarge greatly and then lyse. Because parenchyma cells form in a radial and axial direction, resin ducts may also be in both directions. The ducts usually form in latewood cells. Some trees produce resin ducts normally—pines—while other trees produce very few to no ducts normally, but do produce them after injury or infection—hemlock, spruce. Some trees seldom produce them in wood, but do produce them in bark—true firs. (Again, you can seldom, or never, get a natural system to fit into one box or one category. But, my aim here is to give more themes than variations.) We will come back to anatomy after a slight detour to look at some boundaries. Then anatomy, boundaries, and compartmentation will begin to fit together in a more meaningful way.

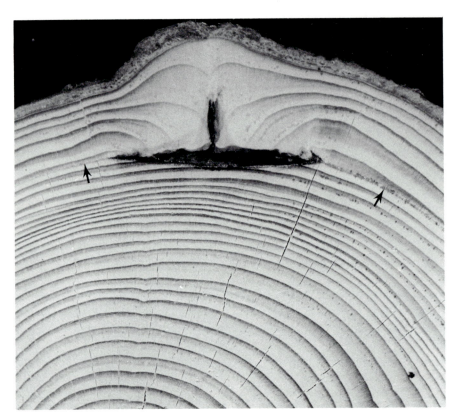

Figure 16-10

Count inward to the sixth growth increment on this Norway spruce (Fig. 10). The arrows show that near the middle of the growth period, the tree was wounded. The arrows show the new tissue, the barrier zone, that formed after the injury. The injury will always be in the tree. Trees can not restore injured cells. In this sense, trees can not heal wounded wood. In 3 years the wound was closed. The wood released the space pressure and cells grew rapidly into the space—callus growth. Callus occurs after injury. Callus can close a wound, but callus is not directly associated with the internal processes of infection. When small wounds, or larger wounds, are closed completely, the infection process is stopped. Large wounds on large trees seldom close completely. More on this subject will come from other samples.

This tree had 18 current growth increments with some resin, indicating that there were living cells within the last 18 growth increments. The small dark dots in the latewood indicate resin flow. The wood inward from the 18 outer increments was much drier than the 18 outer increments.

Note that there were no resin droplets in the wood behind the wound. This suggests that the living cells were killed in the wood behind the wound. And, the wound stimulated the flow of resin in the cells to the right of the wound.

Figure 16-11

The thin section shown here (Fig. 11) was cut from the wood at the point of the arrow at right of the wound shown in figure 10. The figure shown here shows several important factors of barrier zones. Barrier zones in conifers have many resin ducts in them, and resin ducts continue to form after the barrier zone has been completed. The parenchyma in the barrier zone are enlarged in the rays, and the enlarged ray cells continue in the wood formed later in the season, and in this section, even into the next growth increment. The barrier zone has many cells with dark contents. These cells formed as axial parenchyma, and the cell contents were changed chemically to antimicrobial substances. Note that some of the cells inward from the distinct barrier zone appear slightly altered. The cambium was actively producing cells at the time of the wound. The cambium was at the position slightly inward from the barrier zone at the time of the wounding. Note also that the cells that formed after the barrier zone was completed were smaller and not so neatly arranged as those cells that formed before the barrier zone started to form. Sometimes barrier zones form far beyond the wound; sometimes they do not. We do not understand the factors that regulate the size and effectiveness of the barrier zone. We do know that a great amount of energy is used to produce it.

Figure 16-12

A beaver wounded this sweetgum, *Liquidambar styraciflua*, 9 years before the tree was cut (Fig. 12). Fungi, bacteria, and insects spread into the tree. The small black arrows show the barrier zone that formed completely about the trunk. Most of the time, sweetgum forms very small barrier zones that hardly develop beyond the wound. Sweetgum produces a gum-like, or even, resin-like material called storax. The barrier zone had an abundance of this material in the cells.

The double arrows show the boundary of discolored wood that acts as a boundary for lateral spread of the pathogens. Note the sharp dark boundary that separates the decayed wood from the discolored wood. This boundary is surely a microorganism—tree interaction boundary. (I use microorganism often because I can not be sure whether we have only a fungus or only a bacterium, or both involved. I believe it is much safer to think in terms of several microorganisms rather than one. Recheck the chapter on microorganisms and dark lines.)

The large arrows show radial cracks that developed outward from the position where the callus rolled inward. This is a common way cracks start in trees. This feature also shows what will happen when a boundary is broken from the inside. Breaking boundaries from the inside is a common practice where cavities are prepared for treatment. Many of the cracks that form on such treated trees are started by the people who break internal boundaries. There are limits to a tree's defense system. We must be careful not to destroy the defense systems of trees.

A New Tree Biology

Boundaries do benefit the microorganisms as well as the tree. This point was made earlier. In figure 13, a dissected red maple helps to reinforce this point. The small arrows show the boundaries of a decay column that has progressed to almost a central hollow. Injuries at a later time set up the second boundary shown by the larger arrows. The wood between the arrows is decayed. The discolored wood in the outer boundary was inhabited by several species of bacteria and fungi that do not decay wood. The boundary shown by the small arrows also was inhabited by similar microorganisms. The decayed wood between the arrows yielded on isolation a decay-causing fungus different from the one isolated from the central column. The central column had many other organisms including insects, slime molds, nematodes, and others. Indeed the boundaries define and protect the niches, and still "give" the tree a chance to grow.

Figure 16-13

Figure 16-14

All the wood in this birch was decayed (Fig. 14). The same story as given in figure 14 applies here. The important point here is that even after all the decay and the death of the tree, the boundaries were still hard and intact (arrows, Fig. 14). The way trees decay make perfect protective homesites for small and large insects, birds, and other animals. The small cavity in this sample provides a place where many organisms live and reproduce. Think what happens when all of these niches are taken away. They all belong to the same webwork. Indeed, we have wounded many forests.

Wood and Boundaries

How many times can you wound a tree before it dies? It seems that many people are constantly working on this question without realizing what is happening. Consider for a moment the trees in fruit orchards. They are some of the most abused trees in the world. The tops are cut off, branches are cut flush to the trunk, roots are constantly injured by heavy machinery, and the trunk literally "gets it from all directions." Equipment for shaking trees heads the list for bumps and bruises. This pear tree, *Pyrus communis*, received many trunk wounds (Fig. 15). Yes, boundaries formed (arrows) but there are limits to any system. This tree was infected by a fungus that produces wedges into the bark (pointers).

After trees are wounded repeatedly, another problem starts that has received very little attention: starvation. Trees, like other living things, starve when water, elements, and food become limiting. Trees also starve in another way. Trees starve when space for storing energy reserves begins to decrease. My point here is that boundaries are important, and the tree does have a remarkable defense system, but there are limits to this system. In the end, the tree may not die directly because of the wounds, but indirectly because of starvation. So, how many wounds does it take to kill a tree?

Figure 16-15

A New Tree Biology

The wound at left on a species of *Tilia* from Europe was open and the wound at right was closed (Fig. 16). The large arrows indicate the tree's defense to resist inward spread of the pathogens. There were not many differences between the defects associated with the open and closed wounds. Insects had infested both wounds. There were no central injuries in the tree at the time of wounding. It was the tree and the internal conditions more than the closure rates that affected the size of the infected wood. Big callus does not mean that a small internal column exists. The small arrows show the tree's defense to resist vertical spread. Again, not much difference between the open and the closed wound. Any treatment that breaks the internal boundaries will destroy the tree's defense system, and the pathogens will spread rapidly.

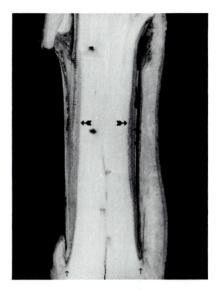

Figure 16-16

Figure 16-17

This sugar maple sample was cut 1 meter below the wound (Fig. 17). The small arrows show the size of the tree at the time of wounding. Note the subtle color change within the cylinder of wood present at the time of wounding. No matter how this wood is dried, it will be a darker shade than the wood formed after wounding. The largest arrows show the radial defense system, and the other arrow shows the barrier zone. Even small wounds will alter the wood. The wound on this tree caused very little injury to the tree — injure is a physiological problem — , but it did cause considerable damage — damage is an economic problem. The color changes could affect the value of wood for high value products.

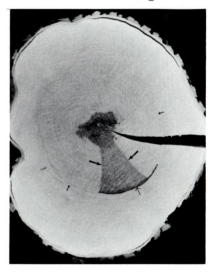

Wood and Boundaries

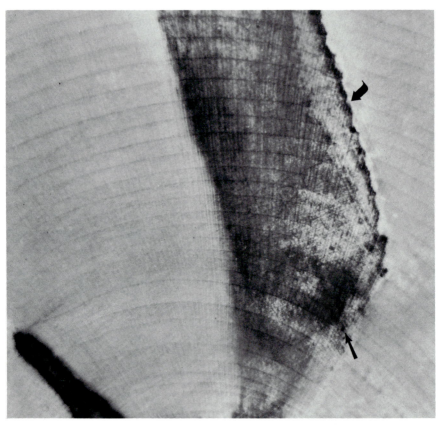

Figure 16-18

The drill bit hole was used in many wounding experiments. The wound could be repeated accurately. And, as already stated, the drill-type hole is common in nature — insect galleries, bird peck holes — and in tree treatments — injections, implants, cabling and bracing, tubes for water drainage, increment borers.

The hole shown in figure 18 was slanted to the right as shown in this cross section sample. The arrow with the curved end points to the dark boundary made up of phenol-based materials. (I used phenol-based here and elsewhere because the number and types of phenols in trees almost seems endless. Trees, especially hardwoods, seem to be full of phenols. Phenols are the basic building blocks for many antimicrobial compounds. Phenols also figure in the tanning process where protein is combined with gallic acid and other substances. When protein is tanned it is no longer available as a food source — leather from hides. The reader more interested in phenol chemistry and the pathways that form the many phenol-based materials should start by reading some chemistry textbooks.)

The other arrow shows the tip of the wound. The wood between the tip of the wound and the other central column of decay died and discolored. Note that the column followed the orientation of the rays inward.

A New Tree Biology

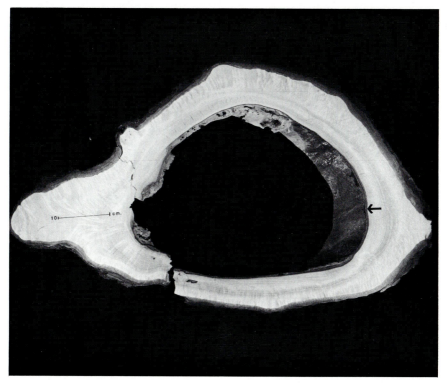

Figure 16-19

Even when all boundaries present in the wood at the time of wounding fail—reaction zones—usually the barrier zone still remains effective. The arrow points to the hard rim that separated the decayed wood from the sound wood in this sugar maple (Fig. 19). (The cracks at left were caused by the felling of the tree.) Again, this remarkable natural boundary should not be destroyed during treatments. Machines that destroy such boundaries and the people who do such disastrous things to beautiful trees are at the top of the list for harmful agents. Lack of understanding of trees was the major reason the horrible practice of breaking internal boundaries with machines got started. People tried to treat trees like humans: clean out the decayed tooth, put a dressing on the wound, "feed" (fertilize) the sick tree! Trees are not people. People heal. Trees compartmentalize. Indeed, lack of understanding about trees has been our major tree problem.

Wood and Boundaries

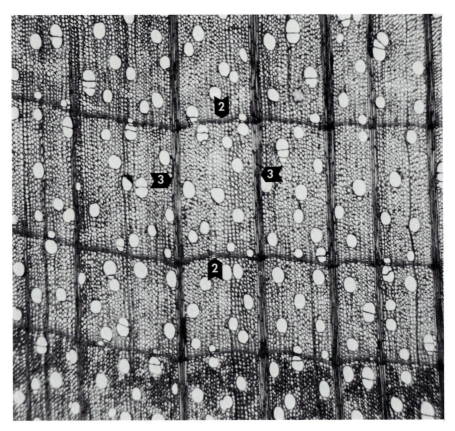

Figure 16-20

Now it is time to tie together wood, boundaries, and compartmentalization. The thin section in figure 20 shows a maple from West Germany. The wood pattern is diffuse porous; evenly spaced vessels. The end of the growth increment is marked by distinct marginal parenchyma (arrows 2). The strong radial sheets of parenchyma impart a grid pattern to the wood (arrows). Each cell is a compartment, and the group of cells are held in boundaries by marginal parenchyma and radial parenchyma. And, each growth ring is a distinct compartment. Just described are the 3 basic orders of compartmentation: 1, the cell; 2, the group of cells within the marginal and radial parenchyma; and 3, the growth increment. These compartments are "built-in" to the tree. These exist as natural boundaries. After injury and infection the 3 basic compartments respond to an altered state of higher protection. The alterations are powered by chemical reactions. The numbers 2 and 3 are the CODIT model walls. Wall 1 (not shown) resists vertical spread of pathogens. Wall 2 resists inward spread, and wall 3 resists lateral spread of pathogens. Wall 1 is the weakest and wall 3 is the strongest. Walls 1, 2 and 3 are model representations of the reaction zone. The highly ordered compartmentation of wood is a wondrous beauty of nature.

274   *A New Tree Biology*

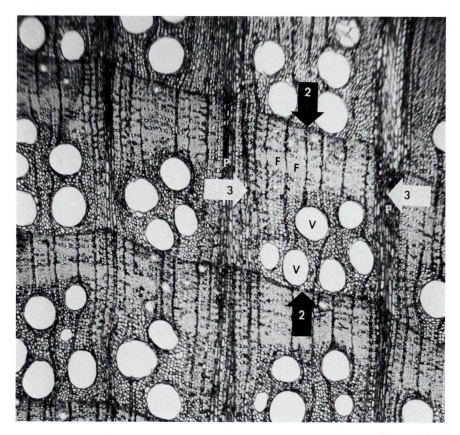

Figure 16-21

The theme of compartmentation (not compartmentalization here; compartmentation is the "built-in" static state of the cells; compartmentalization is the dynamic defense process that starts after injury and infection) is shown again in this red oak thin section (Fig. 21). There are variations on the theme; the vessels formed early in the growth period are very large and the vessels formed later are much smaller, there are many single sheets of radial parenchyma within the wide radial sheets of parenchyma. The large earlywood vessels (V) are surrounded by living parenchyma cells. The thick-walled fibers (F) are mostly in the latewood. The radial sheets of parenchyma cells (P) are very thick. The CODIT walls 2 and 3 are shown. The same pattern of "rooms" or compartments can be seen in the wood. The growth ring is subdivided into earlywood and latewood. In this species of oak, the parenchyma surrounds the large earlywood vessels. In other species of trees, the parenchyma may only connect with a portion of the vessels. When the wood is injured or infected, the parenchyma surrounding the vessels balloon out their contents into the vessel — a tylosis. This blocks the vessel. In white oaks, especially *Quercus alba*, tyloses form within the 2 and 3 year old vessels; normally, without injury and infection. This is why white oaks make good, tight whiskey barrels.

Wood and Boundaries

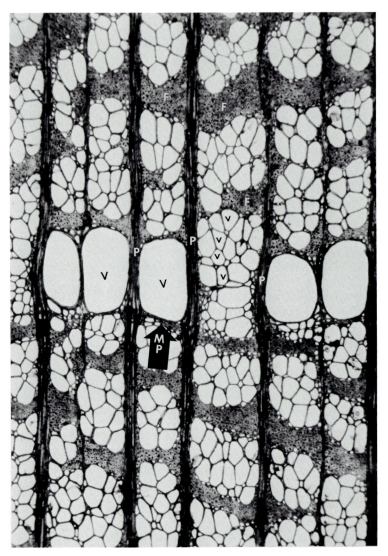

Figure 16-22

American elm has received a great amount of attention in the last few decades because of Dutch elm disease. This is what American elm looks like under the microscope, 100X (Fig. 22). The tree has enormous earlywood vessels (V). Later in the growing season, or even in earlywood, the vessels may be clumped like foam or bubbles (v). The fibers have thick walls and a "gelatinous" type of make up (F). The radial parenchyma (P) are usually distinct. The trees usually have a very thin to nonexistent marginal parenchyma (MP). In some trees, the cells from one growth period seem to form directly into the next growth ring. The vascular cambium is towards the top of the figure 22.

The variations in cell patterns in American elm are extremely great. Some elm wood seems to be more air than wood. Other trees have thickly packed, thick-walled cells. Research has suggested that cell arrangements may play a role in resistance to the spread of the pathogen. But, you can not take one cell feature and say that that feature alone is responsible for high or low resistance. It seems that the combination of cell types and patterns do play some role in resistance.

The theme of compartmentation is very obvious in the section shown. When the pathogen does infect the wood, the pathogens do stay within the compartments. When many pathogens are spreading in the wood from many infection courts, it is difficult to see the confinement of the pathogens to the compartments. When bark is peeled from an elm, the many dark streaks indicate that each infecting pathogen is staying in its own compartment.

Here is a very important point. The pathogen may be spreading in the vessels or other cells, but not touching the vascular cambium. Yet, the cambium responds by forming a barrier zone. The first description of a barrrier zone was in 1935 by Dr. Chrisiana Buisman from Holland. She was studying elm infected by *Ceratocystis ulmi*.

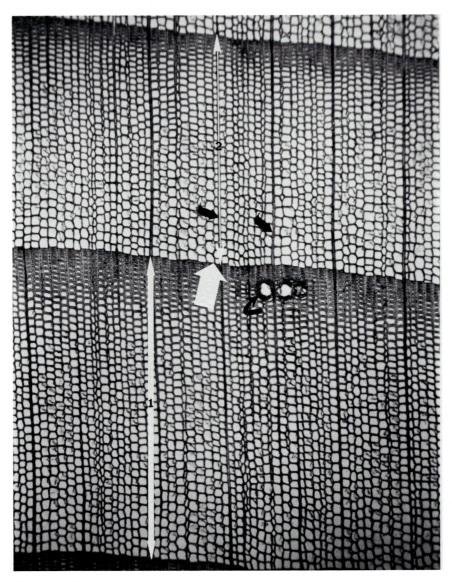

Figure 16-23

Arrows 1 and 2 show the size of the growth increments in this Engleman spruce (Fig. 23). The arrows with the curved backs show the thin sheets of parenchyma. The large white arrow points to the end of the growth ring. Note how the latewood cells developed thicker walls. The curved arrow points to resin ducts in the latewood. The thick-walled latewood cells give the spruce a distinct ring appearance when viewed from the cross section.

The section was cut through the sapwood. The cutting process pulled away the inner walls of the tracheids. The theme of compartmentation is still very clear in this section.

If microorganisms could spread at will, or freely, in wood, trees would not live very long. The "building" of compartments from the cell upward gives the tree unique survival features.

Cellulose has about the same specific gravity regardless where it is in the cell wall: 1.53. The specific gravity of wood is then determined by how closely "packed" the cells are, and how thick the walls are. Extractives, or materials deposited in cell walls also add to the specific gravity of wood.

Figure 16-24

A New Tree Biology

The curved arrows show a compartment in the growth ring of this red spruce (Fig. 24). Note the decrease in the width of the growth rings toward the cambium; top of the figure. The number and width of the earlywood decreases but not so with the latewood. The latewood stays about the same.

Picea abies, Norway spruce, has been used for centuries for the top plate of musical instruments. The sides and back have been made mostly of hard maple, *Acer plantanoides*. Both spruce and maple are woods that do not have abrupt changes in their cell patterns. The maple resists cracks. Defects usually end abruptly in maple. The spruce plate on a violin (family name) is like a vibrating reed. Spruce with open pits may have the best resonating features. Pits are open in sapwood. Pits can be opened in cut wood by treating the wood with cellulases to digest the pit membranes. Pits may also be opened by bacteria. When freshly cut wood is ponded or floated in water, the bacteria may attack the pits. Maybe this is the old secret! (We are working on it.)

Figure 16-25

Take a section of wood, sand it as smooth as possible, and then touch it, look at it, and see how many things you can see in the wood. It is a delightful way to learn about trees. There is a magic in touching ultra-smooth wood. How many features can you see in this eastern hemlock sample (Fig. 25)? You can determine the age. You know it has had some good times, and some bad times. It started growth rapidly. Then suddenly trouble; between the 2 arrows at left. But, the bad times even had worse times. Note the growth increments between the 4 arrow points. The tree was also growing faster on the right side. It must have had some wounds or branches die; note the circumferential cracks. Where are the cracks? Within the growth rings. This means the problem occurred during the middle of the growth period. Look at the radial cracks. Note where they seem to start; between the latewood and the earlywood in the next ring. When was this tree cut? If the last few growth rings can be trusted, the tree was cut at the beginning of its growth period. Why do you need to know all this stuff? Once you learn to "read" trees outside and inside, you will feel the power of understanding a little bit of how some of the parts fit. The more you can "read" trees, the more you will be able to do to help them. And, that is what this conversation is all about.

CHAPTER 17

Heartwood and Discolored Wood and the System

Controversy and Confusion surround the subject of heartwood and discolored wood. There seems to be as many explanations of these wood conditions as there are people trying to explain them. It is sad that so much of the literature on heartwood can not be accepted because the type of wood under study is not known. Discolored wood has been called heartwood or a type of heartwood—false heartwood—in many publications. The major underriding problem has been that the studies involved small pieces of wood or wood collected after the tree was cut and sawn into boards. Very few, if any, heartwood studies started in the forest with the living tree. This is a problem that has followed tree biology from the beginning. But, as already stated, it was difficult, to almost impossible, to cut many mature trees for study, and especially to cut them in a longitudinal section as well as a cross section. Trees and tree processes do develop in a longitudinal way as well as in a radial way. Wood forms and ages in an axial way as well as in a radial way. Heartwood, discolored wood, decayed wood, wetwood, and so on, have been studied primarily in the radial path from cross sections. Heartwood and discolored wood do form in both directions. If this simple point can be accepted, then a great step forward will be made in understanding both processes.

Trees age and die and decompose no matter how big and strong they are. The important difference among species is that the decomposing processes develop at different rates. We know only one time clock: our own. And, we want to use our time clock for everything. It won't work for trees. Yes, aging is the process of going from a highly ordered state to a lower ordered state over time. But, the marking or measurement of the events that take place from the highly ordered to the lower ordered state will differ for different organisms. Aging is not a simple subject. In humans, aging can be measured as a ratio of cell breakdown—autolysis—to restoration. If you live to be 70 years old, the autolysis—restoration processes, will go on 270 billion times in your body! Trees can not do it one time, because trees can not restore parts or processes. So human aging is a time ratio of autolysis to restoration. So long as restoration is equal to autolysis, aging will go slowly. As restoration begins to lag behind autolysis over time, aging goes faster.

Trees have another type of aging ratio. In trees the ratio of aging is based on volume of wood that can store energy—dynamic mass—to volume of wood that can no longer store energy. The tree must "protect its dynamic mass," and its mechanical support system. A constant danger a tree has is that it can grow itself to death because it is a generating system. As the dynamic mass of the organism increases, so does the amount of energy needed to run the system. If dynamic mass begins to increase faster than energy can be stored, the tree is in trouble because its growth activities are all on a time commitment base. When spring comes, the buds must come out, or else. And, the energy system is based on space to store it. You can not separate these 2 factors: energy reserves, and space to store energy—dynamic mass. The tree sheds parts to keep dynamic mass and energy in balance. Yes, if more wood develops in the trunk, the wood can store more energy. But, it is not that simple. There is no direct, or linear relationship between dynamic mass and energy needs. As dynamic mass doubles, the amount of energy needed to maintain the mass may more than double. Remember, the wood that stores the energy must also get some of the energy to live.

The next point that must be understood is the opening. Trees have natural openings—dying branches and roots, twigs, lenticels, etc.—and traumatic openings—wounds by a great variety of agents. The natural openings have some "built-in" boundary to resist infection. But, every natural boundary is not perfect all the time. Plus, the systems are "designed" to resist pathogens, not gases (oxygen, etc.) and moisture.

The final point that must be mentioned in this heartwood-discolored wood subject is that there are many variations on the theme of making wood resistant to breakdown by pathogens. The trees use them all! And we often get too close to a variation and miss the theme, or worse yet, try to make the variation into a theme. That is one of the major reasons for the confusion and controversy in this subject. There are many ways that wood can be altered to resist breakdown. I say this with care, because the real problem is breakdown. Mechanical disruption can kill a tree. Of course, starvation can lead to death also, but starvation still gives a tree a chance. It gives the tree a chance to generate more tissues faster and to get back on a healthy course. Mechanical disruption gives no chance for the tree. A broken trunk *is* the end. Mechanical support is the tree's unique characteristic, and the tree "gives" this feature top priority for protection. The protection may take the form of denser wood, cell arrangements, chemicals within cell contents and cell walls to resist pathogens—extractives, antimicrobial substances—alteration of micro environment—extremes in oxygen, moisture, pH, elements, electrical state—and another "last ditch" method that is seldom considered: "invite" some mild pathogen in that does not break down wood but will keep out others that rapidly break down wood—wetwood.

The historic problem with the heartwood subject is that it was taken out of the natural system and studied as a single subject. This is impossible. If this method is continued, confusion will continue. We must start looking at the entire system, not one of its parts. But, once we focus on the part—heartwood—within the system, then some clarification will come. I will try this approach here. I hope it works!

Figure 17-1

Figure 17-2

All black walnut trees, *Juglans nigra*, have a dark central core (Figs. 1 and 2). Trunks of trees over 40 years old usually have 10 to 14 growth increments of light-colored sapwood. Young trees, 10 to 14 years old will also have a central core of dark wood. In young trees the light-colored sapwood growth increments may number 5 to 8. The tops of mature trees will have sapwood-heartwood patterns similar to trunks of young trees. The trunks of mature trees stay at 10 to 14 growth increments. The point here is that the young trees and the young tops of old trees do have similar sapwood-heartwood patterns, and these patterns differ from trunks of mature trees. Heartwood formation is a way of maintaining the energy-dynamic mass ratio in trees. Trees must regulate total mass to resist mechanical disruption, and they must regulate dynamic mass to resist starvation. There is no perfect way to do this against the forces of the environment and other organisms. But there are ways to do this for periods of time. Heartwood forma-

tion is one way that serves both the protection of the total mass against mechanical disruption and the protection of the dynamic mass against starvation. The other way trees die is by dysfunction. This is primarily a genetic problem. Trees that do not have the genetic amplitude to adapt or to resist moderate and common stresses die early. The death of a weak individual is a survival factor for the group of trees.

Figure 1 shows the common view—cross section—of sapwood and heartwood. Figure 2 shows a longitudinal view. Some other points of interest are shown on figure 2. The small black arrows show the boundary that formed after the branch died. The large arrows show pockets of decayed sapwood. The color looks the same as heartwood. The chemistry of the discolored wood is different from the heartwood. The open arrows show the core of heartwood in the branch. When decay starts in branches that have heartwood, it is the sapwood that usually decays first.

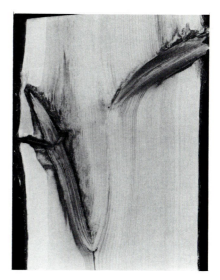

Figure 17-3

Figure 17-4

What name should we use for the darker wood within the margins of the small arrows in this *Pinus rigida*, pitch pine (Fig. 3)? The electrical resistance measurements of the light-colored wood was much lower than the colored wood. The colored wood was directly associated with the old dead branches. The large arrows show the end of one branch. The column of colored wood associated with similar branches gave the pointed pattern to the colored wood as viewed in this cross section. Pathogens were not associated with the colored wood. The colored wood had much less moisture, hence the high electrical resistance, than the clear wood. The columns of branch-associated colored wood were developing in an axial direction as well as in a radial direction.

What name or names should we use for the many types of altered and colored wood in this *Pinus strobus*, white pine (Fig. 4)? The outer growth increments can be called sapwood. The wood inward from the sapwood has many bands of color. Resin has impregnated some of the wood. The real problem is that too many names have been given to wood on the basis of color. The names imply understanding. The names are another reason for the heartwood-discolored wood confusion.

Please keep in mind some basic facts. All wood cells start out alive. All wood cells differentiate, age, and eventually die. All living cells require energy. Trees must maintain mechanical support or they die. Trees must maintain energy levels to support life processes and defense. The many natural and traumatic openings in trees give the ever present pathogens continuous opportunities to digest the tree: break it down. Time is the key. How long can the tree avoid running out of energy or breaking down!

Heartwood and Discolored Wood and the System

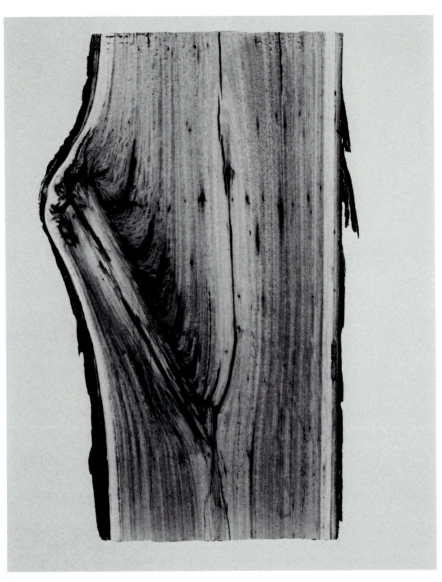

Figure 17-5

The subjects discussed so far are not unique to conifers and hardwood in the northern hemisphere. Trees such as the eucalypt shown here (Fig. 5) from Australia have all the same problems. Insects are in the wood and bark, the branch was infected, there are bands of colored wood within the central core, veins of kino spread upward from the branch corewood, and the very center of the tree has a light-colored zone. The easy way out of this one is to say it has an outer layer of clear sapwood and that everything to the inner side of the sapwood is heartwood. But why the bands or light streaks in the heartwood? Why the dark streaks associated with the insect holes? If heartwood is dead and nonreactive, as the textbooks say, why the discolored streaks? The light-colored center is called brittleheart—another name. What *is* brittleheart? I hope you are starting to feel as disgusted about all of this as I have been for a long time. Let us go back and reexamine how wood is altered and try to make some order out of chaos.

The 2 sugar maples, 100S and 97S, in figure 6 are about the same age. They both were wounded at their base (double arrows) 8 years before they were dissected. Tree 97S had only a slight color change in the center of the trunk. Tree 100S had a column of dark wood in the center of the trunk before it was wounded at the base. Only a dark line at the barrier zone formed after 97S was wounded. A large column of discolored and decayed wood developed after 100S was wounded. These trees show some important points. Sugar maple, *Acer saccharum*, may have clear wood with living cells for many years. Yet, some trees have central columns of sound colored wood. The columns of discolored wood are associated with dead branches and wounds. But, not all dead branches and wounds lead to discolored wood. That is the rub. The system can go both ways. The decayed wood at the double arrow points in 100S was spreading through discolored wood. Yet, the discolored wood was formed as a result of the tree defense system. But, there was a wound, and some organisms had an opportunity to grow into the tree, and they did. The same type of wound was on 97S, but the pathogens did not grow into the tree. The point here is that sometimes the tree defense system (97S) functions very effectively, while other times (100S) they do not. However, even when they do not, the pathogens are still faced with other obstacles.   *Figure 17-6*

In this sugar maple (Fig. 7), some parts of the trunk, the base section at left, had no discolored wood while other parts had small and large columns of discolored wood. Does this tree have heartwood or not? When we review the 3 sugar maples in figure 6 and 7 we see that according to the old school of heartwood, tree 100S had heartwood, tree 97S did not have heartwood, and the tree in figure 7 had heartwood here and there in the trunk. Of course, the answer is that what had been called heartwood in maple (and beech, birch, aspen, ash and many other species) is really not an obligatory type of altered wood. It may be there, but it may not be there. Wounds and dead branches may start the process, but, then again they may not. And, to add more fuel to this discussion; the discolored wood that forms is first protective, but the pathogens when they do spread into the tree, spread through the protective discolored wood. The pathogens either have great difficulty doing this and it takes a great amount of time to spread, or the pathogens spread quickly because they have the enzymes to break down the protective chemicals. The tree still has a chance because, if the pathogen spreads, even in the protective wood, they are still within compartments. *Figure 17-7*

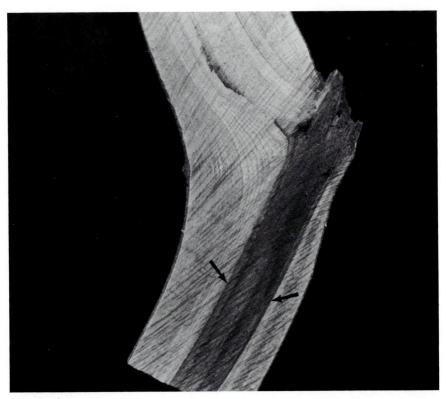

Figure 17-8

The American beech in figure 8 had its trunk broken when it was the diameter between the arrows. Only the trunk wood present at the time of the breakage has discolored and decayed over a 25 year period. This sample is similar to figure 7 in that one part of the sample has heartwood and one part of the sample above the old trunk wound does not have heartwood. Heartwood is used here in the sense of the old school. Heartrot was defined as the rot of the heartwood. Therefore the sample has rot below the old leader stub because the heartwood was only below the broken leader. Once the old concepts of heartwood and heartrot are examined they become silly. The discolored and decayed wood developed in the wood exposed by the traumatic opening. It is that simple. If that wood had not discolored first, the decay would have spread rapidly downward. So discolored wood is a type of protection wood, but protection is not an absolute feature. The all important difference between discolored wood and heartwood is beginning to emerge. *Both are types of protection wood*, but discolored wood is formed within the compartments associated with a natural or traumatic opening. Heartwood forms within the normal compartments of the tree. More details will follow as we examine some other samples.

A New Tree Biology

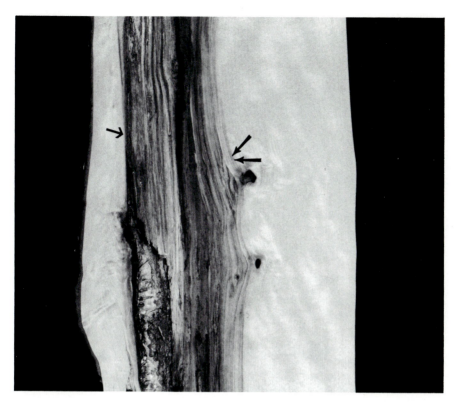

Figure 17-9

The yellow birch in figure 9 has a hollow on the left side of the trunk. The single arrow shows the barrier zone that formed after wounding. The double arrows show the middle of the tree. Again, and not to push this point too far, the old concept would have heartwood and heartrot on the left side of the trunk but not on the right side.

The natural and traumatic openings in wood determine the potential configuration of the infected wood. As seen in the sample (Fig. 6, tree 97S) the defense system may be so effective that little discolored wood or infection takes place. In other samples a gradation of changes took place until figure 9 shows the complete digestion of the wood compartment opened by the wound.

Discolored wood is not "bad" because it invites decay. Discolored wood is "good" because it is the tree's response to an opening that allows pathogens to enter the tree. If discolored wood did not form, the pathogens would rapidly spread through the tree and the smallest wounds would spell instant death. But, we can not take discolored wood too far away from compartmentalization. The discolored wood does form, after an opening, in compartments. The other side of the story is the pathogen. Some pathogens have developed ways to breakdown the defense products. My point over and over again is that the systems are vibrating, they are zigging and zigging, or zagging and zagging, and all of this takes time.

Heartwood and Discolored Wood and the System   293

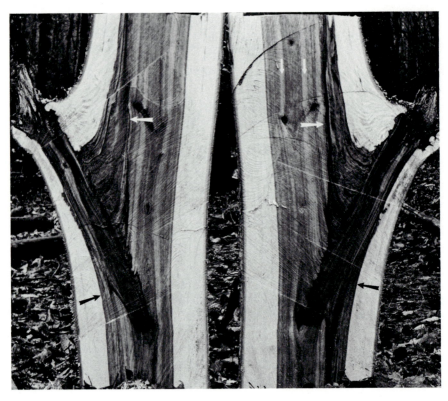

Figure 17-10

All trees have branches (not palms), and all trees have some branches die. The tree forms a protection zone at the base of dying branches, or after a branch is cut properly. But, things do go wrong, and some pathogens are very aggressive, and they grow through the protection zones. When the branch protection zones are breached, compartmentalization still limits the pathogens to the wood present when the branch died as shown by the black arrows (Fig. 10). When the pathogens spread to the trunk below the branch, they then have access to the trunk collar that connects the trunk tissues above the branch (see the pull apart diagram of a branch in the chapter on the branch). When this happens, the new branch associated column of discolored wood (or later decayed wood) does not spread into the older, already established columns (large white arrows). Each major column of discolored or decayed wood is limited to the compartments that were exposed by some opening (some exceptions will be discussed later when we examine perennial cankers, root rots, and canker rots). The 2 small white arrows show columns that were formed early in the life of the tree. The major point here is that the compartment is the last resort to survival. The protection wood, discolored wood, stalls the breakdown of the wood in the compartments.

A New Tree Biology

Figure 17-11

Black walnut does have a central core of colored heartwood (Fig. 11). Heartwood is a wood that no longer is active in transport or storage of energy for use by the tree. (I say it that way because residual starch, or other energy releasing compounds may be found in heartwood. They are not available to the tree.) The sapwood has the power of life as its main defense. When sapwood is wounded it responds in a chemical way to form antimicrobial substances. How rapidly the response occurs is an important part of effectiveness of the response. The response does result in discolored wood. When heartwood is wounded it does not respond in a living sense, but it does react in a chemical sense. Heartwood in living trees does discolor.

The 2 branches shown by the fingers in figure 11 were pruned on this black walnut 25 years before the tree was cut and dissected. The cuts were proper and the branch protection zone effectively resisted spread of pathogens that would have digested the wood. However, the arrows (1) show streaks of discolored heartwood below the branches. The wood below the branches was sapwood at the time of pruning. The central arrows (2) show another dark column. The point here is that the altered wood formed when it was sapwood and not yet heartwood. Once altered, it could not be altered further to heartwood. The banding patterns shown here are common in heartwood-forming trees. It is impossible to say that only one thing happened to the wood. It is not an easy story to understand.

Figure 17-12

The osage orange, *Maclura pomifera*, has one of the thinnest bands of sapwood. Trees may have only 1 or 2 sapwood increments. Another tree that comes close to osage orange is black locust, *Robinia pseudoacacia*, shown here (Fig. 12). It has 3 or 4 growth increments of sapwood. Once cut and used for poles in the soil, it will last for years. So it must be very resistant. Maybe that is so after it is cut, but some pathogens rapidly invade the wood in the living tree. One such pathogen is *Fomes rimosus*. No matter how tough nature gets on one side, there seems to be another side to the story. There are some long-lived exceptions like the coastal redwood, *Sequoia sempirvirens*, and swamp ash, *Eucalyptus regnans* in Australia. However, they too have their problems, man being the main one.

A New Tree Biology

The locust shown here was wounded when it was the size of the hollow. The white arrows show internal cracks that could break out. The point of this sample is that the pathogens have had over 30 years to digest the heartwood beyond the hollow. They have not done it! The heartrot concept often indicates that the decay of heartwood is done by heartwood-rotting fungi. If they are heartwood-rotting fungi why don't they rot the heartwood beyond the hollow? The old barrier zone is still effective. It is hard to believe, but the pathogens have no access to the heartwood. The heartwood is outside the compartment. There is much more to the story.

Heartwood is the result of an aging process. The aging sapwood that no longer transports material or stores energy reserves, and therefore has no living cells, is altered to maintain a protective state. The altered wood maintains mechanical support but no longer makes demands on the energy reserves. A new division of labor begins. At the same time, the ratio of total mass to dynamic mass is regulated. However, there is an initial cost for this altered wood. Materials are converted to chemicals that preserve the aged wood. The natural chemical preservatives can be extracted from the wood and hence the term extractives for the chemicals. In hardwoods they (again) have a phenol base in many cases, and in conifers they have a terpene or resin base. The system must have survival value because the longest-lived trees have heartwood with high amounts of extractives.

Why have compartmentalization when the extractives, and especially extractive plus highly dense wood, will surely prevent pathogens from digesting the wood? Not so. The extractives and dense wood do slow down most pathogens, but the pathogens are not stopped. In the end it is still the combination of extractives, wood density, and compartmentalization that give some trees unique abilities to live for long periods.

There is still much more to the story. When heartwood is wounded it reacts to set boundaries. How can a "dead" tissue do this? It may be a dead tissue according to animal standards, but it still compartmentalizes pathogens.

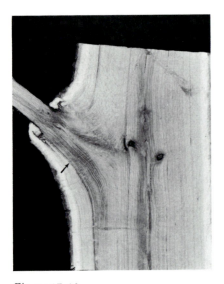

Figure 17-13

Figure 17-14

Discolored heartwood is common in trees. If the background heartwood were removed, you would see the same patterns of discolored wood in maples and oaks (Figs. 13 and 14). Yes, heartwood with its extractives is protective, but not that protective. Protection is a static feature. It stands still. Anything that stands still in nature is an easy target. Many pathogens have developed ways—enzymes—that digest extractives. Defense is dynamic. Compartmentalization is a dynamic process. It is more difficult to destroy something that is on the move, or even more difficult to destroy something that is not there until *after* you get there. A tree is wounded and the competition for colonization goes on on the wound surface. The pathogen that wins the battle on the wound may not be the one best suited for the internal battle. My point is that the surface battle must come first so the "winner does not know" what the internal problems will be. This gives the first advantage to the tree.

The arrow in figure 13 shows the size of the tree when the branch died. The discolored column is 13 growth increments; several increments more than the sapwood indicating that the column has developed inward slightly. Figure 14 shows 2 logs, A and D, that have fairly clear heartwood. Logs B and C have large central columns of discolored heartwood (white arrows). A very interesting point is that fungi that grow on discolored sapwood also grow on discolored heartwood. Again, heartwood indeed is a protective wood, but it still can be infected, and when it is, the pathogens are compartmentalized.

A New Tree Biology

Figure 17-15

Let's talk about boundaries again. Discolored wood is a "boundaried" wood (poor term). Heartwood is not a "boundaried" wood. Heartwood is being formed continuously in an axial and radial direction. Heartwood is a preserved wood that resists infection. If boundaries did not form in heartwood the pathogens would rapidly spread radially outward to the cambium. This would not only kill the tree but it would kill the pathogen. Boundaries not only protect the tree but they protect the pathogen.

The oak section in figure 15 shows many boundaries in the heartwood. Each column has its boundary. The exact nature of the openings that started the columns is not known. The columns developed about the central column of discolored wood. The important point here is that each column has its own boundary. How does such a boundary develop in heartwood? We believe that heartwood still maintains some energy. When oxygen combines with some materials in heartwood there is an enzyme-triggered oxidation process, similar to releasing the trigger on a cocked mousetrap. As heartwood is formed, I believe that some compounds are "cocked" in a chemical way. When oxygen or certain enzymes reach the "cocked" compounds, the triggers are released, and the still available energy is used to build boundaries. The pathogens may play a major role in this process. Remember, boundaries are beneficial for the pathogens as well as the tree.

Heartwood and Discolored Wood and the System

Figure 17-16

Figure 17-17

Much has been written about false heartwood in species of beech, *Fagus grandifolia* (Figs. 16 and 17). In figure 16 the discolored central core is sound. A circle or partial "doughnut" of decayed wood was associated with the death of the large branch. The large arrow shows the boundary between the inner column and the decayed wood. The smaller arrow shows the outer boundary of the decayed wood and another column of discolored wood. Species of *Fagus* do not have heartwood that forms continuously as wood tissues age. Species of *Fagus* do have a colored protective wood that forms as branches die. As branches die, the trunk tissues below the branch also die. The discolored wood is not associated with pathogens, but with the rapid aging and death of trunk tissues associated with the branches. The same processes occur with species of *Fraxinus* (ash), and *Betula* (birch).

Figure 17 shows the many compartments associated with wounds and dead branches in this American beech, *F. grandifolia*. The curved arrows show colored bands associated with death of branches. The straight arrows show that the decayed wood associated with the wound did not spread into the discolored wood. Oaks, walnut and other species have a continuing heartwood formation. Beech, ash, and birch have an altered wood associated with branch death.

Wounds on beech, *Fagus*, also start
the processes that result in discolored
wood and possible decay (Fig. 18). But,
the wounds start a different type of discolored wood. The colored or discolored wood or false heartwood in
beech is the result of trunk aging due
to branch death. In one sense, there is
an opening: the branch, but the opening is *not* an opening for pathogens.
The trunk tissues associated with the
dying branch also wane because their
connection to a water, mineral, and
energy source is discontinued as the
branch dies. The trunk tissues age, exhaust their energy reserves, decrease
their moisture content, and discolor.
When a beech tree is wounded as
shown here in figure 18, or when
pathogens break through the protection zone in the branch corewood, then
the same process as described before
starts within tissues that have not aged,
or within tissues that have aged and
begun to change to a light pink or light
orange color. Also, very important to
note that beech wood altered by
wounds or infected branch core wood
truly discolors first and then turns
darker (arrows). Discolor really means
"away from color" or lighter than the
background. Note the bleached wood
above the wound. It is discolored
wood.

Figure 17-18

Compare the red maple in figure 19 with the American beech in figure 18. The outer rims of the wound-induced column in beech was bleached (see arrows, figure 18). The outer rim of the wound-induced column in this (Fig. 18) red maple infected by *Fomes igniarius* and *Phialophora melinii*, and a host of other organisms including bacteria, was dark. The white arrows show the dark edges of the column as they were developing upward. The central column in the red maple was initiated by branch death and the basal wound. Maples can have the same type of false heartwood as beech and ash. The false heartwood is associated with the death of branches where trunk tissues age and discolor, but are not infected. The great difficulty in understanding these various types of altered wood depends on an understanding of many, not one or two features of wood; and an understanding of tree-microorganism interaction processes, and the aging processes, and the energy flow systems, and the differences between protection and defense, and the factors affecting compartmentalization, and the list goes on.

Figure 17-19

A New Tree Biology

Over and over again I am trying to make the point that if pathogens could spread freely in trees it would be worse for the pathogens than the trees. We are all organisms that live with boundaries. If a pathogen grew in a radial or complete circumferential path, the tree would die. The decay-causing pathogens do not come in contact with living or nonaltered (bad word) wood. There is always a boundary. Figure 20 shows (arrows) the boundaries that surround the decayed wood. The same boundaries are shown for figure 21 (large arrows). The open arrow shows the decayed branch corewood. The small arrows show internal cracks.

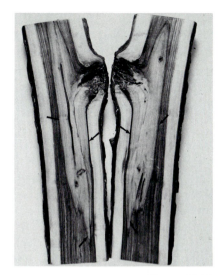

Figure 17-20

Figure 17-21

The all important point, again, is that compartmentalization is superimposed over heartwood and false heartwood. Compartmentalization means boundaries. Boundaries mean the pathogens *and* the tree have *TIME*. The pathogen will have time to get what energy it can and to reproduce. The tree will have time to grow and to support the reproductive bodies of the pathogens. The webwork is the way the system works, not as isolated unit parts. When we treat trees in cities, backyards, orchards, and forests, we must understand the power of the webwork. It will give the tree time and it will buy time for us to enjoy the trees. Time, time, time! Isn't that what it's all about!

A Diversion

The worse possible situation to be in is to be alive but without a defense system. A new human problem is spreading that takes away the defense system. When you are without defense, anybody, or anything, can get you anyway they please. The greatest problem ever faced by mankind centered about such a problem. The worse situation ever faced by humankind was the *fear* of witchcraft, not witchcraft; the *fear* of witchcraft. If you were not a witch, somebody was bewitching you. If you were not bewitched, for sure you were suspect of being a witch. You could not win.

Some examples of being still alive but without a defense system are known for trees. As oaks, especially the red oaks, begin to die from oak wilt, and as American beech begins to die from the beech bark disease, species of *Hypoxylon* spread within days throughout the entire sapwood of the trees. The rate of spread is so fast it is difficult to believe; a matter of days! The sapwood is really not dead, it just does not have enough energy to resist the spread of *Hypoxylon* species. The same story goes for American elms. The trees reach a point where the defense system is gone. The insects breed and so does the fungus as the tree dies. Believe it or not, the fast early death is still the rule in nature. If it were not so we would be up to our eyeballs in turtles, alligators and any number of organisms that reproduce by the millions or even billions. They do serve the purpose of trapping energy for a short time and then passing it on. The same goes for trees. Almost all trees that start life in the forest die at an early age. The fear in the world today is that the trees that have survived the natural stresses are getting "hit" with some "new" problems. Some of this is true. Some is not so true. Trees, as we are seeing, have a complex system of redundancies built in, and they seem to have another new survival "track" every time we turn around. This is great, so long as we do not destroy one important part of this story. Their niche. The niche for trees is special and the niche for tree-inhabiting organisms is special. Trees have evolved to "respect" boundaries. Tree-inhabiting pathogens also "respect" boundaries. Those trees that have weak boundaries do not help the survival of the group of trees, or the pathogens. My major point for this diversion from heartwood for a moment is to say that none of these factors, or systems, or processes are absolute. They all buy time. And, that is what we can do as we work to help trees. Buy time!

Back to heartwood. Heartwood is a wood that buys time for the tree. Heartwood with its array of extractives makes life difficult for the pathogens. Seldom can one pathogen invade alone. Usually many pathogens are associated in a microbial succession. It is really not correct to say they are associated, because pathogens are not altruistic. They do not kill themselves so another pathogen can live. But the protection and defense redundancies get so numerous and complex, that one or two, or even three pathogens can not break down the system.

Figure 22 shows a sporophore of a decay-causing pathogen on black cherry, *Prunus serotina*. The fungus tissues have spread upward into the bark (black arrows). Many sporophores "use" this tactic to "keep the wound" open. Note the growth increments in the sporophore, 5. The white arrows show the boundary between decayed heartwood and sound heartwood. The white lines in the center of the tree are large plates of fungus tissue.

Figure 23 shows a large red oak, *Quercus rubra*, that started life as a 3-stemmed tree (black arrows). The white arrows show the boundaries — chemicals — that separate the decayed heartwood from the sound heartwood. Note that the decayed wood is light colored. The pathogens are breaking down the extractives. The fungi often get help from the bacteria.

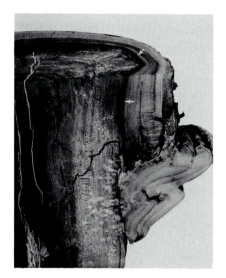

Figure 17-22

Figure 17-23

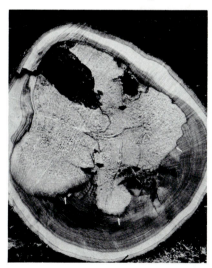

Heartwood-Discolored Wood
Summary — Figure 17-24

Heartwood is age-altered wood. Discolored wood is injury-altered wood. Heartwood forms in an axial and radial direction. Discolored wood forms within the reaction zone and the barrier zone. Heartwood maintains mechanical support and it maintains a high protection and defense system. It forms within the natural boundaries of the noninjured or noninfected wood. As branches die, the trunk tissues associated with the branch also age and die and may be altered to heartwood. I say may here because in some trees this type of heartwood is more common than other trees. This type of heartwood formation has been called false heartwood and it has been studied extensively in beech and ash. Discolored wood is also a protection wood, but it is formed in the direct pathway of pathogens. Discolored wood forms in sapwood and heartwood after injury and infection. Now comes the part that has been difficult to explain. The discolored wood is protective by nature of its chemistry. But some pathogens have developed ways to breakdown the protective chemicals. The battle is still kept within the confines of the reaction zone, which may be moving, and the barrier zone, which does not move, or if it does, that tree part or the entire tree is killed. Also, some of the inhabitants of the wood exposed by natural and traumatic openings serve to keep out others that would spread more rapidly and digest the wood. The bacteria are the major pathogens in this category. They may rapidly infect the wood exposed by dying branches and wounds. They fill the compartments, and many of the bacteria "push" the boundaries of the reaction zone to their end point. Then only the barrier zone confines the pathogens. The part that makes this story difficult to understand is that some of these pathogens alter only very slightly the color of the sapwood or the heartwood. The infected wood is called wetwood when it has a high moisture content most of the time but not all of the time. The pH and available elements are high giving the wood a very low electrical resistance to a pulsed current.

Figure 24 shows 4 columns of discolored and decayed wood in a white oak, *Quercus alba*. The center of the tree was sound. Pathogens do not "rush" to the center of the tree where the wood is weaker. The columns were associated with root and basal trunk injuries. Note the triangular shapes of the columns. Note the boundaries of dark wood about each column. Indeed, heartwood is a protective tissue, but that is not enough. Compartmentalization keeps the pathogens in their places. The arrow shows that heartwood formation is stalled where wounds are severe. The tree "keeps" more wood alive at these points.

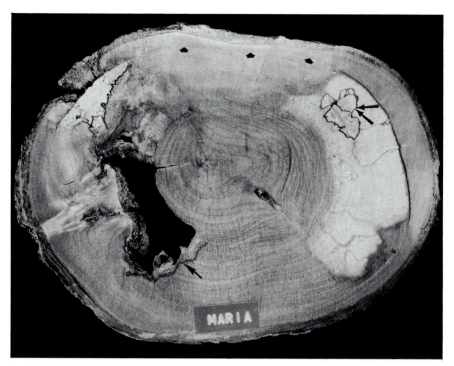

Figure 17-25

Tropical trees like this Maria (Fig. 25) are no different from other trees when it comes to heartwood, discolored wood, wounds, and boundaries. This tree had a thin layer of sapwood and a deep red-brown heartwood. The center of the tree was sound. The center wood was altered as a result of an early wound. Wounds inflicted later were infected, but the infections did not spread inward to the wood that was already altered. If we knew how to regulate this injury-altered state of wood, we could greatly reduce the injuries from accidental wounding. The small arrows show the continuation of the barrier zone. The larger arrow shows the dark boundary that formed in the heartwood. The double arrows show zone lines or boundaries formed by the microorganisms. If you look very closely, you will see that the decayed wood on the inner parts of the boundary is different from the decayed wood on the outside.

One of the many problems in trying to understand how natural systems function is that any one item could be both beneficial or destructive, depending on concentrations. Is water good for you, is salt good for you? Of course they are if they are in the proper concentration. Too much or too little water or salt will kill you! The same game goes for many of the points we are discussing. Is discolored wood "good" or "bad." The answer is yes. At one concentration, altered wood has extraordinary features for long protection or preservation. Yet, when some pathogen "pushes" the concentration one way or another, the wood may go from one extreme state to another. In the end, good or bad, the systems buy time.

Heartwood and Discolored Wood and the System 307

Figure 17-26

Color is the word that has caused the confusion. Any wood alteration that had a color different from sound, healthy sapwood had to be heartwood, or worse yet, a type of heartwood. Color was easy to see, and most of the time the observations were correct until decay was discussed. When discolored wood as we know it now was called heartwood, then indeed, the pathogens digested the "heartwood." In the old forest, most columns of decay were in the center of the tree because most of the columns here started by dead branches. Central rot changed to rot in the heart—*location*—of the tree, to heartrot, which was later changed *to a process* rather than to a *location*. Heartrot was the rot of the heartwood, and chemists in laboratories described accurately all the ways heartrot progressed. Then came more wounds to the outer core as machines went into the forests, then came a closer look at wetwood, and most confusing were the canker rots. Why did the "heartwood" in one pocket rot while the pocket was still surrounded by sound heartwood? Why did some maple trees and birch trees have no heartwood? And if they do not have heartwood how can they have heartrot? If you look even casually at the whole background to this mess you will see that the problem centers about *color*. Then all types of names were given to colored wood: bluebutt (one of my favorites), redheart, pink heart, black butt, mineral stain, green heart. The false impression was that by giving some unknown a name, it suddenly becomes understood. It does not work that way.

Spruce is a tree in point (fig. 26). It has age-altered wood but the aged wood is not a dark color. After wounding the wood discolors. The arrows show the barrier zone.

You can not use color in nature as the basis for a process!

A hole was drilled in this hybrid poplar (fig. 27) 1 year before the tree was examined and photographed. Should we assign different names to the different colored woods at positions A, B, C, and D? Study the figure very carefully because it shows many important points about wounding and boundaries. The wood in position A directly above and below the wound

Figure 17-27

was killed by the wound. The wood was dry and hard. The tree responded to the wound by forming antimicrobial substances in position B. The living cells in the wood at position B discolored and died. This is a hypersensitive reaction. It is different from wood that ages, starves, dies, and discolors. This second type of discolored wood, or better, altered colored wood, is the type that forms in trunks as branches die (false heartwood). Note that the B wood continues about the hole, and that no dead wood is at the sides of the hole. The arrows at the sides of the hole represent walls 3 of CODIT, and the vertical arrows represent walls 1. As pathogens spread, the antimicrobial wood now at B will fall back to C, and then to D, but the boundaries at the sides set by antimicrobial wood will usually hold. How does all of this fit with the heartwood subject? Heartwood is not a wood in gradations. Once formed, heartwood remains in that state until it is injured or infected. Discolored wood is on the move as changes over time are considered. Discolored wood means 2 forces are interacting — tree built up, tree against break down, pathogens. Heartwood is not reacting to another force until it is injured and infected, then the process of discolored wood starts within the heartwood. Heartwood is a static state. Discolored wood is a dynamic state.

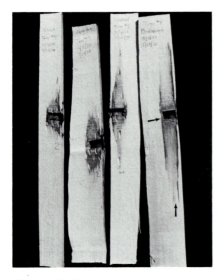

Figure 17-28

Here is an inside longitudinal view of a red maple that received 4 drill wounds in March and was dissected in July of the same year (Fig. 28). The arrow opposite the wound represents wall 2 of Codit and the vertical arrow represents wall 1. The wound in the sample at right with the arrows was inoculated with *Phialophora melinii.* This fungus does not digest cellulose but it can live in the wood that contains phenol-based antimicrobial materials. Back to heartwood for another major point. Heartwood is initiated by aging processes, and microorganisms are not involved in the wood alteration process. Discolored wood is an injury initiated process and microorganisms are involved in the process. Some traumatic opening is the initiator of discolored wood. No traumatic opening is needed for wood to age, starve, die, and change color. The color of heartwood is formed by the protective chemicals called extractives. The color of discolored wood is formed as the result of a dynamic-injury-infection-initiated defense process. The extractives in heartwood "stand still." The antimicrobial materials in discolored wood are under attack and are changing. When discolored wood starts in heartwood, the extractives, and possibly other energy-releasing compounds, are used to block or stall the pathogens. When this happens, the natural boundaries in the heartwood are strengthened even more. I have seen the more resistant species of Eucalyptus with rot holes in them. Resistance is a relative feature that buys time for the tree.

Thousands of trees were wounded, dissected, and studied over a 26-year period. The wound in figure 29 was made by a drill bit and then by a chainsaw in a sugar maple. The limits of the discolored wood were set by the wound. The decayed wood developed within the discolored wood. The cracks developed within the discolored wood.

Figure 30 shows more drill wounds in a sugar maple. The tip of the drill bit in wound A "trapped" the wood between the tip and the older internal column. The wood aged, starved, died, and changed color. Call it by any name you please, but please know the process before you use the name. Names or terms are only as good as the understanding behind them.

Wound B was well compartmentalized. The wood on the inner side of the wound was still able to connect to the transport system for water, elements, and food. The 4 drill holes in this tree initiated a barrier zone completely around the tree (curved arrows).

What happens to the wood within the boundaries will be determined by many factors. Trying to assign one term or name for the process is like trying to give one color for the rainbow. We need terms like rainbow or terms that will imply changes over time. Living systems do not stand still. Heartwood is a feature that "tries" to hold the clock in favor of the tree. Discolored wood is a feature that is thrust into the arena with a pathogen. And there are no intermissions in the game.

Figure 17-29

Figure 17-30

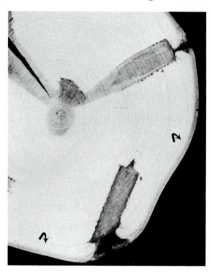

Figure 17-31

Oaks, *Quercus* species, such as this *Q. rubra*, have a colored heartwood (pointers, Fig. 31). When drill bit wounds were inflicted in oak trees, the same patterns of discolored wood formed on the cross sections as did on maples. When the oak trees were killed by removing the bark at the base, and then drilling the holes higher in the trunk through intact bark, the darkly stained drill patterns were not as clear as those in the still living trees. Heartwood is still a part of a living tree. To say the heartwood is dead and nonreactive, and to take the dead nonreactive wood into

A New Tree Biology

the laboratory for studies, and to try to use the answers from such studies to answer the questions in living trees is foolishness. Yet, this is what was done. Yes, in the *final* stages of wood breakdown, there are little chemical differences between the block of dead wood in the laboratory and an equal "block" of old dead wood in a tree. However, how the "block" of dead wood in the tree gets to that state is the part that separates laboratory studies of dead blocks of wood from wood under attack in a living tree. In the laboratory, one fungus under optimum condition may be placed on a block of sound, stabilized wood, and the wood could be almost completely decomposed in a matter of a few weeks (depending on the wood and the fungus, of course). Such a comparable process would be impossible in nature. We need laboratory work, but we must be careful how the results are used in a natural system. Heartwood in a tree and heartwood in a laboratory flask are 2 different things. They should not be confused.

Beech, *Fagus*, and Ash, *Fraxinus*, are trees that form false heartwood. (The term is a poor one, but I use it here because most people will know what I am referring to.) The colored false heartwood is triggered by the death of branches. The trunk wood connected to the dying branch ages, starves, dies, and changes color. The protective features of the wood are not so much because of chemicals that are impregnated in the cell walls, like extractive, but because the wood has a very low moisture content. You can burn such wood easily immediately after it is cut from ash trees. The confusion comes to this story when some of the dead branches are infected, and now a column of discolored wood begins to superimpose, or develop within the "false heartwood." Investigators studying this wood in beech got very confused when this happened. They started giving the same subdivisions and variations to false heartwood that were given to heartwood. Some false heartwood had no organisms while other wood did. Some false heartwood had one set of characteristics while other false heartwood had another set. Just as some heartwood was called light heartwood and dark heartwood, all in the same tree. The processes are really very simple if they are considered from the view of aging, wounding, and compartmentalization (maybe *now* they are simple, but it is unfair to say they were simple several decades ago). (I do hope you are still with me. You must understand, please, that for over a century there has been a great amount of confusion on this subject. It will take a great deal of discussion to clarify the many parts of this story.)

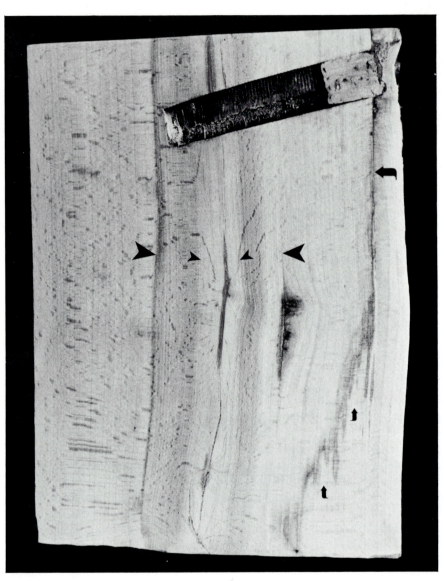

Figure 17-32

Now it is time to add a few more ingredients. In several previous figures (Figs. 27, 28, 29, 30, 31) I showed that wounds in maple that has no colored heartwood and in red oak that does, the same dark patterns formed on the cross section face of samples. When wounds such as the drill hole shown here in an American beech (Fig. 32) penetrate sound sapwood *and* false heartwood, we now have another ingredient for the story. The hole penetrated the central column of light-colored false heartwood (small pointers) and a larger, slightly darker column (larger pointers). The large arrow with the curved back shows the barrier zone and the size of the tree when wounded. The smaller vertical arrows show the advancing margin of the column of discolored wood that formed in the clear, noncolored wood. A new column of discolored wood did not form within the column of false heartwood. This indicates that false heartwood, unlike the heartwood in the red oak, has already responded, and can not respond further. (Reexamine figures 16, 17, and 25.) The starved wood in false heartwood apparently has no energy reserves left to even be oxidized as in red oak heartwood. The other possibility is that the ultra dry wood does not act as a substrate for oxidative reactions or for infection by pathogens that could interact with the wood and cause a change in color. The specific reasons for no added discoloration after the wounding of false heartwood are not known. It is of interest to note that columns of discolored wood associated with wounds, do not discolor further when they are rewounded. Again, the energy levels for a further response may be exhausted. The major point here is that false heartwood or wood altered by aging and starvation that is also very dry does have some very long-lasting protection features. If some pathogen could bring about the rewetting of the wood, then further alteration or even breakdown could start. We are back to concentrations again: too dry or too wet will stall the processes of breakdown. Later when we discuss wetwood, the opposite condition of too wet will be discussed.

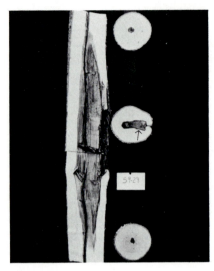

Figure 17-33

Figure 17-34

When a drill bit wound is inflicted deep into a sugar maple (Fig. 33), the discolored and decayed wood spread above and below the wound as shown here. The wound was much more than the drill wound. Note the great amount of dieback above and below the wound. Decay (arrow) did not start deep in the tree, but within the outer portion of the wound. The decayed wood was surrounded by a boundary of discolored wood. The wound was 8-years old.

In figure 34 a drill wound penetrated the sapwood, sound heartwood, and the discolored central heartwood of a chestnut oak. The tree was cut and dissected after 6 years. The arrow shows the barrier zone that formed after wounding. The disc shown at right was cut below the wound. The pointer on the disc shows that the decay did not spread into the central column of discolored heartwood. The decay did spread in the wounded sapwood and sound heartwood. The wound did penetrate to the center of the tree. When wounds penetrate into sound wood in a maple, the columns of defect enlarge as the center of the tree is approached (Fig. 33). When wounds penetrate sapwood and sound heartwood of oaks, the pathogens spread farthest along the sapwood-heartwood boundary present at the time of wounding.

A New Tree Biology

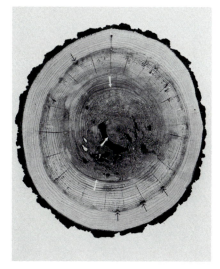

Mature eastern white pine, *Pinus strobus*, has 16 to 22 growth increments of sapwood in the trunk. Young white pine, and the tops of old white pine will have 4 to 8 growth increments of sapwood. The pine shown here (Fig. 35) was wounded 3 different times when it was young (white arrows) and later it was wounded in experiments that used shallow injection-type

Figure 17-35

wounds (black arrows). The tree has 12 sapwood growth increments, and what appears to be heartwood on the inner side of the dark arrows is really wound-altered wood, not heartwood. When sapwood is wounded and it responds to form discolored wood, that discolored wood is dead and it will not age farther to form heartwood. This process is common in many trees. The central columns of young trees may be altered as branches die, as the trunk is wounded, or as the top is killed. Once the central column of wood is altered, it can not age further to form heartwood. The wood in the center may be the same color as heartwood in that tree, or it may be a different color—lighter or darker. In forests where tops of young trees are killed by fire, as in Australia, the central columns are changed as a result of the top killing. Much of the brittleheart in the trees is wood altered as a result of injury. All trees start life as sapwood-only trees. When any type of disruption occurs to the early sapwood, normal heartwood does not form. This is one of the reasons why centers of trees may be very resistant to breakdown or why the center may be rapidly broken down.

Figure 17-36

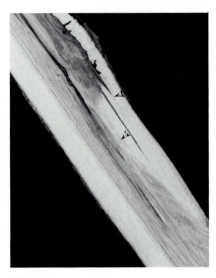

Figure 17-37

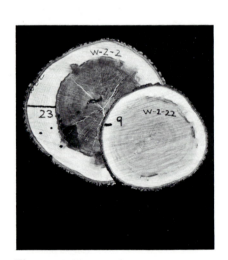

Figure 17-38

Figure 17-39

When a tree that normally forms heartwood is wounded severely, heartwood formation is stalled for years. The post oak, *Quercus stellata*, was wounded severely 21 years before it was cut and dissected (Fig. 36). The small black arrows show the strong barrier zone. The pointer shows the heartwood forming downward into the clear sapwood. The large black arrow points to one of the heartwood dark lines that formed every year. This tree had 10 growth increments of sapwood. The dark heartwood lines number 10 or 11, indicating that the heartwood has been forming downward in an axial way for at least the last 10 years. The dark heartwood lines are common on the cross-section face of logs (see figure 1), but they often blend in with the thick, darkly colored latewood. The dark heartwood lines forming in an axial direction show that they are directly associated with heartwood formation, and that aging can indeed proceed in an axial direction.

In figure 37, the pointer at A shows the barrier zone beyond the wound in this red oak. Pointer B shows the stalled heartwood.

Figure 38 shows the base of a white oak, *Quercus alba*, that had received severe axe wounds 23 years before the tree was cut, in experiments on ways to kill unwanted trees. The advanced decay was confined to the wood present at the time of wounding. There were 23 growth increments of sapwood. A section 22 feet above ground showed that the tree has 9 growth increments of sapwood.

Figure 39 shows a white oak that received severe fire wounds 30 years before the tree was cut. Heartwood was stalled and beginning to reappear in some portions of the trunk. The decayed wood was confined to the diameter of the tree at the time of the fire wounds.

These samples show that wounds stall heartwood formation in oaks. Yet, one of the old terms for colored wood in oaks was wound heartwood. What was called wound heartwood was indeed discolored wood. Wounding, when severe, stalls heartwood formation, not initiates it. Another confused part of this is that the wound that started the so-called heartwood really started the processes that lead to decay. The decay was completely within the boundaries of the so-called wound heartwood. This helped to confirm that heartrot is indeed the digestion of the heartwood. It was not heartwood, but discolored wood.

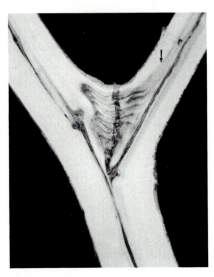

Figure 17-40

The heartwood subject touches many other subjects in trees as we have seen. The major problems still center about color, examination of cross-sections mostly, and the extrapolation of laboratory results to the living tree. The confusion probably reaches its zenith in aspen, mainly because so many studies have been done on aspen, *Populus tremuloides*. (A tree that is more confusing than aspen is southern beech, *Nothofagus* species.) Aspen wood is extremely difficult to understand for many reasons: the wood responds rapidly in a color way to even the slightest injury, the branches have weak or absent branch protection zones that "allow" everything from the branch to spread into the trunk, the bacteria are common in the wood, some of the branch infecting fungi cause canker rots, cankers abound, and that's a lot!

Figure 40 shows the infection from the branch (arrow) spreading rapidly into the trunk. As the trunk "fills" with dead spots, the tree is slowly starved.

Figure 41 shows a dead branch and the continuation of the discolored wood in the trunk. Aspen does not have time to have heartwood in most trees. Before tissues can age and be altered, the wood is altered because of dead twigs and branches mostly. Each column from each branch spreads into the trunk. Some columns have fungi, some have bacteria, some have both. Later we will discuss some genotypes of hybrid poplar that are tough and can resist many of these problems.

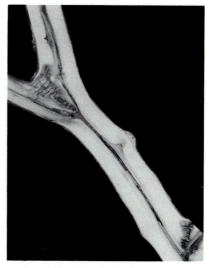

Figure 17-41

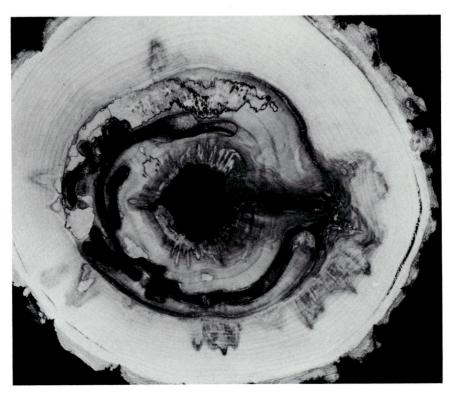

Figure 17-42

A New Tree Biology

If I had to name one, and only one factor, that has caused more confusion throughout the research history of trees than any other factor, I should name the *study of the cross section alone*. Color is a close second. It would rank at the top of the list for heartwood, but for the entire field of tree biology, I still feel that the cross-section alone has been the real problem. The cross-section is really important when it is combined with longitudinal sections. As I have repeated so many times, you will always (one of the few times you can safely use that word) get into trouble when you study only one part of a multipart system. The cross-section of the aspen in figure 42 is a good case in point. To "read" that sample from the cross section shown would imply that the discolored wood is spreading outward, that the crack from frost spread inward and caused the central hollow, that the heartwood was being selectively decayed, and that the insects were boring at random in the tree. All points just made are not correct. All points that I have stated have been repeated many times, and are still believed by most people. We still have a lot of problems.

For the record, here are some comments on those just made.

Starting with the central hollow, if you look carefully you will see the curve of the growth rings indicating a wound when the tree was that size. A crack developed where the callus ribs met. The crack is lined with bark indicating the inroll after the wound. The tree was wounded later and the barrier zone separated several places. A new radial crack formed, and it was surrounded by discolored wood. Other radial cracks developing outward at different positions caused the column of discolored wood beyond the barrier zone. The boring insects may have been the second wounding agent. Note where they entered near the barrier zone. The insects stayed within the second "doughnut" of discolored wood because that is all the wood that was there at the time they infested the tree.

Heartwood, discolored wood, and the natural system must all be tied together. Heartwood is age-altered wood. Discolored wood is injury-altered wood. These are the themes. The variations on false heartwood, hypersensitive reactions, starving wood, and wetwood all center about ways to survive for as long as possible; survival for trees and organisms that live in, on, and about trees.

CHAPTER 18

Wetwood

Fox in the chicken coop is the way I see wetwood. It is better to have one fox that eats one chicken a day and protects all the chickens, than having no fox in the chicken coop, and having the risk of all the chickens being taken by a group of foxes at any time. Protection is a costly feature. Protection in trees either costs a great deal of energy, or the tree must "pay" in some other way. The top priority of the tree is still to maintain mechanical support for as long a time as possible. Wetwood is like salt and water. It is not all good, or all bad. Concentration is important.

Wetwood is a disease of wood: sapwood, heartwood, false heartwood. Bacteria are the primary agents, but fungi and yeasts (which are fungi) may also be involved. The wetwood pathogens get their energy from cell contents. The pathogens are "masters" of recycling essential materials. As a result of their actions, the membranes or walls of the cells become "leaky." Elements accumulate in the infected wood, and along with the concentration of elements, the pH is usually very high, and the resistance to a pulsed electric current is very low. The unique feature of wetwood is its high moisture content. However, there are no absolutes, and in some cases, especially conifers, the moisture content of the wetwood may be no different from the sound, healthy sapwood; but the infected wood just looks more moist. In some species, the infected wood has a "glassy" appearance.

The high pH, elements, and usually water, make for an environment that does not support the growth of the aerobic pathogens — fungi mostly — that breakdown wood. In such an environment, the anaerobic bacteria live. The anaerobes can live in the absence of free oxygen. We must remember, that the anaerobes were probably on earth before the aerobes, because early earth did not have free oxygen. Free oxygen is oxygen not tied to other molecules. Some wetwood bacteria are facultative forms. This means they can exist as aerobes or anaerobes.

Methane, which is an odorless, tasteless, colorless, gas is produced by the anaerobes as a product of their living processes. The methane may build up in a tree and burst outward through weak spots or cracks. It is possible to ignite the methane that comes out of a hole bored into methane-containing wetwood. I have seen a flame several feet long after being ignited.

Wetwood is another confused subject. Many comments made about wetwood are just not correct. Wetwood does not spread outward until it kills the cambium. Wetwood fluids do not kill cambium and enlarge wounds. In a very simple summary way, wetwood infections follow the patterns that form after tree branches and roots die and as trees are wounded. Wetwood will also follow the patterns set up by false heartwood. In some patterns, wetwood is within boundaries formed after wounding—reaction zones, CODIT walls 1, 2, 3, and barrier zones, CODIT wall 4. With the false heartwood-type of patterns, the wetwood may form within the preset patterns of wood anatomy. Here I mean that the trunk tissues that are associated with a dying branch are set aside from other trunk tissues. When the branch dies, usually the trunk tissues that are connected to the branch also die. The patterns of false heartwood are set by wood anatomy, not by wounding. But, if the branch protection zones do not resist the inward spread of wetwood pathogens, the pathogens will spread into the trunk and into the wood that would be called false heartwood. The pattern C type of branch infection would occur. Wetwood would be completely superimposed over false heartwood. But, if this happens, you really never get heartwood or false heartwood because the bacteria are moving as fast as the wood is aging and dying. My point is that the wetwood wood patterns would be the same as those set up by wounds, branches and roots, and by false heartwood. This is an important point, especially with some species of *Populus* and *Ulmus*. The wetwood pathogens move or spread so fast that the normal aging and dying features of the wood are seldom seen. Of course, it does happen in some trees, and when these tissue changes are seen, they just add to the confusion.

The points again: some tree compartments are set up because of normal tree anatomy, some tree compartments are set up because of injury. The normal tree compartments may be altered by aging processes as the case may be for the normal compartments and false heartwood, or by the infection of organisms other than those that cause wetwood. The wetwood pathogens may occupy both compartments or they may not. It is really that simple. However, you must first understand how the tree anatomy, and especially branch-trunk anatomy is set, and how trees respond to injuries and infection. The trunk-branch anatomy was only described for the first time in 1985, and compartmentalization only began to be widely understood and recognized in 1985. So it is understandable why these other problems are still in a state of confusion.

Back to the fox and protection. Wetwood is a disease, but it does stall the breakdown of mechanical support. When wood is too wet or too dry, the wood decay fungi can not grow. The best way to change wetwood into decayed wood is to make the wood drier. The use of drain holes and pipes helps the decay fungi and destroys the tree's protection. Too many times people who work with trees think like people and not like trees. What may be good for us, may not be good for trees. Wetwood is a good case in point.

We must understand that trees have made many "survival deals" over their 200 million year period. Tree 3, the community tree, gets the highest priority in the "deals." However, man wants everything for the individual tree. Knowing how trees and pathogens interact will give us better chances to do the best things for trees.

Figure 18-1

Figure 18-2

Wetwood fluids are external signs of wetwood infection by bacteria. Where does all the liquid come from? Why is the liquid more common at certain times of the year? What do the bacteria live on? These are only a few of the many questions about wetwood. I will try to cover these and many more in this discussion. The black walnut in figure 1 has wetwood fluid flowing from an old branch opening, and the black walnut in figure 2 has fluids flowing from a basal crack (commonly called a frost crack).

All wetwood columns are connected to some opening: branch, root, wound, crack. The opening gives liquids just as easy a chance to flow in as to flow out. The bacteria are not in a rapid state of growth all year. They grow when conditions inside the tree are best for them. They digest the remains of cell contents, and some portions of the cell walls, and the layers between the cells. As new wounds, branches and roots, open to energy sources for them, they spread rapidly within those new compartments. The bacteria recycle many of the essential elements, and some also build up to high amounts, and that is why the pH rises so dramatically.

Consider for a moment a few well known points about wood and water. Wood floats. If logs absorbed water, the old log runs down the rivers would never have happened. The logs stay afloat for long periods because wood is full of air spaces, and just as important is the fact that the wood fibers do not take in high amounts of water. If they did, wood would not float. In the laboratory it is very difficult to rewet sound wood that has been dried. It must be placed under a vacuum to

A New Tree Biology

force the water in. My point in all of this is to make it clear that water does not move about easily in healthy sapwood and heartwood (false heartwood also). So, if a water pocket or column of water in a cavity of an old branch or from a wound is against sound wood, the water will not rush into the sound wood. To make my point even stronger, it is highly unlikely that any cavity or pocket of wetwood or decayed wood will exist without some type of boundary between the cavity and the sound wood. If you drill a hole into sound wood and add water to the hole, the water will move into the vessels, or tracheids, but not into the wood fibers in the walls.

However, when wood-inhabiting pathogens alter the wood fibers, now we have an altogether different story. When the bacteria or fungi alter the fibers, water will move into them. This is the whole "secret" of the so-called dry-rot fungi in wood products. Once the wood fibers are altered, water will move in and be stored. The fungi then grow until they use all the water, but in doing so they have had a new chance to increase the size of their reservoir. I am still talking about a wood product here, but the same process takes place in trees. Once the bacteria and fungi alter the wood fibers, the wood can now hold more water. This is beneficial for the wetwood organisms but not beneficial for the fungi that require some free oxygen. Remember, in nature organisms are not altruistic. The wetwood pathogens can live in such an environment. Back to the fox again. Of course, this is not all good for the tree, but it is still better than having the decay-causing fungi in the tree. The wetwood bacteria do more than just maintain a high moisture condition, they also bring about the high concentration of elements and the concomitant high pH. The decay-causing fungi seldom grow in substrates that have a high pH.

So, what to do if your tree has wetwood? Drain the water? Make it easy for the wood-rotting fungi? The real problem centers about letting the wetwood pathogens start their infections. Improperly pruned branches head the list of prime infection courts. Compacted soil, and soil disruptions prevent the protection zone from forming in the shedding roots, and this gives the bacteria another chance to get in.

Many times we can live with problems, and even pain, when we know what it is, and especially when we know many others also have it; and most important, it may hurt now and then, but it won't kill you. So be it also with wetwood.

Figure 18-3

The arrow in figure 3 shows a central column of wetwood in a recently cut log of an oak. Note the crack to the right of the column. Another internal crack is at the other side of the column, but it hasn't split out to the surface, yet. The middle log has an internal column of decayed wood (arrow), and the third log at right has a central hollow (arrow). Not all columns of wetwood progress to decayed wood and a hollow, but many do. Note that sound heartwood surrounds all the central columns.

You can dry wood that has wetwood. But, when the wood is placed in a moist environment, the wetwood will take up water rapidly and the wood could be easily infected by decay-causing fungi. Wetwood used for products will not hold paint. It is also the first wood that will be attacked by ants and termites that follow the fungi. The point is that the problems of wetwood go far beyond the living tree when wood products are made from the tree.

A New Tree Biology

Wetwood is common in conifers wounded by fire in the Pacific Northwest. The wounds start barrier zones and radial cracks (Fig. 4). The wetwood liquids flow out the cracks. The fire wound may be minor, but the wound opens the way for wetwood and cracks.

The dissected sample from Oregon shows the old central hollow surrounded by advanced decay and many internal radial cracks. Cracks from more recent wounds have split out to the surface (Fig. 5, arrow). Note that the wetwood column surrounds the crack. Other cracks above the wound start star-shaped patterns of wetwood in the log, as viewed from cross-section. The central decay was probably wetwood first before it began to dry. Rot, wetwood, and cracks add up to an impossible condition. Even chips from such a log will cause problems, because the wetwood chips will still take up water after they are made into a product. The paint will peel from such areas also. Defective chips make defective products.

Figure 18-4

Figure 18-5

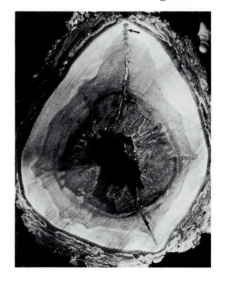

Figure 18-6

The many small dead branches on this western hemlock were the starting points for columns of wetwood (Fig. 6). The arrows (right sample) show the natural anatomical limits or compartment for the wetwood. The altered wood first is bleached, and then it turns darker. The all important point again is that the bacteria infected the trunk through the dying branch, and the bacteria will grow within the natural branch-trunk anatomical compartment. Think how this tree trunk will look after hundreds of columns coalesce!!

The arrows on the left side of the split sample help to make a very important point about wetwood. As stated several times, the major reason for confusion about wetwood is that cross sections are studied. If cross sections are cut from the bottom arrow upward, the dark column of wetwood would appear to be spreading outward. The truth is that the dark wetwood spreads upward or downward within the column provided. Given more time, the now bleached column would be dark. But, at the lower vertical tip of the column you would still see the same pattern as shown here. The reason some columns are seen at the edge of the cambium is because the root or trunk has been wounded at that point, or the root has died and the column is spreading upward within the wood present at the time of root death.

(I have the deep concern in writing this book that I keep talking about problems and confusions that many people are not even aware of, and it might be better to not even mention them. It is a problem, and I may be causing some readers troubles because they may not be able to really believe that some of the problems I discuss could ever be problems. Yet, I do have other readers that I know have written about the problems. The problems are in the literature. Therefore, I feel it is better to discuss them now, rather than have you learn about them later, and then think I was not well informed.)

Figures 7 and 8 show true firs from Oregon with bands of wetwood. Tree 58 in figure 7 has a central ring of wetwood and a larger ring in the younger wood. Such a pattern would make it impossible to saw a board that did not have some wetwood, and a drying problem. The white pointers show the bands of wetwood in figure 8. In both samples, note how sharp the boundaries are between the wetwood and sound wood (arrows).

Electrical resistance is a simple, rapid way for detecting wetwood in standing trees, on the cut ends of recently cut logs, and even on boards cut from logs after being in the yard a month. Feasibility studies showed that electrical resistance methods could be used to sort boards that had a great amount of wetwood from boards that had little or no wetwood.

Figure 18-7

Figure 18-8

Figure 18-9

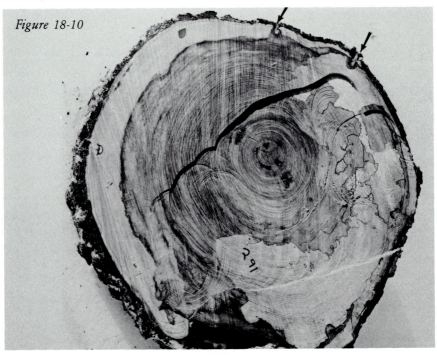

Figure 18-10

A New Tree Biology

American elm, *Ulmus americana*, has a close association with wetwood causing pathogens (Fig. 9). There is hardly an elm, young or old, that does not have some wetwood. Elms grow best in wet, deep, rich soils. Decay is not common in younger trees, but it is common in over mature or old trees over 150 years. When elms are wounded, decay spreads rapidly (Fig. 10). When elms die from Dutch elm disease, again, decay spreads rapidly, and if trees are not cut soon after they die, they decay and fall away in 5 to 10 years. This is a very short time for trees to breakdown after death. (Consider the other extreme, the pines that stand in their dead position for 20 and 30 years, or more.) I believe the large columns of wetwood in elms and cottonwood help maintain mechanical support. When these trees die, and the "fox leaves the chicken coup," the decay-causing fungi rush in rapidly.

The American elm in figure 9 had 18 growth increments of healthy sapwood that stored starch. American elm stores starch all year. The American elm in figure 10 also had 18 growth increments of starch-storing sapwood. The tree received several root and butt wounds 5 years before the tree was cut. Decay spread rapidly within the wetwood.

Note the injection wounds (arrows) with small columns of decayed wood. When injection wounds penetrate, or even come close to wetwood, and the wetwood begins to dry, decay will set in rapidly.

Figure 18-11

A New Tree Biology

Wetwood often spreads upward into the trunk from dying and infected roots. Very important: When a woody root dies, all the tissues in the root and the tissues above the root that connect with the tree can easily be infected with the wetwood-causing bacteria. The new compartment open to the bacteria is the entire root and a cone-shaped column upward into the trunk. Figure 11 shows how columns develop upward from roots. If you saw only the uppermost cross section and the one below it, it would appear that the wetwood is spreading outward and killing the cambium. Yet, when you study the bottom cross section, you will see the decayed wood between the 2 roots. When the bottoms of roots die, the columns spread upward to the trunk tissues between two roots, as shown here. The bottom tissues of roots connect with the trunk tissues between roots. As the column spreads upward, the tree continues to grow new increments of wood. The column stays within trunk tissues that were present at the time the root died (arrows). The root died 8 years before the balsam fir was cut. The wetwood columns could have continued to spread upward within the wood inward of the 8 healthy sapwood increments. Note how the healthy portions of the roots grew faster after the several root infections occurred.

The tree was doing very well what trees do best for survival: generate new tissues and maintain mechanical support. And by doing this, the tree is also increasing storage space for energy reserves. With a system like this, the tree can overcome many problems. But, when the problems come faster than generation increased storage space, and new mechanical support, then the end is near.

We must understand what we can and can not do for trees. We can not restore their infected and decayed parts. We can help them to generate new parts rapidly by proper culture methods. When possible, we must avoid injuries that repeat faster than the tree can respond with new tissues.

Figure 18-12

Drill a hole and drain the wetwood has been an old treatment that is still in use today. When a large hole penetrates a column of decayed wood or wetwood, the pathogens in the column will grow out to the cambium. In figure 12, a column was penetrated by a 14 millimeter diameter hole. The two inner arrows show the original diameter of the internal column. The double arrows show the new extension of the column. The cambium died back above and below the hole. When holes are drilled to drain wetwood fluids, the drain hole extends the column to the cambium. Drilling into columns of decayed wood is much worse than drilling into wetwood because the decay column will be increased in size. I have seen trees with 5 and 6 drain tubes below a wound! This practice must be stopped. The concern is that the fluids will freeze and cause cracks. In most cases the cracks are already present within the trunk.

A New Tree Biology

Figure 18-13

Wetwood fluids, tree sap, and yeast-infected sap (shown in figure 13) are often confused. People are afraid to cut branches on maples and birch late in the dormant season because they "bleed" (what an ugly, poor term!). Sap flowing from a cut branch is part of the tree's defense system. The sap will stop when the vessels clog. Such sap flow will cause minimal injury to the tree, and it will decrease the chances for infection. The sap flow may wet the bark and the bark inhabiting organisms, but it will not kill them. The wetwood fluids will kill most species of bark inhabiting organisms. An easy way to find insect borer damage on young smooth bark of oaks is to look for the white patches on the trunk. White patches also form where tight branch crotches kill tissues. The white patches indicate a flow of wetwood fluids. When sap, or in some cases wetwood fluids, are inhabited by yeasts, bubbles will form. The yeast-inhabiting sap provides "spring tonic" for many organisms.

Wetwood 337

An Intermission

Time to leave the subject for a moment. Time to wander away and not feel any one specific point. Time to feel all the points. Trees are wonderful. Pathogens are wonderful, too, in a strange sort of way. Trees and pathogens have an association that is difficult to understand. We want to crush them—pathogens. Then all will be good, we think. It is difficult to think that the pathogens are really good. If that *is* so, then why learn how to stop them? Maybe this is the point in the intermission that needs some attention. Are we really trying to stop them? If that is what we are really trying to do, then we are fools! They have been at their game for hundreds of millions of years, and we think we can stop them? I am sure if they can laugh, this is the time they would do so. Stop them, indeed!

If that is so ridiculous, then what should we be doing? Maybe we should stop for a moment and learn who they—the pathogens—are, and how do they fit into the whole story. Maybe we should learn something about them, rather than say they are bad, and because they are bad, we should kill them! (Have you ever thought that the pathogens consider us the bad guys?)

Remember the statement about witchcraft. It was not witchcraft, but the FEAR of witchcraft that caused so much trouble. We really fear things we do not understand. The common impulse is to kill anything that will interfere with our lives. Pathogens are bad; kill them.

Maybe the real problem begins to emerge, and that is why we get concerned. People have been the real problem for trees. It is easy to say, and it is being said over and over again. So, what do we do with this new tree pathogen? Kill them? Hardly. We have met the enemy, Pogo said, and he is us.

Nobody wants anybody to know he or she has ever done anything bad or wrong for trees. Especially when a great deal of profit was made doing the right (wrong?) things. Believe me, please, I am getting to the major problem we have now worldwide with trees. Many people have really hurt trees. Some have hurt trees because they did not understand. That can be forgiven. Some have hurt trees because they really never thought about it, but they have not set out to hurt them or anything. They can be forgiven. Some have hurt trees because it meant a constant supply of profit. Dante has an inner circle chair for these people, and they know it. Still, some in this group need a way out. That is fine. Change. Adjust. Learn. Be brave enough to reexamine and adjust. Now we come to the remaining group that resists all for the sake of profit. They will never disappear. Sad. But, we must not spend too much time on this. A new tree biology is here, and the people who really want to help trees will do so. And, make a great deal of honest profit.

The real problem with the new tree biology is that it demands your mind as well as your muscles. The old tree care methods demanded your mind for common sense, and your muscles to do the job; hard jobs. The charter members of the tree working groups in forests, orchards, and cities really worked hard. This was the major trait of the tree person, a hard worker. But, somewhere along the way some strange things happened. Machines came, new policies came, expanded cities and parks came, roads got wider, pollution increased, buildings got bigger, people kept getting closer and closer to trees. The trees could not move away in forests and cities. More roads came, drainage patterns were changed, the biggest and best trees were cut, the "forest weeds" (man's definition) were removed, greed set in for more and more of a natural product that just had to be taken. We all know the story, but some people still do not want to recognize what has happened. The cure was always there; paint it with some stuff, and if you can not see it, you do not have to worry about it.

Now city trees are in trouble. Orchards have a new problem called short life. Forests are dying. The tree problem has the attention of many people. Governments want action. People who never went into a forest or touched a tree are now new world tree experts. The old myths and misconceptions in the textbooks are being still used to try to answer new problems.

It won't work. We have new problems with the oldest continuing living organism on the earth. It is time for some action set in understanding. I believe it is time for a new tree biology. It is time to do something different. To do something better. To make sure that we are not still zigging while the world and the trees are zagging.

The first part of this book has focused on themes; the tree, problems, and care. The second part looks more closely at some of the variations on the themes.

The best way to understand how any organism or industry survives is to study how they respond to hits and hurts. Know how the organism or industry responds to a stimulus. This will tell you a great deal about the industries and organisms that live. We will now look at some tree problems. We will also discuss how best to care for trees that have the problems. Never lose sight of the number one problem trees have — people. If people are the problem, people can also be the answer.

Figure 19-1

A New Tree Biology

CHAPTER 19

Chestnut Blight

Chestnut blight, caused by the fungus *Endothia* (*Cryphonectria*) *parasitica*, is a tree disease that attracted more attention than any other tree disease. Dutch elm disease and white pine blister rust have come very close to receiving almost equal attention. The story of chestnut blight is well known. The fungus was introduced from Asia and it spread rapidly on its new host. The fungus had reached an equilibrium with trees in its own area. The American chestnut tree did not have a chance to adapt. However, the American chestnut (*Castanea dentata*) is still very much alive and living throughout upper Appalachia and vicinity. The large trees are not with us. The tree is now a small tree or even a bush. The tree is not extinct, or even near extinction. Other trees quickly took over the space occupied by chestnut. The niche for chestnut has been changed. The pathogen still attacks the young trees and they die. Sprouts from the roots as shown in figure 1 start a new group of trees. The trees may live for 20 or more years before they are killed. Many trees produce nuts before they die. Do not give up on the American chestnut. It is a tough tree. Let's look at some of its tough features.

Figure 19-2

A New Tree Biology

The chestnut tree does not stand there and die as soon as the pathogen arrives! The tree does have a strong defense system built about boundaries and generation of new tissues. The disease is a canker disease. The pathogen attacks the bark and kills the vascular cambium. The pathogen usually infects branch crotches, but it may also infect small wounds made by a variety of agents that include insects that normally bore into bark. The pathogen has the unique ability to spread laterally in bark rapidly and then inward, which results in the death of the cambium. Apparently the lateral growth of the pathogen in the bark does not trigger the defense response of the tree. By the time the tree recognizes the pathogen, large patches of cambium are set for death. When the tree does recognize the pathogen it begins to form boundaries in bark and wood to wall it off. In figure 2 the straight arrows show a site of attack and bark boundaries. The curved arrow shows the barrier zone that formed in the wood after the attack. Note also how much wider the growth increment is on the side of the tree opposite the infection.

I believe almost every aspect of this disease has been thoroughly studied except the defense system of the tree. The tree does not lie back and die without a fight! The theme continues; we must go back and reexamine trees, and try to help them by treatments and actions that enhance their own built in defense systems.

When the defense boundaries keep small portions of the vascular cambium alive (Fig. 3), the cambium (arrows) will form new wood and bark. All cankers do not lead to death on all trees! Many infections are stalled or walled off, and the tree forms, or generates enough new tissues to store enough energy to maintain life processes. An interesting point from our studies showed that some trees maintained a high amount of starch reserves while others had only low amounts. The trees were cut at the same time in the very early spring and the trees did not have infections. Starch studies showed that starch reserves were rapidly depleted in wood beneath most cankers, but not all. Those trees that were able to wall off the cankers maintained high amounts of starch reserves in the wood. Energy is still the basic need for defense.

Figure 19-3

A New Tree Biology

Hypovirulence means low virulence. Virulence is the amount of or number of pathogen propagules required to cause a specific degree of disease symptoms in a certain time. If a few bits of a pathogen cause disease symptoms it is very virulent. If it takes a great amount of the pathogen to cause similar symptoms, the pathogen is weakly virulent. I believe the so-called hypovirulent strain of the pathogen is anything but below virulence. I believe it is so virulent that it triggers the tree's defense system immediately, and the tree does what it genetically is geared to do; wall off the pathogen. The shape of the cankers are elliptic which is the normal shape of walled off cankers.

Figure 4 shows a peg (black pointer) with a needle behind it. The dead bark about the peg was taken away for the photograph. The peg then formed a new zone of wood and bark. Figure 5 shows a closer view of some pegs that formed out beyond the killed bark. The point here is that chestnut can do some very strong defense actions. Let's not write off American chestnut.

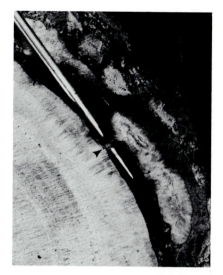

Figure 19-4

Figure 19-5

Figure 20-1

Figure 20-2

A New Tree Biology

CHAPTER 20

Hypoxylon Canker

Hypoxylon canker on aspen, *Populus tremuloides*, is caused by *Hypoxylon mammatum*. The disease can take a heavy toll of aspen. The fungus usually infects the branch crotch. The broken bark cambium, the phellogen, is highly suspect as the major infection court. (Review chapter on branch development.) The fungus spreads rapidly in the bark, and the infected bark appears water soaked (Fig. 1). Large patches of cambium may be killed and the fungus begins to form a hard, dark layer of material called a stroma. The layer may appear as a thick layer of tar. Within this layer, the sexual stage of the fungus develops, the perithecia. Inside the perithecia are bodies called asci, and in each ascus there are 8 spores. The fungus has a unique feature for removing the outer bark. Pillars of fungus material develop under the outer bark. The pillars expand and push away the bark, thus exposing the tar-like stroma with the perithecia. Insects commonly gnaw on the stroma. The role they may play in long range dissemination of spores is not clear. Insects often gnaw in branch crotches.

After the fungus has spread in the bark, there does come a time when the tree recognizes the infection and boundaries begin to form. Some trees respond so effectively that cankers are held to small dead spots, and the tree continues to live for many years. In other trees, the defense boundaries are weak, and the tree may be killed in a few years.

When the tree does wall off the infected tissue, it also walls off wood that normally stores energy reserves. The fungus is primarily a bark pathogen, but it does grow into the wood beneath the killed bark. The fungi may be temporarily walled off for the remainder of the growing period. Then when the fungus begins to grow again the next season, it spreads again in the bark. Bark boundaries only are effective for one growing period. The fungus spreads again as a wedge deep into the bark. The second season may be the end for weak trees. For strong trees the new fungus bark wedge is short.

The all important point here is that the fungus spreads in the bark *first* and then in the wood beneath the killed cambium. The fungus does not move vertically in the wood and then spread outward to the cambium. If it did do this, it would only do it one time, because this would kill the tree.

The pathogen that causes hypoxylon cankers is a switching pathogen: it goes from bark to wood, to bark and wood. The weak Achilles' heel is the bark that can not set a boundary to resist the fungus. This bark-wood seesaw is the way perennial cankers, canker rots, and root rots operate.

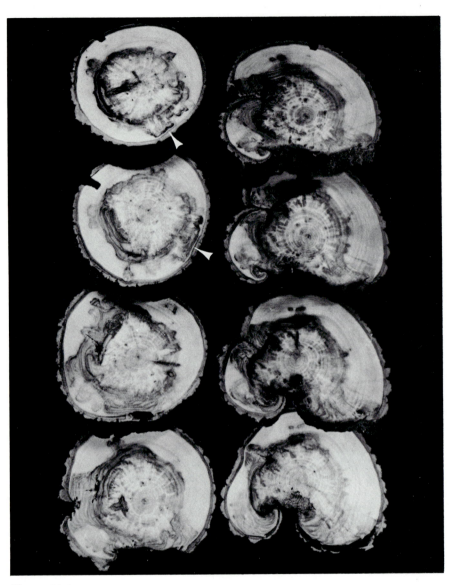

Figure 20-3

A New Tree Biology

The 8 discs shown in figure 3 were cut above and below a canker. The important point is that the *still living* cambium does wall off the pathogen. The pathogen may go a short distance or a long distance in the bark. There is a time — phenology — when bark tissues do not form strong boundaries. This is the time the pathogen has to spread. There is also a time when the tree begins to form boundaries in bark that resists the spread of the pathogen — the theme is the same. Pathogens have their time when the physiological Achilles' heel is present. Then the tree recognizes the pathogen and begins to wall it off. But, and so very important, only the living cambium, or the cambium that still remains alive after the attack by the pathogen, can form a boundary to resist spread of the pathogen.

The white markers show the clear wood that separates the infected wood from the clear, healthy wood. The pathogen was walled off, but only a thin strip of healthy wood now separates the infected wood from the healthy bark. The current year wood does not store energy reserves until the end of the growth period. And, even when it does store energy reserves, the amount of energy reserves in one thin growth increment may not be enough to stop an attacking pathogen. As the tree loses space to store energy reserves, it also loses it ability to resist additional attacks by the pathogen.

The important point about pathogens that live in bark and wood, is that they can "move" from one place to another to stay alive. They keep "hitting" the tree and the tree keeps responding to form barrier zones, until the tree has worked itself into a corner: no energy is left, or no space to store energy.

The same story keeps repeating. The pathogen only "takes" a small amount of space, but the taking repeats faster than the tree can generate new tissues. You can not study one part of the system. Boundary-setting is very good. Boundary-setting is very bad! So long as the tree can generate new tissues faster than the pathogen can spread into new tissues, the tree will stay alive. What we must do is to recognize this natural biological tree pathogen game, and do what we can to keep the balance in favor of the tree.

Figure 20-4

Figure 20-5

A New Tree Biology

When the bark "wakes up" and recognizes it is being invaded, it responds to start forming a boundary to resist further spread. The best way to resist a bark infecting pathogen is to put a boundary of wood in front of it. That is exactly what the tree does (white arrow). A wedge of wood forms as the growth increment turns upward as shown in figure 4. Figure 5 shows a section from the vertical tip of a canker. The old infected bark is beneath the back of the white arrow. The theme is that bark boundaries of wood form to resist spread of the pathogens. In both figures, note the decrease in the width of the last few growth increments, indicating that the trees are slowing their growth rate. Note also the abundance of vessels in aspen. There is more empty space than wood. And, the radial sheets of ray cells are very thin. This gives the pathogens little resistance to spread in a lateral direction.

In some ways, hypoxylon canker is the same above ground as *Armillaria mellea* is in the roots below ground. Both are primarily bark infecting fungi. Then they grow into the trapped wood beneath the killed cambium. If the wood is a weak compartmentalizer, then the next time the fungus infects in the bark, the farther it can penetrate. Remember, even the strongest bark boundaries rupture every year. The fungus usually infects along the bark cambium. This wedge-type of penetration will be shown in several other figures.

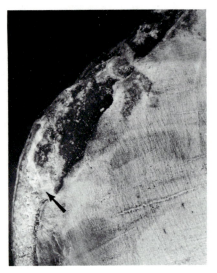

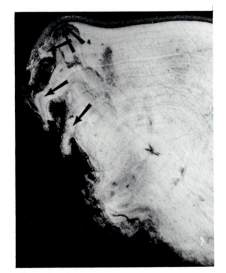

Figure 20-6

Figure 20-7

Figure 20-8

Figure 20-9

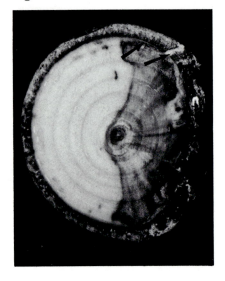

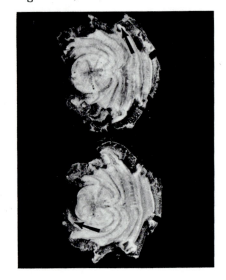

A New Tree Biology

Here are some additional samples that show the wood boundary in the bark of aspen. The arrow in figure 6 shows a long wood boundary. The arrows in figure 7 show several old wood boundaries. This tree was a strong compartmentalizer. Note the double arrows and the thin band of wood that separates the discolored, and infected wood from the healthy cambium. When the next bark wedge of the pathogen spreads, the cambium and wood in this area will hold no resistance for the pathogen. But, the important point is that the pathogen will not grow from the wood to the bark, but instead, the pathogen will advance through the bark.

In figure 8, the arrow at right shows a wood boundary in bark, and the arrow at left points to the thin strip of clear wood between the infected wood and the bark. In figure 9, the arrow shows one of many wood boundaries.

Results by geneticists have shown that some individual trees within several species had much stronger systems for compartmentalization than other individuals. We need to use this information in our search for resistant trees. We know the stronger individuals exist, and the ability to be a strong compartmentalizer is not closely associated with growth rate. We have focused too much on growth rate and not enough on defense systems. We just grow defective trees faster!

Figure 21-1

Figure 21-2

Figure 21-3

Figure 21-4

A New Tree Biology

CHAPTER 21

Strumella Canker

The theme for strumella canker on red and white oak is similar to the theme for hypoxylon canker on aspen. The canker is caused by *Urnula craterium*, which is the name of the perfect or sexual stage of the fungus. The name of the imperfect or asexual stage is *Strumella corynoidea*. The canker is found almost exclusively about old dead branch stubs. Observations showed that the cankers start within the branch crotch of living or dying branches. Cankers can be at the base of trees when an old stub was there (Fig. 1). Cankers are usually higher on the trunk (Figs. 2 and 4). The sexual stage develops when the infected tree falls to the ground (Fig. 3). The arrow points to a sexual fruit body on an infected stub at the base of a living tree (Fig. 1). The cankers may develop on some trees for over 25 years (Fig. 4). The crowns of the trees are not affected until the trunk is girdled. Then the crowns die suddenly. If the infected tree falls but does not touch the ground, the perfect stage will not form. The cups of the perfect stage contain perethecia which hold the asci with the spores. The cups and spores mature at the time oak leaves are forming. When oak leaves are forming, the phellogen is growing rapidly within the branch-trunk crotch. The spores leave the cups in great dark clouds. The fruit bodies begin to form on the bottom of old infected logs during the late fall. In the spring they mature rapidly. Their numbers are determined by fall conditions mostly. (I have been making observations on many logs that produce fruit bodies for over 8 years. On one log that was 8 inches in diameter, 60 cups formed in the spring of 1984 over a 1 meter portion. The fall of 1984 was very dry, and the spring of 1985 was also dry. The same section of log produced only 12 cups in 1985.)

The cankered trees often occur in clusters. The exact reason for this is not known. Many tree problems do occur in clusters. Healthy, high quality trees also occur in clusters. Natural boundaries may be a major reason or natural soil conditions: streams, rock outcrops, heavy or light amounts of essential elements in one area, especially where there were "recent" glaciers, past logging patterns, road and other construction that changed water drainage patterns, soil compaction by machines, changes in soil microflora brought on by man and his activities. Be on the alert for clusters of "good" trees and "bad" trees. Some of the same types of cluster can be found in parks, and even along city streets. It is not just a forest phenomenon.

Figure 21-5

A New Tree Biology

There is much more to strumella canker than a fungus and a tree. Many other bark and wood microorganisms grow on and in the cankers. Insects bore into the dying and dead bark, and others bore into the decaying wood. The canker fungus, *Urnula craterium* will cause some breakdown of wood. Other decay-causing fungi often enter the canker. The story of associates continues. Squirrels and birds visit the cankers to search for insects. Figure 5 shows a canker that was pecked by a hungry bird in search of insects. The birds are most active in this type of work late in winter or early in spring. Small pieces of infected wood must stick to parts of the birds, or squirrels. I believe that small animals and birds play an important role in long distance spread of this disease, and of others that are similar to strumella canker.

There is a canker on *Quercus robur* in Europe that is similar to strumella canker. The fungus associated with the canker is a species of *Pezicula*.

Cankers on trees are often signs of other problems. Cankers are very common on young trees in the forest, and the cankers cause the death of many young trees. This is one of nature's ways of early elimination of the weak. Our practices often go directly against these natural processes. We want 90% germination from a given seed lot. Then the young seedlings are protected and cared for until they leave the nursery. In the forest 98% of the trees would have died by that time. When the trees are planted, cankers of all types may start appearing. I have seen this story repeated many times! The trees looked perfect as they left the laboratory, or greenhouse, or nursery. And, then the canker fungi and bacteria "hit." Everybody then wants a quick "cure"; some spray treatment to kill the pathogens. I have told people that what was happening was a quick kill of the weak. Sometimes the weaklings do not get infected until a much later time because of the care given to the young tree. My point here is that when you see many cankers on young trees, or even older trees, look for the real causes. And do not be mislead by rapid growth. Trees that grow fast are not always healthy trees. Here are some real causes for the cankers: trees that normally grow in sun, growing in shade, and the opposite condition; trees that grow best in dry soils growing in wet soils, and the opposite condition; trees over pruned, and at the time leaves were forming; soil compaction; root injuries and root death.

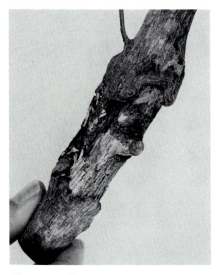

Figure 21-6

Figure 21-7

Figure 21-8

Figure 21-9

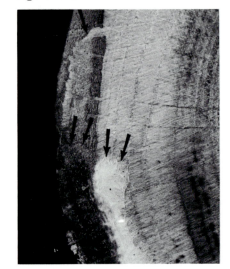

Strumella cankers will also form on hickory, as shown here on *Carya ovata* (Figs. 6 and 7). The young trees may break at the cankers. Hickory trees often overgrow the cankers. Figure 7 shows a young hickory with a current year canker. The pathogen entered at the branch crotch (arrow). The branch was healthy 5 cm distal to the crotch. The ruptured phellogen in the branch crotch is highly suspect as the major infection court for the pathogen. The canker fungi are reported to spread downward from branches to the trunk. If that were so, the cankers would only be below the branch on the trunk. Such a patten is seen where *Nectria cinnabarina* does spread downward from dying branches on several species of trees in Europe.

A canker is defined as a localized lesion; a dead spot. On young trees, many canker pathogens spread so far so fast that the trees die rapidly from a complete lesion. The small oak in figure 8 died 2 years after the first infections. In nature, many young trees die the first season after infection, and it is difficult to believe that a canker pathogen could be so aggressive. We see only those trees that were strong enough to resist the complete invasion of the bark.

Figure 9 shows how an oak resists spread of the pathogen. The single arrows show the bark boundary of wood. Wood will form in bark. Note that the bark ray parenchyma have differentiated to form wood. The double arrows in the wood show the mycelium — fungus vegetative body — of the pathogen. The canker was cut into cross section discs. The discs were placed back in order, and after a week, the fungus grew out of the wood and onto the wood surface. This is the natural, easy way to see a pathogen that is in the wood. The double arrows in the bark show the bark boundary that separates the infected bark from the healthy bark. The bark boundary is the first line of tree defense. The large patch of wood in the bark is the second line of defense. Unlike *Hypoxylon mammatum* in aspen, *Urnula craterium* in oak seldom spreads laterally in the wood beyond its position in the bark. The 4 arrows are in a line. This is one reason why most oaks live with strumella cankers longer than aspens live with hypoxylon cankers. Of course, there are always exceptions. The points here are that some young trees are overwhelmed by canker pathogens and the trees die. Other trees play a seesaw game with the pathogen for 30 or more years. There are times when the tree does stop the spread of the pathogen.

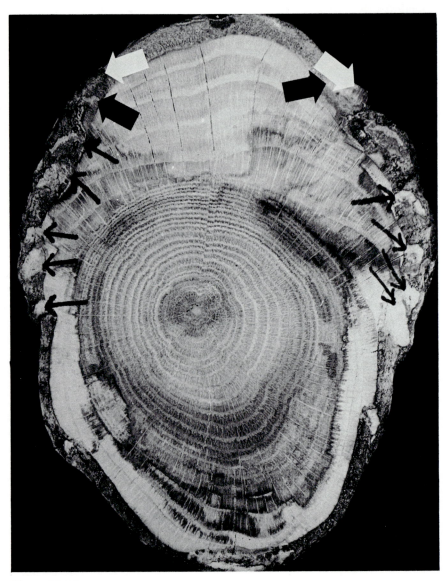

Figure 21-10

A New Tree Biology

How does the tree-pathogen seesaw function? A quick review first. The sexual spores are produced at the time leaves are forming. Nature does time events for results. To me, this means that trees must be at their best physiological or phenological positions for infection. We know that most cankers, or with strumella cankers, all cankers, have an old branch stub in the center. We know that at the time oak leaves are forming, the phellogen is beginning to expand in the branch crotch. We know that the phellogen may come near or completely to the surface for a short time. If the pathogen infects, it may grow rapidly and kill the young tree in 1 or 2 seasons. If the pathogen infects, but the tree responds to resist infection, then the seesaw starts. The pathogen spreads first in the bark. The bark boundaries form to resist spread. Next, wood boundaries may form in the bark. The spreading pathogen is stalled, but the vascular cambium beneath the infected bark dies. The cambium that is still alive beyond the infected bark, and the wood beneath the infected bark and the wood beyond this area begin to compartmentalize the pathogen. The wood forms reaction zones. The cambium forms a barrier zone. Tree growth continues. The next spring before growth starts, the pathogen begins to grow again in the bark. The pathogen expands at the position where the bark cambium meets the phelloderm, or outmost phloem. The pathogen grows as a wedge between these tissues. As growth starts, and the bark begins to expand, the natural, old, bark boundary begins to rupture. They rupture because of normal growth expansion pressures, plus the pathogen may have already made an entrance into the phellogen-phelloderm area. The pathogen expands into the outer bark, and the base of the pathogen spreads downward in the phloem until the vascular cambium is killed. By this time the tree is beginning its normal growth processes. The killed cambium — the smell of death — produces chemicals that initiate defense reactions. The necrobiotic chemicals trigger the reactions far beyond the actual infection site. The tree speeds its bark boundary and wood in bark boundary processes. Now the seesaw action tips toward the tree. The points made here are recorded in the section shown in figure 10. The smaller, black arrows drawn on the wood show the wood boundary that formed the season before this red oak tree was cut. The white arrows show the pathogen "coming around the pass" and invading new bark. The section was cut in June, and the new wood had not yet started to form. This tree was rapidly losing the battle with the pathogen. Strong lateral resistance — CODIT walls 3 — were the only reason the tree was still living.

Figure 22-1

Figure 22-2

Figure 22-3

Figure 22-4

CHAPTER 22

Cankers

Cankers are localized dead spots. A lesion is any dead spot. A dead area may develop over the entire tree. When an infection kills a large portion of a tree, or any organism, the term systemic is used. It means, throughout the system. Cankers are lesions, but not systemic lesions. There are 3 basic types of cankers: 1, annual cankers; 2, perennial cankers; and 3, canker rots. Annual cankers are most common on twigs and small woody roots. Annual cankers may result from insect oviposition wounds, from bird pecks, squirrel wounds, etc. The annual canker does not continue to spread. The perennial canker does spread every year until the tree dies or until it breaks at the canker site. Perennial cankers may be associated with some rot, but usually only a small amount. In fact, most perennial cankers have discolored wood that is high in density and it resists rot. The canker rots are perennial type cankers where the primary infecting pathogen does cause wood rot. Perennial cankers are caused by pathogens that spread from bark to wood, and back to bark and wood. The roots also have cankers that are perennial. And again, some root cankers cause very little rot while others cause considerable rot. Details on root cankers will be given later. It is important to know now that the canker themes above ground on trunks and branches are not so different from those on roots below ground.

Figures 1 and 2 show a typical nectria canker on a sugar maple. Fungi in the genus *Nectria* cause many cankers on many species of trees. (Genus — your last name; species, your first name.) The canker may have a target appearance as each year's seesaw process causes spread by the pathogen and resistance or a callus boundary by the tree. The tissue killing and the tree response result in swollen areas in the trunk or branches. The wood in the canker is often very dense and almost appears like burl wood. The wood may be impregnated with gums and other substances that resist infection by decay-causing pathogens.

Figure 3 shows a nectria canker on a young yellow birch. The lenticels — air openings into the outer bark — are enlarged and corky near the canker. The sexual stage of Nectria looks like bright orange to red dots. A sharp eye or magnifying glass is needed to find them. They are usually at the border of recently killed wood and bark and still healthy wood and bark. As pointed out before, cankers can kill young trees. And as also stated many times already in our conversation, nature does not deal in absolutes. Some decay-causing fungi may infect nectria cankers (Fig. 4). The tree can form antimicrobial substances, but it seems that some organisms adapt to the substance and break it down. The time games are a central theme.

Cankers can be cut out of trees by cutting into the bark *far* beyond the canker, and doing the cutting in mid growing season for the tree. In most cases the tree is weakened and disfigured by the treatment. Once portions of the canker infect more than a half of the trunk, removal becomes difficult to impossible.

Figure 22-5

Figure 22-6

The 2 sugar maples have a canker caused by *Eutypella parasitica* (Figs. 5 and 6). Both trees have central columns of discolored wood associated with old branch openings. Note that the decayed wood in the cankers end abruptly above and below the cankers.

Many pathogens incite cankers on hardwoods. Twig cankers usually break off. Trunk cankers may kill the tree quickly or persist for many years. Most canker pathogens do not spread far in bark or wood. The perennial cankers are inhabitants of bark and wood.

Cankers on trees in parks and along streets can lead to breakage. Be on the alert for cankers on trees that have leaning trunks.

The pathogens that cause cankers usually require some opening to enter the bark and wood. Insects and small animals can also break bark and give the pathogens a point for entrance. A disease called canker strain causes serious problems for the London plane tree, a tree that is very tough and can survive after many types of abuse and mistreatment. The fungus *Ceratocystis fimbriata* infects wounds on the tree. The fungus is in the same genus as the fungi that cause Dutch elm disease and oak wilt. Wound prevention and proper pruning will greatly reduce the injury caused by the pathogen. The pathogen is a problem in warmer, southern limits for the range of the London plane trees.

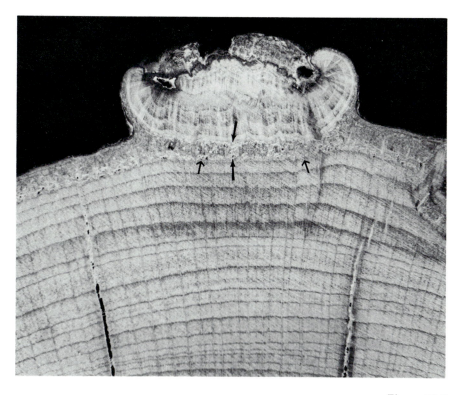

Figure 22-7

Nectria coccinea var. *faginata*, and *N. galligena* are associated with the beech bark disease in the U.S.A. and Europe. Europe does not have the same Nectria (*N. coccinea* var. *faginata*) as the one infecting trees in the U.S.A. The pathogen may cause localized cankers, or the entire tree trunk can be infected. Some tree trunks are bright red with the millions of perithecia—fruit bodies. Back to the tree and defense. The tree does wall off the localized dead spots, even when they may be several meters long on the trunk. The pathogen may also form small knob-like cankers. These cankers are not only walled off, but some are actually shed as shown in this figure 7. At the central longitudinal point in the canker, the trunk bark (small arrows) separate the canker from the trunk. The knob-like growth has a vascular cambium (large arrows). The knob shown was 8 years old. The knob forms as the pathogen kills islands of vascular cambium, but some small portions of cambium stay alive (see the pillars formed by American chestnut in the chapter on chestnut blight). It is remarkable to see the many variations on the theme of setting boundaries, and generating new cells in new positions.

CHAPTER 23

Canker Rots

Canker rots are perennial cankers incited by fungi that can rot wood, the Hymenomycetes. Canker rots are some of the most difficult tree problems to understand. Canker rots are major causes of economic damage to timber trees. To understand canker rots, trunks *must* be studied from the longitudinal view as well as from the cross sectional view. Trees with canker rots were some of the first wood defect problems to be studied by pathologists. This was very unfortunate because cross sections of trunks with canker rots revealed a maze of boundaries and of wood in various stages of discoloration and decay. And, the defects did appear to spread outward from wood to bark. These early observations are some of the major reasons why the compartmentalization concept never surfaced until G. Hepting's work in 1935. The canker rots did appear as if the heartwood (discolored wood) was being continually infected by the "saprophytes" that cause decay. The "saprophytes" — organisms that live on dead organic material, like wood, or *for certain* heartwood — spreading in the dead, nonresponsive heartwood, and such a process could not be called a disease. Breakdown of dead wood can not be called a disease, they said. Decay was not a disease!

Many of the misconceptions brought on by studies on cross sections of canker rotted wood are still with us today! Studies of such cross sections are studies of an artifact, as a means of explaining the process.

Canker rots on birch, maple, and oak will be discussed first, and then canker rots (ring rots) on conifers after this. The common root rots *are* canker rots, and again the confusion still is with us on this subject. The major problem centers about thinking that all wood is dead and nonreactive, heartwood for certain, and that the fungi can spread freely in trunks of trees. If these 2 incorrect points were really true, trees as we know them today would not exist. Wood does have many living cells in sapwood, and heartwood does react to set boundaries. Pathogens do not spread freely in wood. Pathogens spread within the limits of the natural preset boundaries and also within the limits of the defense set boundaries.

Pathogens that cause canker rots grow in bark and wood. The canker rot pathogens are unique because they did "find" a temporary way to avoid being compartmentalized. This is not so different from the pathogens that cause perennial cankers like *Nectria*, *Cytospora*, *Hypoxylon*, and *Endothia*. These pathogens are short term killers compared to the canker rots. But, the canker rot pathogens are "smart." If they killed the tree, they would not have a long food supply — to rot the wood. The perennial canker pathogens live primarily in wood and go to the bark for a short time. The seesaw process operates for both groups.

Let us start by discussing some canker rots on hardwood, and then we will go to the conifers.

Figure 23-1

Figure 23-2

Poria obliqua (now *Inonotus obliquus*) causes a conspicuous canker on yellow and paper birch. Figure 1 shows the swollen "bowling pin" shape of an infected paper birch. The black mass of fungus tissue has been called a sterile conk. Conk means a fertile body. The term is a contradiction of terms—"a sterile fertile." The hard, coal-like mass is a type of pressure pad. The mass does not produce spores. When the tree dies, a fertile, flat spore-bearing layer of fungus tissue forms under and within the bark. The outer bark falls away to reveal the spore-bearing layer. The layer will form on trees that have fallen as well as on standing dead trees.

The dissection (Fig. 2) shows the stripes of discolored wood and the light-colored decayed wood. The fungus causes a white rot—cellulose and lignin are digested at about equal rates.

The infection started when the tree was very small. In some yet unknown process, the infection stimulates tree growth above and below the canker.

The hard fungus material has been studied as a possible source of substances that would combat some types of cancer. Nothing positive has come from the research.

Here is another type of canker rot on paper birch (Figs. 3 and 4) that has a sunker canker caused by *Fomes igniarius* var. *laevigatus*. The fungus produces small flat sporophores on the canker surface. On larger cankers, the sporophores can be much larger. The dissected trunk section, below, shows an old branch stub (arrow) as the possible original infection court. The section at left shows the size of the tree (arrows) where the pathogen infected.

The center of the tree had sound discolored wood. The dark stripes in the discolored wood mark the boundaries that formed as branches died. The wood above and below the canker was decayed. The fungus causes a white rot. It is important to note that the decay did not spread into the central column of discolored wood. Pathogens do not grow freely in trees. The longitudinal view of the trunk below the canker presents an artifact. The chainsaw cut a straight line through a curved base. Once you know you have an artifact, you can treat it as an artifact and not as the correct view. The central column of discolored wood appears to end in the tree base. In truth, the column of discolored wood curved to one side. The view above the canker is directly through the central pith, a correct view.

Figure 23-3

Figure 23-4

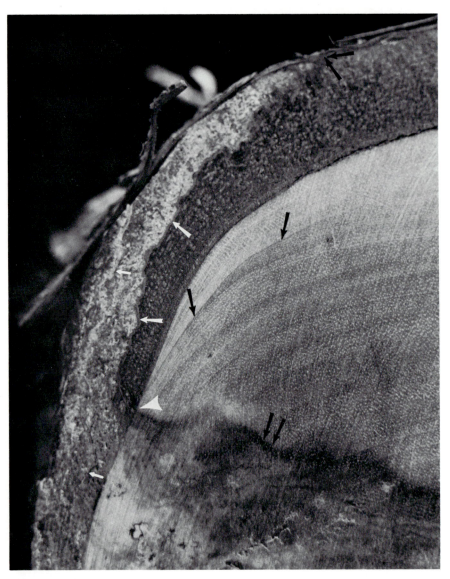

Figure 23-5

A New Tree Biology

The canker rot pathogens produce wedges of fungus material into the bark (Fig. 5). The larger white arrows show the boundary of the wedge that penetrated the bark of this paper birch 3 years before the tree was cut. The double black arrows in the bark show the tip of the wedge. The wedge is pushing into the thin sheets of outer bark. How much of the wedge boundary shown by the large white arrows is outer bark corky sheets, and how much is newly formed boundary material in the bark, is not well understood. The small white arrows show an earlier boundary. The white pointer indicates the position where the wedge meets the living cambium. The barrier zone that formed in the wood is shown by the black arrows in the wood. Three clear growth increments formed after the barrier zone was completed, indicating that the fungus wedge had formed 3 years before the tree was cut. The double arrows in the wood show the reaction zone, or wall 3 of CODIT. Wall 3 persists lateral spread of the pathogen, but the wood on the inner side of the barrier zone begins to starve and discolor slightly. The fungus wedges did not advance every year on this tree. The bark thickens greatly distal to the fungus wedge.

This seesaw of fungus wedges, tree bark boundaries, and wood reaction zones and barrier zones must all be understood to understand canker rots. This is not easy. And there is still much that we do not know. In some way, the pathogen and tree interact to keep the seesaw under control. If this were not so, the pathogen would soon girdle the tree. The tree circumference increases greatly near the canker, giving the seesaw more room to swing. The decayed wood is not one solid mass of broken down wood, but instead, the hard old boundaries of the reaction zones and barrier zones give the trunk with decayed wood strength.

When I see systems such as these, I often wonder whether the tree is a single organism or really a part of a network that we have not learned to recognize or appreciate yet. The real question is what bonds or holds such systems together. They all seem to support each other for the longest possible time.

Figure 24-1

Figure 24-2

Figure 24-3

Figure 24-4

A New Tree Biology

CHAPTER 24

Polyporous glomeratus

Polyporous glomeratus causes a canker rot on maples (Figs. 1, 2, 3, 4). It is typical of many canker rots caused by other pathogens. The white arrow in figure 1 shows a spindle-shaped canker caused by *P. glomeratus* on red maple. Some cankers appear as swollen knobs on tree trunks. The shape or type of canker is determined by the fungus wedges that penetrate the bark. If the wedges circle the canker, a knob-like swollen spot results; if the fungus wedges advance into the bark farther above and below the canker than to the sides, a long, spindle-shaped swollen canker results. Figure 2 shows the dissection of the tree shown in figure 1. Note the wide band of discolored wood that surrounds the central column of decayed wood. The discolored wood usually contains bacteria and a number of imperfect fungi such as *Phialophora* species. The rot has a distinctive medicinal odor. The decayed wood seldom spreads to the base of the tree.

Figure 3 shows 2 cankers joining to form a long spindle-shaped canker. This red maple had many cankers while another red maple only 15 feet away, and at the same size, did not have a single canker.

Figure 4 shows a close up of a dissected canker on a red maple. The opening is plugged by the dark mass of fungus material. The infection court appeared to be a broken branch. The arrow shows where the old branch broke. Dissection of many cankers revealed that broken branches were major infection courts. The mass of fungus material keeps the wound open and the wedges expand the wound.

Once canker rots start in trees, the rot will increase over time. The canker rot fungi temporarily grow around the old boundaries by enlarging the wound. Every time the fungus wedge spreads into the bark the size of the wound is increased. Then the tree compartmentalizes the newly exposed wood. This type of seesaw action is best called intermittent compartmentalization.

Figure 24-5

The paper birch wedge was shown in cross section. The wedge by *Polyporous glomeratus* is best shown in a longitudinal section (Fig. 5). The white point in figure 5 shows where the living cambium meets the recently killed cambium. The white arrow shows the vertical tip of a fungus wedge. Note how neatly it slices through the bark. It is often difficult to find good examples of the wedges because the lateral wedges may be more active in some samples, while in other samples there will be more vertical wedges.

In forest improvement work, trees with canker rots should be removed as soon as possible. The defects will only get worse. It is also best to remove the trees from the forest and destroy them or use them as soon as possible for chips, or other low-grade products. Be on the alert for clusters of trees with canker rots.

A New Tree Biology

Canker rots were found on several species of *Eucalyptus* in Australia. The dissected tree in figure 6 shows the typical broken branch and the decay spreading in the inner branch core-wood. As the fungus wedge spread into the bark and rewounded the tree, bands of kino formed. The canker was young and only beginning to swell. Note the similarity in this section with the red maple section in figure 4.

Figure 7 shows another eucalypt with a canker rot. The large black arrows show where the branch broke. The branch core wood is decayed. This is not usual, because the branch core-wood is usually not rapidly decayed by fungi. The canker rot fungi seem to "thrive" on wood impregnated with protective materials. The smaller black arrow shows a kino band that formed after the wound was enlarged by the fungus wedge.

Why broken branches seem to be good infection courts is not really understood. It may be that the branch is weakened and dies a slow death. In cities and parks it is always wise to remove broken branches as soon as possible. Broken branches may also lead to problems for property and people.

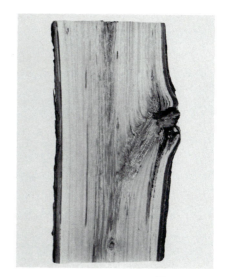

Figure 24-6

Figure 24-7

Figure 25-1

A New Tree Biology

CHAPTER 25

Fomes everhartii

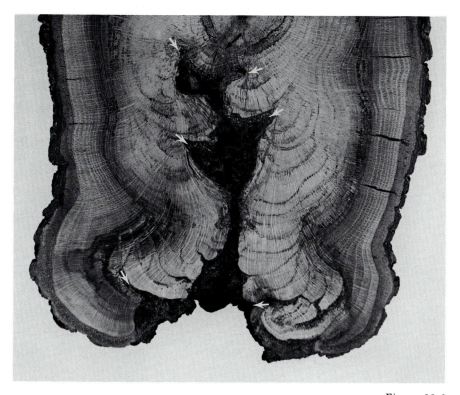

Figure 25-2

Fomes everhartii causes a canker rot on oaks. This fungus produces masses of fungus tissues just as the other canker rot fungi described. But this fungus also produces a fertile sporophore on the cankers. At left on the sample in figure 1 is a mass of fungus tissue. On the upper part of the sample, a large woody sporophore formed. This fungus also produces wedges into the wood (white arrows). The black arrow shows where the infection started.

Figure 2 shows a sample with a large mass of fungus tissue, but no sporophore. The white arrows show the persistent fungus wedges in the bark. Note the tree bark that separates the wedges from the wood. The fungus seems to force the bark and wood to roll inward. Note how the growth increments turn inward at the points of the inner wedges.

Observations on oak with this fungus indicate that the openings must be large with a great amount of fungus material before a sporophore will form.

Figure 26-1

A New Tree Biology

CHAPTER 26

Fomes pini

Fomes pini causes a canker rot. Defect caused by this fungus ranks first for economic loss. The fungus, and its variants, attack all but a few members of the pine family, a very large family! The defect is often called red ring rot, again named from its appearance from the end of a log; a cross cut view.

Figure 1 shows a longitudinal view of *F. pini* in an eastern white pine. The infections are closely associated with old dead stubs. This does not mean that they spread downward into the trunk through dead and dying branches. This is highly unlikely. They probably follow the same infection process as many other canker rot pathogens, and infect the protective wood in the trunk that forms after branches die. More on that as we look at many samples.

The dark arrow shows the sporophore of *F. pini*. It may develop to form a shelf-like conk. Sporophores are usually found where the old branch wood still protrudes. The white arrows show the fungus wedges penetrating the bark and keeping the wound open. The cavity above the branch corewood is filled with the hard fungus material. Note also that the branch corewood is digested by the fungus. This fungus can breakdown the resin-soaked protective wood in the branches. For this reason I call the theme "don't throw me in the briar patch." If you recall in the children's story about the bear and the rabbit, the rabbit said to the bear that the worst thing that could happen to him would be to be thrown into a briar patch. Of course, that is what the bear did to the rabbit. The rabbit then survived where others could not go. The same with *Fomes pini*. It survives in the protective wood that does not support other organisms. The fungus has no competition in the protection wood. In fact, this is why the ring rot pattern forms. The fungus grows in resin-soaked wood.

When the branch stub falls away, the fungus fills the cavity with the hard material. In advanced stages of decay, the entire branch corewood is replaced by the fungus plug of material and a "punk knot" results. Figure 2 shows the beginning of a punk knot in an eastern white pine.

The wood between the 2 black pointers is resin-soaked. It formed at the boundary of the heartwood and sapwood. *Fomes pini* does not attack sapwood or heartwood, but the protection-altered wood that forms at the sapwood-heartwood boundary. The protection wood often includes 10 to 30 growth increments. The fungus grows only in the band of protection wood, and thus the rings of rot.

The center of the tree shows advanced decay. The rot is called a pocket rot because small pockets of wood are decayed leaving borders of hard wood. The fungus is a white rot fungus, but it does digest lignin more readily than cellulose. This could have some very beneficial commercial value as a means of delignifying wood for pulp or for cattle food. *Figure 26-2*

A New Tree Biology

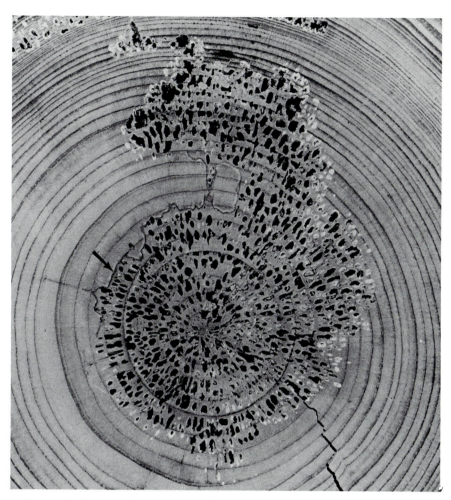

The rot is often seen in the center of trees. How can this be? We must remember that all trees start as sapwood trees. When the young sapwood tree begins to have branches die, and the central wood has aged enough that it is not yet heartwood, but again, it is aging sapwood that fills its resin ducts with protection materials. The fungus "goes" for the resin ducts as dead branches give the pathway into the trunk. The selective digestion of the resin ducts leads to the pattern of decay pockets shown in figure 3. The arrow shows a dark boundary about the decayed wood. Care must be taken in viewing this cross section sample. The cross section does expose several separate columns of decay. Note also the slightly discolored wood about each column of decay.

Figure 26-3

Figure 26-4

Figure 4 is a full view of the wood shown in figure 3. A ring of decay is associated with each dead branch. The center of the tree was decayed, sound heartwood surrounded the decayed wood, and the rings of decayed wood were surrounded on their inner and outer sides by sound wood.

A philosophical point or question: what survival value is there in this pattern of ring decay or in the pocket rot pattern? If decay-causing fungi decayed the wood at random, without boundaries, the tree would break. The survival "deal" again is to maintain the tree's mechanical support while it is being decayed. This sounds like a paradox. The ring rot pattern and the pocket rot pattern help to accomplish this. So long as the tree is standing and alive, the fungus has food and a home. The fungus also has a sturdy structure for its reproductive bodies. I think the system is incredibly smart!

A New Tree Biology

The early stages of *Fomes pini* central decay are shown in the longitudinal dissection in an eastern white pine (Fig. 5). The wood between the black arrows is a light pink to red. Note the decayed wood at the base of the branches. The rot has started and will advance into the central column of red wood. The white arrows show the limits of the heartwood.

Figure 6 shows an eastern white pine with advanced central decay in the lower half of the sample. The smallest black arrows show the central column of rot on equal sides of the central pith. The decay column in the upper half of the sample is only to the right of the central pith (medium-sized arrows). The large arrow shows the rot in the center of the old leader that died. Note the rot in the large branch stub at left, and in the dead branch corewood at lower right. The sample shown in figure 5 would have developed to the stage shown by the lower half of the sample in figure 6.

It is easy to understand why people who see such patterns of rot say that CODIT and compartmentalization are not correct. It does take a great amount of study to understand patterns of rot caused by canker rots. I always start with the view that nature is orderly, and when I don't see the order, I am wrong, or I have not seen enough material the right way. CODIT and compartmentalization are built on the order of natural systems.

Figure 26-5

Figure 26-6

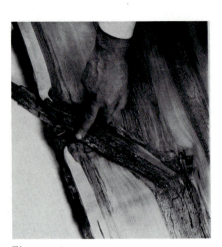

Figure 26-7

Figure 26-8

Figure 26-9

Figure 26-10

A New Tree Biology

Fomes pini is too important to leave without some additional details. Figure 7 shows a large eastern white pine sample that was sound in the center and bands of rot surrounded the sound center wood. Healthy heartwood surrounded the columns of rot, and the finger shows a new column of rot beginning to spread into the newly-formed column of resin-soaked wood. The tip of the finger is on the plug of fungus material.

Figure 8 shows that each growth increment has "its own" column of rot. Note the sharp boundaries between the small rot pockets as they are spaced in each growth increment. Note also the discolored wood about the infected wood. The white cottony dots are portions of rays filled with fungus mycelium. The initial infections appear to be more in the ray cells, and axial-formed resin ducts. Resin ducts come from living parenchyma cells, and parenchyma can be in a radial or axial direction. Regardless, the initial rot pattern is not at random in all wood; the process is highly ordered.

Figure 9 shows that the rot columns usually attenuate as they develop downward. Figure 10 gives another view of punk knots. The old branch corewood has been replaced by fungus material. Note the rings of decay surrounded by sound wood. Indeed, it appears complex, but it really is not. Disorder always appears complex. Once you learn to see the order in things, they become simple. Complexity usually comes before simplicity.

CHAPTER 27

Caution

At this point in our conversation, in our snowball rolling, I am getting concerned that tree people with special interests may begin to skip over material they feel is not germane to their needs. I hope you will not do this. I caution you against this, because the points I keep trying to make all focus on the tree and how it manages to survive against an unending number of agents and pathogens that "try" to "outwit" the tree. Or, better yet, pathogens that "try" to establish as long a relationship as possible with the tree. In a way, the pathogens (our word, not nature's) and the tree work together as a life force. The tree and pathogens, and all living things that live in, on, and about trees have a common friend and foe in the ever-changing environment, and natural events—storms, earthquakes, volcanoes, landslides, etc. The tree and associates can "work out" their best survival "deals" and these survival methods must be beneficial for the tree and associates if some unexpected natural environment problem occurs. In a sense, we have the living group and the non-living group. Both have regulating forces within them.

The usual way this subject is discussed is to first draw a triangle that represents the host, pathogen and environment. Then the discussion proceeds as each can affect the other. I can not accept that 3-part system. I believe natural events and processes vibrate between 2's. The first two parts are the living and non-living. Within the living we have those that survive by building up matter, and those that survive by breaking down matter; 2's again. Indeed there are many agents, living and non-living that enter this story, but we must be careful to put them in a flow chart that always shows one force against the other.

Why all of this now? Because many of the details on how these systems function are brought out in the different ways the trees and pathogens operate over time. An arborist or orchardist might feel that to know *Fomes pini* is not necessary because *Fomes pini* is not one of their problems. Again, and again, I do not mean this to be a pathology book, or an anatomy or physiology book! It is a tree biology book. The information on specific problems helps to show how the tree survives. There is more to come, so I hope you will stay with me.

Figure 28-1

A New Tree Biology

CHAPTER 28

Fomes pini and Related Species

Fomes pini and its variants cause serious economic problems in western U.S.A. and Canada. The first section on *Fomes pini* was on eastern white pine. This section will be on Douglas fir, true or white fir, and western hemlock from Oregon, Washington, and northern California.

The large sample in figure 1 came from California. Without an understanding of CODIT, compartmentalization, and canker rot patterns, an explanation of the sample would be impossible. Or, the decay patterns would all be considered random. This was the way it was in the past. Let us start in the center and work outward. The center or A region is sound except for a few columns. The B region is decayed. The black arrows in the B region are resin soaked spots that are common at the margins of wounds. The small white arrow shows where the tree was wounded to start the B region. The B region decay did not spread into the A region because the wood in the A region was already altered to a more protective state, a type of false heartwood. The large white arrow shows where the wound — fire, logging? — started the decay in region C. Note the resin-soaked spots (black arrows) at the tangential-lateral margin of region C. (It appears that region C may be 2 regions.) Insects infested region C. Note the turn of the growth increments at the position of the large white arrow. This is an indicator of a wound. The large resin-soaked spots beyond the white arrow indicate that the tree was wounded above or below where our sample was cut. The circumferential cracks indicate serious wounds above or below where the sample was cut. Note that the radial cracks developed outward from the circumferential cracks. The sample has several large rings of *Fomes pini* — rotted wood. The wood in D is the largest ring. Note the bands of sound wood between the rings of pocket-rotted wood.

Figure 28-2

A New Tree Biology

Figure 28-3

A fungus very closely related to *Fomes pini* is *Fomes chrysoloma*. It causes a canker rot on some western conifers that can lead to death. The position of infection and spread are similar to *Fomes pini*. A major difference between the fungi is that *F. chrysoloma* produces a very large fungus wedge, especially in the lateral direction (large white arrows, Fig. 2). When many wedges meet or coalesce about the trunk, the tree is girdled, and it dies.

It is very difficult to recognize the fungus wedges because they are the same color, and almost the same texture, as the bark. Note how flat the wood in the trunk is below the fungus wedge. The wedge was associated with the dead branch.

A ring rot pattern is obvious in this sample. The small white arrows show the chemical boundaries that formed internal to the ring rot. A close look will reveal 2 boundaries. The significance of the 2 lines is not known. The lines or dark boundaries do turn at sharp right angles as they go from compartment to compartment.

The sample in figure 3 shows a longitudinal and cross-sectional view of the rings of pocket rot. The arrow shows a new column starting from the branch corewood.

Figure 28-4

A New Tree Biology

The many sporophores on this white fir indicate that the fungus wedges of *Fomes chrysoloma* have coalesced and the tree is near death (Fig. 4). It takes a long time for this to happen. The fungus will produce billions of spores, and the process will start again on another tree.

Death has always been a subject that most people do not like to discuss. We think of it as the end, which, for the individual, is so. The religious beliefs of many people deal with death in a way that still gives them another chance someplace else. That is not the point here. I am talking about the death of trees and their associates. The tree provides much for many long after it dies. Death is far from the end. There is all that energy trapped in cellulose that is awaiting use. The cavities in the tree will continue to be home sites for many organisms. A tree may lose life, but it surely does not immediately lose all the life that surrounds it. But, in a sense, there is a changing of the guard after tree death. A new group of competitors enters the stage. New rules for survival of the competitors for the new energy source and space are made. The saprophytes enter. The saprophytes are those that get their energy from dead organic matter (that is usually redundant). The boundaries set while the tree was alive still remain as boundaries for a few to many years. The protection materials often still remain in materials that resist breakdown. Some woods are called durable because even after death, few organisms can break them down. The real meaning of durable woods does not come clear until you see the dead trees in the moist, warm, rain forests. The fungi and termites rapidly break down almost all dead organic matter. But, some tree trunks remain sound as they lie woven together with others on the forest floor, or high above the forest floor. In a rain forest it is often difficult to know where the forest floor is! The down durable trunks greatly increase the area for other plants to grow. Just how durability of down trees may give a survival advantage to their own species is not well understood. My major point here is that the benefits of trees do not stop when the trees die. I often wonder how man has changed all of this by cutting them and taking them away. I am not against harvesting trees. I just wonder whether our harvesting methods do not need a complete reexamination. We still want too much, too fast from our forests. Over and over we have discussed the time game.

The American Indians viewed nature from the inside. They were part of the web, and they made their decisions from the inside. Modern man has drifted too far out of the web for decision making, but man can never really get out of the web.

Figure 29-1

A New Tree Biology

Chapter 29

Armillaria mellea

Now it is time to turn the tree upside down and discuss the canker rots of roots, the root rots. *Armillaria mellea* is the pathogen that receives the most attention (Fig. 1). It is doubtful that this one species is responsible for all the root rot that is called *Armillaria* rot, or shoestring root rot — because of the black strands of fungus material it produces. The strands are properly called rhizomorphs. They are fungus strands that look like roots, or black shoe laces. There are other species and varieties involved in the *Armillaria* complex. The fruit body is a typical mushroom (Fig. 1) and in culture mycelium and rhizomorphs develop, especially on selected media.

Of course there are some major differences between the above ground trunk canker rots and the below ground root canker rots. The trunk canker rots are usually several meters above the ground and several meters on the trunk below the living crown. This is the trunk area that has many old, large, dead branches. Root canker rots, usually but definitely not always, are more common nearer the ends of the woody roots. This is bad because the root is a cone, and when the end portions are killed, all wood directly connected to the end portions may also be killed. The straight line connection to the tree butt is disrupted by other large branching roots. But, the root rots do have opportunities to grow upward toward the tree butt within the root tissues present at the time of infection. The tree does have safeguards against the straight path to the trunk. We will discuss these.

Woody "branch" roots age and die just as branches on trunks age and die. A root pathogen does not need to look long for openings into the woody roots; they are plentiful. They are at least as numerous as the dead branches and stubs. All branch stubs are not infected and all "branch" root stubs are not infected. Infections in trunks through dead branch openings take place when the branch protection zone does not resist the spread of a pathogen. As pointed out, some pathogens are well adapted to digesting the protection materials. Woody root openings from branch roots also have protection zones. The formation of effective protection zones takes a great amount of stored energy. When trees are stressed — stress is a reversible condition resulting from some disruption, drain, shunt, or blockage of energy — the defense system may suffer. Any abiotic or biotic agent that stresses a tree — energy — has the potential to weaken a defense system. When defense systems are weakened and a pathogen is present, infection usually takes place. Roots may also die as soil conditions block the formation of protection periderms in nonwoody roots. Pathogens may then enter the woody roots through the openings provided by the defenseless nonwoody roots.

There are 4 major parts to the *Armillaria mellea* disease: 1, infection; 2, bark spread and bark boundaries; 3, wood spread and wood boundaries; 4, breakdown of wood—rot—within the boundaries. A major part of the confusion with armillaria root rot is the mixing of all 4 parts.

The rhizomorphs are abundant in nature. The black fungus strands encircle dead roots and healthy roots. It appears that stress, or energy drain, is a major predisposing factor for root rot. If this were not the case, every tree would have the disease. The fungus can overwhelm young trees where the inoculum is so very high from roots and stumps of large recently cut trees. The fungus can be very aggressive, but this is not the usual way the fungus attacks. The fungus is a coassociate of many other diseases. As beech trees die from beech bark disease, Armillaria is there. The same can be said for species of Eucalyptus with other types of diseases. The Armillaria pathogen can be such a rapid secondary that it often appears as the primary agent of the problem.

Stress is a temporary energy alteration condition. It is not correct to call stress a problem until the condition progresses to an irreversible state. That irreversible state is best described as strain. When animals are strained, they heal. When trees are strained, they compartmentalize. Animal healing requires high amounts of energy. Tree compartmentalization also requires high amounts of energy. If compartmentalization must occur when energy reserves are low, the pathogen will have the advantage, and when they get the advantage they usually take it. The tree can still eventually set boundaries and wall off the pathogen, but at the great price of losing a great volume of wood that normally stores energy reserves. This is still not so bad, so long as the tree has time to generate new energy storing tissues in a new spatial location. The generation of such new cells also demands more energy. Now comes the risky part: If the tree does not get infected again while it is at this low energy point, it will regain its energy reserves. But, if new agents cause more tree problems, the tree will be in serious trouble. This is the time when new insect defoliation could be very difficult for the tree.

What can be done? The first answer is always prevention. Try to keep stress from going to strain. Some early warning signals are insect defoliators that repeat their feeding within the growth period, or that repeat the next year, soil moisture extremes—too wet, too dry—compaction, salt applications repeated, over pruning, especially at bud break, over use of soil chemicals for killing weeds, construction damage to roots and trunks, change in drainage patterns, new swimming pools or new decks and patios, new overuse and improper use of injections and implants, over fertilization, soil fill, wrong tree in the wrong place, and the list goes on. You know them all. The real problem is that tree help is not wanted until it is too late. The new tree biology says that we must focus on health, and maintaining health, and not trying to bring the trees back from the dead.

Armillaria root rot, like so many tree problems, has been greatly enhanced by the action of people. If people are the problem, the solution will be to inform people how they hurt trees.

Once armillaria root rot starts spreading, most trees die very quickly. The problem again, is that the disease may be spreading under ground and unseen for many years. The tree then reaches a threshold, and the curve bends abruptly to death.

Trees can generate (not *regenerate*) new roots. I have dug out many trees that had root rot. In some cases, the trees produced an abundance of bushy, small woody roots close to the base of the tree. The leaves and general condition of the trees appeared very good. Yet, the trees had very few large, woody, healthy, support roots. The trees were in a forest, so they were "braced" by their neighbors. If the same trees were in an open situation, they would fall over. The point remains that some trees can produce new roots as fast as the pathogen takes old roots. The new roots will support the life process of the tree but not the mechanical support of the tree. When a tree falls down and there are no more roots, the tree will die. Loss of mechanical support is one of the ways all organisms die. If such a new root system can be encouraged by proper watering and fertilization, an infected tree could be kept alive. The tree would require crown reduction, and a frequent visual checking to make certain it was not losing mechanical support. Watering and fertilization close to the trunk may encourage new roots on those trees that produce them.

If a suspect root rot tree is a tree that was released from a group of trees within the last 10, or 15, years, the tree should be viewed as a very high risk for failure. Be on the alert for recent edge trees—trees now on the edge, that were protected by others at an earlier time. Be quick to inform clients, or supervisors, of any suspect hazard trees. Do it in writing. This point can not be emphasized enough. Too many people have been killed!

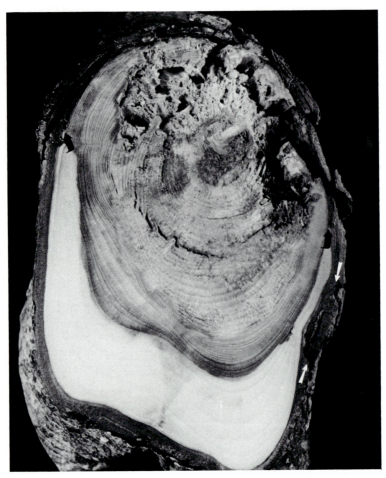

This butt sample of red spruce, *Picea rubra*, shows some of the points discussed (Fig. 2). The black arrow at right shows where the first fungus bark wedge was stopped. Follow the growth increment around the trunk to see where the wedge stopped on the other side. The black arrow at left shows a more recent fungus wedge. Only a thin strip of clear wood remains at this point. The fungus does have access to all the wood present in the butt at the time the wedge was stopped. How far the fungus spreads will be determined by the resisting force of the reaction zone. The white arrows show the vertical tip of a wedge starting from a lower point on the sample. The fungus spreads in the bark first. In eucalyptus trees, bark spread has been measured in meters up from the base. The bottom of the sample shows the increase in growth rate after infection. The tree rapidly began to regain the space for storing enough reserves. Note also that the decay spread to the center of the tree. *Armillaria mellea* will spread rapidly into wood that is starving behind the killed cambium. If the wood had been altered previously, the *Armillaria* fungus seldom grows into such wood.

Figure 29-2

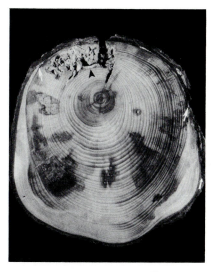

Figure 29-3

The 2 samples shown here are from the same red spruce. Figure 3 is from the butt, and figure 2 is 20 centimeters above the butt. The fungus did not spread into the center of this spruce (pointer). As already pointed out, *Armillaria* does not grow in heartwood, or wood altered by other injuries or altered by the false heartwood type of alteration. The 2 upper white arrows show the limits of the first 2 bark wedges. The lower arrow at right shows another wedge. The butt has lost almost all of its storage space. The tree is set for starvation. The upper sample shows the thin band of clear wood capable of storing energy. The white arrows show the barrier zone from the first infection. The discolored wood outward beyond the arrow is from the newer infection. As new roots die, new columns of infected wood form.

Note the many growth increments in the center of the tree.

Figure 29-4

Figure 29-5

Figure 29-6

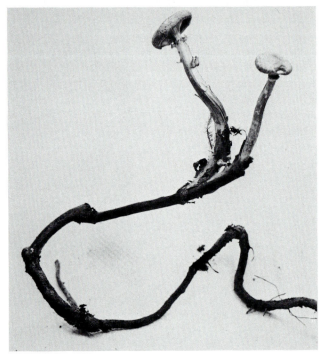

Mushrooms or fruit bodies of *Armillaria mellea* and other species usually develop late in the growing season for the trees. Some mushrooms also form mid-season. And, others are still forming long after the leaves have fallen. I believe we may have many varieties of the fungus. I have seen many cluster areas of *Armillaria*. The trees will be dead, and many new sprouts will be forming from the base. The sprouts usually do not persist. I have also seen fruit bodies on stumps 3 and 4 years after apparently healthy trees were cut. The fungus may have already been in the roots. Another point of interest about the fruit bodies is that they are quickly infested by fungus gnats and other insect larvae. Spores of some fungi pass through the guts of insects before they germinate. It is difficult to germinate the spores of *A. mellea*. I wonder whether the *Armillaria* spores must also pass through an insect gut. The fungus gnats do go back into the soil to complete their life cycle.

On living and dying trees, the mushrooms often appear in the sunken area between 2 roots, as shown in figure 5. The bottom of roots decay first, and the decayed root bottoms meet at the sunken spot at the base of the trunk. Note the crack above the mushrooms. Root rots are common starting points for basal cracks on balsam fir, birch, and many other species. Be suspect of basal cracks as an indicator of root rot. Be especially suspect when dark liquids flow from the cracks. On some tree species the bark at the base of root rotted trees will appear water-soaked. Thin strips of sunken bark vertical on the trunk to over several meters may also signal root rot. Another strange indicator that is usually reliable, but poorly understood, is the heavy resin pitching from old branch openings on conifers with root rots, especially the spruces.

Figure 6 shows the mushrooms on a dead root. The mushrooms may grow on dead roots in the soil and appear as if they are growing directly out of the soil. Mushrooms may also grow for several meters up the trunk of recently infected trees.

The fungus also produces large patches of fungus material that looks like white sheets of thin rubber. The mycelial fans, as they are called, form under infected bark. They are reliable indicators of *Armillaria*.

Other features of the infected roots are the rhizomorphs about the roots. A root that has been infected will crackle when squeezed.

Figure 29-7

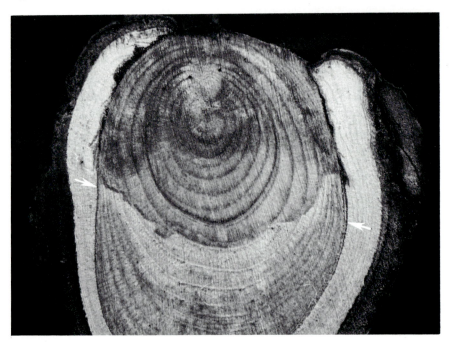

Figure 29-8

402

The patterns and some of the features of *Armillaria mellea* are similar to those of other fungi that rot roots. It should also be mentioned that fungi other than the Hymenomycetes also rot roots; the nonwoody roots. The most infamous fungi in this group are the *Phytophthora* species—*P. cactorum,* and *P. cinnamomii.* These fungi have mobile spores that can swim to their infection courts. They attack the fine nonwoody absorbing roots. When the root periderm is weak at the base of the absorbing roots, the fungi spread into woody roots and kill cambium. These fungi are the principle agents involved in the dieback of jarrah in Australia. When the trees are stressed, and the defense systems are not functioning properly, the pathogens spread and kill. The same story over and over again. The only different part of this over repeated story is that man never wants to assume the blame for starting the problem. Instead, man will spend enormous amounts of money trying to blame some other agent.

Figure 7 shows a root wound and the white arrows show the root barrier zones. Portions of roots die for a number of reasons. The tree compartmentalizes the infected wood. And, again, this is at the high risk of losing valuable storage space for energy. We have dug roots in the forest where no machine had gone. We still find many roots with dead spots.

Figure 8 shows a close up of a hemlock root that is 2 centimeters in diameter. The white arrows show the sharp barrier zone. The boundaries of the reaction can be seen in the sample. Roots do compartmentalize. Roots have 2 major functions: absorption of water and elements for the entire tree, and mechanical support for the tree. I question whether a major function of roots is to store energy for other parts of the tree! I believe roots store energy *mainly* for themselves, and for generating new roots. Roots are captive organs. They must "trade" their elements, water, and mechanical support for *food.* They can not make food. (And, of course, fertilizers or elements are *not tree food.*) When roots do not get food, they starve. When roots starve, the entire water and element balance of the tree is disrupted. To fertilize heavily roots that are starving is "the kiss of death." The fertilizers— nitrogen mostly—will stimulate the roots to use their low food supplies all the faster.

Trees seldom die from starvation. Long before they can ever starve to death, any number of opportunistic organisms infect and drain the last amounts of energy from the still living but defenseless tree. We then blame the most obvious pathogen for the death of the tree.

Figure 30-1

A New Tree Biology

CHAPTER 30

Root Rot

No, we are not done with root rots, and especially *Armillaria mellea*, yet. There is still much more to show and tell. We will now concentrate more on hardwoods.

Figure 1 shows an aspen that had a large root killed by *Armillaria*. The black arrows on the cross section of the trunk show the barrier zone. The longer arrows on the cut surface of the root show another barrier zone.

Root rots are some of the major trees problems worldwide. Soils and niches for trees and associated organisms have been so damaged, that root pathogens are spreading rapidly. Before the axe and saw, nature did not know a stump. Trees rarely broke at the base. Trees either fell, pulling up their roots, or trunks broke several meters from the ground. The cutting of forests has left an unbelievable amount of dying wood underground. When trees die and break in the virgin forest, rot is advanced in most cases. The harvesting of healthy trees and the abandoning of roots, leaves the roots in a trapped condition for starvation. There was no way for the living roots to get food, unless they were grafted to roots that were still part of the whole tree. The point is, that harvesting did give these pathogens that grow best on starving roots optimum conditions. The pathogens built up their populations to great amounts. So great that they could attack roots that were only beginning to starve, or even healthy roots.

I am not against harvesting trees. I believe in cutting trees to serve many of the needs of man. I am against poor forestry practices that take so much so fast that the trees *and* their soil associates do not have time to recover from the shock. To continue to have ultramodern, rapid harvesting methods, and no *long term* forest plans will cause the health of our forests to decline. We are beginning to see some of this now. And, again, we are looking for a short-term destructive agent to blame.

The organisms in the soil are doing only what they do best: take out the weaklings. What is the answer? Long term management plans. It has taken a few centuries to get into the problem. It will take us a few centuries to get out of it.

Root rots are also city tree problems, and orchard tree problems. Damaged soils and associates are the major cause. Trees depend on their soil associates. And, the soil associates depend on the trees. If the top is changed—the trees—then the bottom—soil associates—will change. When the top is zigging and the bottom is still zagging, problems will result, and root rots are the major types of problems.

We must find better ways to help soil associates after tree harvesting. Adding fertilizer may or may not be the answer. It may be necessary to treat the soil in other ways. We need this type of information badly.

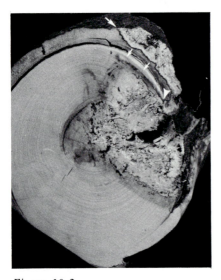

Figure 30-2

Figure 30-3

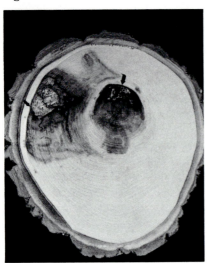

The fungus wedge in the bark of this aspen is very clear (Fig. 2, large white arrow). Dark, bark defense boundaries separate the wedge from the phloem and vascular cambium. The small white arrows show the size of the trunk when the cambium was killed to the point of the white pointer. When the bark wedge advances again, only the small band of clear wood beyond the small white arrows will have stored energy for defense. Note that the decayed wood is surrounded by discolored wood—the reaction zone. Wall 2 of CODIT has been pushed to the pith, so it no longer exists. Walls 3 are very strong in the tree. They resist lateral spread. Isolations for microorganisms from the discolored wood commonly yield bacteria and imperfect fungi. Note the dark lines between the decayed wood and the discolored wood.

Figure 3 is a section from the trunk of an aspen that has 2 pockets of decayed wood associated with *Armillaria mellea*. The arrows show the barrier zones and the places where the decay was most advanced. Note the band of clear wood separating the 2 columns. We suspect that the wood that forms after wounding may be more resistant to further infection than normally produced wood. Not to belabor the point of multiple columns, but it is always beautiful to see how the columns from different sources remain separate.

Figure 30-4   *Figure 30-5*

Figure 30-6   *Figure 30-7*

The white patches of mycelium — mycelial fans — of *Armillaria mellea* are shown in figure 4. The bark above and to the sides is cut away to show the limits of the fungus in the bark.

The bark was removed from the wet-appearing bark at the base of this paper birch (Fig. 5). Some mycelial fans were present.

Basal cracks, collar cracks, may be associated with root infections of *Armillaria mellea* (Fig. 6). The cracks are usually at the base only (Fig. 7), but they may start secondary cracks that propagate high on the trunk (Fig. 6). The cracks may be started by *Armillaria mellea*, but frequently other fungi, such as *Fomes igniarius* (Fig. 7, arrow), will infect the wood exposed by the cracks.

Root Rot   407

Figure 30-8

Figure 30-9   Figure 30-10

Many fungi other than *Armillaria mellea* cause root rots. Most root rotting fungi do not spread from roots far into trunks. There are always exceptions. *Fomes applanatus*, the artist's conk, is a fungus that will attack the roots, butt, and trunk of trees. The fungus is unique in its amplitude; it will grow in living trees and for longer periods in wood after the tree is dead. (The fungus, *Hypoxylon deustum*, I think, takes the record for amplitude. It will remain for many years on dead, rotting wood. The fungus is called the "coal fungus" because the black fungus tissue that holds the sexual bodies looks like chunks of tar or coal.) American beech and European beech have very strong butts. This is one reason they live so long in spite of many injuries. When a basal wound on beech is infected with *F. applanatus* (Fig. 8), the fungus will grow rapidly in the butt and roots (Fig. 9). Figure 10 shows the normal pattern of defect associated with wounds low on the trunk.

A special note about beech: Beech is a tough tree, but it has a very sensitive root system. This may be because it has an obligatory association with mycorrhizae. Soil damage near beech usually results in serious problems for the beech.

City trees also have many root and butt problems. This large eucalypt in California (Figs. 11 and 12) is a high risk hazard tree. The tree was topped and there were many large, high dead branches. The road limited root spread, and the fungus *Polyporus sulphureus* was fruiting on the roots, and in a crack (arrows) high on the trunk. Such trees with dead tops, dead horizontal branches, trunk cracks, and sporophores of aggressive decay fungi on the roots and trunk are flashing red lights for high risk hazard to property and people.

Hazard trees are on the increase because people are squeezing trees into smaller spaces and mutilating them in a variety of ways. It is bad enough when power lines and property are destroyed, but when people are injured, and killed, then it is time to wake up.

The eucalypts in California are a case in point. People like them because they grow fast. I am always told how fast they grow. Then when they get big, the same people want them small again. So, the loppers come in and do the job—cheap. I believe this is not only not right for the people who get injured by falling limbs, but it is unjust for the trees.

Figure 30-11

Figure 30-12

CHAPTER 31

Fomes annosus

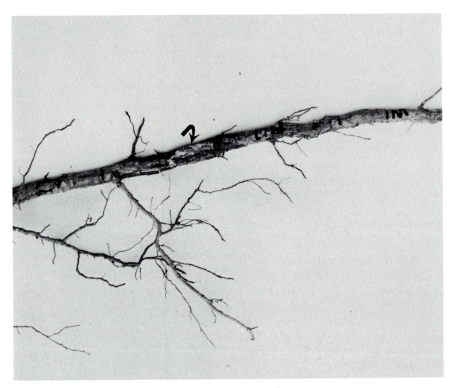

Figure 31-1

Fomes annosus (*Heterobasidion annosum*) is another root rot fungus that causes considerable damage, especially to conifers in plantations in warm climates. The fungus infects trees through roots that are injured (Fig. 1, arrow) and openings left by branch roots. The fungus also infects the surface of recently cut stumps. As the healthy wood begins to die, it is an easy target for the fungus. The fungus can then grow into all the roots. If some of the roots are grafted to roots of trees that are still living, the fungus can spread to the living trees. Root grafts are ways root rot pathogens can spread from one tree to another. In attempts to control the fungus, many stump treatments have been tried. The few that now appear effective are the application of borax and the introduction of the fungus *Peniophora gigantea*, which quickly colonizes the stump surface and resists colonization by *H. annosum*.

Figure 31-2

Figure 31-3

Infections in the roots are compartmentalized, but as more and more roots are infected, large portions of the tap root are killed. Roots that survive or portion of roots, grow rapidly. The points in figure 2 show the size of the tree base (*Pinus resinosa*) when several large roots and most of the thick tap root were killed. A barrier zone formed. The still living roots within the pointer area increased their growth rates. The new root wood could maintain energy reserves and mechanical support. Note that the decayed wood spreads within the resin-soaked wood.

Figure 3 shows a longitudinal section of an infected red pine, *Pinus resinosa*. The arrows show where the trunk wood resisted upward spread of the pathogen.

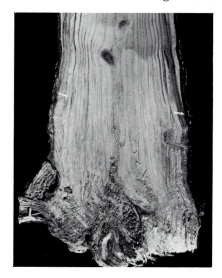

Figure 31-4

A New Tree Biology

The long dead spots on the roots and trunk of this hemlock *Tsuga canadensis* (Fig. 4), were caused by a fungus that does not rot the wood, *Verticicladiella* spp. (or a species in the *Leptographium* complex). The dead areas follow the tissues associated with the roots. Stress is a major factor for these root problems. Trees with injured roots and trees that were in and near recently logged areas often are infected. When many dead spots connect, the tree will die. Wet spots at the bases of the trees are early signs of problems. The wet spots usually are most obvious near the end of summer while temperatures are still high.

Stress seems to be the major predisposing factor for a great number of root rots. Stress means energy problems. By the time the problem is recognized, the chances for helping the tree are not good. People often think that trees are easy to treat, and "cure." We just can not turn some situations around once they go to a point of threshold. When this happens then risks for damage to property and people must get first priority. We must also remind ourselves that with all the billions spent on many human diseases, people still die. There are limits to what can be done in some cases. It is often better to start over again with a new tree than try to save a tree that has many problems. I am very much aware of the other side of the story. Some people want nothing spared in attempts to save an "old friend" or an historic tree. I have seen some trees in Europe that have more iron in them than wood. I believe trees should be trees, and look like trees, and when their time comes, they should die with dignity. It is sad to see the old trees full of braces. Yet, some people feel this is not only proper, but that the trees (?) are attractive. Now we get to the subject of what one person finds attractive and another finds sad. The world is full of exceptions, and I agree some old veterans still look attractive in spite of many braces. But, they are very rare. In the U.S.A., geriatric tree care is not so common. I am all for maintaining traditions — trees — that are still healthy. But, to maintain a tradition (trees and tree care is my subject) just to maintain the tradition, while the trees are reduced to grotesque figures, is something I do not understand. But, then, there is much that I do not understand.

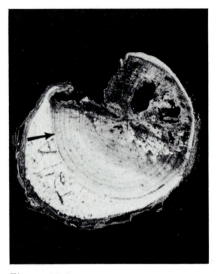

Figure 31-5

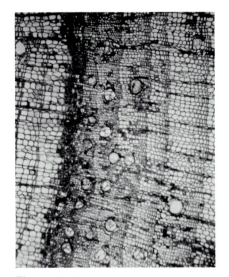

Figure 31-6

Figure 31-7

Figure 31-8

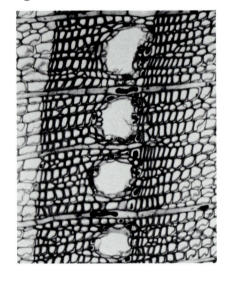

A New Tree Biology

Before we end this section, let us look again into some roots to see their make up.

Figure 5 shows a well-compartmentalized column of discolored and decayed wood in a larch, *Larix laricina*. The arrow shows the barrier zone.

Figure 6 shows a white pine root near a natural wound. Many resin ducts formed in the wood formed 5 years after the wound. The normal patterns of cells did not resume until 5 years after the wound. Root storage is still only in the parenchyma cells, and they are not too abundant in conifers.

Figure 7 is a section from a hemlock root, *Tsuga canadensis*. The dark cells are the barrier zone. Cells that normally would have differentiated to form tracheids, remained as cells with living contents that were changed to protection substances.

Figure 8 is a barrier zone in larch. Large resin ducts were in the thick-walled barrier zone.

Injury and infection leads to changes in anatomy and physiology. Roots have strong protection features and defense systems. If this were not the case, trees could never survive with the abundance of potential pathogens in the soil. When pathogen populations are very high, they may be able to attack some portions of healthy tissues. We must also remember that most of the trees that start life do not live very long. The root pathogens are always at work with plenty of material. Indeed, only the very strongest trees have a chance to survive.

CHAPTER 32

Tree Treatments

A third of the people in the world still use wood as the major fuel for cooking and heating. Wood is the major building material in many places on earth. Trees and people have always had a close association. The association has been primarily a taking situation for man. Man still wants more and more from trees. It is time to do something for trees. That is what this book is all about.

Over the last few centuries many people have tried to help trees, and many people have helped trees. There have been many programs designed to plant more trees, to prune and fertilize trees, and to treat their wounds and to give them medicines for their diseases. The intentions have been very good. It would be very unkind to criticize the people who have tried to help. They did many correct and proper treatments for trees in line with the conditions of their time. They were not wrong in their concerns and actions for trees. They did the best with the information available. But, time changes many things. We now have bigger machines in the forest, more pollution, bigger cities, wider roads; and you know the whole story. We must keep pace with these changes in our attempts to help trees.

Science advances as old concepts and principles are reexamined and adjustments are made. To survive, a constant feedback system must be in action all the time. Send out a signal to learn how everything is functioning, and be quick to recognize the response that comes back, and make the necessary corrections or adjustments.

The major intention of this book is to give a new view of trees, and their problems and care. It is not the intention to say anybody was wrong. The world around trees has gone from zig to zag, and we must also go from zig to zag in the way we perceive trees. Just think for a moment all the recent discoveries about our own bodies that have lead to new ways to treat old problems. Think of the problems that were "cured" by heat, and now we are told to do just the opposite; apply cold! We have made an about face on many human treatments. We also have human problems from pollution and radiation that did not exist a few decades ago. My point is that we must constantly reexamine and adjust, we must have a constant feedback system, or we will be zigging while something else will be zagging.

A major problem with tree treatments in the last few centuries is that they have followed too closely the treatments given to people. Cover the wound with a dressing, clean the cavity, sterilize the exposed wood, stimulate "healing by stimulating callus," blame the frost for everything that you don't understand, etc. It is interesting to note that few wounds resulting from surgery today are covered with dressing. The doctors want the wound to be exposed to the air as soon as possible.

Let's talk about cavities for awhile. Carries, or decay of teeth, has been the most common human disease for centuries. False teeth were common on most people (who could afford them) 50 years ago. False teeth or few teeth in people over 50 years old was common. Today, most people over 50 still have most of their teeth. Yes, better methods for filling cavities have been developed, but that is not the answer to fewer people with false teeth. The answer is better diets, better programs for prevention, better sanitation, and better programs on awareness of the potential problem. This is the way we must go with trees! We need to focus more on what makes trees healthy, and less on trying to bring back the dead. We need a new attitude about tree care. The most difficult thing to adjust is an attitude. The only way the attitude will be adjusted is when people see that new methods not only help trees to be more healthy, attractive, and safe, but the methods will save them money or make them money. This goes all the way from forest industries, to orchards, to cities, and to the trees about your house.

Figure 33-1

A New Tree Biology

CHAPTER 33

Pruning

Pruning is one of the oldest agricultural treatments. It is still the major tree treatment where people come in contact with trees throughout the world. Pruning is essential in orchards, along power lines, where fast growing conifers are grown in plantations, for bonsai; and the list goes on. Pruning is done for many reasons; regulating shape, size, health, flowers, fruit, wood quality, safety, and again, the list goes on. You know all of this!

Pruning has been the subject of hundreds of studies for 2 centuries. In spite of some people saying that the branch collar should not be cut, the recommendations have been to cut branches as close as possible to the joining stem — a flush cut — and then paint the wound with some material to prevent rot. Although this has been the recommendation, many people did not follow it because they felt that the "shoulder wood," or "heal collar" should not be injured and removed. Many people over the last 50 years, at least, have questioned the benefits of wound dressing.

When the hand saw was the major tool for pruning, most cuts were proper. It was much faster and took less work to cut the branch at its smallest point, which was the position where the branch met the branch collar. The real troubles started when small power saws were used for pruning. The raised ridge within the branch crotch just made a natural fit for the powerful saws. But, this was good, they thought, because now the old recommendations were being followed. And, the flush cut did stimulate rapid growth of callus that "healed" the wound. So, all this was thought to be good. Of course, we know that it was anything but good.

Flush cuts and cuts that leave stubs are major starting points for many tree problems: discolored wood, decayed wood, cavities, resin pockets that do not accept preservatives in wood products, circumferential cracks (ring shakes), radial cracks and seams (frost and sun cracks), wetwood, a host of different cankers, energy depletion about the wound that invites insects, and dead strips on the trunk that may continue downward to roots. This information is not new to many people who have worked closely with trees for years.

As people and trees get even closer, pruning will become more important for the health of the tree, and for our safety. Power lines and trees can be compatible, if we start early with planting and pruning programs (Fig. 1). Let us discuss some specific points of the subject.

Figure 33-2

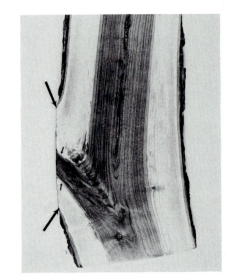

Figure 33-3

Figure 33-4

Figure 33-5

Black walnut trees, *Juglans nigra*, that had 13 and 25-year-old pruning cuts were dissected and studied starting in 1976. The trees were in Kansas (25-year-old pruning cuts) and southern Illinois (13-year-old pruning cuts).

Figure 1 shows a black walnut being cut for study. Note the well-closed pruning wound at 18 feet on the trunk. The trees that were pruned appeared very good. The type of pruning cut used on the trees is shown in figure 2. The large black arrows show the size of the typical flush cut. The small arrows show the width of the heartwood. Figure 3 shows the inside of a tree similar to that in figure 2, 13 years after a flush cut. The wound was closed. The open arrows show the band of discolored and decayed wood that developed in the branch above and below the wound. Note that the branch corewood was not decayed. The small arrows show the internal cracks associated or started by the wound. The finger points to the crack that opened at the end of the sample. Trees with internal defects of these types can not be used for high quality products such as veneer and gun stocks. The cracks cause the most serious degrade. The cracks may go far beyond the wound.

Figure 5 shows another flush cut after 25 years. The branch corewood is still sound. The decay-causing fungi, and insects spread above and below the wound in the trunk. The flush cut exposes the trunk tissues to the organism. The wound was closed. The black arrows show the decayed wood. The open arrows show the discolored heartwood. It is important to note that the wounds did close. The flush cut does stimulate callus formation. But, callus formation is not healing. The pathogens and insects quickly invaded the trunk tissues. Nature never knew this type of wound — flush cut — until saws and axes came. Nature developed a very effective protection system in the branch corewood. The flush cut removes the protection zone in the branch. But, even then some branch core wood still resists the pathogen. But, the sudden exposure of the trunk wood above and below the wound destroys the bands or circles of trunk collars that hold the branch onto the trunk. The flush cut removes the remarkable trunk collars. The pathogens and insects have the advantage, and they take it.

Figure 33-6

Figure 33-7

Black walnut, like most trees, forms a protection zone at the base of branches (Fig. 6, arrows). The decay-causing pathogens spread downward to the zone, and the decay facilitates shedding. The old thought was that longer lengths of clear wood could be obtained by cutting off the swollen branch collar. The removal of the collar made the quality much worse, not better. This was known for over a century. Foresters knew that the flush cut trees had more defects than trees that were not flush cut. So, why did they continue to do it? The answer: They still confused callus growth with healing. The flush cut did give large callus ribs. The thought was that "we know how to prune to promote healing, now we need a wound dressing to stop the rot." The search for that magic material still continues, while flush cuts take away nature's effective wound dressing!

Figure 7 shows a properly pruned branch (an accident, or a lazy technician?) after 25 years. Yes, there is still a small bump. But compare the bump with the well "healed" wounds in figures 4 and 5. The tree "healing" process will die slowly, or not at all with some people. Treating trees like people is fine in some ways, but in other ways, it will only cause problems.

A New Tree Biology

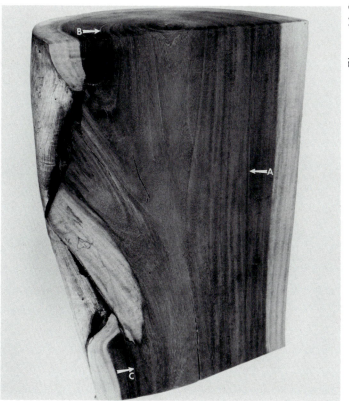

Figure 33-8

Tropical trees like this greenheart, *Hibiscus* species, or mahoe, respond as other trees to improper pruning cuts (Fig. 8). Many tropical trees form very large branch collars. Decay developed in the sapwood exposed by the wound. Much worse than the decay were the cracks that formed below (C), above (B), and to the opposite side of the wound (A). Because of the cracks, flush cuts greatly increase the risk for hazard trees. The cracks also greatly reduce the value of the trees for high value wood products.

Tropical trees have some unique problems associated with flush cuts or cuts that leave long stubs. Most tropical trees grow rapidly, and after a flush cut or stub cut, callus forms to close, or better, to almost close the wound. The fungi and termites work together to enter the nonprotected wood exposed by the wound. The rapid callus growth gives the impression that all is very well. I have heard it many times that "healing" is so rapid in the tropics that they do not need to worry about the type of pruning cut made. Then I ask, "What kind of problems do you have?" Termites. Termites. The fungi and termites spread rapidly into the exposed wood, and the thick callus growth give the impression of a well "healed" wound. Meanwhile, under optimum conditions — an almost closed wound, and freshly exposed wood with no protection zone — the fungi and termites have an easy life. Proper pruning is very important on *all* trees, and that means tropical trees.

Pruning

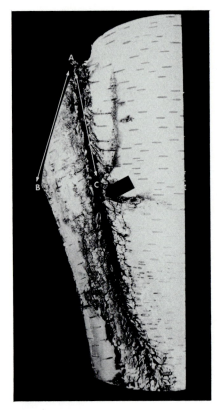 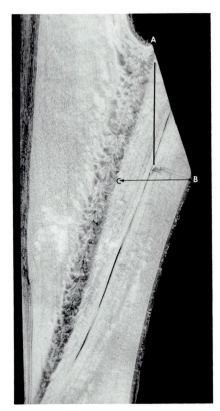

Figure 33-9   *Figure 33-10*

Figures 9 and 10 show the same paper birch sample on the outside and inside. The black arrow in figure 9 shows the upturned branch bark ridge (BBR). A proper cut goes from targets A to B. The angle of the cut, A to B, is at an angle opposite the BBR, or A to C.

Figure 10 shows the same targets from the inside. When target B can not be found, drop an imaginary line down from A; the target ABC makes a triangle where angle ABC = angle ACB, and the imaginary line bisects the triangle to form right angle on the line CB.

Never put any cutting tool behind target A.

The best time to prune for health is in the dormant period, especially near the end of the period. Be very careful when pruning at the time of leaf formation. Be very careful when pruning at the time of leaf shedding. If possible, avoid pruning at these times.

424   *A New Tree Biology*

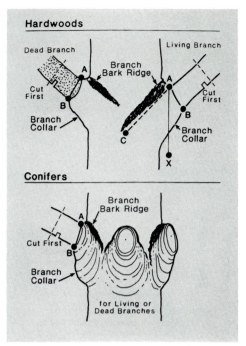

Figure 33-11

Here are diagrams (Fig. 9) that give the themes for proper pruning. I say themes because there are variations, as you will see later. Pruning properly done is one of the most difficult tree treatments. Every branch will be different.

Unless a branch is very small, a double cut method should be used; remove the branch safely leaving a stub and then remove the stub. Start by locating the branch bark ridge (BBR). Place the cutting tool as close as possible to the outer edge of the BBR within the branch crotch, target A. Target B is where the branch meets the bottom of the branch collar. Make your final cut from A to B. On large branches, it may be easier to cut from B to A with power tools. Use great care if you do this. Kick back could cause serious problems if the operator does not have great skill with the tools. When target B can not be found, then drop a line in your mind from target A downward (to target X). Angle XAC is approximately the same as angle XAB. It is still best to try to locate target B, if possible. The angle method is an approximation. When pruning dead branches, cut as close as possible to the swollen callus collar that surrounds the dead branch. Do not injure or remove the callus collar (called a branch collar in the diagram. See chapter on the branch).

The branch collar and BBR in conifers may circle the living and dead branches. Most conifers have very obvious swollen collars.

The pruning method is called Natural Target Pruning (NTP). Aim for the targets. Try to hit them. Do not try to "be safe" and leave a stub. A stub gives the pathogen a food source while they grow into the branch corewood. Do not leave stubs! Do not flush cut. Do not paint the cuts. Within a year the cut surfaces will turn the same color as the bark. Learn to recognize collars and the BBR.

Pruning   425

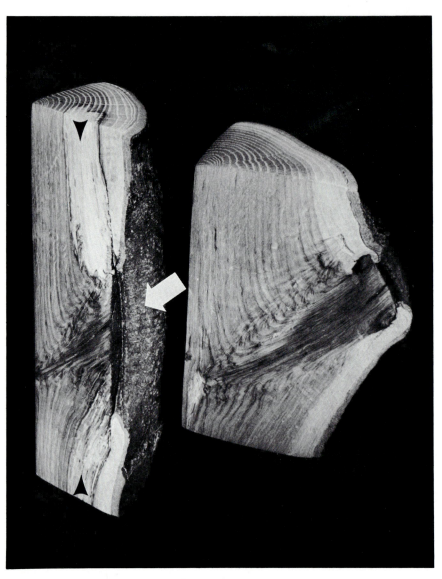

Figure 33-12

A New Tree Biology

The 2 red oaks, *Quercus rubra*, samples (Fig. 12) came from the same tree. Two living branches the same size were pruned—left, flush; right, proper—6 years before the tree was cut and dissected. The sample at left had large ribs of callus (white arrow) and a large pocket of decayed wood (pointers). The sample at right had a branch protection zone slightly below the cut surface, and no decay. The samples were typical of hundreds of others treated the same ways. Over an 8-year-period, 1200 trees of 12 species were pruned, cut at different time intervals after pruning, dissected longitudinally through the pruning cuts, and studied.

Decay developed rapidly in the trunk above and below the flush cut. The branch corewood did not decay. The wood behind the flush cut was hard and sound. Here lies one of the deceptions with flush cuts and wound dressings. The wood behind the flush cut may appear sound, and the wound dressing gets the credit. Many comments and claims about wound dressings have come without experiments with controls and without dissections. There are no data to show that wound dressings stop rot. There are no data to show that flush cuts that remove the protection zone and expose the trunk wood lead to less decay than properly cut branches.

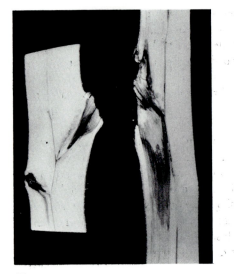

Figure 33-13

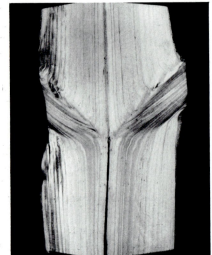

Figure 33-14

Figure 33-15

Figure 33-16

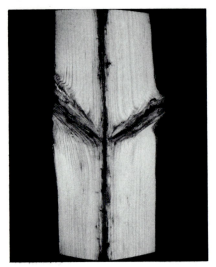

A New Tree Biology

The theme of flush cutting and proper cutting are shown in other samples in figures 13, 14, 15, and 16. The oak in figure 12 represented a heartwood forming hardwood. Figure 13 shows a birch, *Betula alleghaniensis*, and again similar sized branches from the same tree, 1 year after pruning. Pathogens spread very rapidly in birch. At left is the proper cut and at right the flush cut. A species of *Stereum* (*S. purpureum?*) infected the flush cut. The corewood was decayed as well as the trunk wood on the sample at right. It should be noted that species of *Stereum* are aggressive pathogens of several species of fruit trees in the genus *Prunus* (plums, mostly). The Stereum enters mainly through harsh, improper flush cuts and topping cuts. Proper pruning would reduce the number of infections.

Figures 14, 15, and 16 show conifers. Figure 14 is a white pine; left improper, right proper after 1 year. Conifers normally have resin-soaked branch corewood. The resin pockets and infections spread into the trunk above and below the flush cut at left. Figure 15 shows a red pine only 5 months after improper, left, and proper, right, pruning. It does not take long to see the internal effects. Figure 16 shows a flush cut on white pine after 6 months. The wound was not that large, but it did expose the trunk above and below the branch.

Conifers in plantations are often pruned. Cracks may also form after flush cutting branches. In Australia, I saw many recently cut logs of *Pinus radiata* that had circumferential cracks caused by flush cuts. Observation on pieces of culled boards — culled because of cracks — gave further proof that the cracks were caused by the old pruning wounds. Because the branches on conifers are in whorls, the wounds caused by several flush cuts about the trunk at one locus compound the injury.

As faster growing trees are developed, the need for pruning, especially pruning conifers in plantations, will increase. All the work done to produce and plant the trees would be wasted if the wood is cracked, discolored, or decayed because of improper pruning.

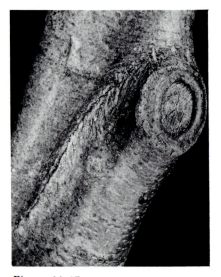

Figure 33-17

Figure 33-18

Figure 33-19

Figure 33-20

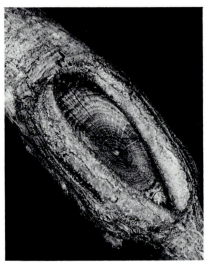

A New Tree Biology

When branches are cut properly, a ring, or "doughnut" of callus will form completely around the wound (Fig. 17). Aim for the targets and try to get the circle callus. The callus will form the growing season after the cut is made. If the pruning cut is too close at the A target in the branch crotch, the callus after the first growing season will not be complete at the top of the cut (Fig. 18). A flush cut will produce an oval shaped callus with weak growth above and below. Because of the shape of some branches, proper cuts will produce a slightly oval-shaped callus also. The point here is that the shape of the callus must be observed after the first growing season. Even a flush cut may produce a continuous callus about the pruning cut after several years. The callus method is a good way to check on your pruning cuts and those of your workers. (Caution: as some branches get larger, and as trunk collars do not close about branch collars below the branch, even proper cuts may leave a dead spot below branches. Another exception deals with included bark, which will be discussed in the next chapter.)

When branches tear out of the trunk as shown in figure 20, or when the cuts are made too close below the branch, the callus will not meet below the branch. When the double cut method for removing branches is not used, branches will often tear. This will cause a problem below the branch.

Callus will form above and below wounds when the cambium is alive about the margin of the wound. A common question is, "Will not wound dressing keep the cambium alive?" If proper cuts are made, the cambium will not be killed on the trunk. Time for a very important point. Proper branch pruning cuts remove the branch along the natural shedding line. The line separates branch from trunk. A proper cut removes the branch and does not injure the trunk. Next question, "Then why not be really safe and leave a stub?" The stub gives pathogens a chance to get established and to spread inward against the branch protection zone. The zone resists, not stops pathogens. The questions continue, "But, I'll cut the stub out the next year along the natural shedding line, and that will be the perfect cut; not so?" Can you imagine the work to recut hundreds of stubs? Not possible in a business world! Plus, many canker causing fungi will move in. Don't do it!

Figure 33-21

Figure 33-22

Figure 33-23

Figure 33-24

A New Tree Biology

Eucalyptus trees and tropical trees respond the same way to improper and proper pruning cuts. In figure 21, the upper pruning cut was proper and the callus rings the cut. The larger pruning cut below on the tree in figure 21, was much too close on the lower left side. Ants were very busy moving in and out of the exposed wood. The pruning cuts on the eucalypt in figure 22 were proper. The flush cut on the eucalypt in figure 23 was well painted. The wound was several years old, but there was still no callus above and below the wound indicating cambial dieback. Note the sunken trunk below the wound. Dark liquids flowed from the wound. The tree had obvious large pockets of decayed wood in the trunk. It was leaning over a heavily trafficked street — people and cars. The tree was a killer tree.

Figure 24 shows a dead branch on a *Chorisia speciosa*. When more than a third of the leaf-bearing branches are cut from the tips of larger branches, the larger branch may wane and die in many species. Some trees can tolerate their tips removed, others can not. The problem is common along power lines. Northern oaks can not tolerate the tips being removed. Some southern oaks will form many branch sprouts after tip pruning. Most of the northern oaks that receive such pruning will have branch decline and death. Trees like the species of *Tilia* and *Platanus* can tolerate harsh pruning.

This subject is a very different one and generalizations will only cause more confusion. A major point that must be considered is how much living wood in a branch is being supported by the branch tips that have leaves. The leaves must support the wood in the branch, and still "send" food for the tree trunk and roots. When small volumes of wood in a branch are supported by many twigs with leaves, such a branch could have more tips or twigs removed than a long branch with a high volume of living cells, and only a relatively small number of twigs with leaves. The ratio of wood in a branch to leaf area of the branch must be considered. The point remains, many dead branches can be seen along power lines where tip pruning has been done. I say, when in doubt, go back to the crotch for removal of the entire branch. Better to remove it than have it die a slow death.

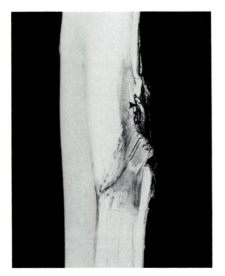

Figure 33-25

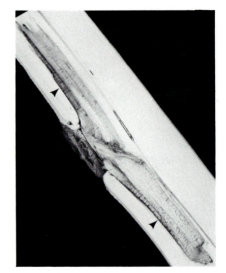

Figure 33-26

Figure 33-27

Figure 33-28

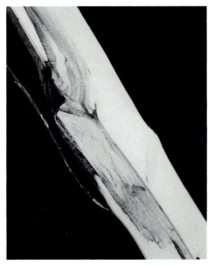

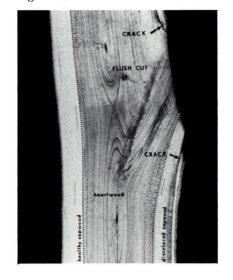

A New Tree Biology

Here are some additional samples that show the problems flush cuts start. Figure 25 is a yellow birch with a 1-year-old flush cut that left the stub with a ragged margin. *Stereum purpureum* (pointer) rapidly infected the wound. Many of the fungi that cause problems on orchard trees are wound pathogens that take advantage of improper pruning cuts and especially topping cuts. Experiments by orchard pathologists showed that proper pruning greatly reduced the incidence of infection by *Cytospora* sp. on peach.

Figure 26 is a red maple with a 2-year-old wound. The pointers show the strong barrier zone. A perennial canker has started in this wound. Two separate callus rings had formed about the wound. In some experiments, the pruning cuts removed the inner branch corewood that would normally be the position for the protection zone (Fig. 27). After 1 year the maple had cambial dieback far below the wound and advanced decay. All in 1 year! When you remove a defense system, the pathogens move swiftly.

Flush cuts are more injurious on some tree species than others. Species of *Prunus* are very sensitive to improper pruning. The black cherry in figure 28 had a 1-year-old flush cut. Cracks were forming above and below the wound (arrows). Note the 8 healthy growth increments on the left side of the sample. This is normal for the species. Above and below the flush cut at right only 1 growth ring of healthy wood is present. Discolored wood is dead wood, and it does not store energy reserves. The current growth increment requires energy until it is fully formed. The current increment will store energy at the end of the growth period. While the new growth ring is forming above and below flush cuts, the tree is starving locally above and below the wound. The tissues are highly vulnerable to insect attack at this time. Canker-causing pathogens also have an easy target. Sudden cold or sudden heat will also cause the single new growth increment to burst, or die. The very worst situation occurs when 2 or more flush cuts are in vertical alignment. We will see more of this, because such injury is common in some nurseries.

Figure 33-29

Figure 33-30

This ornamental pear in a nursery in California had a flush cut a year before the photograph was taken (figure 29). The callus ribs are only to the side of the wound. A sunken spot above the cut indicates cambial dieback. The wound was on the southwest side of the trunk. Heat injury occurred above and below the cut. Figure 30 shows another tree in the planting. The pruning cuts started the problem and the sun or heat did the rest. The trunk injury spread to the roots.

Sun and frost are commonly cited as the cause of all types of bark injuries. Yes, the heat or cold are a part of the problem, but, they seldom start such problems. The flush cut is a type of predisposition. The injury makes the tissues very vulnerable to other agents. We will discuss a similar problem that starts with incomplete graft unions. Heat and cold take the blame for this one also.

A practice in some nurseries is to let the young trees grow with low branches, because growth is increased, and especially diameter growth. Trees are often sold by their diameter measurement or caliper at a set position on the trunk. When sale time is near, the trees may receive a severe pruning. It is shortly after this time that I get to see some of the horror stories. Everything is blamed except the real cause: Severe over-pruning, and worse yet, flush cuts. Figure 31 shows an example of this treatment. The part that confuses the nursery person is that the bark or trunk injuries are usually much lower on the trunk than where most of the pruning cuts are. So, they think it must be cold, or heat, or something. As the columns of defect spread downward they coalesce and the columns get larger. Yes, cold or heat could also be a part of the story, but it is not the starter. If cold or heat were the only cause, then every tree should be affected. That is rarely the case.

Figure 32 is a reminder of a point made in the beginning of the book. It is not the size of the flush cut that makes it so injurious. It is the fact that the cut removes the protection zones and also exposes the trunk tissues. The 2 mechanical wounds on the samples were the same area as the flush cuts. The samples were prepared 1 year after the flush cuts and mechanical wounds were made.

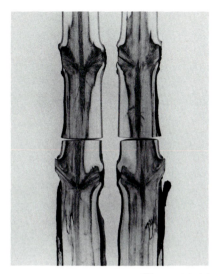

Figure 33-31

Figure 33-32

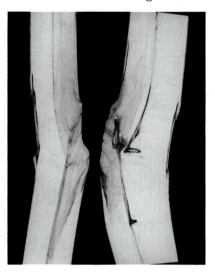

The point must be emphasized strongly that stubs, even small ones, should not be left after pruning branches. This is especially true for small trees in nurseries. In Europe, Nectria canker often start on small stubs, or on the injured trunk tissues from flush cuts. Figure 33 shows a black walnut that had a pruning cut that left a small stub. The pointers show the advance of a canker pathogen over 3 growing periods. I agree, you can not prune all branches perfectly, all the time. But, I do believe that the targets for pruning should be the aim of the person doing the pruning. In nursery work, be very careful with any type of pruning tool that crushes or tears the bark, especially if pruning is done when the bark is loose. Proper pruning does take skill and practice, but like any art form, once learned, the person can operate very quickly. I have seen too many horror stories that started in the nursery with poor pruning. Improper pruning on some trees such as species of *Tilia* and *Ulmus* will lead to trunk sprouts. Some trees do form basal sprouts and trunk sprouts normally (crepe myrtle, Linden). *Figure 33-33*

A New Tree Biology

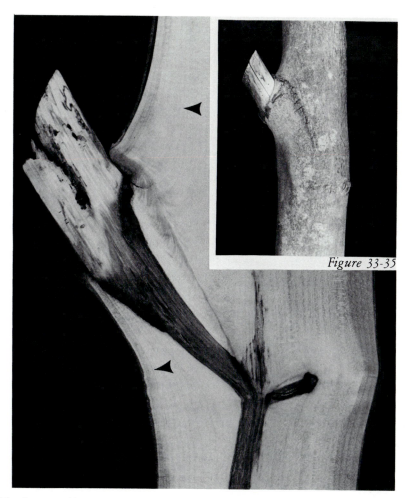

Figure 33-35

The longer stubs make perfect homesites for insects and potential pathogens (Figs. 34 and 35). The combination of insects and microorganisms have "pushed" the branch protection zone, and the microorganisms have spread to the center of the tree. The pointer below the branch (Fig. 35) shows the barrier zone. The pointer above the branch shows the diameter of the trunk above the branch when the branch died, or was cut leaving the long stub. Note the sunken spot under the branch in figure 34. As the trunk tissues below the branch that are connected to the branch wane after the branch was cut, the sunken spot results. As branches age and die normally on trees, the trunk tissues below the branches slow their growth while the trunk tissues above the branch continue to grow at their normal rate. This process results in a more cylindrical trunk. Trees that have large living branches low on the trunk usually have pyramidically shaped trunks. Branch death is a major factor affecting stem or trunk form.

Figure 33-34

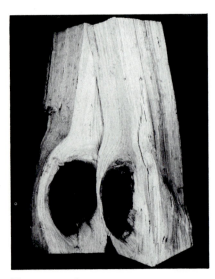

Figure 33-36

Figure 33-37

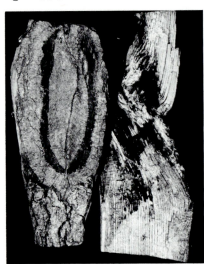

Arborists provided samples from old trees that had received many pruning cuts. The samples made it possible to study large, old cuts on large, old trees that were in the city. The sections in figures 36 and 37 came from the same old red oak from Iowa. Figure 36 shows a sample of a 6 inch branch cut properly 50 years before the tree was cut. The wound was closed and there had been no decay. Figure 37 shows a 6 inch branch that was flush cut to a wound of 11 inches 35 years before the tree was cut. The section at left (Fig. 37) was covering the flush cut. It is turned at a right angle here to expose the bark. Advanced decay and many insect galleries were in the wood exposed by the large wound. The original length of the cut is shown by the length of the crack and the length of the oval shown by the old wound dressing (left section). The wound was treated with a wound dressing. The wound never closed. The long vertical crack was on an opening that made conditions optimum for the pathogens. The pruning cut on the sample in figure 36 was closed. An almost closed wound does make conditions near perfect for pathogens. Be suspect of "closed" wounds that have liquids flowing from them.

The same common sense question must be repeated: If flush cuts are the best way to remove branches to promote healing, and wound dressings do stop rot, why do so many flush cut branch wounds that have been dressed have large pockets of decay? And further, why are so many of the old treated wounds so rotted that they must be cleaned out with all types of machines? This is primarily a practice in Europe.

A New Tree Biology

Axes, handsaws, shears, knives, and chainsaws are commonly used for pruning. Axe handle pruning is also used on conifers that have small dead branches. This is a dangerous practice for the person doing the job, and is injurious for the tree when crushed stubs are left. It is best not to try that type of pruning. Some people can use knives with great skill on small trees. Most hand shears make

Figure 33-38

straight cuts that injure or remove the branch collar. Some hand shears crush the trunk bark at the branch base. Small and large handsaws can be used to make proper cuts. Thin-bladed saws can make curved cuts. Chainsaws, especially small ones used by one hand, can cause serious injuries to people and trees. The blade fits too easily behind the branch bark ridge within the crotch. Big flush cuts increased in numbers when chainsaws came.

Hydraulically operated saws and shears are commonly used by arborists, especially when pruning trees near power lines. Figure 38 shows a circular saw, shears, and a chainsaw that are hydraulically operated. It is possible to make proper cuts with the tools, but you must be at right angles to

Figure 33-39

the branch to do it. Most all of the time spent in pruning is spent getting into the proper position for the cut while being in an aerial lift. Figure 39 shows a proper cut being made by the circular saw. The branch was removed on the down stroke, and the final cut made on the up stroke. The circular saw is not allowed on some power line jobs because it is too easy for operators to hedge cut the branches.

People who clear power lines from branches have a very difficult job. They need better tools.

The subject of pruning trees under and near power lines needs some additional comments. As stated, the job is a dangerous one and a difficult one. People demand electric power at all times. People want power restored very soon after trees fall on the lines during a storm. People also want big beautiful trees under and near power lines. There is no doubt that power line clearing injures and kills many trees. It is sad to see the topped trees dying. What can be done? Is there a way for trees and power lines to coexist? I believe that the answer is yes, but some changes must come from both directions; the power line owners, and the people who want trees near power lines.

If you start early, you can train a tree to be any size or shape. Consider the bonsai trees! The point is that the pruning must be started early. Trees that have the genetic capacity to grow fast and tall should not be planted near power lines. The elm was long thought to be an exception because it grew fast and big, but the branches developed far above the power lines. Many elms have died in the last few decades, and removal has been very costly near power lines. The new pruning information is being rapidly accepted by most power line companies. This is good because the workers now know how to properly remove branches. New tools are needed badly. New tools must be able to make proper cuts, not stub cuts or flush cuts.

Here is the real problem: money! It costs a great deal of money to keep lines clear of branches. Even small branches that may drain power from a line must be removed. It is not known how much power is drained by small branches touching the lines. Many of these branches come from branch sprouts that come from pruning wounds. Proper pruning will not stop sprouting on some trees, but proper pruning will decrease the number of sprouts. Sprouting means that the workers must return after 2 years with some trees. This short time interval really costs money. Money could be saved if longer contracts were given for the pruning. If longer contracts that started earlier were given the workers would do their very best to make certain they could minimize their repeat visits. So long as the specifications for clear lines was held, there would be no need for more frequent pruning.

The orchard people know how to grow dwarf trees. We need dwarf trees under power lines. It is better to see dwarf trees than mutilated trees.

During one of our last bad storms, many trees broke power lines. The trees that did this were not under the power lines, or even very near. The trees were those that had been released in the last 10 years because of house construction. The trees became edge trees with large tops and weak root systems.

I doubt that there is a way to make everybody happy (except the contract line clearing companies). We need some awareness programs to let the people know some of the problems. It is amazing how some people will make adjustments in their thinking after the third day without power.

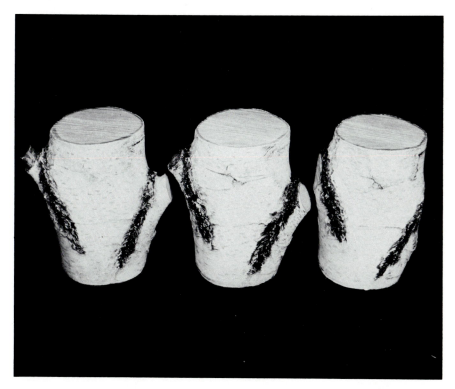

Figure 33-40

The 3 rubber models of paper birch bolts summarize the pruning story (Fig. 40). The model at left has a dead branch (left) and a living branch (right) cut too long. Do not leave stubs of dead or living branches. The model at right has a dead branch (left) and a living branch (right) cut too short. The callus collar was removed when the dead branch was cut, and the branch collar was removed when the living branch was cut — flush cut. Do not remove callus collars. Do not remove branch collars. Do not make flush cuts. The center model shows proper cuts for the dead branch (left) and the living branch (right). Do not paint the cuts. The color of the wound surface will blend with the bark within a year. If possible, prune during the dormant period, or after the leaves have matured. You can prune any time, but try to avoid pruning branches at the time leaves are forming and at the time leaves are falling.

Pruning can be dangerous. Small branches can cause serious problems, especially to eyes. If you are not a professional, call one if you must get on a ladder to do the job. Think safety.

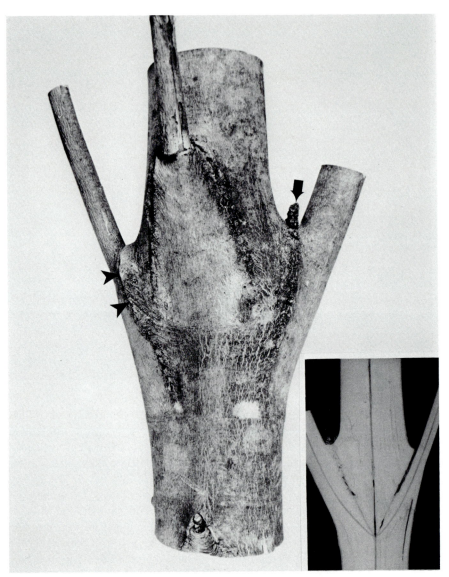

Figure 34-1   Figure 34-2

CHAPTER 34

Included Bark and Pruning

Proper pruning not only takes a great amount of skill; it also requires an understanding of the various tree parts that are to be removed. We loosely use the word branch for tree parts that have different patterns of tissues as they form unions with the other parts. What this means is that branches have different tissue arrangements from codominant stems, and both are different from epicormic branches—dormant buds, adventitious buds—and, to make matters more complex, we must also add the tissue patterns associated with included bark. Once these different tissue arrangements and their outer bark signs are recognized and understood, we will return to clarity and simplicity.

Let us start in the middle with included bark and work toward the ends—how it starts and how to deal with it. Start with the branch bark ridge, the outer bark ridge that forms as the cylinder of the branch expands and later—asynchronously— the joining stem or trunk expands. The branch bark ridge is bark tissue that gets pushed upward within the branch-trunk crotch. The bark ridge starts as a circle about young branches (review chapter on branches). A strong branch-trunk union is shown by a branch bark ridge that pushes upward.

Included bark means inner and outer bark that forms between the expanding cylinder of the branch and the trunk. The vascular cambium "turns" inward within the branch-trunk crotch. The branch bark ridge also turns inward to form an invaginated structure. If you hold your hands together with fingers extended, you have a strong branch bark ridge. If fingers from both hands are turned inward, you have a weak branch bark ridge because of included bark.

On some young branches, the vascular cambium turns inward as soon as the branch begins to form. The trunk cylinder and branch cylinder both expand, the inturned cambium becomes a wedge between the two cylinders. The expanding wedge greatly weakens the branch and may cause it to break off under very slight loading. What starts such early development of included bark is not known. It does cause some young branches to shed soon after they are formed.

Included bark may also have an intermittent pattern where it forms in the crotch for one or two years or more, and then the normal upward turning of the tissues will form for a few years. Included bark usually forms where branches have a tight or close angle with the trunk, but included bark also forms where the branch is horizontal. The point here is that angle alone does not start included bark. Included bark is common between codominant stems, but, again, this is not a rule because tight unions with an upward turning stem bark ridge also is common between codominant stems. These points indicate that the cause is not under strong, or even moderate, genetic control. It must be some local, short-term condition that starts the included bark. We do not know exactly what that condition is, but the synchronous development of branch and trunk may be one of the major factors. This condition could change over time, and this could help to explain intermittent included bark. It is also possible that a synchrony of branch and trunk could be under moderate genetic control. Another possibility is that local conditions or treatments of planted trees may bring about synchrony of branch and trunk.

On young trees, the sooner the branches with included bark are pruned, the better. If a young tree has many branches with included bark, and the branch is in a place where failure could damage property or people, the branch should be removed. Bracing a large branch that has included bark may not be a long-term solution.

Figure 1 shows some of the points discussed. The pointers show the inward turned bark. The arrow shows the upward turned bark that was so extensive that a pillar of bark formed within the crotch. Figure 2 shows the internal view of the red maple sample.

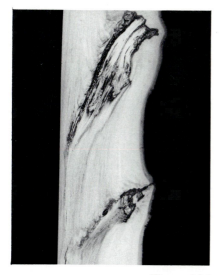 

Figure 34-3   *Figure 34-4*

The upper branch on the yellow birch had included bark. The decay was advanced within the branch corewood, but the decay did not spread into the trunk above or below the branch corewood. The included bark does act as a very strong protection boundary for upward spread of decay. (Upward spread of decay from branches is not common even where there is no included bark.) The lower branch had a small pocket of included bark. It is always good to see how well compartmentalization does function in trees. Trees do have very effective ways for confining their problems. Our health treatments must respect the natural boundaries.

The black cherry sample shown in figure 4 shows the inturned branch bark ridge, indicating included bark. The branch was killed by leaving a long stub, one year before the tree was cut. The strong, swollen living collar about the branch shows the position for a proper pruning cut (arrow). The targets for proper pruning are effective for removing branches that have included bark. If this branch were alive, the line of cut would be the same as shown here by the swollen basal ring. Cut as close as possible to the swollen ring, but do not injure it or remove it. This branch would require the final cut to be made on the up stroke.

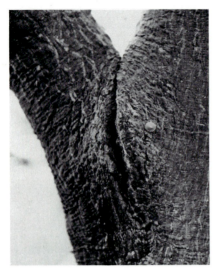

Figure 34-5

Figure 34-6

Back to a tropical tree, the silk floss tree, *Chorisia speciosa*, to show some points about included bark and pruning. Figure 5 shows a deeply inturned branch bark ridge. In figure 6 there is triple trouble: included bark, a sharp bend in the branch to horizontal, and an old flush cut wound exactly at the weakest point on the branch. Be on the alert for this combination. It ranks at the top of the list for potential failure. Learn to examine the bend in the

A New Tree Biology

Figure 34-7

Figure 34-8

branch, and look for cracks, wounds, or old stubs near the bend. Figure 7 shows the very obvious collar (arrow) on the branch. To the right of the branch is a recent flush cut. Figure 8 shows a swollen, healthy, collar about a living branch. The collar should not be injured or removed. (People who make flush cuts should be made to slide down this tree.)

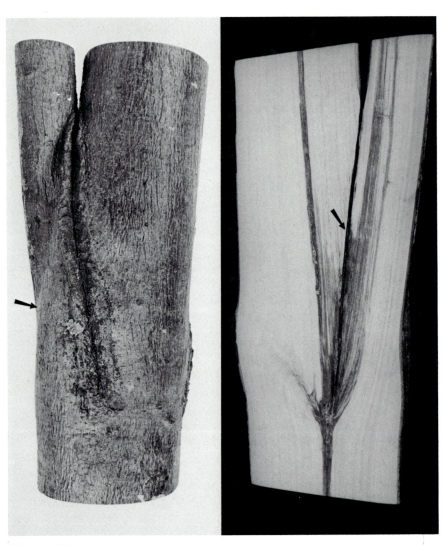

Figure 34-9

Included bark is on young and old trees, hardwood trees, tropical trees, and conifers (Fig. 9). Note the sunken spot (arrow) at the base of the branch at left on the eastern white pine. The inside view also shows the sunken spot. Bark separates the trunk from the branch. The expanding cylinders of trunk and bark squeezed the vascular cambium to death midway in the sample. The trunk and branch responded to the double cambial injury and death by forming resin-soaked wood. The band of resin-soaked wood developed much farther up the branch than the trunk. Spots, or dots or resin ducts, did form in the trunk wood above the point of cambial death. In a sense, the trunk has been competing with the branch that turned upward as both buds began to develop at the same time.

A New Tree Biology

Figure 34-10

This red oak sample adds a few more factors to the story of included bark (Fig. 10). The small white arrows point to the dormant bud trace that grew later into the branch. The open small white arrows point to the dead spot that formed as the included bark of trunk and branch squeezed the vascular cambium to death. The white pointer shows where the heartwood formed. Note the dark lines in the bark. The large white arrow shows a point of rejoining the wood of the branch and the trunk. The sample also gives us an opportunity to see very wide, large bands of rays (black pointers).

Learn to read trees, inside and out. It is always exciting to see the many many variations on a theme. It is much better to think of them as variations rather than exceptions to a rule. Rules are just too absolute for mother nature. The sample in figure 10 could be the basis for a long discussion. How many other things do you see in this sample? From all we have discussed, I hope you can see at least 10.

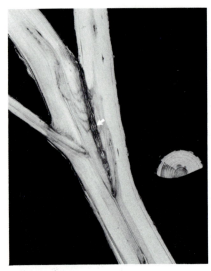

Figure 34-11

Figure 34-12

Included bark (arrow) in American elm (Fig. 11) and a species of *Angophora* (white arrows) (close to *Eucalyptus*) from Australia (Fig. 12). In the elm sample, note the dark lines that formed as the cambium was killed. The lines are midway in the sample. In the *Angophora* sample, instead of dark lines, veins of kino (small arrows) formed. The included bark in the *Angophora* formed in large pockets. The kino veins and the dark lines in figure 10 (see white pointer); again, we have a theme. As cells age and die as they are squeezed to death, the tree responds to form a chemical boundary. The variations are in elm, oak, and *Angophora*. The included bark in the elm sample is between codominant stems. The stem at left was infected by *Ceratocystis ulmi*, the fungus that causes Dutch elm disease. The fungus was in the other stem at right, also. Only one thin growth increment was healthy in this sample.

The large white arrow on the red maple sample (Fig. 13) points to the inrolled cambium indicating included bark. The union between the 2 codominant stems are very weak and the disc below shows the patterns of infected wood associated with the included bark. Note the upturned branch bark ridge at the upper right on the sample. Some species of trees normally have many codominant stems with included bark. Silver maple and Norway maple head the list for these characteristics. They are trees that often split during storms or when the branches are loaded with snow. Be on the alert for codominant stems that turn from an upright position to a horizontal position. Look for these hazard indicators on old, open grown trees or trees that were released to become edge trees.

Figure 34-13

Figure 34-14

All 3 leader buds developed rapidly on this red maple (Fig. 14). The branch at left was removed at the proper angle 2 years before the tree was cut for study. The pointers show the included bark. The branch at right was cut after the tree was cut. The angle of cut is proper for such a branch. When branches with included bark are pruned, discolored and decayed wood will develop rapidly, regardless of how the branch is cut. The defect seldom spreads upward. The C pattern for branch infection is common when there is included bark.

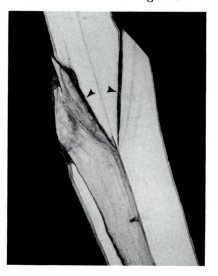

Figure 34-15

A New Tree Biology

When a branch with included bark is pruned properly, the result is the same as cutting a main trunk and leaving a long stub. The included bark separates the trunk from the branch so the branch is more like a separate trunk that is squeezed into or included within the larger trunk. Very important: The branches with included bark are not attached to the trunk by trunk collars as branch collars are. The pruning cut does leave a long trunk stub. The maple sample at left (Fig. 15) had a proper cut 2 years before the tree was cut. The branch corewood was decayed. A small portion of the infected wood spread into the center of the tree. The sample of red maple at right had a pruning cut that was slightly too close above and below the branch. A thin column of discolored wood developed above the branch and the C pattern for branch infection developed below the branch. The pruning cut was 1 year old. On the sample at right, opposite the pruned branch, is a 1-year-old wound that was the same area as the primary wound. It is not the size of the primary wounds that are flush with the trunk that are so injurious. It is the fact that the branch protection zone is removed and that the trunk is wounded.

When branches with included bark are pruned and the decay-causing pathogens digest all the branch corewood, or digest the wood within the trunk present at the time of wounding, a hollow will result. The hollow may fill with water. Do not drill holes into the tree to drain the water. If the water is unsightly and must be prevented, siphon it out and fill the hole with some nonabrasive material. It is best to leave the hole alone. While water is in the hole, decay will be stalled. The water may even kill some aerobic pathogens if the water remains for a long time. Water pockets may form in dead spots between large trunks growing side by side. Again, do not drill holes. Leave it alone, or brace the crown after proper pruning. Try to foresee such situations with young trees and don't let it happen. Like so many tree problems, once they happen and are recognized, there is no way to restore the condition.

Figure 34-16

Leaving a stub when removing a branch with included bark will give the advantage to the pathogens for easy spread into the tree (Fig. 16). The branch with included bark is already set as a leader trunk and the protruding stubs give the pathogens all the more food for their growth into the tree. The sample of white oak shown here has a multitude of interesting points. The branch had intermittent included bark and the large pointer shows where the branch "rejoined" the trunk. The curved white arrows point to the large pocket of included bark similar to that shown in figure 12 for *Angophora*. The open arrows point to the strong barrier zone that formed after the branch was cut. The long branch stub was a prize food source and the pathogens formed protective zone lines (small black pointers) to "protect" their conquered compartments.

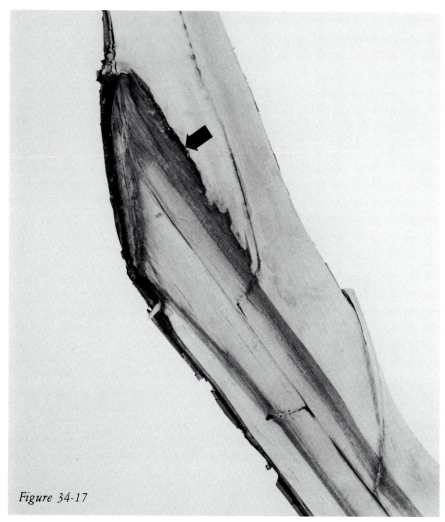

Figure 34-17

Here is the answer to a common question: What happens when you cut one stem of a codominant pair? If there is no included bark, the chances are good that the infection will not spread deeply into the trunk below the cut. When there is included bark, no matter how the stem is cut, the C pattern of infection (see chapter on branches and pruning for A, B, and C patterns: A, stop at protection zone; B, spread within branch corewood; C, spread within trunk wood below the branch present at the time branch died or was cut). Figure 17 shows a sample of yellow birch 2 years after a proper cut to remove one of the codominant stems. The arrow shows the included bark. Remember: There is no built in protection zone at the base of codominant stems! This is why pathogens spread to the C pattern so quickly. Removing a codominant stem is like cutting the top off a tree. But, the injury can be minimized by following the targets as given for branches.

CHAPTER 35

Topping

A hundred times, at least, I have heard it said, "... the client wants their trees topped, and we (the arborist talking) give them what they want and what they will pay for. We must make a profit, or we will not be in business long. And, believe me, the next company that comes along will take the topping job." A dilemma begins to happen. If the arborist does not do the requested topping, somebody else will and the trees still will be injured, so the first arborist often feels that he might as well do the injurious job and get the profit. Some arborists will refuse to top trees. I accept the fact that there is a dilemma. And, I believe that like wound dressings, topping will never go away, but I also believe that there are ways to greatly reduce this injurious practice and still make profit, or even more profit.

First, some order is needed on the subject. Let us not confuse topping—the internodal removal of a leader trunk—with early pruning or training of young trees, pollarding, bonsai pruning, crown reduction by cutting at crotches (many names for this: drop crotch pruning, dehorning, etc.). Topping is done internodal; proper crown reduction is done at nodes, or at crotches. So the first separation must be nodes—good, internodes—bad.

The next point that needs clarification is size or diameter of trunk or branch removed. You could make a nodal cut by removing a trunk 10 inches in diameter at the place it has contact with a one inch branch. This is cut at a node. Is this then not a proper nodal cut? No! The part removed should be at least a third smaller in diameter than the part that remains. There are always exceptions. There is no exact rule here because you can do almost anything to some trees, like linden, plane tree, and willows, and they will keep growing. My only point here is that when I say nodal cuts are better than internodal cuts, some common sense must come to play when size of parts removed is considered.

More. We live in a society that wants everything fast. We want fast growing trees to fill small areas. Then when the fast growing tree continues to grow, it must be cut back to size again. We equate rapid growth and large size with health and vigor. Heavy fertilization is often used to make the tree grow even faster and bigger. Over and over again, the story ends with a topping cut.

Let us not confuse topping with early training of trees. If you start early, you can train most trees to grow almost any shape and to regulate size by periodic pruning. Topiary proves that many trees, especially conifers, can be pruned to assume many shapes. The important point is that the pruning must *start early*. Then, even some small topping cuts do not cause serious injury.

458

In the Orient they bonsai prune trees that are several meters high. The training still starts when the trees are relatively small. In South Korea I saw trees that were 4 and 5 meters tall pulled partially out of the soil and tied down to start training as a procumbent tree. It can be done when started early. As trees get larger and older, the harsh pruning methods cause more serious injuries.

Pollarding is different from topping. Pollarding starts when trees are relatively small and young. The tree is topped once and a number of new shoots form. Every year, the shoots are cut off without cutting into the tissue *below* the origin of the buds. Ground pollarding for biomass or fuelwood is commonly done on species of alder and willow in Europe. The first cut is made at ground line. After a few to several years, the shoots are cut back to their base without cutting into the swollen basal mass of tissue that produces the buds. Tilia (linden) and plane trees can survive constant pollarding, just as *Catalpa* species. Problems start when other species such as maples, elms, and oaks are pollarded. Pollarding must be started early in the life of the tree and kept up every year. The sprouts are usually cut after the leaves fall.

Some people try pollarding conifers. Trees such as hemlocks and firs and some pines can be sheared or hedged, but this is not pollarding. When the tops are cut from spruces, the tree may live, but the dignity of the tree is destroyed.

On the tree species that can withstand pollarding, the treatment is not harmful so long as it is kept up.

What can an arborist do when asked to top trees? The best solution is to discuss the work with the client and indicate that the trees can be reduced in size, but to do the work in a way that will not injure the trees, the pruning should be done over a 3 or 4 year period. At the same time, attention should be drawn to young trees owned by the client. Try to get a pruning program started on the young trees so they will not need topping later.

We must work together to stop topping of mature trees. We must work with landscapers and developers to help get the right trees in the right sites. Topping also is a major starting point for hazard trees. Malpractice suits may be in the near future for people who continue to top trees. As people and trees get closer, greater care must be exercised in treating trees. We must push hard to let people know that if it must be topped, then it would be better to remove the tree and start over again with a new tree. And to start pruning early.

Figure 35-1

Figure 35-2

Figure 35-3

Figure 35-4

Figures 1, 2, 3, 4 show topped eucalypts in southern California. People want the eucalypts, especially the gums, because they grow so rapidly. It is common practice to top them. Some trees still live, but large dead snags persist. Some trees do produce new branches, but older branches continue to die. On young eucalypts, topping is not so injurious because the trees grow so rapidly. But, branches with very weak attachments to the trunk begin to develop. Topping and flush pruning are major starting points for branches that fall from the trees. Dormant buds, or new buds form in the cambial zone. The branches grow in a horizontal direction very rapidly. The tips of the branches may later begin to produce vertical twigs. This adds weight to the branches. The trunk collars at the base of the branch could squeeze the branch until it fractures.

Note the children under the large dead trunks in figure 1. This tree is a high hazard risk. In figure 2, the large dead trunk is above a heavily trafficked road and also near a sidewalk. Again, this is a high hazard tree. The large dead branches on the tree in figure 3 are high hazards to people. Topping combined with flush cuts (Fig. 4) not only leads to hazards, but the trees begin to lose their beauty.

The hazard trees shown here are the types that could or should be recognized easily by a person with the responsibility to care for trees in the city.

Figure 35-5

Figure 35-6

Figure 35-7

Figure 35-8

A New Tree Biology

Topping is not only a problem on the West coast. It is also a problem on the East coast, and throughout the United States, and other countries in the world. Trees under power lines are major targets for topping. People insist on planting trees directly under the power lines. Topping is the only solution (Fig. 5). I believe it is better for the tree and the scenery to remove it. Some trees are so mutilated that they are no longer attractive, and they die a slow death. I believe that trees should be allowed to die with dignity. The tree in figure 6 has been denied this privilege. The tree was old and decayed except for one small branch. Yes, this is a triumph for compartmentalization; but is this what a tree should look like? Other strange shapes are shown in figures 7 and 8. The removal of large portions of a tree could lead to a serious imbalance in weight. The tree then becomes a high hazard risk.

We tree people have a responsibility to stop the injurious practice of topping. We need to reach people on this subject. We need to start more long range tree maintenance programs early in the life of trees. If a large tree really needs to be topped, then it should be removed.

Figure 35-9

Figure 35-10

Figure 35-11

A New Tree Biology

Topping is a major starting point to many problems on orchard trees (Fig. 9) and ornamental trees (Fig. 10). When a long trunk stub is left on trees, the pathogens have easy access to the dying wood. The trunk stub is alive but defenseless. The tissues begin to die from the cut surface downward. The gradation of events associated with the dying tissues gives every pathogen just the perfect conditions for its establishment. If a pathogen requires freshly exposed wood, that condition is there. If a pathogen requires wood slightly altered after wounding, that condition will be there in a few days. The trunk stub is a large food source for the pathogens. Coating the cut surface with fungicides and other materials may have short-term benefits for a few pathogens. But, pathogens are patient. If it takes a few more weeks, they will wait. Some pathogens must have fresh wounds, and the fungicides may keep these pathogens away. Other pathogens will come later. The worst pathogens are those that rot the wood. They are very patient. There are no materials known that will keep these pathogens away.

The cherry tree in figure 10 had received many harsh internodal cuts. Scale insects, borers, and fungi were abundant on the tree. Figure 11 shows a willow that was topped. The branches have a very weak attachment to the trunk. The hollow will fill with water.

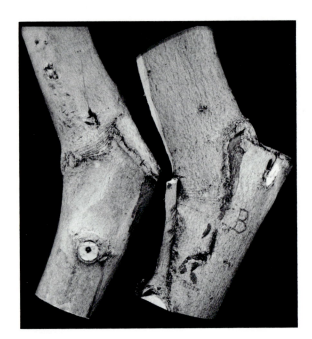

Figure 35-12

Figure 35-13

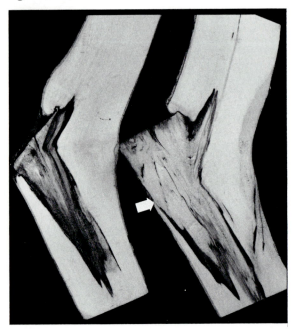

A New Tree Biology

Studies that involved cutting and dissecting trees 3 years after proper and improper topping cuts were made showed that pathogens always infected the trunk tissues below the cuts regardless of how the cuts were made. Topping cuts that left a flat-topped trunk stub were infected rapidly by pathogens that caused decay. Although the term "proper topping cut" is used here, there is no topping cut that will not cause a tree serious injury. The "proper" cut does reduce the amount of injury. Topping cuts could be made to young trees. When they are made on young trees the cuts should never leave a trunk stub. A "proper" topping cut is shown at left in figure 13. The flat-topped cut is at right in figures 12 and 13. The arrow in figure 13 shows where the tree began to wall off the pathogen. The arrow is also the point where the "proper" cut should be made. To remove a leader or codominant stem from the left of 2 stems, target A will be to the left of the bark ridge on the trunk as shown by the white arrow in figure 13.

Topping cuts, like codominant stem cuts, will always have infections because there are no natural protection zones at the bases of the stems.

Figure 35-14

Figure 35-15

Figure 35-16

Figure 35-17

Here are some photographs from Europe that help to reinforce the points made about topping.

The time to start training a tree is when it is young (Fig. 14). Note the small topping cuts on this maple in Sweden. This tree is being properly trained. The topping cuts on this mature tree in Denmark will lead to serious injury (Fig. 15). Figure 16 shows a well-maintained group of plane trees with pollarded branches. The trees were shaped early in their life. The recently inflicted flush cuts and the long trunk stubs on this linden (Fig. 17) will lead to injury. This is not a proper treatment.

A New Tree Biology

Figure 35-18

Figure 35-19

Figure 35-20

Figure 35-21

The branch growing from this topped ash will not have a strong attachment (Fig. 18). Trees should have the right to die with dignity. This old linden tree is only a shell (Fig. 19). The 2 codominant stems of this thornless locust are growing into each other (Fig. 20). There is included bark between the stems. One of the stems should have been removed when the tree was small. It is too late now. One stem could be removed, but such a treatment would disfigure the tree. It would be best to replant a tree in this site. The maple tree in figure 21 has a strong union between the 2 codominant stems. Note the upward turning stem bark ridge that indicates a strong union.

Topping

CHAPTER 36

Cracks

Cracks or seams are separations of bark or wood. The separations are circumferential or radial in wood and usually vertical in bark. In wood, the circumferential separations or the weakened areas that are prone to separation are called ring shakes. In wood of some living trees, the shakes are open. In other cases, the weakened zones are called shake lines. Cup shake is a ring shake that circles the central portion of a trunk. Heart shake means wood separations in the center of the trunk. The separations may be both circumferential and radial. Radial shakes or ray shakes usually follow the sheets of ray parenchyma and the shakes usually start from a circumferential shake. Many wood separations do not become apparent until after the tree is cut and the wood begins to dry. There is a basic difference between shakes that result in separations and cracks, from wood separations that occur as healthy wood begins to dry after cutting of the trunk. These separations are called checks. They appear at the ends of logs. Checks may start and end within the wood cylinder, but they are most common near the margin of the log where the separations — checks — start from the cambial zone and develop inward. Cracks usually start from the inner portions of the trunk and they propagate outward toward the bark.

In the bark there are 2 basic — themes — types of vertical separations. One type starts in the outer bark and the separation may propagate inward to the inner bark, or even into the cambial zone. The other type of bark crack is formed as wood cracks continue to propagate outward from the wood, to the cambial zone, and further into the outer bark. The shallow bark cracks that seldom injure the cambium cause little injury. The cracks may form as tree growth increases at a rapid rate. It is possible that the temperature extremes could cause some cracking of the outer bark. The sun and frost are commonly blamed for all types of cracks in and on trees. Wind is a common agent blamed for cracks in wood. Then there are falling cracks, and drying cracks.

The type of crack that is a problem for living trees is the type that starts from wounds and dead branches and roots. In a structural way, the circumferential cracks are not so injurious for trees.

The barrier zones are zones of chemical strength but of structural weakness. The barrier zone may form after wounds and the death of branches and roots. (Barrier zones do not form after the death of every branch or root. Barrier zones may be very small and they may not form beyond the lateral limits of a wound.) The real problem for trees starts when radial cracks begin to form. The cracks cause the trunk or branches to act as 2 or more separate beams. Such a condition greatly weakens the mechanical support of the trunk or branch. Cracks are one of the major problems for trees.

There is a great amount of confusion on the subject of cracks. Once you understand how they start, much can be done to prevent them.

Figure 36-1

Figure 36-2

Figure 36-3

Figure 36-4

Here are some examples of common types of cracks on trees. The shallow crack in the bark of the beech shown in figure 1 formed above an old wound. Holes for implants started the cracks in the maples (Fig. 2). Construction damage killed many roots on this beech (Fig. 3). The crack formed above the dead roots. Roots killed by *Armillaria mellea* started the cracks in this balsam fir (Fig. 4).

A New Tree Biology

Figure 36-5

Figure 36-6

Figure 36-7

Figure 36-8

Fire wounds and logging wounds are common starting points for wounds on conifers in the West (Fig. 5). A logging wound started the cracks on this paper birch (Fig. 6). Branches that tear the trunk bark as they break start cracks (Fig. 7). The old branch may close but the crack will persist (Fig. 8).

The important point shown by all the trees is that some type of wound started the crack. A wound disrupts the circular form of the trunk. If some other agent — heat, cold, wind, drying, felling — causes the trunk wood or bark to expand or shrink, or to respond to impact, a crack will start. Cracks do not "just happen."

Figure 36-9

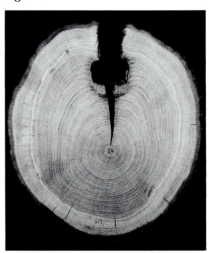

Figure 36-10

Figure 36-11

Figure 36-12

Internal wounds show how some cracks start. The white arrows in the peach disc (Fig. 9) show that the tree was wounded when it was 1 year old. The crack continued to widen as the tree grew. When grafts do not connect completely about the young trunk, similar cracks will form. A wound started the crack in the white pine (Fig. 10). The cracks usually start at the edge of the old wound (large arrow). This crack split after the sample began to dry. The small arrows show the primary crack that formed as the wound closed. The small black walnut (Fig. 11) was wounded when it was 1 inch in diameter. The callus rolled inward to start a crack on the opposite side of the wound. The other separations in the sample are drying checks. Note that they are in sapwood. An old dead basal sprout was the weak spot that started the crack in the red oak (Fig. 12).

474   *A New Tree Biology*

Figure 36-13

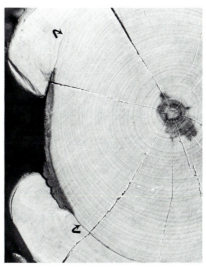

Figure 36-14

Figure 36-16

Figure 36-15

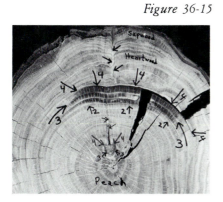

Root rot in the balsam fir advanced to cause the central hollow (Fig. 13). Wet-wood (see chapter on wetwood) was throughout the base. Cracks developed outward from the hollow. The cracks were between the roots, except for the double crack at left. The oak stump in figure 14 was cut below the groundline to show the central hollow that was the source of the cracks. Old dead roots lead to the hollow. The peach sample in figure 15 has many cracks. The labeled arrows show the old wounds. The crack inward from near the center of the wound and the crack outward from the edge of the wound at right, are typical cracking patterns for large wounds. Figure 16 shows a sugar maple with a well compartmentalized wound. The arrows point to the barrier zone, which was a separation. The long radial separations are drying cracks.

Cracks 475

Figure 36-17

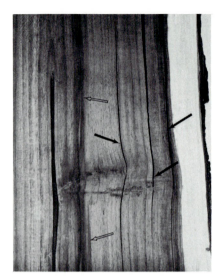

Figure 36-18

Flush cut branch wounds are major starting points for internal cracks—ring shakes, vertical stems. The black walnut sample (Fig. 17) at left received a flush cut wound 6 inches long for a branch that was 2 inches in diameter at the base. The tree was cut 13 years after the cut was made. The wound closed very well (left, center of sample). A large crack developed above and below the wound. The solid black arrows in figure 18 show cracks that were started by pruning wounds and mechanical wounds in a black walnut. The cracks are commonly called shakes. The open arrows show a streak of discolored heartwood that was associated with an old branch opening. Shakes are very costly defects in walnut and other woods used for high value products. Shakes make it impossible to cut veneer. Shakes are also major defects in many species of *Eucalyptus* in Australia. The shakes are commonly associated with fire wounds. Little decay develops from the fire wounds, but the trees respond to the wounds by producing large barrier zones. When the trees are felled and when the wood begins to dry, the barrier zones start many long cracks. The cracks are much more damaging than rot.

Cracks mean "frost cracks" to most people. The belief for centuries has been that frost or sudden cold starts frost cracks. The sharp loud sound in a forest in winter means a crack started by the cold. The loud, sharp cracks are real. I have heard them. The cold temperature may "pull the trigger" for the crack, but some wound or dead branch starts the process—loads the gun. Figure 19 shows a crack above a fire wound on an oak. The oak in figure 20 has several long cracks. The primary

A New Tree Biology

Figure 36-19   Figure 36-20

Figure 36-21   Figure 36-22

crack forms as the wound callus closes the wound. The secondary cracks often split outward to the bark. A "frost crack" may close every summer and open every winter. A raised rib of callus ridges form when the crack opens and closes every year (Fig. 21). The ribs of callus indicate the number of years that the wound has been opening and closing. The large white arrow below the large callus rib on the white oak (Fig. 22) shows where the callus closed the original wound. The small white arrows at the edges of the wound show the early formation of secondary cracks.

Cracks   477

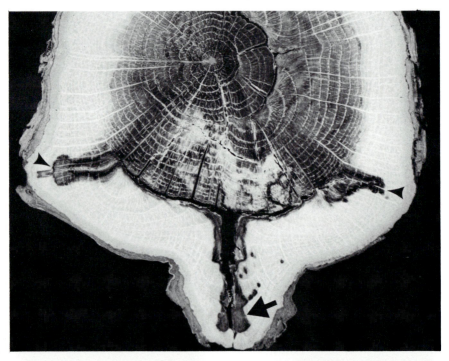

A New Tree Biology

Wounds or weak spots due to branch death or root death start potential "frost cracks." It takes three events to fire a gun: 1, load the gun; 2, cock the gun; 3, pull the trigger. Frost, sun, drying, felling, and aging are trigger pullers. The wound cocks the gun with the formation of barrier zones and potential radial weak spots. The pathogens that infect the wounded wood determine the magnitude of the charge. The frost or sun alone rarely start "frost" cracks or "sun" injury. (I am not talking about winter sun injury where the soil is frozen while the leaves may be far above freezing. This will lead to dehydration and death of leaves and twigs.) Figure 23 shows a section from a small red oak. The large arrows point to the crack that formed as the wound callus closed the wound. This is the primary crack. The small pointers show the secondary cracks that formed where the callus began to inroll over the wound surface. The primary cracks may close and stay closed, but once the secondary cracks begin to form, they seldom close. Of great interest is the fact that the cambium distal to the ends of the secondary cracks responds to the crack even though the cambium is not directly injured. The cells formed by the cambium distal to the ends of the secondary cracks may be more prone to cracking. In a way, the secondary cracks set up conditions that favor the extension of the cracks. Note the cracks forming outward from growth increment seven from the tree center. When cold does suddenly shrink the trunk, the secondary cracks may split outward with a loud, sharp sound. Indeed, frost or cold is a part of the process, but it is the second or third part and not the first part. Frost does *not start* "frost cracks." The shallow bark cracks may be started by sudden cold or sudden heat.

Figure 24 shows 3 sections from a white oak that had primary and secondary cracks. The primary cracks formed as the wound closed. The wound, a fire wound, almost circled the trunk. Several secondary cracks developed at each edge of the wound where the callus began to inroll over the wound surface. Note that heartwood formation as indicated by color (?) was disrupted near the cracks. The all important point is that wounds are the major starting point for "frost cracks." The primary crack forms as callus inrolls, and the secondary cracks form at the edges of the wound.

Figure 36-23 — Figure 36-24 (bottom).

Figure 36-25

Fire wounds and logging wounds are major starting points for cracks in western conifers. The arrows point to the primary crack in a western hemlock (Fig. 25). Note the triangular-shaped hollow behind the old wound face. Several secondary cracks developed outward from the circumferential crack about the wood present at the time of wounding.

Fire wounds are usually deltoid-shaped from the tree base upward. On small trees—less than 10 inches in diameter at the base—that have long vertical deltoid-shaped wounds, the callus will begin to close the wound rapidly on fast-growing trees. The callus grows inward at the edges of the wounds and mechanically disrupts the newly developing sheets of ray tissues. A crack starts. When similar-shaped wounds are inflicted on larger trees or on slower growing trees, the callus does not inroll or "cut back on itself" as it would on a smaller, faster growing tree. The western hemlock shown here fits this pattern better than the patterns shown in figures 23 and 24. The point here is that "frost cracks" develop more readily on smaller, faster growing trees that received long, vertical deltoid-shaped wounds. Fire wounds are normally narrow deltoid shaped.

Wetwood is a common disease in wounded western conifers. The wounds start the problem. The wetwood pathogens live in the wood present at the time of wounding. The bacterial ooze flows out of the cracks—primary and secondary. The wounds or dead branches and roots still start the processes.

Why do you need to know this? Because for centuries frost has been blamed for all "frost cracks." The thought was that you can not regulate or prevent frost, so we must accept "frost cracks." That is not so! We can prevent frost cracks by preventing wounds, by making proper pruning cuts, and by preventing root injuries. Once we understand how a natural process starts, much can be done to prevent, predict, or regulate the process.

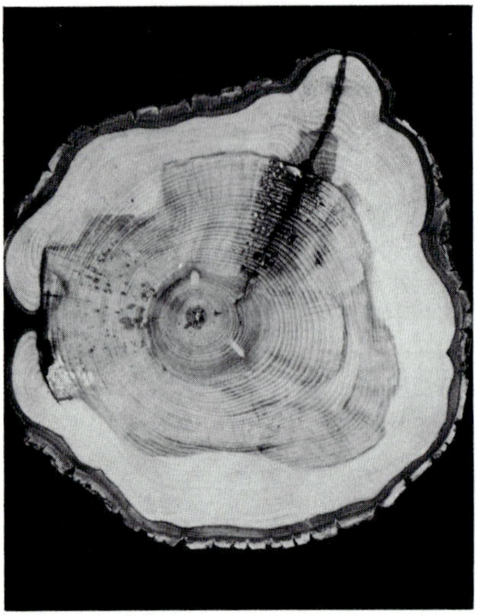

Figure 36-26

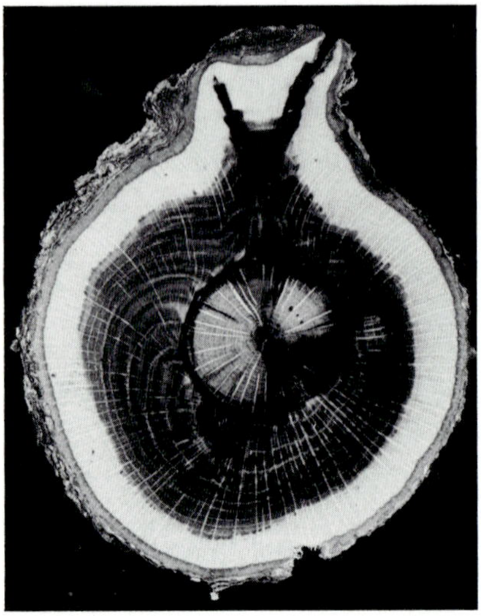

Figure 36-27

Figure 36-28

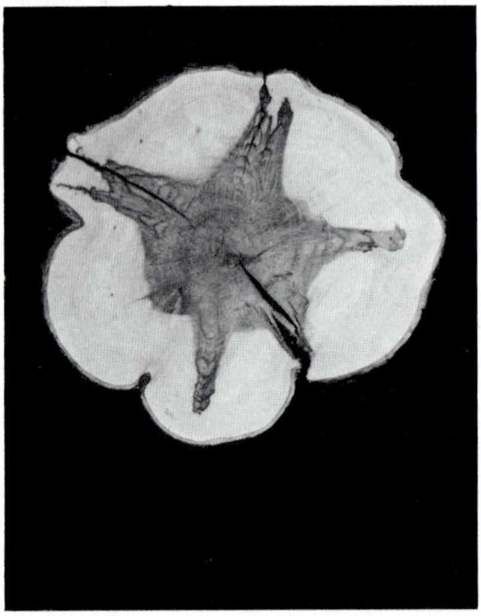

Figure 36-29

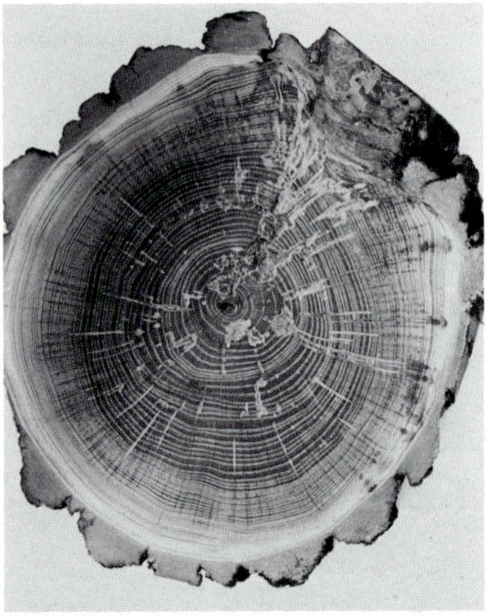

The theme for internal cracks starts with a wound. The primary crack starts as the wound closes (Fig. 26). In figure 26, the wound at left on the ash is almost closed. The wound at the top of the sample is almost closed and the primary crack is well developed. Note the triangular-shaped column of decayed wood that formed on the inner side of the wound. The primary crack may bifurcate as shown in figure 27 for the red oak. Repeated bifurcations caused the pattern in the red maple sample (Fig. 28).

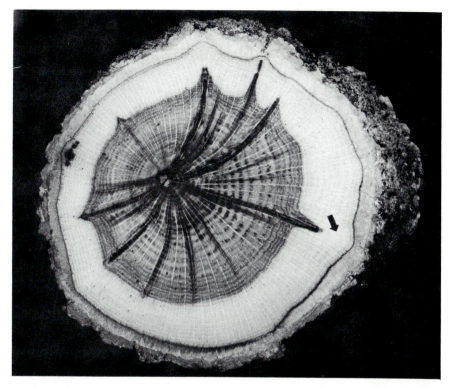

Figure 36-30

Note that the cracks did not spread to the center of the trunks and a star-shaped pattern formed in the red maple. Figure 29 is a sample of black locust infected by *Fomes rimosus*. The fungus causes a canker rot. Note the darker heartwood within the central 30 growth increments. The infection of the trunk through the large branch occurred at that time (review chapter on canker rots).

The star-shaped crack pattern shown in the red oak sample (Fig. 30) is a variation on the crack theme. Note the small central core of decayed wood. The tree was wounded when it was only a few years old. Radial shake lines developed. Cracks started when the tree was 6 years old. (I can see the curve of discolored wood about the crack in the 6th growth increment.) The developing cracks wound the xylem on the inner side of the cambium. The situation is similar to that explained for the "almost through wounds" (see chapter on cambium). As the crack spreads outward toward the cambium the cells formed by the cambium differentiate to form ray parenchyma cells that are weak or more prone to cracking. The cracks begat cracks in this case. Note the swollen growth increments distal to the ends of the cracks (arrow). Once such a pattern starts, it is highly unlikely that it will ever stop. This pattern also shows that the symplast—network of living material in sapwood—regulates the activities of the cambium and the differentiation of the cells formed by the cambium.

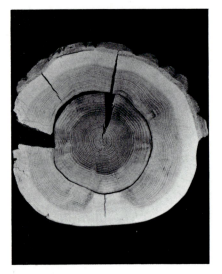

Figure 36-31

Figure 36-32

Figure 36-33

Figure 36-34

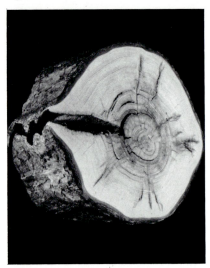

A New Tree Biology

The post oak in figure 31 shows cup shake or the complete separation of the central portion of the tree. This defect is also called loose heart. Note that the dark center of the tree is surrounded by a lighter ring of heartwood. The open circumferential crack surrounds the ring of light heartwood. Note the sudden decrease in width of the growth increments after the crack. The tree received several basal wounds from fire. The tree was almost girdled by the wounds. The tree was in Missouri. The white oak in figure 32 came from West Virginia. Note that the radial cracks spread outward from a circumferential shake. The radial cracks did not start in the center of the tree. The terms "spider heart" or "star shake" are used for this type of cracking. The eastern hemlock section (Fig. 33) shows a combination of cracks. Heart shake is often used for this pattern. Hemlocks are known for their ease in forming cracks. Figure 34 shows typical drying checks in a thin disc of red oak. On a sound disc, the combined widths of all the drying checks will nearly equal a circumferential reduction equal to pi of the original moist circumference of the disc.

Figure 36-35

A New Tree Biology

Studies were done with engineers to determine how trees fail under heavy loading by wind or snow. The tree studied was the balsam fir because basal cracks are common and trees often fail in the forest (Fig. 35). We had an abundance of sound and cracked trees to study. The basal cracks are usually associated with root decay caused by *Armillaria mellea*. The studies started by examining trees that had failed. The trees were cut and dissected. The second part of the study was done in the engineering laboratory. Trunks from sound trees and trees with rot and with rot and cracks were tested with machines that measured amount of force required to fracture the wood. The third part of the study developed models based on the field and laboratory results. The fourth part of the study took the model to the field, and trees were loaded by a winch to the point of fracture. The real forces needed to fracture the trees were compared with those predicted by the models. There was very close agreement.

The force of loading caused cracks to form at right angles to the pull by the winch. When cracks formed, or if they were already formed, the tree trunk acted as 2 beams, one on top of the other. As the loading force "pulled" the top of the trunk toward the winch the top "beam" began to slide over the bottom "beam." The bending toward the pull of the winch caused compression while the opposite side or upper side of the trunk had tension. The top "beam" sliding over the bottom "beam" caused the cracks to propagate to the cambium and then upward in the trunk toward sound wood. When the loading force caused the cracks to propagate to the point where the sound wood was stronger than the force of loading, the trunk fractured, or sheared. The same events occur when branches shear. When a loading force causes cracks to form, a double beam action starts. When branches or trunk shear as a result of the double beam action, one portion of the trunk or branch will protrude far above the other portion. A similar event occurs where branches bend to a more horizontal position from a more vertical position. Be on the alert for trunks that have major cracks on opposite sides. The trunk is then a double beam. Be on the alert for branches or large codominant trunks that have old branch stubs or wounds near the abrupt bending point from a vertical to a horizontal position.

It is important to reinforce some of the points made about cracks. Cracks are signs of problems for trees and for property and people near trees. Cracks seldom just happen. Planting injuries often start cracks. Wounds to the young trunks or to the small woody roots could start cracks that could persist for years in the tree. Many so-called frost injuries or cold injuries are really injuries that were inflicted at the time of planting. We must also add graft incompatability to the planting problems. The incomplete graft union can cause cracks to form, or worse yet, to cause the cambium to grow inward to form a ball and socket union that can easily break. It is happening now to trees that are over 6 inches in diameter.

Be on the alert for cracks on recently planted trees. Look at the base where roots come together, not the root ridges, but in the depressions. Cut off injured roots. They generate (not *regenerate*) new roots. If large cracks are seen on young trees, remove the tree when it is small.

Check young plants for flush cut branches, especially flush cuts low on the trunk. Check for sunken spots below the pruning cuts. Do not accept trees from the nursery that have flush cut branch wounds. Do not accept trees that have minor cracks. Never accept a tree with a painted or wrapped trunk! If trees are in containers or in balls, *carefully* remove some of the soil to inspect the roots. Indeed, make certain there are roots. Some trees are balled and tied at a higher point than their groundline point. Do not bury such trees. Find the groundline point. Take away the string, or rope, or wire to make certain you know where the groundline point is on the trunk. If your tree is in a wire basket, cut the wires with a wire cutter. Do not plant the entire basket! The roots will girdle themselves. And, cracks may form at the tree base, even after 5 or more years.

Cracks that have fruit bodies of fungi indicate advanced decay. On mature trees such signs are indicators of high risk hazard trees. (Remember: Symptom, *function* is altered; sign, visual manifestation of an agent that causes a problem.)

Cracks that are wet indicate wetwood. Cracks that have inrolling or invaginating callus indicate more internal problems than cracks that have outward or upward rolls or ribs of callus.

Cracks at or near the bending position of branches indicate a high risk hazard condition.

Cracks that are shallow or only in the bark cause little injury to the tree.

Cracks that form after a tree fails or shears will not have inrolled cambium or callus. Cracks on trunks present at the time of shearing or failure will have inrolled cambium or callus.

There are no data to show that bolting a trunk with cracks will stop the cracks or add strength to the trunk. When a crack is held steady at one position, other cracks will develop at other positions.

Cracks can be prevented by preventing wounds and by pruning properly. Wounds inflicted by lawn mowers are major causes of basal cracks on trees. The best way to reduce lawn mower damage is to let the person who caused the wounds to have a few days off—without pay. It works!

Train your eyes to look for cracks. Cracks are the major signs for hazard trees. If you decide to cable and brace a tree that has cracks, make certain that you inspect the tree at relatively short intervals.

Cracks are the Achilles' heel of the tree. The tree has greath strength so long as the trunk is solid. Hollow centers may be an advantage for older trees because the trunk will bend as a pipe and not break. Remember the double beam theme. Be on the alert for large cracks on opposite sides of a tree.

CHAPTER 37

Basal Sprouts

Myths and misunderstandings about basal sprouts are plentiful. Sprout stems can grow to be attractive, healthy trees that can produce high value wood. Decay does not spread rapidly from the old parent stump into the sprout stem. The heartwood of the parent stump and the heartwood of the sprout stem do not connect and allow "heartrot" to spread from heartwood core to heartwood core.

If these points are true, then why do so many sprout stems have a short life; and why is the wood often so defective and decayed? There does seem to be some confusion. The theme of this book is to clarify how trees are built up, how they stay built up—defense—and how they break down. We must look a little closer at how sprouts start, how they survive, and how they break down.

Basal sprouts start from epicormic buds—dormant buds that were "carried" in the bark, or adventitious, or newly formed buds. The names are not so important as knowing that some buds were there and some buds start as new tissues. Some trees, such as beech (*Fagus* species) will form new buds along the cambial zone on the surface of the cut stump. The stems are often called "stool shoots." They may persist for several years, but stool shoots usually do not continue to grow into mature trees. Beech, aspen, and other species may "send up" new stems from roots. The stems are called "root suckers."

On oaks, maples, and birches the sprouts grow on the parent stump, or at the groundline on the stump. Now comes the important point. Some sprouts start from single buds, while others start from groups of buds. Those that start from single buds usually grow very rapidly, and, again very important, the lower branches on the single-stemmed sprouts are small. The sprouts from the group of buds may produce low branches that persist for several years. Some of the branches are only a few inches above the base of the sprout on the stump.

In Sweden I saw plantings of willow and alder from small cut stumps—coppicing for biomass. Some genotypes had small group sprouts while others had mainly single sprouts. It did appear that the single or group factor for buds may have been under moderate to strong genetic control.

The new sprouts are takers of reserve energy. The sprouts, like newly forming twigs, must depend on the previous years transport system for water and elements. The sprout must also depend on energy reserves in nearby wood for growth to start. The sprout generates new cells in a new spatial position. As the sprout and still-living stump, and roots grow, a new growth increment develops. After a tree is cut, the stump does not suddenly die. Some stumps may form callus, and the entire stump wound may close. This occurs when the cut tree has root connections or grafts with other still-living trees nearby. Root grafting is common in the forest. The woody roots also develop a new growth increment. The newly formed sprout has the advantage of having all the volume, or better, the area of root surface that was "serving" the entire tree before it was cut. If the stump is root grafted, the sprouts still grow rapidly the first few years. Hundreds of sprouts may develop on a stump. Many of the sprouts are really low branches on the sprouts. Then after 2 to 6 years, the number of surviving sprouts decreases greatly. The survivors are usually those that started as single stems.

The roots present at the time of the felling begin to die. Root rot pathogens commonly attack the still living but defenseless roots. But, the root tissues that formed after the felling may continue to live so long as they are receiving food from the sprout. If root pathogens do spread quickly, the thin growth increments covering large roots under attack can not support the entire root. Roots do begin to die. New woody roots that are near the stump begin to be the major support — water, elements — for the sprouts. The point here is that the surviving sprouts begin to establish their own root systems.

Time for a few comments about compartmentalization. The pathogens that attack the stump and the root wood present at the time of felling are compartmentalized within the wood present at the time of felling. The new root and stump tissues, and sprout tissues, are not exposed to the pathogens. But, there are limits to compartmentalization. When 99% of a root is under attack, the newly formed 1% may not have a chance to survive, regardless of barrier zones or reaction zones.

Back to the survivors. Some sprouts do establish new root systems, or the sprouts were able to "keep" old roots that were small. As time passes, decay may spread into the wood present at the time of felling because all of this wood is open to attack. But, it takes time. The decay does not spread from the old wood into the sprout. The heartwood core of the sprout and the heartwood core of the old stump do not join and allow the pathogens to spread freely. The problem here comes from the old "heartrot" concept that implies that rot or the pathogens will spread freely in heartwood. Therefore, if heartwood is connected to heartwood (which is not the case in sprout-stump unions), then the rot must spread from one heartwood location to another.

Finally, why so much rot in sprouts? Here are some answers: 1, The low dead branches serve as ideal infection courts; 2, The multiple sprouts from groups of buds squeeze and kill the cambium, thus causing dead spots; 3, Death of low vigor sprouts that are part of groups of sprouts serve as infection courts; 4, Root rots may spread from the old roots to the new roots, and continue to spread upward to the base of the sprouts; 5, Single or multiple sprouts may squeeze against the parent stump and cause cambial killing and dead spots. The samples shown in the figures will show all of these points.

Figure 37-1

Figure 37-2

Trees cut during the dormant season produce many basal stump sprouts the following spring as shown in this red maple clump (Fig. 1). Within 2 years, several to many stems still survive. Note the cluster of sprouts at the left of the red maple clump (Fig. 2) and the single stem at right. The single stem has low, large branches. Note the branch callus (arrows). The branch bark ridge on the lower branch is invaginated, indicating included bark. When large low branches die, pathogens may invade the sprout. The red oak in figure 3 has

Figure 37-3

a single sprout at left and a multiple sprout clump at right. They are all the same age. The single stem is much larger. The red oak in figure 4 has a sprout cluster and the stems are beginning to squeeze the cambium to death. Note the white patches in the crotch (arrow) indicating bacterial ooze that killed bark microflora. The sprouts have many low, dying branches that will serve as infection courts. A cluster sprout should be removed or reduced to one sprout as soon as possible.

Figure 37-4

Figure 37-5

Figure 37-6

The red maple cluster sprouts in figure 5 (left) appear as single stems. When the leaves were removed (right) the stems are seen as a cluster all joined at the base. As the stems become weak or suppressed and die, they serve as perfect infection courts for wood-rotting pathogens. The large sprout clump of red maple stems in figure 6 shows the many large branch openings at the 5 foot height above ground. Before assessing the base of sprouts, it is more important to assess the old branch openings. A more mature red

Figure 37-7

Figure 37-8

maple sprout clump is shown in figure 7. The old parent stump has decayed completely. (Extra note: the target shaped patterns on the bark are signs of an outer bark disease of red maple. This has never (?) been reported or studied to my knowledge.) Dissection of the trees in figure 7 shows the very clear and healthy stump (Fig. 8) and the defects associated with branch openings higher on the trunk. The center trunk section has a canker rot associated with *Polyporous glomeratus* (arrow).

Figure 37-9

Figure 37-10

Figure 37-11

Figure 37-12

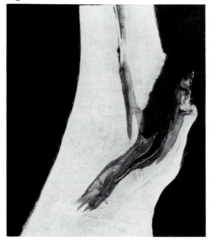

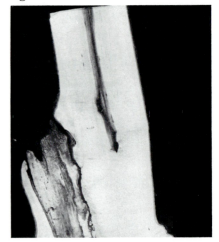

The basal sprout that died on the yellow birch sample (Fig. 9) did not join the main stem or trunk. The sprout was decayed completely, but the decay did not spread into the main trunk. The remaining trunk and the old sprout started life from separate buds. The red maple in figure 10 is slightly different because the remaining trunk and the old sprout were close together when they both started to grow. A close examination will reveal that the decay from the old sprout did not spread into the central column of the remaining trunk. Included bark separates the dead sprout from the remaining trunk.

Figures 11 and 12 give another view of this type of separation in maples. The important point here is that the decay from the basal sprouts does not spread freely into the remaining trunk. If sprouts are cut properly, this is the pattern of decay that will follow. If the remaining trunk is injured at the time the sprout is cut, the decay could develop within the wood of the living trunk present at the time of injury.

The red maple sprout in figure 13 has been growing for 18 years. The sprout is separate from the parent stump. The hollow in the parent stump was there before the tree was cut 18 years before we cut the tree. Note the inroll of bark under the sprout (arrow). This could weaken the sprout in time. The red oak sprout in figure 14 is also 18 years old. And, again, the sprout is separate from the parent stump. Note that the colored central core of heartwood in the sprout attenuates abruptly at the base of the sprout. Note also the inrolling of the bark at the upper crotch of sprout and old stump. Sprout stems are really epicormic stems. The sooner a sprout can grow away from the stump, or the sooner the stump decomposes, the better for the growing sprout stem. Sprouts high on a stump that is slow to rot will become a weakly joined sprout.

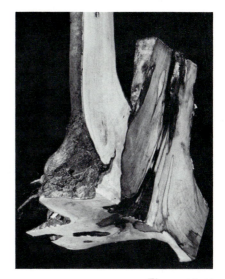

Figure 37-13

Figure 37-14

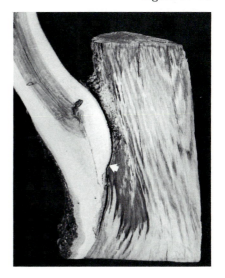

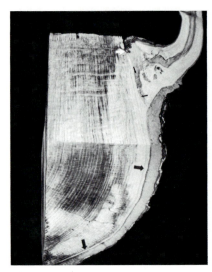

Figure 37-15

Figure 37-16

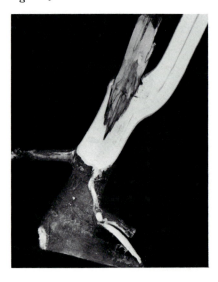

The 1-year-old sprout on the red oak in figure 15 has all the characteristics of an epicormic branch. One of the problems with epicormic branches is that the cambium often inrolls and the growing branch "grows itself away from the trunk." This is happening in the red oak. The small arrows show the new bark that separates the sprout from the stump. The large arrows show the barrier zone. A strange phenomenon begins to take place. When there is an inrolling cambium (white arrow), the faster the sprout grows, the shorter its life will be because it decreases its attachment below the sprout, or branch if we talk topping of a tree. The sprouts could grow themselves to an early death. Of course, many sprouts do this.

Sprouts on sprouts further complicate the situation. Soon after the original sprout on the red maple shown in figure 16 died and broke away, a new sprout formed near the base of the dying sprout. The decaying base of the original sprout will weaken greatly the base for the new sprout. If the new sprout continues to live, it will appear as if the decay entered the base of the sprout from the parent stump. Not so.

A New Tree Biology

Sprouts can squeeze other sprouts until the cambia of both sprouts die along the squeezed areas. The arrows on the beech sample in figure 17 show the dead spot caused by the squeeze of cambia. The decay-causing fungi can then easily enter the living stem because the dead spot is the same as a wound. This is a point that has confused the subject of decay spreading from one sprout to another, or from parent stump to sprout. If the cambium is killed at any place, the fungi will spread freely from one position to another. The small sprout stems in figure 18 show the included bark between the stems. The larger sprout was cut 2 months before the sample was cut. Note the bark and wood boundary that resisted spread of pathogens (arrow).

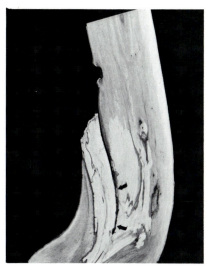

Figure 37-17

Figure 37-18

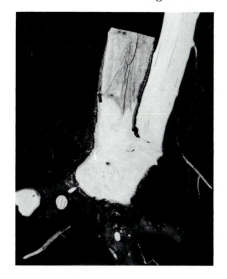

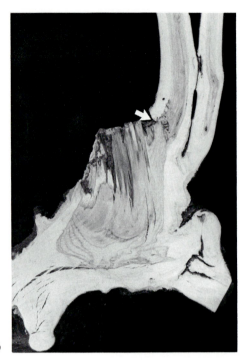

Figure 37-19

Figure 37-20

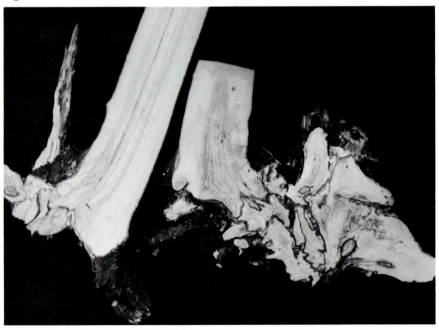

A New Tree Biology

The dissected red oak stump in figure 19 shows some of the problems with sprouts (arrow). The faster growing sprout near the top of the stump has cambium inroll. It appears that the heartwood of stump and sprout join, but they do not. Included bark separates the sprout from the stump. The smaller, lower sprout is squeezing against the upper sprout. Some cambial killing has taken place already. Note that decay is more advanced on the opposite side of the stump that has the sprouts. You will see the same pattern in figure 15. The sprouts do decrease the rate of decay in the parent stump. But, this is not beneficial for the sprouts, because the sound stump wood enhances the cambial inroll and the squeezing of the sprout cambium.

Sprouts, like all trees, can be invaded from below by root rotting pathogens. When roots and stump wood are rapidly rotted by pathogens, no boundaries remain strong. Figure 20 shows an abundance of rotted roots and stump wood and the upward invasion of the sprouts of black cherry.

Sprout management is not easy. But, once you understand how sprouts form, management for high quality trees is possible. And, all important, pathogens do not spread freely from stump to sprouts!

CHAPTER 38

Callus and Wound Closure

Wounds close, not heal. Trees do not restore injured and infected wood. Trees are generating systems. Trees produce new wood in new spatial positions. Even the vascular cambium changes its spatial position in reference to the center of the tree every growth period. Every wound a tree receives will remain in the wood for the life of the tree. Trees wall off, or compartmentalize, injured and infected wood. Some injured wood and bark may be walled off and shed. It is really not so important to argue over a word as it is to understand a process. If the word heal is to be used for trees—and some people insist on it—then we should say "tree healing," so it can be distinguished from animal healing. We have borrowed too many terms from animal sciences without an understanding of the process they are to describe for trees. Terms are means for communications. The level of any scientific discipline, or any discipline for that matter, is measured by the terms that are used by people in the discipline.

It seems very trite to repeat that trees are different from animals. Yet, in many ways they are similar. Trees and animals do require the same factors for survival, but animals move to get them while trees stand still. Trees and animals have transport systems. Animals have a circulatory system, while trees have a one way system. My point in all of this is to say that we indeed must recognize the basic biotic similarities between trees and animals, but we must also recognize their differences.

The real problem with healing centers about the long belief that closure by callus equals healing. And, any treatment or material, or magic, that promotes callus closure is promoting healing. Call the closure process anything you wish, but do not confuse the closure process that takes place after injury and infection and takes place in a new spatial position with the process that goes on within the tissues present at the time of injury and infection. They are 2 distinctly different processes. They are not closely related. The inside processes may be very effective, and the pathogens do not spread into the wood, but the wound does not close. Is this poor healing or strong healing? If the wound closes with large thick callus ribs, but the pathogen spreads very rapidly with the tree during the time of wound closure, is this poor or strong healing? Calling 2 separate processes by the same name has been, and still is, a great source of confusion. If you still insist on "heal" then we need a "tree heal, part I," and a "tree heal, part II." It is getting silly!

The major treatments on trees all have been confused because of this subject. Wound dressings were developed to heal wounds. Many materials will stimulate callus growth. Flush pruning will stimulate callus growth so flush pruning must be beneficial. Digging deep into wounds and breaking the cambium will stimulate new callus, so this treatment must also promote healing. For centuries, the outside, visible callus has been the measure for healing. Everybody (I did it also) wants to measure callus and talk about healing in trees.

If you still feel that a word or two are not important, consider what Robert Hartig did when he reversed a few words. Before his research, people said, "Decay caused fungi." Hartig said, "Fungi caused decay." From that word change, an entire new concept evolved.

How trees grow *is* different from how animals grow. Trees do have another method for survival. It functions very well for trees. Trees are highly compartmented. Trees do set boundaries. The boundaries resist spread of pathogens. Callus does close wounds.

A major problem in tree biology is that we have too many terms that do not fit the processes they are used for. To use a term implies that the process it describes is understood. We have gotten into trouble because too many terms have been used where the processes have not been understood. But, the use of the term indicates understanding of the process. And, the circle route continues. This is the same problem with many textbooks. One author repeats another without touching a tree in between. When 5 transfers take place from one book to another, "truth" takes place. That is why there are so many myths in our textbooks.

Figure 38-1

Figure 38-2

The Indian almond, a tropical tree, in figure 1 shows how injured and infected wood is compartmentalized. The discolored wood was not restored. The growth increments increased near the wound, and the cambium inrolled to close the wound. Bark was buried in the wood where the two rolls of callus met. The bark will remain in the wood. The all important point is that the wound will not be restored. This process functions for tropical trees and other trees. It is a major survival theme.

Figure 2 shows a wound in a sugar maple. Four inches of sound wood covered the wood. The portion of the wood with the sound wood was pulled away from the sample. Note the twisted grain in the wood surrounding the wound. Wood that has such twisted grain may chip veneer knives. The wound will not be restored. Trees are different from animals.

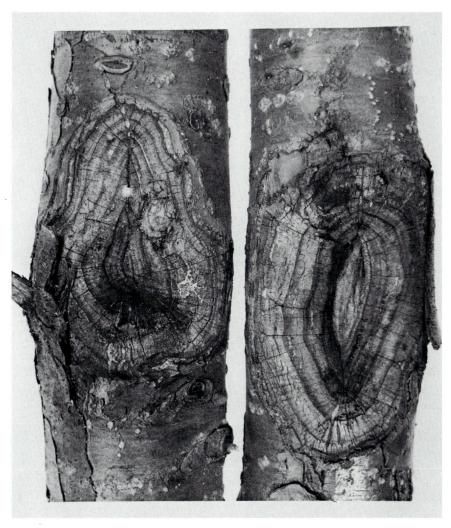

Figure 38-3

   Callus ribs formed every growth period are distinctive on some trees, such as the eastern hemlock shown in figure 3. The 6 bands of callus indicated a 6-year-old wound. Most of the time, the first callus rib is much larger than the others. On most wounds, the callus ribs decrease their growth rate after 3 to 5 years. Trouble starts when the cambium turns inward to form a callus roll. When this happens, the wounds may never really close. There will be a fine hairline crack between the inrolling callus ribs. An almost closed wound make internal conditions optimum for pathogens. Closure is best when the cambium "slides" over the wound surface.

Figure 38-4

Figure 38-5

Figure 38-6

Figure 38-7

Wounds do close. The arrow shows a closed wound on a yellow birch (Fig. 4). The pointers in figure 5 show the inside of the closed wound. Twisted wood surrounds the wound area. The wounded wood is never restored.

Branch openings also close. Figure 6 shows a closed branch opening on a paper birch, and figure 7 shows the sample from the inside.

When wounds or branch openings close, active growth of organisms stops in that area, unless other openings nearby allow oxygen into the tree. When small isolated wounds close, growth of organisms does stop. As wound size increases, the time it takes to close the wound also increases. Large wounds and large branch openings seldom close. Closure is important and we should prune properly and scribe wounds properly (see chapter on scribing, ahead) to stimulate closure. Closure does take time, and the pathogens can spread rapidly. I am not saying that closure is not important. I am saying that closure is different from compartmentalization.

Figure 38-8

Figure 38-9

Figure 38-10

Figure 38-11

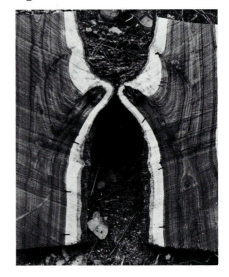

A New Tree Biology

The arrows in figure 8 show 2 closed wounds on a black walnut. The pruning cuts were made 12 years before the photo was taken. The wounds are closed. But, cracks and pathogens had already altered the wood. Figure 9 shows a closed pruning wound after 25 years on a black walnut. The pruning cut was not a harsh flush cut, but it was not a proper cut either. The arrows show the dark band of discolored wood that formed while the wound was open. The band will always be in the wood. The large bumps on the black walnut in figure 10 formed as long dead branch stubs were closed by callus. This is common on black walnuts. Figure 11 shows the dissection of one of the bumps. The arrows show the dark band of discolored wood that formed while the stub was open. The point over and over again is that it takes time to close a wound. The pathogens spread into trees during that time.

As small wounds and branch openings close, the wood pathogens are walled off in small pockets. Propagules of the organisms may remain inactive, but still capable of growing again, when conditions are proper. Many of the pockets of organisms are in wood that appears normal. When isolations are made from the pockets and organisms grow, some people interpret that as proof of an indiginous population or organisms in healthy wood. It is proof of compartmentalization.

CHAPTER 39

Cavities

Cavities and compartmentalization go hand in hand. Cavities form because trees compartmentalize injured and infected wood. Anthropomorphism strikes hard again with this subject. If a person has a cavity in a tooth, what do you do? You clean away all the decayed material until only healthy tissue remains, sterilize all newly exposed surfaces, and fill the cavity. If that is good and and proper for humans, it must be good and proper for trees. Here we go again! You can treat teeth that way, but there are some problems with trying to treat trees that way. The cavity in the tooth is a random pattern determined by points of infection by pathogens. Given enough time, the entire tooth will be digested, and no new tooth will form (second teeth, of course). Before we go to the tree to discuss how cavities form, it is of interest to point out that cavities, or caries, or tooth decay, is the most common disease of humans. Yet, tooth decay has been dramatically reduced in the last 2 decades in the U.S.A. The decrease has come not because better methods for treating cavities have been developed, but because better methods for prevention have been developed and put into practice. More attention on diet, tooth sanitation, and regular examinations have been the answer. If we insist on treating trees like humans, then why not follow this example for reducing decay in trees? It can be done.

Cavities in trees start when some natural or accidental opening is infected by pathogens. Boundaries form, but some pathogens "push" the boundaries. Reaction zones can be "pushed" until walls 1, 2, and 3 of CODIT all fail, and only wall 4 or the barrier zone remains. If the barrier zone does not form, or if it is "pushed" by the pathogens, that part of the tree is killed, or the entire tree may be killed. It takes time for the pathogens to gain space within the tissues present at the time of wounding. During this time, the tree produces or generates new wood beyond the barrier zone. The barrier zone is a nonconducting tissue, and in some trees (oaks) suberin has been found to line the inner walls of the cells.

The pathogens spread within the wood present at the time of infection, far beyond the visible areas of wound decay.

Any treatment that destroys the reaction zone will increase the rate of spread of pathogens within the column of wood present at the time of infection. Treatments that destroy the barrier zones will give the pathogens access to the healthy wood that was generated after the tree was infected.

Cavities hold water because the natural protection boundaries act as walls against spread of pathogens and water. Holes should never be drilled to drain water from a cavity.

Cavity-filling techniques came to the United States from Europe after the turn of the century. To have cavities filled in trees was a sign of affluence. Only the very rich could afford such service for their trees. Some early tree workers did respect boundaries. Whether this was by accident or design is not known. Most workers dug deep into trees.

Europe to this day has 3 major trees in the cities, linden, (lime, *Tilia* spp.), London plane (*Platanus acerifolia*) and horse chestnut (*Aesculus hippocastanum*). Plane trees and linden are very strong compartmentalizers, and they could survive after harsh treatments. The horse chestnuts are weak compartmentalizers, and they do not survive well after harsh pruning or cavity treatments. The problems in the United States started when cavities in other weak trees were treated. The practice of filling cavities has decreased rapidly during the last 50 years. Very few arborists fill cavities now in the United States.

Meanwhile, in Europe, cavities are still being treated. All types and sizes of mean machines have been developed to destroy boundaries in a great variety of ways. Most cavities are no longer filled, but they are "cleaned" to healthy wood, sterilized (?), painted with a great variety of wound dressings and wound sealants, and covered with screening to prevent people from throwing trash into the trees. Also, at the bottom of the cavity, a hole is drilled and a pipe inserted to drain water.

The harsh flush cut has been the major starting point for cavities. The closer the cut, the bigger the callus, the bigger the callus, the better the healing (they thought). So, we are back to healing again as a major cause of many years of cruel treatment to trees.

The new natural target pruning methods are being accepted. In time, proper pruning should greatly reduce the number of cavities. In time, the points about destroying boundaries may be understood, and then a giant step forward for helping trees will take place. I hope it comes soon.

Figure 39-1

Figure 39-2

Figure 39-3

Figure 39-4

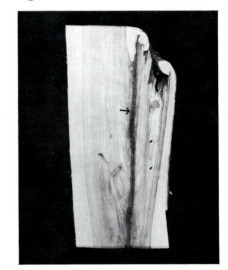

A New Tree Biology

Cavities form in forest trees when the main leader trunk breaks or dies and a branch becomes the new leader. This is shown in the yellow birch in figures 1 and 2. The abrupt turn in a stem is a sign of an old broken leader. Note the large callus "doughnut" about the old leader wound. The dissected trunk shows that the hollow formed downward because the decay spread in the wood present at the time the leader broke or died. The discolored column in the tree is from other wounds and branch openings.

The dissected branch in figure 3 shows a similar pattern for the central hollow. The tree was bent before the top died. Note how sound the wood is in the base. The stump shows only a small amount of discolored wood. Cavities make safe homes for wildlife.

Hollows also form as large codominant stems die (Fig. 4). The large arrow in the sample in figure 4 shows the included bark between the stems. The small arrows show zone lines that formed within the decayed wood.

The cavities form within the boundaries of the barrier zones. The reaction zones resist the downward development of decay.

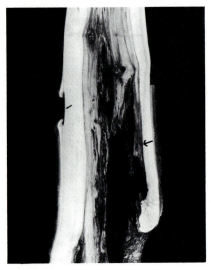

Figure 39-5

Figure 39-6

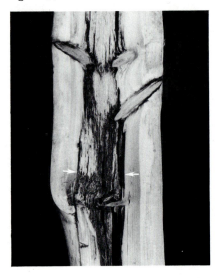

Wounds also start cavities. The large arrow on the sugar maple sample in figure 5 shows the diameter of the tree when it was wounded. Note the small wound and the barrier zone (small arrow). The column of decayed wood in the sample ends abruptly above the large, old wound. Insects also infested the wound.

The eastern white pine in figure 6 was wounded by fire. The arrows show the diameter of the tree at the time of wounding. The column of decayed wood was surrounded by sound heartwood. The pathogens did not spread from the decayed wood in a radial direction to the sound heartwood.

Figure 39-7

Study this red oak sample (Fig. 7) very carefully. How many points that have been discussed do you see? The tree was wounded and pathogens have infected and caused decayed wood. The white pointer shows the diameter of the tree at the time of wounding. The small arrows show the reaction zone in the heartwood. Givne enough time, the reaction zone would "retreat" to the white pointer. A hollow would form to the limits of the white pointer. The mechanisms involved in the reaction zone in the heartwood is poorly understood. The boundary must be the result of an interaction between tree *and* pathogen. The reaction zone buys time for the tree *and* the pathogen that can maintain or occupy the niche. The radial cracks shown by the curved arrows would eventually cause problems. Note how the callus has inrolled at right but not at left. At left the callus is "sliding" over the wood surface. At right the callus is "cutting" into the trunk and causing cracks. Why do you need to know all this stuff? *Because the more you see and understand the more you can regulate.*

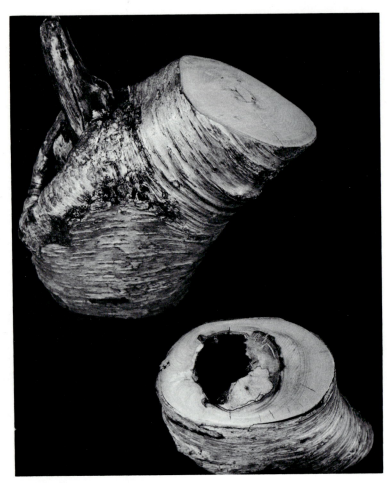

Figure 39-8

Here is the same sample from 2 views (Fig. 8). The leader stem on the yellow birch died. A branch became the new leader. Note that the new leader is sound (upper photo). The lower photo of the same sample shows the cavity associated with the old wound. Decay is still digesting the wood present at the time of wounding.

What should you do with a tree with such a problem? First, you could understand what is happening and leave it alone. Second, you could take the water out, and remove the decayed wood without breaking the boundary, and then fill the hole with some nonabrasive materials. Expandable foam has been used by some people. It might be best to cover the hole with screening. The all important point here is that the decay is spreading in an orderly way. It is not going up. It is not going into new wood that formed after the trunk broke or died. Do not drill holes

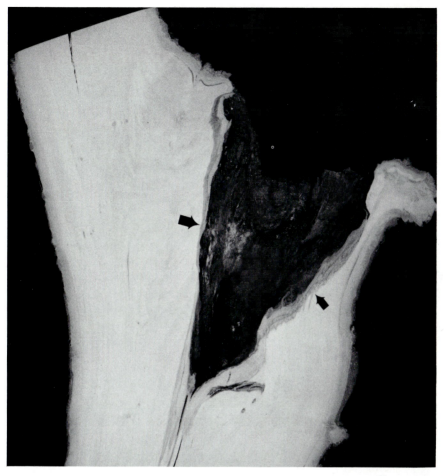

Figure 39-9

to drain water! Do not disrupt the callus about the wound. Show your client this photo, and spend 5 minutes with her or him and that will be the best answer!

This sample is from Frankfurt, West Germany (Fig. 9). The tree is a species of *Tilia*, a lime or linden tree. I have never seen trees that compartmentalize so effectively (olive trees are very close). The strong boundaries (arrow) are effectively resisting spread of the pathogens. The wood beyond the boundaries is perfectly healthy. I have seen samples similar to this one *many* times in Europe. The lime tree and the plane tree are major reasons why the harsh treatments do not kill trees. Or, it may be that the lime and plane trees became the trees of Europe because they were the only ones to survive the harsh treatments! Of course, there are other trees there, but few live so long as the lime and plane tree. The elm trees come close, but Dutch elm disease has caused them serious problems.

Cavities

Figure 39-10

Thousands of trees have been dissected in our studies over the last 25 years. The advantage I had was access to many trees for all types of studies. I also studied city trees that were cut by arborists. Results have come from small trees and large trees, and from trees in the forest and trees in the cities. The theme of all the studies was to dissect and study the inside of the trees. After dissections of over *15,000* trees, themes began to repeat and repeat and variations were easy to recognize.

The sample of red maple shown in figure 10 shows what happens when large holes are drilled into columns of decayed wood. The arrows with curved ends show the size of the decay column before we drilled a hole at the position of the large arrow. The pointer shows the cambial dieback from the drill hole. Note that the pathogens spread outward to the cambium killed by the drill hole. Hole size is important. Very small holes cause less injury than large holes. (The small depressions in the sample are places where wood chips were taken for isolation of microorganisms.)

Figure 39-11

STOP! Think! Before you decide to destroy boundaries in a tree, stop and think what you are about to do. Nature has "spent" over 200 million years developing a defense system that makes trees unique as organisms on this earth. Do not destroy this remarkable boundary.

Figure 39-12

Figure 39-13

Figure 39-14

Figure 39-15

Here are some photos from Europe. Figure 12 shows one of the machines used to grind into cavities. Different types of cutting heads are used for various types of work. The machines break internal boundaries and destroy callus as shown here.

Figure 13 shows a tree that was machine treated shortly before the photo was taken. The cavity started when the large branch was cut too close below the collar. The tree had been routed before. The callus has been destroyed.

Figure 14 shows the typical pointed tips of a treated cavity. This tree had several drain tubes. The arrow shows where a fungus fruit body formed at the end of a drain tube.

The large lime tree in figure 15 has been treated many times. Several long steel poles also brace the branches. I believe trees should be allowed to die with dignity!

CHAPTER 40

Injections and Implants

Injections, like wound dressings and topping, will never go away. But, unlike wound dressings and tree topping, injections may be beneficial when properly done. *I am not against proper injections.* I am very much against improper injections and implants when large, deep holes are inflicted on trees. Proper injection means very shallow holes no deeper than the current growth increment. The holes should be at the base of the tree, not above or not into the roots. The holes should be checked after one growing season to determine whether or not they are closing. If holes are not closing, additional injections should not be done.

We know very little about the efficacy of the many materials that are being injected and implanted into trees. Nitrogen will always give a response. Microelements like iron will always give a response. I have not researched the efficacy of the materials so I will not comment further. I do know that the injection and implant wounds plus some materials will cause long streaks of discolored wood. Discolored wood is dead wood.

Dutch elm disease has been the major impetus for injections and implants. The claims for quick cures, and long prevention are just as common now as they were a decade ago. The elms still die. The ones that die were always the ones that did not get the treatment soon enough, or not the proper chemical. There is no doubt that the chemicals being used will stall the fungus. That is absolutely not my point. Getting the material to the right place at the right time is the major point.

So few people who have used injections and implants have seen the inside of treated trees. Yes, trees can compartmentalize, but there are limits to how much tissue can be walled off. Then there are the treatments coming from Europe that say that large holes must be drilled into the trees, some to the center of the tree. This is sad indeed!

I don't think that injections or implants have *directly* killed any tree, or directly caused so much rot that the tree died or fell over; but I do know that over injection and over use of implants have seriously injured many trees. The large deep holes have caused cambial dieback, wetwood, discolored wood, decayed wood, cracks, and cankers. I know this is so because I have dissected over a 100 mature trees that were injected and implanted by others. I have dissected many city trees that died after the treatments. The sad, but true part of this story is that injections and implants have been a people profit scheme first, and a save tree or help tree scheme second. There are the exceptions to this, but they are few. If all of this is true, and I believe it is, why am I not speaking out totally against injections and implants? I still believe that the treatments may have some benefits when they are used properly. Many methods now call for very shallow holes. This is good. Many methods inject only at the base. This is good. Many people are using the methods only as a last resort. This is good.

We come back to healing and playing human doctor again. We are so used to quick cures. Sick one day; get an injection; better the next day. If we can do it for humans, why not for trees, we think. The confusion between trees and humans repeats.

Another very delicate, but basic point, is that few people who are using injections or implants really understand what is happening when the materials are put into trees. This is why we need to reexamine tree biology. It is one thing to have the perfect medicine. It is another thing to get the medicine to the right place at the right time.

Figure 40-1

Figure 40-2

Figure 40-3

Figure 40-4

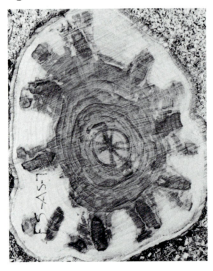

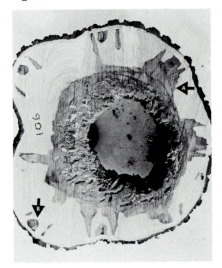

A New Tree Biology

Here are a few typical samples from the over 100 elms that I have dissected (Figs. 1, 2, 3 and 4). All trees were injected by others. Most people are not using the deep injection holes now; yet some are even using larger holes. Figure 1 shows the many columns of discolored and decayed wood associated with injections. Figure 2 shows that the injections have reduced the tree to only a few growth increments of healthy wood. American elm normally has 18, or up to 30, growth increments of healthy wood. The volume of wood for storage of energy reserves is greatly reduced. The injection wounds do the same thing to the tree as the pathogens, the storage space for energy reserves is drastically reduced. The arrows in figure 2 show where the normal, healthy, energy storing growth increments should be. Figure 3 shows a young tree injected with deep wounds. The discolored wood is not heartwood; it is dead wood. Figure 4 shows that injections into healthy wood cause little injury (arrow B). Injections that go close to older internal columns quickly united with the older column (arrow A). As more and more large injection or implant holes are inflicted into trees, the internal columns begin to coalesce to form larger and larger columns of dead wood.

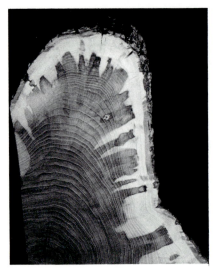

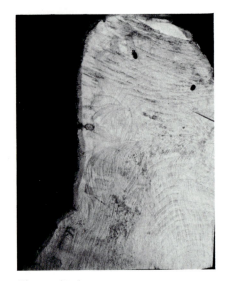

Figure 40-5   *Figure 40-6*

This is *not* a book on tree care alone. It *is* a book on tree biology. My points here are to show you what infection and implant injuries look like on the inside. Figure 5 shows a "root flare" that was injected several times. Only two healthy growth increments remain. There should be at least eighteen. Over injection, and over implantation reduces storage space for energy reserves. That is a fact. How bad or destructive that fact is must be weighed against many other points, such as saving a tree that would otherwise die. I tire of hearing the same points made. A tourniquet will definitely stop a nose bleed, but that is a hard way to go!

Figure 6 shows the opposite side of the sample shown in figure 5. It has all the information on it that is shown in figure 5. What I am trying to do here is to show you the other side.

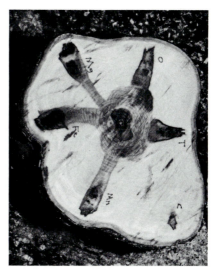

Figure 40-7 Figure 40-8

Experiments were done on injection wounds and on wounds made by implants. All trees were cut and dissected. Unless dissection studies are done, a person will *never* know what is really happening. (Beware of people who talk about things they have never done, or seen, or touched.)

Figure 40-9

Figure 7 shows a variety of implants in a very healthy tree: very little injury. Figure 8 shows the same variety of implants in a tree that had a central column of discolored wood. Except for the control that was far from the center (at lower right) all columns coalesced with the center column. My point here is that the treatments were exactly the same on the same species of tree — red maple — on the same site.

Figure 9 shows longitudinal views of implants in a red maple. The section at left was the control. The wound itself is not so injurious. The wound plus the chemicals cause the serious injuries.

Injections and Implants

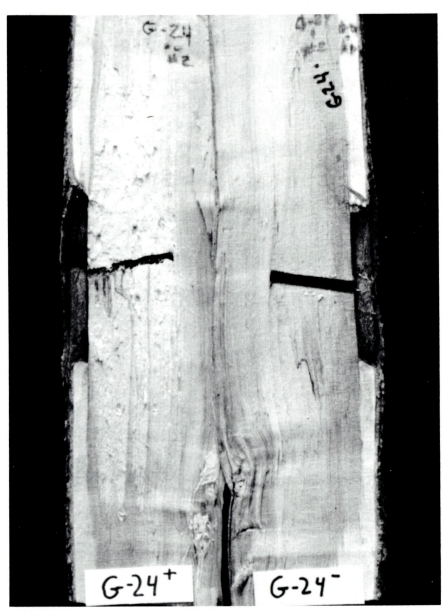

Figure 40-10

A New Tree Biology

Long before research was done on injections and implants, research was done on sugar maple trees that were treated with pills of paraformaldehyde to increase the period of sap flow for maple syrup production. Again, hundreds of trees were treated—and controls—and dissected. Isolations were made from all sections. Dissections started after a few months to 8 years. It was the wound plus the pill that caused rapid development of decay. The paraformaldehyde blocked the plugging of the vessels. The sap flowed freely out of the wounds. The open vessels were easy pathways for the pathogens. They had the advantage, and they took it.

The paraformaldehyde selectively killed the axial parenchyma that surrounded the vessels. These cells are called contact parenchyma because they connect with the vessels and with the radial parenchyma. *In a sense*, they are the "brain cells" that govern many activities of other cells. Once they were killed, the plugging mechanism for defense was destroyed. Figure 10 shows a typical pattern from the same tree. At left, the hole received a pill, while the hole at right did not. The tree was cut after 8 years. There were no differences between the column sizes of discolored wood between treated and control, but there was a highly significant difference between the columns of decayed wood associated with the treated wounds and the columns of decayed wood in the control samples. My point again, for all of this, is to bring home the message that wound alone is not the problem. It is wound plus chemical that causes the problem.

If all else fails and you will inject or implant, please try to follow these simple guidelines: small holes, shallow holes, treat at groundline, check holes after one growth period, do not inject or implant above or below wounds or old injection or implant holes, anticipate future hole positions, do not use the same holes, and use injections and implants only along with other cultural health treatments such as proper pruning, watering, aeration, fertilization, and cable and bracing.

As bad as the situation is now with improper injection and over implantation, I still am optimistic that we will learn to use these techniques in such a way that they will help trees; of course, along with other cultural health treatments.

It is difficult to treat trees. This is why I believe we must start by understanding how the tree functions to survive. And, then to help the tree help itself. You never do only one thing to a tree. You never treat only the wound, or only one disease. You must treat the whole tree. And, the time is coming when we must also learn how to treat the groups of trees. It is not going to be easy.

CHAPTER 41

Wound Dressings

Wound dressings take us back to confusion between trees and people again. When you were a child, your mother put some medicine on your cuts and bruises. If you love trees, you should also put some medicine on their cuts and bruises. A well-painted wound has been the hallmark of the arborists for centuries. Flush cut and paint have been the recommendations for centuries.

Wound dressings will never go away. The search for a magic medicine to stop rot and to undo all the injurious treatments inflicted on trees by man will continue. The major problem in this entire area is the lack of understanding about trees. Once a person begins to understand how trees are constructed, and how trees respond to wounds, it will be clear to them that wound dressings may hurt more than help the tree.

Wound dressings have been with the tree business in cities, forests, and orchards for many centuries. There were awards given for the best concoctions. Many of the ingredients used are not "nice" to write about. The driving force was to find a material that would block the infection by pathogens. Some other materials were used because they kept the cambium moist, or helped to dry the wound surface, or to kill the pathogens, or to stimulate callus formation, or to keep insects out that carried pathogens, or to keep everything out but to let the wound "breathe." Everybody wants to make the perfect dressing, but few people have designed experiments with controls to test their product. Now comes the callus healing confusion again. Many materials will stimulate callus formation. Well! Is this not a stimulation of the healing process? The confusion over basics of tree biology strike again. Callus formation is easy to measure. It is difficult to cut and dissect trees.

Then there are those who say that wound dressings are needed to keep out insects that carry pathogens. These people prune when leaves are forming. This is the natural high period for infection. Flush cuts are also made. So, two serious mistakes are made and now a medicine to undo these mistakes is wanted. Also, there is a difference between dissemination of a pathogen — to carry it from place to place — and transmission of a disease — taking the pathogen to an infection court and having infection occur. My old professor, Dr. J. G. Leach wrote the book on insect transmission of plant diseases. This point he stressed over and over again. People are still missing his point. If branches are pruned properly, and if a pathogen could infect, only a small strip of tissue on the trunk below the branch would be infected (see chapter on branches).

Of the hundreds of papers and claims about wound dressing, only a few include experiments with controls and dissections.

I spent 5 years trying to find a beneficial wound dressing. My early work on the subject was to find a better product, not to discredit wound dressings. I immediately fell into the same trap all others fell into. I conducted short-term experiments. Some products did stimulate callus. Some products did significantly reduce the amount of discolored wood. Studies by other scientists showed the same results. We thought we really had the answer. Then some rude awakening began. As time went on, the callus on the controls began to equal the callus on the treated wounds. And, some very bad news with growth regulators. Those that stimulated callus also stimulated the pathogens! As time went to 5 and 7 years, the treatments that "looked great" after 1 or 2 years, had more decay than the controls. Later we learned that discolored wood can be a beneficial wood alteration that could stall the decay-causing pathogens. Slow the process of discolored wood, and you give the advantage to the decay pathogens. By our 5 and 7 year studies, there were little differences between treated and controls, except treated wounds on some trees such as white oaks had more decay than controls.

In Europe where thick coats of wound dressing are used, especially one product that covers wounds with a rubber-like film, fruit bodies of fungi breaking through the wound dressing are common. The dressings protect the fungi, keep the wounds moist, and make conditions perfect for rapid growth. Never put wound dressings over a large wound that has some infected wood. You will then protect the pathogens. Most large branches already have some internal infections. Wound dressing over a pruning wound that removes a large branch will help the pathogens.

But, will not the dressing stimulate callus, and if the wound closes rapidly, the pathogens will not spread? Yes, in theory this is correct. On small wounds, callus will normally close the wounds rapidly, so no dressing is needed. On large wounds, the callus rarely closes the wound, and the dressing will protect the pathogens. If branches are pruned properly, the pathogens will seldom spread into the tree. If branches are pruned improperly, no amount or type of material will keep the pathogens out.

Nature has a wound dressing that does resist pathogens. The material is made on the inside of wounds. What we must not do is to destroy the only wound dressing that works!

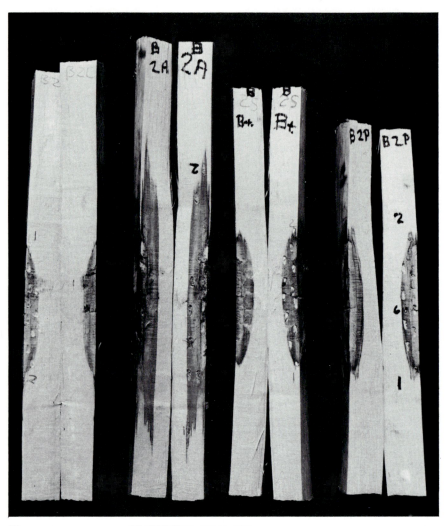

Figure 41-1

In all our wound dressing studies the same tree received at least 4 wounds. Three of the wounds were treated immediately after they were inflicted and one wound was left without treatment. Three different materials were used on one tree. After a few months to several years the trees were cut, all wounds were dissected, and isolations were made for microorganisms. Shallow wounds and deep wounds were inflicted. Figure 1 shows one red maple 6 months after treatment; from left: control, asphalt based material, orange shellac, and polyethylene varnish. The small holes show where wood chips were taken for isolations of microorganisms. People who make claims about their product, but have not made tests such as these are very *dishonest*!

A New Tree Biology

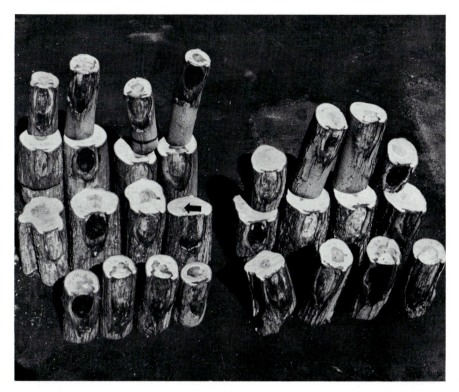

Figure 41-2

Here are samples cut from 7 red maple trees, 7 years after the wounds were inflicted and treated (Fig. 2). Each horizontal row of 4 bolts is from the same tree. A template was used to make certain all wounds were the same size. Each wound received 4 cuts into the surface with a sharp tool. Note that all wounds on tree 18 (arrow) had very little discolored or decayed wood even though some wounds had cambial dieback. Compare this with tree 15 (4 bolts, lower left). All wounds except the top wound at right had large columns of decayed wood. Two factors are important: 1) genetics of the tree; 2) the proximity of new wounds to older internal columns of discolored and decayed wood. Note, that open wounds and dieback of cambium were *NOT* associated with columns of discolored and decayed wood. Take some time to study this figure. It will make you a believer.

Red oaks were also in the same long range studies. Figure 3 shows sections from 2 red oaks after 7 years. The 4 sections at vertical left are from an oak that closed all wounds and all columns of infected wood were small. The 4 sections at vertical right are from another oak that did not close any wounds, and all columns of infected wood were large. You must experiment with a large enough sample to see these extremes. When only a few trees are tested it is possible to see only a few very strong or a few very weak trees. We cut and dissected over 400 trees in our wound dressing experiments. The results have been published in several papers.

Figure 41-3

A New Tree Biology

Here are some samples from experiments that had deep wounds. The holes were drilled to a depth of 2 centimeters. In conducting experiments great care must be taken to inflict exactly the same injury to each tree. The size of the wound was kept constant by a template and the pattern and depth of the holes were repeated on every wound. These experiments were testing a foreign product. Many products (over 40) were tested over a 7 year period. The 2 upper samples are from strong compartmentalizing trees and the bottom 2 samples are from weakly compartmentalizing trees. Treated wounds are at left, and controls at right. The treatments were 2 years old. We must start selecting and growing strong compartmentalizing trees. *Figure 41-4*

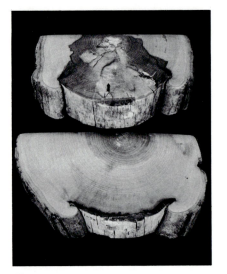
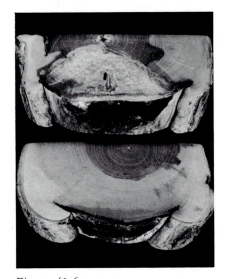

Figure 41-5 *Figure 41-6* ·

Over and over again our results showed that tree genetics and past wounding were much more significant than the dressings for development of decay. Figure 5 shows 2 control wounds: top, weak; bottom, strong. The weak tree was not able to resist pathogens from branch openings and wounds. It had a large central column of infection *before* we wounded the tree. Our new wound was less than 5 centimeters from the inner column. Our results show that with red maples, 5 centimeters is the distance that must separate new wounds from old internal columns. The bottom disc had no decay. The new wound was farther than 5 centimeters from the old slightly discolored center column. The same patterns are shown in figure 6. The arrows show where the old columns were at the time we wounded the trees. The wounds in figure 6 were both treated. The results: controls can have decay or not have decay; treatments can have decay or not have decay! Conclusion: it is the tree more than the treatment.

A New Tree Biology

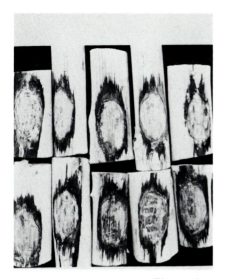
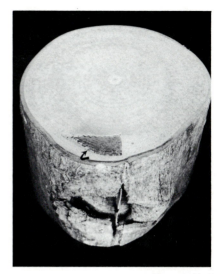

Figure 41-7   *Figure 41-8*

Cambial dieback was common on treated and control wounds (Fig. 7). Wounds inflicted in spring when leaves were forming had the most cambial dieback. Insects often infested the dying bark above and below the wounds. The dieback patterns shown in figure 7 are primarily associated with ambrosia beetles. Again, the beetles did not attack the wound face but the bark above and below the wound.

Another series of wound treatment experiments was done with cooperators (Dr. C. Leben, Univ. of Ohio, Columbus). A wound was made with a chainsaw, and a metal plate (straight arrow) was forced into the wound. One side of the wound was treated and the other side was the control. Compartmentalization made this technique possible. The curved arrow shows the infection associated with a treatment at left of the wound, while the control was at right.

Once a person appreciates how orderly trees are, better tree care treatments will come.

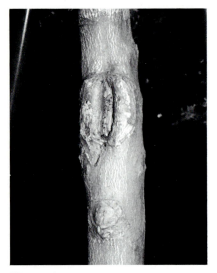

Figure 41-9

Figure 41-10

Figure 41-11

Figure 41-12

Here are some wound dressing photos from Europe. Figure 9 shows dark beads of wetwood fluids breaking through a 1-year-old flush cut that was heavily painted. The young horse chestnut is being trained early to have wetwood. The entire trunk was covered with an ugly (I think) wound dressing! Figure 10 shows wound dressing over a central pocket of decay. The large branch was flush cut. Note the weak callus only to the sides. Again, a horse chestnut being trained for problems. The large flush cut on the maple was well covered with wound dressing. Note the large fungus fruitbody on the wound face and the weak callus. The cut stimulated sprouts. Figure 12 shows several pointed wounds that were rotted and painted. The wetwood fluids were flowing from the wounds.

Figure 13 shows an old flush cut that was recently painted again. Note the 2 fungus fruit bodies indicating advanced decay. Figure 14 is an elm. The wound dressing did not hold back the bacteria.

Wound dressings are not only a waste of money and time, but they help the pathogens. Can we continue to afford this kind of waste and injury?

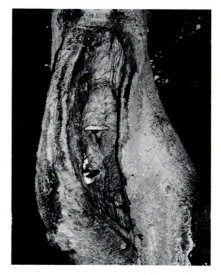

Figure 41-13

Figure 41-14

CHAPTER 42

Trichoderma and Biocontrol

Trichoderma is a genus of fungi known to attack other fungi. Fungi that parasitize other fungi are called mycoparasites. Species of *Trichoderma* have other unique characteristics. They are usually fungi that grow very rapidly in culture. Many species have a strong odor. They are usually late in the succession line in nature. They seem to be everywhere; soils, wood, etc. Some species can live in wood that has high amounts of protective antimicrobial substances. Many experiments have demonstrated their abilities to attack other fungi and to stall the spread of pathogens in nature. They have been used for short-term problems in agriculture. There is no doubt about their ability to hold back other fungi.

If all of this is so, then why not use them for wound treatments? This is exactly what we did. Wounds were inflicted and treated with living spores and mycelium of *Trichoderma harzianum*. Some of the inoculum was mixed with glycerol. Within a 2 year period, the *Trichoderma*-treated wounds had significantly less decay than the controls. Excitement again! Treatments in cold weather were no better than the controls. After 2 years there was no significant difference between treated and controls.

Other experiments by Dr. Walter Shortle and Dr. Kevin Smith showed that the *Trichoderma* fungus could live in the phenol-based antimicrobial materials, while the decay-causing pathogens could not. It is very difficult to "hold" a niche too long in nature.

Experiments were conducted to determine how far the spores or mycelium moved in the wood exposed by wounds. Results showed that the mycelium did not move and the spores collapsed and did not germinate. The fungus had to grow into the wood from the inner wound surface.

There are reports that products of the fungus can move great distances in trees, and that the products can stall or inhibit pathogens. It is very difficult to understand how this could happen when all the data show that the fungus is a contract mycoparasite. Or, at best, some of its products could spread slightly beyond the mycelium.

Other experiments were conducted to determine more about the best substrate for the fungus (Fig. 1). Growing cultures of the fungus were placed on steam autoclaved healthy wood (A); living healthy wood (B); steam autoclaved discolored wood (C); and fresh sections on nontreated discolored wood (D). The fungus only grew on the healthy wood that was killed by autoclaving. Then, how does it live in discolored wood in the tree? After wounding, the fungus is introduced into the tree with glycerol. The fungus grows poorly if introduced without glycerol. The glycerol either acts as an added nutrient or it keeps the spores and mycelium moist long enough for infection to occur. The fungus grows very slowly in the wood as it dies and discolors.

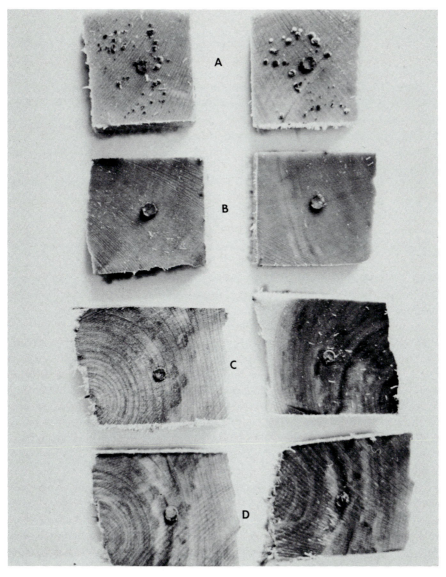

Figure 42-1

CHAPTER 43

Cabling and Bracing

Proper cabling and bracing can extend the time trees remain healthy, attractive, and hazard free. Proper cabling and bracing require skill, hard work, and a keen understanding of tree construction. The treatment does wound the trees. The wounds must be made in the least injurious ways, and when possible, at the time when the tree can best respond to the wound. The treatment is a tradeoff; some injury for a longer safe life.

When cables and braces are put into a tree, the treatment indicates that the tree, or a tree part, is a potential hazard. The cables and braces must be checked periodically. The time between checks depends on the nature of the job, and the potential hazard risk of the tree, or the tree part.

Cabling and bracing is always a part of a treatment, never the complete treatment. Before the tree is braced, a thorough hazard potential check should be made. Will the treatment really help the tree, or will it increase a hazard condition? Should the tree be removed and another tree planted? Are there other ways to lower the hazard risk—fence, signs, etc.? Does the client really know what is involved? Will crown reduction alone solve the problems?

Before a tree is braced, all necessary pruning should be done. All other necessary tree work should also be done (if needed); soil aeration, fertilization, watering, etc.

(My comments deal with the wounding aspects of bracing, and not with the mechanics of using the hardware or the placement of the hardware.)

On small trees, or small stems that are free of internal infection, screw lags may be used. Never dead end a screw lag into infected wood. The hook should always be vertical with the stem. The open hooks should never be turned into the bark. When in doubt about internal infections, check with a Shigometer. Or, when in doubt, use a bolt or rod through the stem.

When making a hole for a rod, use sharp tools. There is no need to sterilize tools. If sterilization is wanted, use a 10% solution of household bleach. Do not use alcohol. Alcohol will help to spread pathogens into wood because it moves into wood very easily. If possible, avoid making wounds into trees at the time leaves are forming and when leaves are falling. Use round or oval washers on *both* sides

542

of the bolt or rod. Nuts are placed over the washers. Do not use washers with sharp points. Seat the washer on the wood, or slightly in the wood so the washer is flat against the wood. Do not seat the washers deep in the wood or on the surface of the bark. Do not paint the wound or the hardware. Install the hardware at an angle that allows the cables to pull straight on the bolts or rods. Make certain that the cables do not pull the rods or bolts to one side or another. The cables should not be so tight that some slight movement can not occur between the connected branches. When checking hardware, examine the wound for cracks, cambial dieback, and fungus fruit bodies. If it appears that decay is developing faster than the closure of the wounds, consider removal of the braced parts, or the entire tree. If the client resists removal, when you know it should be done, get your recommendation in writing.

Remember, long term holding power of cables and braces takes place when new wood covers the washers and bolts. It is the new wood that forms after the treatment that provides the long-range holding power, not the wood present at the time of treatment.

Use extra caution when working near electrical conductors. Cables can flip through the air and do strange things. Cabling and bracing can be a dangerous job in many ways. Make certain all plans are made while you are on the ground. If you plan to use a jack or a come-a-long to pull branches up, make certain that the branches are not held taut by the cable when you release the come-a-long.

Never put cables or wire around a trunk or branch. Never use iron bands to brace a trunk. Never drill holes for rods or bolts above or below wounds or large old branch stubs. Be alert for included bark. It signals a very weak crotch. Do not bolt trunks that have long vertical "frost cracks."

(Many arborists provided samples for study; special thanks to William Rae, Frost and Higgens; Byron Kirby, Ralston Tree Service; and Robert Keller, Frankfurt, West Germany.)

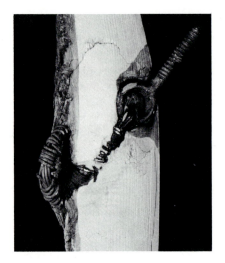

Figure 43-1

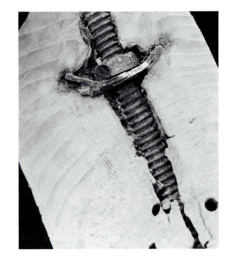

Figure 43-2

Figure 43-3

Figure 43-4

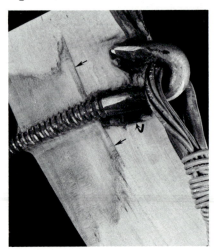

Figure 1 shows a well-compartmentalized screw lag in an ash. The sample broke away at the position where the screw was inserted. Decayed wood was interior to the round end of the screw. Decayed wood surrounded the rod in the American elm in figure 2. The holding power was provided by the sound wood about the washer. If a washer were not on the opposite side that holds the cable, the rod and washer would be pulled into the decayed wood.

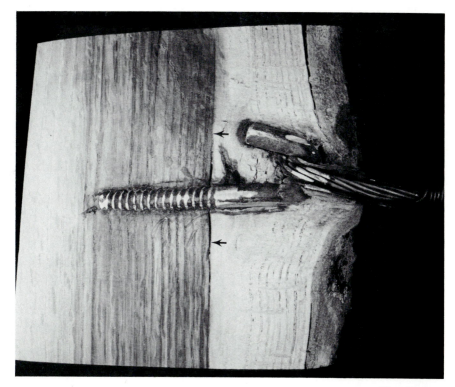

Figure 43-5

The arrows on the elm sample in figure 3 show the barrier zone that formed after the screw was inserted. The discolored wood about the outer portion of the screw indicates movement and not a strong attachment. This screw would pull out after the wood about the inner screw decayed. The straight arrows in figure 4 show the barrier zone that formed after insertion of the screw. The curved arrow shows a cavity indicating movement of the screw. When the wood interior to the straight arrow decayed, such a screw would pull out.

A well-placed screw lag in a red oak (Fig. 5). The arrows show the barrier zone and the size of the tree when the screw was inserted. Note the crack or separation along the barrier zone. This is common. The wood about the inner screw portion was stained blue because of the strong iron reaction with the tannins in oak. The slightly bleached wood about the screw indicates the early stages of decay. The tree has closed the wound, and even if internal decay develops interior to the arrows, the lag should maintain its holding power. The tree was cut 14 years after the lag was inserted.

Figure 43-6

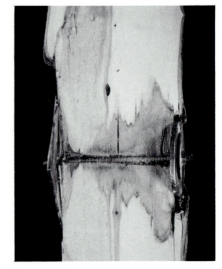

Figure 43-7

Figure 43-8

Figure 43-9

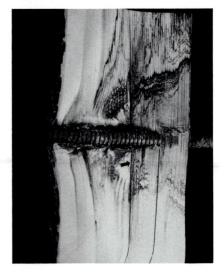

The sharp-pointed diamond-shaped washer in the cherry sample (Fig. 6) prevented closure. It would be similar to trying to clasp a razor blade. Experiments showed that round washers did not cause as much injury, especially cracking, as other washers (Fig. 7).

The threaded rod in the pine sample in figure 8 was steady while the bent rod in the sample in figure 9 moved constantly. The arrows show when the rods were inserted. The pine samples have many zone lines. A possible explanation is that the wound for the rod introduced new fungi into the old column of decay caused by *Fomes pini*. The 2 fungi started setting their own boundaries.

Here are 2 samples from Frankfurt, West Germany (Figs. 10 and 11). Figure 10 shows the rod with washers on both sides (large arrows). The small arrows show a barrier zone that was associated with an older rod. Figure 11 shows the long cracks that formed above and below the bolt. The arrow shows the barrier zone. The washer tilted inward above the bolt, and the crack was guided inward. The crack below the bolt followed the barrier zone. Cracks are commonly started by hardware in trees.

Never place bolts or rods in vertical alignment. This will enhance cracking. The same rule should be followed when other types of wounds must be inflicted in trees. It is best to always offset the wounds.

Use great caution when you cable and brace trees. Safety first!

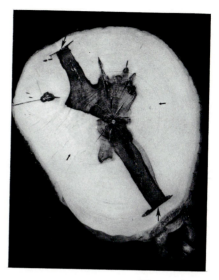

Figure 43-10

Figure 43-11

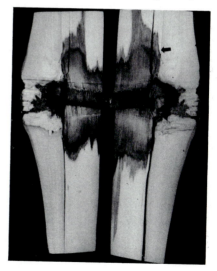

CHAPTER 44

Other Treatments and Problems

There are many other tree treatments and tree problems that should be mentioned: drain tubes, climbing spikes, increment borer wounds, tapping wounds for sap, scribing or tracing wounds, black plastic and mossing, grafting incompatability, construction damage, hazard tree identification and prevention, and shigometry.

Drain tubes: If you drill into a cavity to drain the water, the pathogens will spread outward in the wood about the hole. The tree will still compartmentalize the pathogens, so the tree is not immediately doomed. The size of the hole is important. The larger the hole the more the advantage goes to the pathogens. There is a difference between draining water from a cavity that has decay-causing fungi, from a column of wetwood that will usually be inhabited by bacteria. The danger of drilling into wetwood is that the central portions of the column will dry slightly, and conditions become proper for the decay-causing fungi. The wetwood bacteria will still spread outward to the tissues exposed by the wound. Many times the wounds and the pathogens may cause cambial dieback—a much larger wound now. Drilling holes and inserting many drain tubes in vertical alignment over time greatly favors the spread of the pathogens. I have seen 5 drain tubes in a vertical row in some horse chestnut trees in Europe. The treatment caused large patches of cambial dieback and an abundance of bacterial ooze. If a client insists on draining a wetwood column, insert a tube that will not be grown over in a few years. If a new tube is needed, it should be placed inside the old tube, not around it. I do not recommend the use of holes for draining water from cavities or the use of tubes for draining wetwood fluids.

Increment borer: The increment borer takes a long core of wood out of a tree. The cores are commonly used for dating the age of the tree or for measurements on growth rate. The cores are also used by dendrochronologists to determine old weather patterns and to establish growth maps that can be used for dating old wooden instruments and paintings. For example, if a certain growth increment pattern was common in spruce trees between the dates of 1600 and 1700, and a violin was said to be made in 1620, but the pattern of growth increments in the top face of the violin—spruce—did not match that period, the age of the violin would be suspect. Cores are also taken from old wooden buildings where the ages are known. But, when increment borers are causally used to wound trees just to see how they are growing, then it is time to examine this technique. The cores are often used to determine whether decay is present in living trees and wood products, especially utility poles. Most borers make an outside diameter hole nearly 1 centimeter. The cores are about 4 to 6 millimeters in diameter. Studies on the injuries made by increment borers were made in the 1930s and 1950s. Results from all the studies showed that the wounds caused long columns of discolored and decayed wood.

548

Some holes were plugged with wooden dowels, and others were filled with all types of wound dressings and wound sealants. There is no doubt, the borer wounds do injure trees, and may also start cracks.

The information gained from the core must be weighed against the injury. In many cases it is very difficult to determine the condition of the wood in the core: discolored, early decay, etc. I have always said that one needs "magic eyes" to read a core for wood condition. If all else fails and you still insist on coring a tree, follow these guidelines to decrease injury: practice with the borer on a cut log, use a sharp borer, do not go in at an angle, do not bore above or below wounds or old branch stubs, bore as low on the trunk as possible, do not bore when leaves are forming or falling, do not plug the hole, do not paint the wound. In research, I believe it is better to sacrifice a few trees and study discs from throughout the tree, rather than a few cores. I do not trust results obtained from a few cores.

Climbing spikes or spurs: Spikes should be carried by all arborists. They should be used on any tree when it is necessary to make a rescue of a fallen worker. All working tree people should know how to make a rescue from a tree, especially if it involves contact with an electrical conductor. The number of arborists being injured by electrical conductors is on the increase. Know what you can and can not touch, or even get close to.

Spikes can be used for taking down dead, dying, or unwanted hazard trees.

Now comes the difficult part of this topic. I do understand that the corky, outer bark of many old trees is very thick. But, as you move up such a tree, the bark gets thinner in the upper trunk and branches. Do you then take off the spikes? Most people do not. The statement that spikes can be used on thick-barked trees is a dangerous one. I would still rather limit spikes to removals and rescues. Or on thick-barked trees only on the trunk, until a line can be secured on the top.

We have conducted research on spike wounds, and we studied samples sent in. (Thanks to Richard Pratt.) When a spike point injures the inner bark and the wood there is a wound. The wounds may be infected by a variety of pathogens; some may cause cankers. The wounds disfigure the bark patterns. Spikes hurt trees, there is no doubt about it, and spikes should not be used on thin-barked portions of trees. I have heard many times that they are needed for the large eucalypts in California. Yes, to top the trees and flush cut branches. I have seen this. This is triple trouble for the trees. We must go from tree lopping to tree care.

Scribing or tracing wounds: People who love trees want to do something good for the tree when it is wounded. The old recommendation was to cut away the torn bark about a wound, and to reshape the wound in the form of a vertical ellipse with pointed tips. The scribing often went deep into the wood. Drain tubes were inserted at the bottom of the wound. The tubes were placed into the bark and usually slightly to one side (why, I do not know). The rationale for all of this was to promote "healing" by stimulating callus growth. It was thought that callus only formed from the sides of wounds, so such a "football-shaped" wound would be the best for strong callus and closure. You can see over and over again how the theme of callus as a sign of healing kept directing many tree treatments. As we have discussed, callus is good, but it is not directly associated with the internal processes of wood infection; callus not only forms from the sides but it will form above and below wounds if the cambium is alive. The pointed tips cause cambial dieback, and callus can not form where the cambium is killed. The drain tube at the base usually extends the lower cambial dieback, and in many cases decay did set in the wound. Still today in Europe all of these procedures are done plus one even more injurious. To really clean the wound, the surface may be routed out by a machine. Then the beginning of a cavity is the result of the treatment. A heavy coating of wound dressing completes the job.

Indeed, it is time to adjust this horrible treatment. On many thick-barked trees, the outer bark is scraped off by a vehicle and the wound is very minor. If possible, give the tree a chance to set callus boundaries. Then gently remove the torn bark. This can be done after one growing season. If it is necesary to treat the wound, shallow or deep, here are some guidelines: Do not enlarge the wound, scribe as shallow as possible into the bark and wood, make all margins rounded, do not make pointed tips anywhere, do not insert drain tubes, do not rout the wound face, do not paint the wound. Then treat the tree: does it need pruning, watering, fertilizing, etc. Never treat only the wound; treat the tree.

Results from our research show that more cracks and cambial dieback were associated with sharp-pointed wounds than with wounds that had rounded margins. The pointed margins will not prevent some cracking or cambial dieback, but it will decrease these added problems.

It is good practice to include a wood chisel that has a rounded edge in your work kit. It is very difficult to scribe thick-barked trees. Do not scribe trees with a chainsaw! I have seen trees that had very minor wounds receive major wounds after chainsaw scribing.

It is possible to cut out cankers on trees. A great amount of bark must be removed. The cuts or scribe should be done in late spring after leaves are mature. You must decide whether such a treatment will really help the tree or whether it will so disfigure the tree that the beauty is gone. It is necessary to scribe far beyond the obvious margin of the canker. I have been moderately successful in this treatment with nectria cankers on birch. I did not cut far enough on some cankers, and the pathogen continued to infect the tree.

Black plastic wound treatment: Covering wounds with wet moss is a very old technique. It is one old treatment that may still have some value. It is not uncommon to have roots grow out of wounds that have been covered with moss and plastic.

Our short-term experiments with black plastic were encouraging. Clear plastic did not provide any benefits over the noncovered controls. The black plastic wrap — the type commonly used for garbage bags — did stimulate callus formation and increase internal compartmentalization. How much of the internal compartmentalization was due to the change of environment under the black plastic wrap and how much due to the many microorganisms on the wound surface is not known. The treatments were done in summer, so we do not know about treatments done in the dormant period. The use of black plastic may be of some value for wounds inflicted during the growing season. The problem with the treatment is the difficulty of wrapping large wounds with plastic and then making certain the plastic is removed. The plastic should be on for at least 6 months. This treatment needs more attention from research.

We have girdled the bases of white pines, red oaks, and red maples and covered the wounds with moss and black plastic. The trees were 5 to 7 inches in diameter at the base. The bark was removed from a 10 inch portion of the base. After 3 years most of the trees were still alive. Some maples produced sprouts below the girdle. This treatment of mossing and covering with black plastic may be of value when valuable trees are girdled by rodents, or after vandals injure a tree. The treatment must be done very soon, within days, after the injury. If portions of the cambium are still alive, a new bark will form. On tropical trees and some species of eucalypts, new bark and roots will form after such a treatment. It has been used for air layering to get rooted cuttings from branches.

Tapping trees for sap: The story goes that Indians saw squirrels biting maple trees in early spring, and then drinking the sweet sap. Tapping maple trees for sap is an old practice. The common question is: "Why can they tap trees for many years, and the tree has no problems, yet you tell us not to put large holes in trees?" There are some very basic differences between maple tree tapping and injections and implants with large holes. First, the rules for tapping maples are 1 hole after the tree is 10 inches in diameter, 2 holes when the tree is 18 inches in diameter, and 3 holes when the tree is larger than 18 inches in diameter. Second, the holes are made in late dormant period or very early spring when the tree can best respond to the wound. Third, sap is being taken out, while with injections materials are being put into the tree. That was the old procedure. Some people still follow them. Others are using power tappers. Many holes are put into the trees in a short time. Some people are putting hoses on the tubes from the tap hole and applying a vacuum to the hose to pull out the sap. Some people are adding pills of paraformaldehyde to the tap hole to increase the time period when sap flows. So, there are new troubles in the sugar bush: over tapping, rapid rot caused by pills, and a disease called sapstain. (Acid rain has been blamed for all the declines, and anything in between.) Some maple producers have cut out all the other species of trees leaving only the sugar maple trees. This has been a disaster. What can be done? It is time to start learning what man can take and what he can not. The major problem is simple: greed! Everybody wants more and more. Pull it out by vacuum, put a pill in that takes away the tree's defense system, cut away all the neighbors, put more holes in the tree. Then the trees begin to decline and acid rain gets the blame. This is worse than silly, it is a horrible crime against nature! The answer is to start learning about trees. Let's take something, but let's give something in return. Let's manage the forests and sugarbushes on the basis of tree biology not on new technology for taking everything out of a tree. We all share the responsibility to get some common sense back into tree management.

Problems similar to those given for maple tapping also exist for slash wounding of trunks for naval stores or pine sap and for rubber in *Hevea* plantations. Chemicals such as paraquat are used to increase the yield period for pine terpenes. Paraquat acts to stall the plugging process, the defense process. This is not so different from paraformaldehyde. Ethylene releasing chemicals are also used to enhance flow of rubber or latex. The point again is that we want more and more from our trees. Special note: Be careful with paraquat-type chemicals on tree wounds. Be alert for any herbicide that gets on tree wounds, such as lawn mower or weed eater wounds on the base of trees. The materials may stall the tree defense processes.

Back to the sugar maples for a moment. The trees do produce an abundance of sap in the early spring. People call this bleeding. It is a very poor term. Pruning of birch and maple during the end of the dormant period has concerned people because of the sap flow. The sap flow is part of the defense system. The pressure is outward. The vessels do plug. Do not be concerned over pruning at this time. Know the difference between sap flow and the flow of wetwood liquids.

Construction Damage: People pressure diseases (PPD) are on the increase everywhere. As more roads, paths, and buildings are constructed, the tree that can not move has more problems. The time is coming in some states where plans for the trees must come before construction. This will be a happy day for trees. Until then, the trees will continue to get hurt. It would be wonderful if developers, or even landscape people talked to tree people BEFORE work was started. (Please note that I separated landscape people from tree people. With all due respect to landscape people, horror stories show that few understand trees. More on this later.) Here is a subject where a little prevention could save many trees. It is extremely difficult to almost impossible to help some trees after construction damage. Some trees such as beech and yellow poplar are very sensitive to construction damage. Barriers should be made to keep machines away from trees. Plans should be made to avoid changing water drainage patterns. Building sites (proposed) should be moved if necessary. And, most important, look the machine operators in the eye and inform them that there will be no tree damage or they will be out of a job. It works. Have very high penalties for damage, and make the penalties real.

Soil compaction, change in drainage patterns, root injuries, branch and trunk injuries, and chemical spills are the major causes for tree problems. If roots are crushed, make new cuts to remove the dying or damaged roots. Roots on most trees will generate new roots if given a chance. Do not pile soil about the base of trees. This can kill some trees. Too often roots are damaged and then a well is constructed about the tree. This is too late for any treatment. There are no general rules for putting walls about trees and then making the grade higher. If the roots are not injured first, and the tree has time to adapt, and the well is large enough, there may be a chance for the tree.

Do not fertilize trees near construction sites until after the leaves mature. Then apply very light amounts of fertilizers. High amounts of nitrogen will stimulate the stressed tree to exhaust its energy reserves.

Starvation is the common symptom of construction damage. The roots do not get enough oxygen. The energy reserves are exhausted, and the many opportunistic pathogens, especially the root pathogens, infect the tree. Remember, the nonwoody roots do the work for absorbing water and essential elements. The nonwoody roots are commonly associated with fungi—mycorrhizae. When new conditions hurt the fungi, the tree suffers. Also, it takes energy to operate a root system. It takes energy to form the periderms that wall off the nonwoody roots. As energy reserves decrease, so do the defense systems. Pathogens can then grow into the woody roots through the nonwoody roots. Most nonwoody roots shed every year or after a few years. It takes energy to grow new roots. We are back to stress and strain again. When natural processes begin to function at the limits of available energy, then we have stress. When stress continues, the natural processes no longer function, and that is strain. Trees, and other organisms, die from strain, not stress.

Hazard Trees: Any tree can be a hazard. Position of the tree is one of the major factors in assessing the potential hazard risk of a tree. Trees near property, power lines, and people should be checked for potential hazards. Yet, we can not cut every tree that is close to property, power lines, and people or few trees would remain.

When assessing a tree for its hazard risk rating consider: 1) the species; 2) the position; 3) tree architecture; 4) recent changes to the tree and its surroundings; 5) external signs of internal defects; 6) internal defects. Here are some comments on these points.

Species: Some tree species are known to be "crackers." Silver maple and Norway maple have many codominant stems with included bark. These trees often split. Trees such as cherry also often split, but they usually do not grow tall enough to cause problems. Species of *Populus*, especially some hybrid poplars, grow fast and go fast. Branches often fall from them. Horse chestnut, red oaks, and most fast growing trees pose potential problems.

Position: Trees leaning over houses, power lines, or recreation sites are high risk. Be on guard for edge trees. Trees that were part of a group, but because of building of roads or buildings the trees were released, and now are at the edge of the group. Trees near heavily trafficked areas get extra points for high risk.

Architecture: How the tree framework looks must be assessed. Trees with wide spreading crowns get extra points for risk. Did an edge tree grow itself into a problem? This commonly happens when a tree suddenly gets new space for growth. Be on the alert for this, especially if the tree or branch has a sharp curve or bend where it "reaches" into the new open space. Some new or recent tree varieties look good when young, but as they mature the crowns spread out to become hazards. The Bradford pear is a good example. When this tree is young it has a beautiful shape or architecture. But, as it gets older, the low branching heavy crown often splits. Be on alert for trees that follow this pattern.

Recent Changes: Root rot or root injuries due to construction can cause problems 10 to 12 years after the injury. The crown of the tree may look better than ever because it is getting water and fertilizers because of a new lawn. The woody support roots rot while the nonwoody absorbing roots flourish. The top gets heavier, and the bottom roots get weaker. The tree uproots in a gentle storm.

External Signs: Yes, rot and fruit bodies are reliable signs of internal problems, but fruit bodies are not always present. Some fungus fruit bodies only last for a few days or a few weeks. The most important external sign is the crack. Be on the alert for vertical cracks, especially when they are on opposite sides of a tree. Look at the base between roots, look under old branch openings, look below codominant stems that have included bark, look below old hardware used for bracing, look for cracks where branches bend downward.

Internal Defects: Shigometry can be used to determine the internal condition of a tree. The method takes practice.

Other Considerations: Large tree fruits can cause serious injuries when they fall on people.

Mistletoes and Dwarf Mistletoes: Mistletoes belong to the genera *Viscum* and *Phoradendron*. (The mistletoe fruits and twigs are used for Christmas decorations.) The leaves of the mistletoes often mimic the host tree. In the fall, the mistletoe leaves are often greener than the tree leaves. Oaks in the southeastern U.S.A. have many mistletoes. Poplars are common hosts in Europe. Mistletoes are common on many tree species in Australia.

Dwarf mistletoes belong to the genus *Arceuthobium*. They are common on many conifer species in western U.S.A. and Mexico. Dwarf mistletoes are usually on suppressed, low vitality trees. The plants can be pruned out of young host trees.

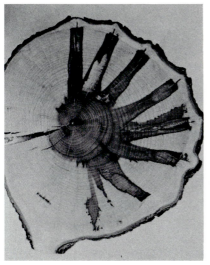

Figure 44-1

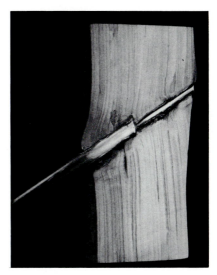

Figure 44-2

Figure 44-3

A drain tube in an American elm (Fig. 1). A larger tube was inserted over a smaller tube. If tubes are to be put in trees, a large tube should be inserted first. Then, if the tree grows over the tube, a smaller tube can be inserted through the large tube. A mechanical power tapper made the deep holes in this sugar maple (Fig. 2). The person could not get to the other side of the tree because there were 2 trunks at this position. Overtapping is a serious problem. Advanced decay was associated with the increment borer wound in the yellow poplar (Fig. 3). Keep increment borers out of trees that are wanted for high quality wood.

Figure 44-4

Figure 44-5

Figure 44-6

Figure 44-7

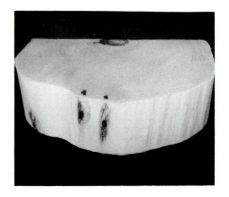

Climbing spikes cause injuries to trees. The wounds on the red oak are 1-year-old (Fig. 4). Figure 5 shows the injuries caused by 1-year-old wounds. Figure 6 shows an oak at left and a red maple at right. Both wounds are 1-year-old. Figure 7 shows 1-year-old spike wounds in a red maple.

Figure 44-8

Figure 44-9

Figure 44-10

Figure 44-11

People are getting injured and killed by trees. Negligence is a major cause of the injuries. The trees shown here (Figs. 8, 9, 10, and 11) are not rare examples. They can be found in many places. We need better programs to reduce the high risk of hazard trees.

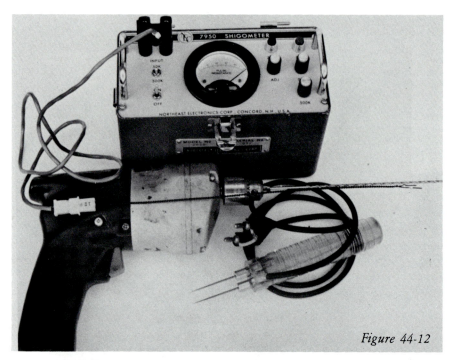

Figure 44-12

Figure 44-13

Figure 44-14

The Shigometer (Fig. 12, dial model) is a battery operated field ohmmeter. It "sends" a pulsed resistant direct current, and with a variety of electrodes, measures the resistance of the current as it passes through a substrate. It can be used to detect decay in living trees and wood products (Fig. 13), and the vitality of trees (Fig. 14). The meter always gives you numbers. How the numbers are interpreted is the important and difficult part of the method. The methods require skill, understanding of CODIT, and lots of practice. When you learn how to use the method, it can give you valuable information about trees. Trying to write and tell you how to use the Shigometer is like writing to tell you how to play the piano. The people who are really interested will learn. For others, please do not try it!

A New Tree Biology

Figure 44-15   Figure 44-16

Figure 44-17   Figure 44-18

Figure 15 shows a tree in California with clumps of *Phoradendron* mistletoe. The thick balls of growth in the red spruce (Fig. 16) in New Hampshire are caused by a dwarf mistletoe *Arcerthobium pusilum*. A closer view of the dwarf mistletoe can be seen among the spruce needles (Fig. 17). The dwarf mistletoe also causes large swollen areas on the trunks of red spruce (Fig. 18).

Other Treatments and Problems   559

Figure 44-19

We still know very little about burls on trees. Figures 19 and 20 show a burl on an ash. Large burls also form when sprouts are removed every year from trunks.

Figure 44-20

CHAPTER 45

Genetics

I dare you to show me the holes or openings in the forest where hundreds of thousands of American chestnut trees died several decades ago. I can show you the holes, or empty spots, where thousands of American elms have died along our city streets during the last few decades.

Forests can heal. They can regenerate new trees in the same positions where older trees died. Forests can repair; they can replace. Forests can do all the things that an individual tree can not do. Forests are groups of trees. How the group functions *is* different from how the individual functions. The group is not the sum of the individuals. The group is something else. It is a multiple organism all to itself. But, what about the elms in the city? Why can not they heal? Are they not a group? We took the elm out of the group and planted it in the city and near our homes. We put cement and asphalt all about it. We took away its ability to operate as a group. We have made it a number of individuals, not a natural group. There was no way the holes could be filled. Only if we fill the holes.

I used to believe in evolution as a slowly organized process where organisms changed over time. I can not believe that any more. Now I believe in the vibration or the resonance of the group. The group is the theme. Each artificial group called a genus has many different types. When environment or any destructive agent goes zig, most of the population dies; except those few that may not even be recognized as part of the group. When the new system zags, a few of these individuals also are able to zag. They stay alive. They reproduce. They form a new group. The group is made up of extremes. Some do not even come close to resembling the "founders" of the group. Another change. Another catastrophe. Another zag to zig. All those that are committed to zagging only, die. The few zigs remain alive. They may be so different from their founders that you would never believe there was a relationship. So the new zagger multiplies rapidly and becomes a new high population because they now have no competition. The extremes in a zagger group appear nothing like their founders. And on it goes. The wider the population the better chances that some individuals will survive the next swing from zig to zag, or zag to zig, whatever it may be. My point in all of this is that the diversity in the population, the size of the population, gives some individuals a better chance to survive when zig goes to zag.

There is hope! I believe the hope is in the group. We must maintain the group. We must make certain that the group is large, is diversified, is allowed to be different. What I mean here is that we have no power or high authority to say which plant is good and which is bad; which is a good tree or a weed tree. All of these mistakes have been made over and over again. We want to determine the mix of the group. That is very, very dangerous.

Back to the urban forest. The individuals we select for our artificial forests—orchards, parks, homeside trees, city trees—all come from the group. I feel a comment here. What about all the selections man has made? And, I say, yes, what about all these selections. Are they not serving man? Maybe man for a short time. Few people are aware of some of the problems with graft incompatability, and diseases that can spread rapidly through one of our master individuals. Consider for a moment what we did with one of the major agricultural plants of the world a few years ago—corn. We got a sterile male. Great. Now we could make hybrids easily by fertilizing the corn with any type of pollen we wanted. Trouble. The sterile male also carried a gene that made it very susceptible to a very virulent pathogen. The pathogen killed almost all the corn produced. Man was not so smart. It is dangerous to play the population game with only a small handful of genes. The pathogens are too worldly smart. What we must do is to make certain that we have as large populations as possible. Then if disaster strikes, the likelihood of having a few survivors increases greatly.

That is all an introduction to genetics, where I believe there are a great many answers to our problems. We must start our artificial forests, but we must keep close touch with the natural forest. This book, or discussion, or conversation, is for all people who work with trees. We must not have barriers between people who work with trees in the forest from those who work with trees in cities, parks, orchards, or for bonsai. We really all need each other. Compartmentalization is great in trees. Compartmentalization is deadly for people who work with trees. The foresters don't talk to arborists, and the nursery people don't talk to tree people at universities. And we must have an increasing system of compartmentation.

Yes, we can encourage natural groups to enlarge as we increase the gene pool. Yes, we can make; and we must; our selections for trees that best suit our needs. When we squeeze the gene pool, we make it very difficult for organisms to survive.

We know now that some individuals of a species can compartmentalize much more effectively than others of the same species. We must start selecting and growing the tough trees in our forests and artificial forests.

Figure 45-1

The white pointers show canker rots on a large red maple (Fig. 1). The red maple to the left and red maple to the rear are free of canker rots. We see this over and over again in our forests. For centuries our forest harvesting system took the disease-free trees and left the infected trees—high grading. Now many of our forests have mostly defective trees.

A New Tree Biology

Figure 45-2

The American beech in the background was killed by the beech bark disease. It was then girdled to hasten death. The beech in the center foreground was infested by *Xylococculus betulae* and *Nectria* sp. The 2 beech trees on both sides were free of infections and infestations. Believe me, genetics works! We must make it work more for us.

Figure 45-3

Figure 45-4

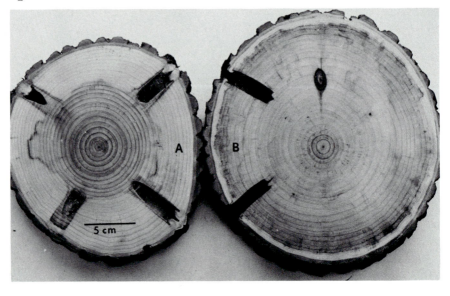

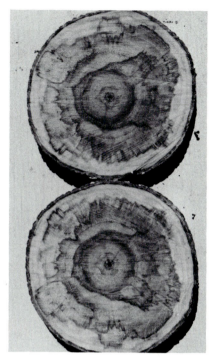
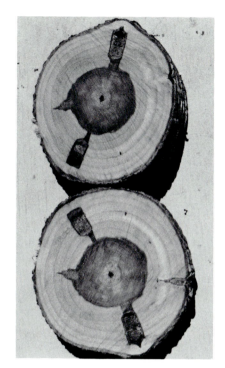

Figure 45-5   Figure 45-6

The 2 hybrid poplars in figure 3 are the same size, same age, and they had the same species for parents: *Populus deltoides* x *P. trichocarpa*. All trees in clone P7 at left had small central columns of colored wood while all trees in clone P6, right, had large columns of central colored wood. When trees in clones similar to P7 were wounded with drill bits very little discolored wood formed as shown in sample A, figure 4. When trees in clones similar to P6 were wounded, the entire trunk discolored, sample B, in figure 4. These experiments showed that compartmentalization was under moderate to strong genetic control.

Wounding studies were conducted on many known clones of *Populus deltoides* in the South. The results were similar to those with the hybrid poplars. Figure 5 shows one of the weakest clones after wounding, and figure 6 shows one of the strongest clones. Similar experiments have been done on yellow birch, paper birch, yellow poplar, black walnut, red maple, silver maple, sugar maple, London plane, and Douglas fir. All studies show similar results: some individuals of each species are stronger compartmentalizers than others of the same species. The experiments on Douglas fir show great differences among the half-sibs (known mother, not known father). It is time to put this information to work for us in the forest and in the cities.

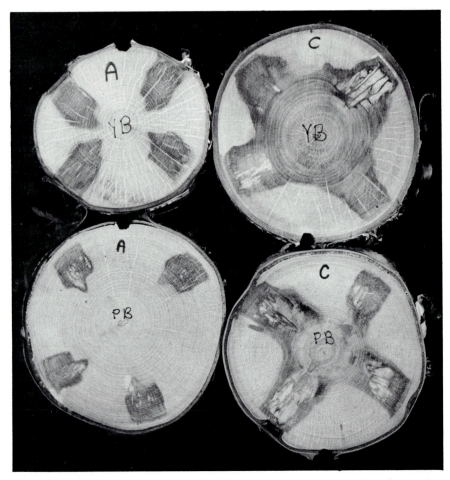

Wounding studies were conducted in the forest on several species of trees that were about the same diameter and age: yellow birch, paper birch, American beech, red maple, sugar maple. Several whorls of drill holes were inflicted in the trunks as shown in figure 7. After 2 years, the trees were cut, dissected, and studied. There were great variations in the amount of discolored and decayed wood associated with the wounds in different individuals within a species. The columns in any single tree were always about the same size. In figure 6, YB and PB, A (yellow birch and paper birch) were strong compartmentalizers before we wounded them, and they were strong after wounding. YB and PB, C were weak before and after wounding. The results show that great differences exist among individuals within a forest population. Growth rate was not correlated with ability to compartmentalize. Callus formation also was not correlated with ability to compartmentalize. Additional studies on samples from the trees were done in West Germany by Prof. Dr. J. Bauch and associates. They showed that there were many anatomical differences between the strong and weak compartmentalizers.

Figure 45-7

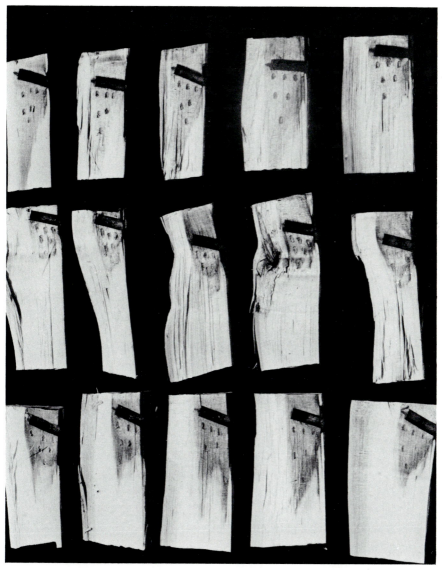

In the wounding studies, all holes were left open to be infected by any pathogens present. The holes were not inoculated. The sample size was large enough to show similarities and differences among individual trees of species. Figure 8 shows samples from 3 red maple trees; 6 samples from each tree, 3 horizontal rows, each row from 1 tree. The small holes in the columns show the positions of wood chips taken for isolation of microorganisms. The same microflora were in the short column as were in the long columns. Again, it was the tree more than the pathogens that set the limits for the column.

Figure 45-8

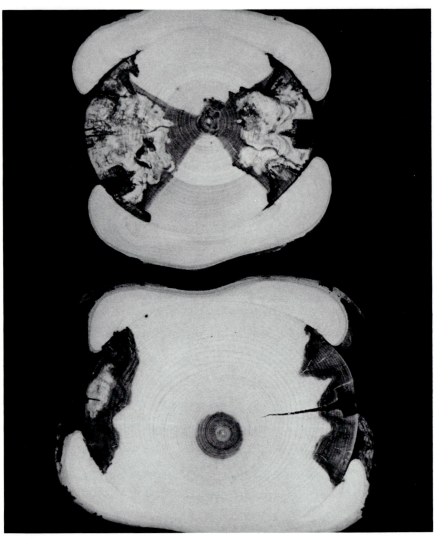

Figure 45-9

Experiments that used larger wounds showed the same results: Some individuals of a species were stronger compartmentalizers than others of the same species. Figure 9 shows 2 red maples: weak, above, strong, below. The wounds were 8 years old. A template was used to make a large trunk wound, and then 5 drill holes were inflicted within the wound. The weak tree had only a small central core of discolored wood. Note that both wounds were still open. The weak tree did have thicker callus. Note the many dark boundaries that the strong tree formed.

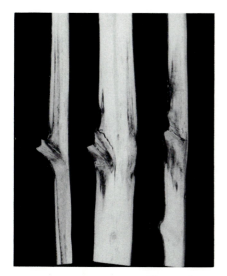 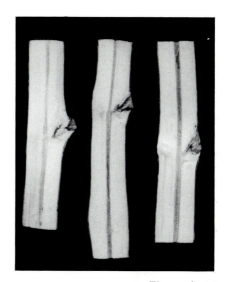

Figure 45-10   *Figure 45-11*

Our forests have been high graded (take the best, leave the worst) for centuries. It would be difficult to prove, but it could be that high grading reduced the gene pool for the strong compartmentalizing trees. We do know that some still exist. We must manage forests in a way that will help to increase their numbers.

Studies were also done on sprout stems, 1 to 3 years old, that came from the same stump. All sprouts from the same stump would all be the same genotype. Figure 10 shows that no matter how some 1-year-old sprouts of red maple were cut — long, flush, proper — cankers and discolored wood formed within a year. Figure 11 shows that 1-year-old sprouts from other stumps had no cankers or discolored wood regardless how the living branches were pruned — long, flush, proper.

Genetics   571

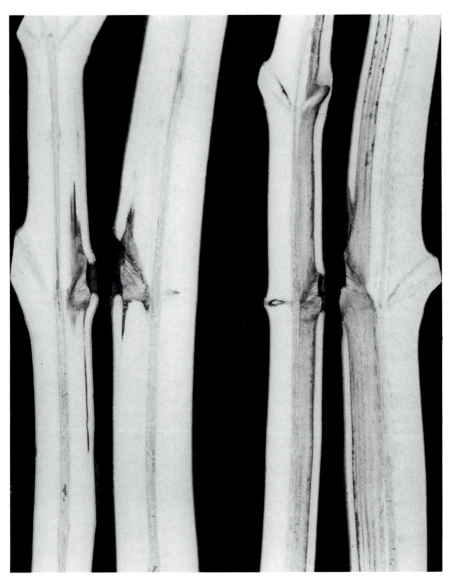

Figure 45-12

A New Tree Biology

Then we did other experiments on 3-year-old sprouts of red maple that used only the flush cut (Fig. 12). And again, some genotypes (left) rapidly responded and very little defect formed. Other genotypes had cankers and long columns of defect (right). Because pruning is one of the most common treatments and mistreatments, these studies show that tough trees can be selected in a year by inflicting flush cuts. If a young tree can "handle" a harsh flush cut, that tree is ready for the city. If it can not, then it is better not to grow that variety.

CHAPTER 46

Dutch Elm Disease

Dutch elm disease (DED) deserves some special attention. The disease is very well known. DED continues to kill elms. There are many accounts of the disease, and I see no point in repeating them here. The disease is caused by a fungus, *Cerotocystis ulmi* (now, *Ophiostoma ulmi*) that is carried to the tree by beetles that feed in the small twig crotches. There is no doubt, the fungus causes the disease. How the tree dies is another matter. Control of any disease can be aimed at the causal agents — *what* causes the disease — or at the way the host dies — *how* the host dies. Almost all the attention on controlling DED has been focused on the causal agents; the fungi and the insect vectors. The rationale is correct: kill the beetles and the fungus will not get to the trees; kill or hold back the fungus, and the trees will survive. All types of chemicals have been used to kill the beetles, and chemicals have been injected into trees to hold back the spread of the fungus. All of these chemicals are effective. The chemical sprays will kill beetles, if they touch the beetles, or if the beetles eat the sprayed tree tissues. The injected chemicals do resist spread of the fungus, if the chemicals move to the sites where the fungi are growing. There are attempts of control by using sex lures to concentrate the beetles on sticky paper, and chemicals that quickly kill dying trees so beetles will not breed in the trees. The best control method is still sanitation, the quick removal of the tree. The tree is then burned or buried to prevent beetles from reproducing in the inner bark. If sanitation is done promptly, the disease could be greatly lessened. It has been done in some places. The search for highly resistant trees continues. Some trees are more resistant than others, but some of the highly resistant trees do not look like the beautiful American elm. So you might as well plant a maple or a London plane. In spite of all types of chemicals, miracle cures, magic medicines, and noble attempts, most of the control programs have not been too successful. They have provided a great amount of money for the people selling the materials. The claims have been ludicrous in some cases, but a desperate tree owner will try anything. I'm sure you are aware of all of this. On to something more exciting.

Many important parts of the disease have been left out or only slightly mentioned. Let us take another look at DED and the tree, the American elm. The tree has been left out of the problem.

Let us start with a healthy tree, or a tree that has no infections by *C. ulmi*. The tree has at least 18 growth increments that store starch. Starch is stored all year in the living parenchyma cells. The story starts at the end of the dormant period. The tree processes start rapidly once the dormancy period is over. Water and elements move up to the twigs through the vessels in the last growth increment. Most of the transport is in the last increment, because the new wood has not formed yet. The buds open and the flowers emerge. Reserve energy is used for the process. The elm flowers are perfect — male and female parts — and almost every stigma on the pistils receives pollen from the anthers, and fertilization takes place. Elms produce heavy seed crops every year whereas other tree species have cyclic seed crops. The seeds begin to mature, and more reserve energy is used. The vascular cambium begins to produce new phloem and new xylem in the twigs. More reserve energy. The leaves begin to develop and mature; more reserve energy. By this time the energy reserves as starch are greatly lowered. Now is the time the new leaves must begin trapping new energy from the sun and making sugar, tree food. But, before this can happen, beetles arrive in some trees and begin to feed on the newly forming tissues in the twig crotches. The beetle eats the crotch tissues in such a way that the tissues above and below the wound are exposed, and also the small branch or the twig. The crotch wound is infected by spores of C. *ulmi* that were on the beetle as it left its overwintering home under the bark of a tree that died the previous year. The crotch wound not only gives the spores access to the branch and the upper and lower portions of the stem that hold the branch, but the wound destroys the tissues that would normally produce the protection zone. So, the fungi get the first advantage to move. The large spring vessels are just completing their development, but the end walls may be still intact. As the end walls break, the spores are there to be pulled inside. The tree recognizes the foreign invaders, and a chemical shunt takes place. Carbohydrate now must go to produce more phenols that will combine with oxygen to produce antimicrobial materials that will inhibit the spread of the fungi. The oxidized phenols appear as dark streaks. The fungus fights back with a chemical called cerato-ulmin. It causes temporary wilting of the leaves. The leaves wilt and are not able to make more food. The reserves from last year are beginning to be exhausted. Still, the cambium is committed to producing new wood cells and new phloem, and this takes reserve energy also. The living cells also require energy to maintain their natural internal processes. The defense system should go into effect to start blocking the pathogen by producing vessel blocks and a barrier zone. The advantage is still with the pathogen because it has access to the tissues above and below the wound, and tissues in the small branch. If the leaves were able to supply enough new energy before the fungus spread, the tree would win the battle. But, if this did not happen, then the branch and joining stem would begin running out of fuel to operate all normal processes and still operate a defense program. And, the leaves have wilted, so no new energy is coming into the system, and water and element systems are also blocked. The twigs and joining branch begin to die a slow death.

The fungus spreads downward as transpiration pressures decrease and as vessels still forming in a downward or basipetal way have end walls breaking. If the fungus is in a branch that has a protection zone at the base, the spread downward may stop if the protection zone forms before the fungi arrive. But, if the fungi are spreading downward in a codominant stem, they can easily keep spreading downward until they reach the trunk. Once in the trunk they have a free path downward into the roots. But, the tree is far from dead, unless this story has been repeated or has occurred over thousands of twigs all at about the same time. The tree would then be overwhelmed, and die suddenly. It is possible. But, most of the time only some branches are killed, and the trunk will have some dark streaks. The same sequence of events could be repeated later in the growing season, but the advantage tips more towards the tree. However, if the small infections reach the trunk or the larger branches, the tree will form barrier zones. The barrier zone walls off the infected wood but in doing so, wood that normally stores energy reserves is also walled off. Add to this the fact that the current growth increment is still taking energy to form, and does not store energy as starch until the end of the growth period. A tree could live for many years by walling off the fungi in branches with protection zones, or by walling off the fungi in the trunk with barrier zones. The tree will stay alive so long as generation of new tissue exceeds the amount of tissues walled off by barrier zones. The decrease in energy reserves is caused by the infections. However, as infections increase over time, and tree reserves continue to decrease, decrease in energy reserves begins to be a part of the cause of death. The elm still forms seeds every year before it forms leaves. This is a strong survival feature for the group. It is not so good for an individual. The elm grows naturally in deep, rich, moist soils, where the early seed production gives it a distinct advantage.

Many pathogens can kill branches and twigs. Many pathogens can kill trees that have been weakened by abiotic factors. This is how many root rots kill. Very few pathogens can kill a tree without the help of abiotic factors. A few pathogens have joined forces with insects, nematodes, and other organisms, and together they kill a tree. However, I still believe that to kill the entire tree was not their real design. The organisms could still survive on dying parts of the tree. I believe we have "forced" many of these organisms to become quick killers. Now back to *C. ulmi* and how it kills a tree. Remember, for *C. ulmi* to kill a branch is not unique. Many fungi can do it. The fungus must do some extra "tricks" to kill the entire tree.

An elm may have many infections throughout the growing season, and yet only a few branches may show symptoms. The tree may have walled off many infections in the trunk, and this is all good.

IF the tree is not infected many times the next spring when leaves mature, the tree could survive another series of attacks later, and still stay alive. But, if the tree is infected many times again the next year, that tree will die suddenly. As the many infections spread downward to the trunk, the barrier zones start to form instead of normal wood tissues. The new barrier zones form against the old barrier zone. The 18 growth increments of energy storing tissues are gone. Only a portion of 1 growth increment now holds energy reserves. Now, the final stages start when the symplast ruptures; the radial parenchyma break away from the cambium. The cambium must get food from the wood. There are no functioning leaves; the leaves are wilted. The insects invade the inner bark and the fungus invades the inner bark because there are no oxidized phenols to stop them. The insects and fungi reproduce in the inner bark on the last remains of the energy reserves. The beetles and fungus reproduce in living but defenseless tissues. No, the tree does not die from starvation. Long before that happens, the natural proccesses slow down and begin to be noneffective. Then the beetles and fungi finish the job.

A few additional points. The aggressive strains of the fungus utilize amino acids (nitrogen, proteins) faster than the nonaggressive strains. They lower the tree's reserves faster. Beetles may infest the trunks of trees late in the growing season. When only a single growth increment is present because of barrier zones, the beetles seem to "know this." When the beetles do infest the trunks, this makes the situation explosive for the next growth period.

American elms are wanted because of their vase-like form. Elms have many codominant stems. The codominant junction makes it easy for the fungi to spread downward because there is no protection zone.

Figure 46-1

The American elm in the foreground has only a few dead branches (Fig. 1). The elm in the background had many dead branches. Spruce, pine, and maples have been planted, knowing that the time will not be long for the elms. Each branch is a separate problem for the tree. When all the infected tissues meet on the trunk, barrier zones wall off the pathogen. The barrier zones also wall off wood that normally stores energy reserves.

A New Tree Biology

Figure 46-2

Figure 46-3

In 1983, the 4 vase-shaped elms were all dying (Fig. 2). Note the clusters of sprouts in the crown. These trees were dying for over 5 years. They were walling off the infected tissues. The oval-shaped elm in the background at left was very healthy. In 1985 the oval-shaped elm had many dead branches (Fig. 3). A great amount of sewer and water pipe construction occurred near the tree. How much injury the construction caused is not known. The highly compartmented nature of the disease is shown by the dead branches and the very healthy branches. The fungus takes a branch at a time.

Dutch Elm Disease

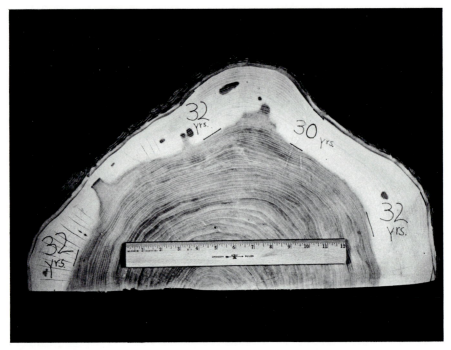

Figure 46-4

Figure 46-5

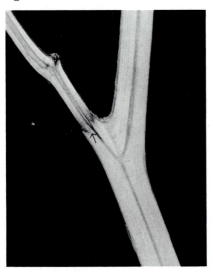

Most elms have large central cores of wetwood (Fig. 4). Elms may have 30 or more growth increments of healthy wood, but elms normally store starch in the most recently formed 18 growth increments. When infections spread downward in branches (Fig. 5), the chemical protection zone at the branch base (arrow) usually resists spread of the pathogen into the trunk.

A New Tree Biology

The sample in figure 6 shows an infected codominant stem at left. The infection continued downward into the stem below 2 codominant stems. The infection did not spread from one codominant stem to the other. One healthy growth increment is at left (arrow), while 11 energy storing growth increments are at right of the trunk. The large arrows on the sample in figure 7 show where many infected compartments were walled off. The small arrows show individual infected compartments. When many are close, large portions of the wood are walled off. The tree had 2 multiple infection periods the 2 years before the tree was cut. Only a portion of the last growth increment was still healthy and storing starch. Arrow A shows an insect hole. Beetles will infest trunks of weakened but still living trees.

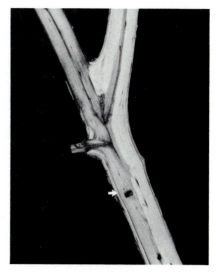

Figure 46-6

Figure 46-7

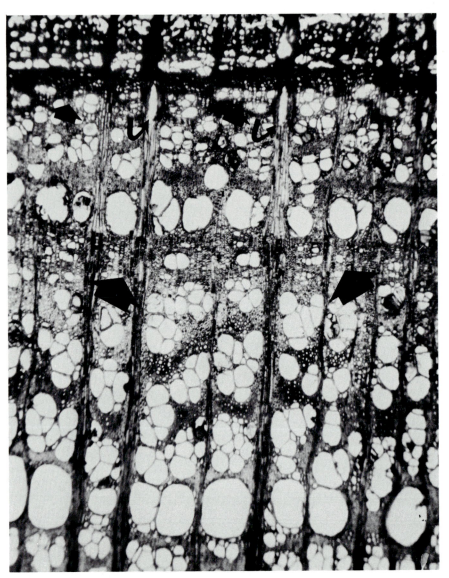

Figure 46-8

The elm that yielded this sample (Fig. 8) was dying in the fall and it was cut midwinter. The curved arrows show the split ray parenchyma. The smaller black arrows show the barrier zone that formed at the end of the growing season. The larger black arrows show the barrier zone that formed at the end of the previous growing season.

What can be done? Sanitation is still the best answer. Prompt removal of dead trees is costly, however, in the long term it is the most cost effective way to stall the disease. Pruning has had mixed comments. The real problem is that most people are making flush cuts. The branch collar should not be injured or removed. Another part of the confusion centers about calling codominant stems regular branches. Codominant stems are pruned differently from branches. Prompt proper pruning is another way to hold back the disease. Spraying to kill beetles is effective, if the spray is always there to reach the beetles. Injections can help prevent infections from spreading, but repeated injection can cause other problems. If holes are very small, very shallow, and at the ground line, injury will be reduced.

I hope that more effort will be given to helping the tree help itself. Why not spray to deblossom the tree? This would conserve reserve energy. Why not inoculate with nonaggressive strains of the fungus? Why not feed the tree! Only a few people in the world have ever fed a tree. Can we introduce sugar and have the tree use it?

The arguments go on and on about pruning and wound dressings. People prune while the leaves are forming. Flush cuts are made. Beetles come to the trees. The people then want a wound dressing to keep the beetles away. Pruning should not be made at the time of leaf formation unless there is storm damage, or unless the pruning is part of a job along a power line. If proper pruning cuts were made, and if the fungus infected the wound, the fungus would only infect a small portion of the trunk below the branch wound. These controversies will never go away. Wounds made by climbing spurs are much worse than the wounds made by proper pruning cuts. If people want to use wound dressing, then every spur wound should be scribed properly and painted, and every pruning cut should be painted. The same goes for oak trees and oak wilt.

Figure 47-1

A New Tree Biology

CHAPTER 47

Fire Blight

Erwinia amylovora is a bacterium that causes fire blight of many woody plants in the rose family — *Rosaceae*. This pathogen can kill trees without the help of other organisms. The only other pathogens that come close to *E. amylovora* are *Endothia* (*Cryphonectria*) *parasitica*, the chestnut blight fungus, and *Cronartium ribicola*, the whie pine blister rust fungus. Fusiform rust, *Cronartium fusiforme*, and maybe a few other pathogens can also kill trees without the help of other organisms or even a wound. There are many wound pathogens that can kill branches, and some may kill trees. How do some of these other pathogens like *Erwinia amylovora* get into the tree? The tree does have natural openings. The fire blight pathogen can infect the natural openings in the flower, the stigma on the pistil. The bacterium can kill the flowers and the primary tissues that hold the flowers; the twigs. But, the bacterium can also infect the tree through another infection court — the ruptured phellogen or other tissues within the branch crotch. Review the chapter on branch attachment. You will see that the phellogen and phellem often wrinkle and break within the branch or twig crotches. The broken tissues serve as a perfect infection court. I believe that the chestnut blight fungus and the white pine blister rust fungus invade also through the same temporary openings. The opening is an Achilles' heel for a short time.

The tree can still compartmentalize the bacterium. Then how does the tree die? Trees die 3 basic ways: 1) mechanical disruption; 2) dysfunction; and 3) infection or starvation (energy drain). Yes, some pathogens produce toxins, but trees do not have a circulatory system, and toxins at best serve as localized problems for the tree. Most trees die when energy reserves are so depleted that defense systems do not function effectively. The tree does not die of starvation. Long before starvation starts, many opportunistic pathogens infect and drain the remaining energy from the still living but defenseless tree.

The species name of the fire blight bacterium — *amylovora* — means "I eat starch." Every time the pathogen is walled off, normal tissues that store starch are also walled off. Defense requires a great amount of energy. It is well known that fertilization of trees with fire blight greatly speeds the progress of the disease. The nitrogen stimulates the tree to rapidly use its already low energy reserves. As defense decreases, the pathogen spreads all the faster.

Figure 1 shows a typical shepherd's crook on pear that results from flower and twig infections.

Figure 47-2

The 4 pear samples in figure 2 all had crotch infections. The arrows on 2 samples at left show dead areas between them. The stem was alive and not infected above and below the arrows.

The arrow on the sample at right shows where an infection spreading downward was stopped. The remaining sample shows infections at the branch crotches.

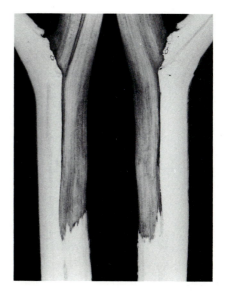

Figure 3 shows the downward spread of the pathogen. The pathogen did not spread from one codominant stem (arrow) to the other.

The 2 trunk sections of peach in figure 4 had wide bands of sapwood. The 2 sections below had narrow bands of sapwood. The lower sections came from peach trees that had many wounds. Only a small volume of wood could store energy reserves in the lower samples. Many root rotting fungi attacked the trees. The peach samples were not infected by fire blight.

Figure 47-3

Figure 47-4

CHAPTER 48

Utility Poles and Wood Products

Many problems in utility poles and other wood products have their origin in the living tree. You will *never* understand defects in wood products if you do not understand the living tree.

After the tree dies or after it is cut, a new group of organisms begins to infect the wood. The tree begins to lose its defense system. The new group of microorganisms compete among themselves for the new space and energy. If the wood is to be used for products, some new problems start for the wood-inhabiting organisms: drying, preservatives. Some fungi and bacteria join forces with insects to invade the wood. The important point here is that many defects in the products had their origin in the tree: cracks, altered wood within boundaries, branch stubs, etc. The new group of microorganisms infect first the wood that was already altered in the tree. The altered wood will take up moisture faster than noninfected wood. The termites and ants follow the organisms that grow within boundaries set in the tree. Barrier zones separate as wood dries, small radial cracks become large radial cracks, and bacterial infections lead to honeycombing.

The wood products industries often think of a log as a uniform cylinder of wood, all sound. I have heard it from pole people many times that rot formed in the pole only because they did not get enough preservative into the right places. That may be partially so, because you can not get preservatives into a resin pocket, and the resin pocket was associated with a flush cut branch on a conifer. My point here is that many defects develop in wood products because the wood is already on the way to breakdown in the living tree, but the wood does not appear decayed. The electrical resistance methods for decay detection will show a decrease of electrical resistance in those areas. But, people say the wood is sound because they think it looks sound. Long before wood begins to breakdown the ionic state of the wood increases. Three separate research projects showed this. Yet, the industry still will not believe a machine; they want to see the decayed wood. By the time you see it, you can do nothing about it! Yet, industry wants a method for early detection of decay. It is a no win situation.

It is getting more and more difficult to get long lengths of high quality, defect-free lumber. Industries have focused on ways to splice and grind and chip and glue the pieces together to make a usable product. All of this work attests to the lower grade material that is available. Yes, we must use the low grade material, but we should also spend more time on growing more high quality material.

The only answer, as I see it, is to start some sorting: sites that will produce high quality wood from sites that will not, young trees that are defective now from young trees that have a good chance to produce high quality wood, etc. We have taken too much too fast from our forests, and we still want more and more. One way to stall this trend is to go back and start reexamining the tree. Let us learn more about the tree, and then base our decisions for management on tree biology.

The greatest advancement in all of humankind came when we understood the benefits of health—sanitation, diet, exercise. It is time to focus more on what makes trees healthy than on what makes them sick. Yes, we have sick trees in cities, parks, orchards, and forests, and it is getting more difficult to get high quality wood.

We know how to prune properly now. We know that some individual trees of a species do resist spread of defects better than other individuals. We have new electrical methods to help us to know more about trees. It is time to put all of these points together and make some much needed adjustments in the way we are managing our trees.

Back to poles. Let us look at some common defects in utility poles.

Figure 48-1

Figure 48-2

Figure 48-3

Figure 48-4

Sound well-treated southern yellow pine (Fig. 1). Decay in outer rim or shell of southern yellow pine (Fig. 2). Decay pockets beneath outer hard rim in cedar (Fig. 3). Central rot infested with ants in cedar (Fig. 4).

Figure 48-5

Figure 48-6

Figure 48-7

Figure 48-8

All samples are southern yellow pines (Figs. 5, 6, 7, 8). Wedge-shaped decay that followed blue stained wood (Fig. 5). Hollow that formed after the wedges were completely decayed (Fig. 6). Note that the fungi did not grow freely in the pole. Inbetween decay pattern that is associated with old branches and flush pruning (Fig. 7). Complete breakdown of wood in the inbetween pattern (Fig. 8).

Figure 48-9

Figure 48-10

Figure 48-11

Figure 48-12

All samples are southern yellow pines (Figs. 9, 10, 11, 12). Central core sound, outer wood decayed (Fig. 9). Complete decay of the pole (Fig. 10). Early stage of wood infection, lower left (Fig. 11). The section at left in figure 12 was below ground and the section at right was above ground. The center was sound (pointer). Note how abruptly the rot ends. The ants kept pace with the decayed wood.

A New Tree Biology

Figure 48-13

Figure 48-14

The double needle electrodes and the Shigometer can be used to rapidly test the outer rim of poles at ground-line. The needle electrodes are below a decayed area that is below an old borer inspection hole. The needle electrode can also be used to find softrot at the ground line. Electrical readings below 50 k ohms are suspect.

The 2 meters in figure 14 show the difference between sound wood at arrow 1, and sound-appearing, but infected wood, at arrow 2. The tips of the twisted-wire electrodes are at arrow point 1 for meter 1 (bottom), and at arrow point 2 for meter 2 (above). Sound wood had a reading above 500 k ohms while the sound-appearing wood beyond the column of brown rot had a reading of 190 k ohms.

Utility Poles and Wood Products

Figure 49-1

CHAPTER 49

The Future

Where do we go from here? I have touched on many points, but have not gone deeply into any of them. My aim was to introduce you to the tree webwork. This book will never teach you about tree biology. I can not teach you tree biology. The book and I can help guide you along the way. You must touch the trees. You must begin "thinking" like a tree.

I am optimistic about the future in spite of all the problems we have with trees. I see a new awareness and concern for our trees. I see new interests and pressures coming from many sources for help for our trees. This is all good. But, we, the keepers of the trees, must be ready to meet those new demands.

I see the day when we will have small electrical gadgets and sensors in trees like that shown in figure 1. It is receiving signals on the electrical changes in the tree. Such sensors could be attached to trees, and through telemetry, send signals to a computer that will unscramble the information and give a printout. I can see it now; the red light is on, the tree at the corner of Main and Elm has been infected, or someone has just made a flush cut. Why not? I believe it can be done. This will be the early warning system of the future. Indeed, the future holds many new and wonderful surprises.

Not to drift from being optimistic, but we must remember that what keeps you alive will eventually kill you. We must learn more about ways to buy more time. A time game is what all of this is about. Time for health.

We must understand the bend in the curve. That point where it gets too expensive or difficult to maintain any condition. So much is free. To get a little more, costs a little more. There comes a time when even a little more is just too costly.

I hope you will use this book as a guide to a better understanding about trees. Have doubts. Work to resolve your doubts. Touch trees.

A NEW TREE BIOLOGY

ADDENDUM

A NEW TREE BIOLOGY was written for people who care about trees. Information in the book comes mainly from research I did for 30 years with the help of many hard-working people.

Because the book is a conversation with you, I thought it would not be polite to keep interrupting our talk by citing literature. And, because the book gives information mainly about my research and research I did with others, I thought it would be bumptious to keep citing our publications.

But, you have asked for references to the research. I am including a list.

Many people have asked also for an index. I did not include an index in the first edition because I thought the dictionary would be a better way to get more information fast on important subjects. You agreed, in part. You still want an index. I am including one.

A very important point emerges. To survive, a system needs constant feedback and adjustments. I wrote the books in a way I thought would be easy to understand. The books were sold. You returned comments. I considered the comments. I made adjustments.

Any system that ignores feedback and making adjustments when needed will perish.

Adjustments are needed now in many tree care practices that hurt more than help trees. We must work together to bring about the adjustments before more trees perish!

NEW INFORMATION

Since the book was published I have learned that what is often called callus should be called woundwood. Here is a brief statement on callus and woundwood.

CALLUS AND WOUNDWOOD

Wounds are injuries to living tissues that usually are inflicted suddenly.

After wounds injure wood in living trees, a long series of physiological and anatomical events take place. The first response is an electrical one. Then chemical changes take place. Stored energy reserves in living parenchyma cells are converted through long biochemical pathways to substances that are inhibitory to most wood-inhabiting microorganisms. The substances form a boundary that resists the spread of microorganisms into the wood. The boundary also defends the liquid transport, energy storage, and mechanical support systems of the tree. The boundary is called the reaction zone.

When the cambial zone about the wound resumes growth, the newly formed cells differentiate to form a boundary that separates the wood present at the time of injury from new wood that will form after the boundary is completed. That separating boundary is called the barrier zone.

On the margin of the wound, the cambial zone produces large, undifferentiated, nonlignified, homogeneous cells called callus. As callus production continues, some of the cells begin to differentiate to form transport cells — vessels, tracheids — and fibers. When these cells become lignified, then we have woundwood. The woundwood expands as ribs or rolls about the wound because there is no pressure to confine the growing cells.

In 1925 Professor Dr. E. Küster at the Botanical Institute of the University of Halle wrote a large detailed book on pathological plant anatomy (Küster, E. 1925. Pathologische Pflanzenanatomie, Fisher, Jena, 558 pp.). In the book he describes in great detail the changes that take place after wounding. He makes strong points for the differences between callus and woundwood, and also woundcork. People interested in details should read the book. An English translation is available in the library of the United States Forest Service Laboratory at Hamden, Connecticut.

REFERENCES

The concepts in this book are based mostly on what I did for 30 years with the help of many hardworking colleagues. Listed here in chronological order are 200 of the 270 publications that discuss the research.

Research by many others helped to develop the concepts. The literature cited in my papers will give easy access to the works of these researchers. The papers by other researchers I consider most important are listed in publications 16, 24, 27, 32, 174, and 186.

PROFESSIONAL PAPERS AND PUBLICATIONS

1. Shigo, A.L. 1959. Fungi isolated from oak wilt trees and their effects on Ceratocystis fagacearum. Mycologia 50: 757-769.
2. Shigo, A.L. 1960. Parasitism of Gonatobotryum fuscum on species of Ceratocystis. Mycologia 53: 584-598.
3. Shigo, A.L. 1960. Mycoparasitism of Gonatobotryum fuscum and Piptocephalis xenophila. Trans. New York Academy of Science. 22: 365-372.
4. Shigo, A.L. and G. Yelenosky. 1960. Nematodes inhabit soils of forest and clear cut areas. USDA For. Serv. Res. Note 101. NE For. Expt. Stn. 4 p.
5. Shigo, A.L., C.D. Anderson, and H.L. Barnett. 1961. Effects of concentration of host nutrients on parasitism of Piptocephalis xenophila and P. virginia. Phytopathology 51: 616-620.
6. Shigo, A.L. 1962. Observations on the succession of fungi on hardwood pulpwood bolts. Plant Disease Reporter 46: 379-380.
7. Shigo, A.L. 1962. Another scale insect on beech. USDA For. Serv. Res. Pap. 168. NE For. Expt. Station. 13 p.
8. Shigo, A.L. 1963. Fungi associated with the discoloration around rot columns caused by Fomes igniarius. Plant Disease Reporter 47: 820-823.
9. Shigo, A.L. 1963. Ring shake associated with sapsucker injury. USDA For. Serv. Res. Pap. NE-8. NE For. Expt. Stn. 10 P.
10. Shigo, A.L. and G. Yelenosky. 1963. Fungus and insect injury to yellow birch seeds and seedlings. USDA For. Serv. Res. Pap. NE-11. NE For. Expt. Stn. 11 P.
11. Shigo, A.L. 1963. Beech bark disease. USDA For. Serv. Pest Leaflet 75. 8 p.
12. Shigo, A.L. 1964. The chainsaw: a valuable tool for research. Chain Saw Age 12: 8-9.
13. Shigo, A.L. 1964. Organism interactions in the beech bark disease. Phytopathology 54: 263-269.
14. Shigo, A.L. 1964. Collar crack of birch. USDA For. Serv. Res. Note. NE For. Expt. Stn. 4 p.
15. Shigo, A.L. 1964. A canker on red maple caused by fungi infecting wounds made by the red squirrel. Plant Disease Reporter 48: 794-796.
16. Shigo, A.L. 1965. The pattern of decay and discoloration in northern hardwoods. Phytopathology 55: 648-652.
17. Shigo, A.L. 1965. Decay and discoloration in sprout red maple. Phytopathology 55: 957-962.
18. Shigo, A.L. 1965. Patterns of defects associated with stem stubs of northern hardwoods. USDA For. Serv. Res. Pap. NE-34. NE For. Expt. Stn. 4 p.
19. Shigo, A.L. 1966. Organism interactions in decay and discoloration in beech, birch, and maple. USDA For. Serv. Res. Pap. NE-43. NE For. Expt. Stn. 43 p.

20. Shigo, A.L. 1966. Decay and discoloration following logging wounds on northern hardwoods. USDA For. Serv. Res. Pap. NE-47. NE For. Expt. Stn. 43 p.

21. Shigo, A.L. 1966. Decay and discoloration in northern hardwoods. A consideration of microorganisms and external signs. Proc. IUFRO Congress, Melbourne, Australia. 15 p.

22. Shigo, A.L. 1966. Organism interaction to decay and discoloration in beech, birch, and maple. Mat. und Org., Duncker and Humbolt, Berlin. 309-324.

23. Shigo, A.L. 1966. Defects in birch associated with injuries made by Xyloterinus politus Say. USDA For. Serv. Res. Note NE-49. NE For. Expt. Stn. 7 p.

24. Shigo, A.L. 1967. Successions of organisms in discoloration and decay of wood. Inter. Rev. For. Res. 2. Academic Press. 65 p.

25. Shigo, A.L. 1976. The early stages of discoloration and decay in living hardwoods in northeastern United States. A consideration of wound-initiated discoloration and heartwood. Proc. IUFRO Congress, Munich, West Germany. 17 p.

26. Shigo, A. L. and L. Kilham. 1968. Sapsuckers and Fomes ingiarius var. populinus. USDA For. Serv. Res. Note NE-84. NE For. Expt. Stn. 2 p.

27. Shigo, A. L. and E. M. Sharon. 1968. Discoloration and decay in hardwoods following inoculations with Hymenomycetes. Phytopathology 58: 1493-1498.

28. Shigo, A. L. 1969. The death and decay of trees. Natural History 78: 42-47.

29. Shigo, A. L. and E. vH. Larson. 1969. A photo guide to the patterns of discoloration and decay in northern hardwood trees. USDA For. Serv. Res. Pap. NE 127. NE For. Expt. Stn. 100 p.

30. Shigo, A. L. 1969. Diseases of birch. Birch Symposium Proc. 147-150. USDA For. Serv., NE For. Expt. Stn. 185 p.

31. Shigo, A. L. 1969. How the canker rot fungi, Poria obliqua and Polyporus glomeratus incite cankers. Phytopathology 59: 1164-1165.

32. Shigo, A. L. and E. M. Sharon. 1970. Mapping columns of discolored and decayed tissues in sugar maple, Acer saccharum Marsh. Phytopathology 60: 232-237.

33. Shigo, A. L. 1970. Growth of Polyporus glomeratus, Poria obliqua. Fomes igniarius, and Pholiota squarrose-adiposa in media amended with manganese, calcium, zinc, and iron. Mycologia 62: 604-607.

34. Shigo, A. L. 1970. An expanded concept of decay in living trees. In: Interaction of organisms in the process of decay of forest trees. Symp. under the chairmanship of Dr. A. L. Shigo, University of Laval, Quebec, Canada. Bull 13: 43 p.

35. Shigo, A. L. and F. M. Laing. 1970. Some effects of paraformaldehyde on wood surrounding tapholes in sugar maple trees. USDA For. Serv. Res. Pap. NE-161. NE For. Expt. Stn. 11 p.

36. Cosenza, B. J., M. McCreary, J. D. Buck, and A. L. Shigo. 1970. Bacteria associated with discolored and decayed tissues in beech, birch, and maple. Phytopathology 60: 1547-1551.

37. Shigo, A. L., J. Stankewich, and B. J. Cosenza. 1971. Clostridium sp. associated with discolored tissues in living oaks. Phytopathology 61: 122-123.

38. Friedrich, J. H., A. E. Rich, and A. L. Shigo. 1971. Diseases of fruits and seeds of northern hardwoods. Rhodora 73: 306-308.

39. Stankewich, J. P., B. J. Cosenza, and A. L. Shigo. 1971. Clostridium quercicolum sp. n., isolated from discolored tissues in living oak trees. Antonie van Leeuwenhoek 37: 299-302.

40. Shigo, A. L. 1971. The beech bark disease in northeastern United States. Proc. IUFRO Congress, Gainesville, Fl. 8 p.

41. Shigo, A. L. 1971. Shakes associated with wounds in trees. Proc. IUFRO Congress, Gainesvills, Fl. 5 p.

42. Shigo, A. L. 1971. Discoloration and decay in oaks. Oak Symp. Proc. USDA For. Serv., NE Forest Expt. Stn. 135-141.

43. Shigo, A. L. and C. L. Wilson. 1971. Are tree wound dressings beneficial? Arborist's News 36: 85-88.

44. Shigo, A. L. 1971. Successions of microorganisms and patterns of discoloration and decay following wounding in deciduous hardwoods. Second International Symposium on Plant Pathology Proceedings. Indian Agricultural Research Institute, New Delhi. 12 p. 175.

45. Shigo, A. L. 1972. Successions of microorganisms and patterns of discoloration and decay after wounding in red oak and white oak. Phytopathology 62: 256-259.

46. Shigo, A. L. 1972. Ring and ray shakes associated with wounds in trees. Holzforschung 26: 60-62.

47. Shigo, A. L. 1972. The beech bark disease today in Northeastern United States. J. Forestry 70: 286-289.

48. Skutt, H. R., A. L. Shigo, and R. A. Lessard. 1972. Detection of discolored and decayed wood in living trees using a pulsed electric current. Can. J. For. Res. 2: 54-56.

49. Hepting, G. H. and A. L. Shigo. 1972. Difference in decay rate following fire between oaks in North Carolina and Maine. Plant Disease Reporter. 56: 406-407.

50. Shigo, A. L. and C. L. Wilson. 1972. Discoloration associated with wounds one year after application of wound dressings. Arborist's News 37: 121-124.

51. Tatter, T. A., A. L. Shigo, and T. Chase. 1972. Relationship between degree of resistance to pulsed electric current and wood in progressive stages of discoloration and decay in living trees. Can. J. For. Res. 2: 236-243.

52. Rier, J. P. and A. L. Shigo. 1972. Some changes in red maple, Acer rubrum, tissues within 34 days after wounding in July. Can. J. Bot. 50: 1783-1784.

53. Shigo, A. L. 1973. Insect and disease control; forest fertilization relations. Proc. For. Symposium. USDA Tech. Rept. NE-3. 117-121.

54. Shigo, A. L. and W. E. Hillis. 1973. Heartwood, discolored wood, and microorganisms in living trees. Ann. Rev. Phytopathology 11: 197-222.

55. Shortle, W. C. and A. L. Shigo. 1973. Concentrations of manganese and microorganisms in discolored and decayed wood in sugar maple. Can. J. For. Res. 3: 354-358.

56. Filip, G. M., A. L. Shigo, M. C. Hoyle, and A. E. Rich. 1973. Effect of fertilizer salt accumulation and low relative humidity on development of stem lesions on yellow birch seedlings. Plant Disease Reporter. 57: 499.

57. Wilson, C. L. and A. L. Shigo. 1973. Dispelling myths in arboriculture today. Amer. Nurseryman 127: 24-28.

58. Shigo, A. L., W. B. Leak, and S. Filip. 1973. Sugar maple borer injury in four hardwood stands in New Hampshire. Can. J. For. Res. 3: 512-515.

59. Shigo, A. L. 1973. A tree hurts too. USDA For. Serv. NE-Inf. 16. 28 p.

60. Shigo, A. L. 1974. Effects of manganese, calcium, zinc, and iron on growth and pigmentation of Trichocladium canadense, Phialophora melinii, Hypoxylon rubiginosum, Daldinia concentrica, and Cystopora decipiens. Mycologia 66: 339-341.

61. Shigo, A. L. 1974. Relative abilities of Phialophora melinii, Fomes connatus, and F. igniarius to invade freshly wounded tissues of Acer rubrum. Phytopathology 64: 708-710.

62. Safford, L. O., A. L. Shigo, and M. Ashley. 1974. Concentrations of cations in discolored and decayed wood in red maple. Can. J. For. Res. 4: 435-440.

63. Sharon, E. M. and A. L. Shigo. 1974. A method for studying the relationship of wounding and microorganisms to the discoloration process in sugar maple. Can. J. For. Res. 4: 146-148.

64. Shigo, A. L. and A. Shigo. 1974. Detection of discoloration and decay in living trees and utility poles. USDA Res. Paper NE-294. 11 p.

65. Shigo, A. L. 1974. A new look at decay. Northern Logger 23: 10-11.

66. Shigo, A. L. 1974. Biology of decay and wood quality. In Biological Transformation of Wood by Microorganisms. Walter Liese, Ed., Proc. Symposium. Wood Products Pathology. Springer-Verlag Co., Berlin, Heidelberg, New York 1975. 1-15.

67. McGinnes, E. A. and A. L. Shigo. 1975. Use of an electronic technique for detection of discoloration and decay and injury associated with ring shake in black walnut. For. Prod. Journal 25: 30-32.

68. McGinnes, E. A. and A. L. Shigo. 1975. Effects of wounds on heartwood formation in white oak. Wood and Fiber 5: 327-331.

69. Pottle, H. W. and A. L. Shigo. 1975. Treatment of wounds on Acer rubrum with Trichoderma viride. Eur. J. For. Pathol. 5: 274-279.

70. Shigo, A. L. 1975. Wounds: Number one problem of city trees. J. For. Proc. 1974 SAF Meeting in New York. 4 p.

71. Shigo, A. L. and P. Berry. 1975. A new tool for detection of decay associated with Fomes annosus in Pinus resinosa. Plant Disease Reporter. 59: 739-742.

72. Shigo, A. L. 1975. Compartmentalization of decay associated with Fomes annosus in trunks of Pinus resinosa. Phytopathology 65: 1038-1039.

73. Shigo, A. L. 1975. Microorganisms associated with wounds inflicted during winter, summer, and fall in Acer rubrum, Betula papyrifera, Fagus grandifolia, and Quercus rubra. Phytopathology 66: 559-563.
74. Shigo, A. L. 1975. Heartwood and discolored wood. Northern Logger 24: 28-29.
75. Shigo, A. L. 1975. Wood decay. McGraw-Hill Book Co. Yearbook of Science and Technology. 417-419.
76. Shigo, A. L. and D. M. Carroll. 1975. Common tree families. Reader's Digest September issue. 8 p.
77. Shigo, A. L. 1975. A new look at decay in trees. New Horizons Hortic. Res. Instit. 10-12.
78. Shigo. A. L. and E. vH. Larson. 1975. Anatomy of a wound: How city trees react—how they can be helped. Weeds, Trees, and Turf 14: 20-22.
79. Shigo, A. L. 1975. New ideas in tree care. J. Arboric. 1: 234-237.
80. Shigo, A. L. 1975. Compartmentalization of discolored and decayed wood in trees. Mat. und Org. Berlin, Belheft 3: 221-226.
81. Shigo, A. L., E. Kerr, G. Lloyd, J. Riddle, and H. Marx. 1975. A guide to help package research for application. USDA For. Serv. 12 p.
82. Shigo, A. L. and R. J. Campana. 1976. Forest disease priorities in the Northeast. NE For. Comm. NE For. Expt. Stn. Upper Darby, PA 37 p.
83. Shigo, A. L. 1976. Decay: A problem in young and old trees. Amer. Nurseryman 144: 24-25.
84. Shigo, A. L. 1976. Rx for wounded trees. USDA For. Serv. Agric. Inf. Bull. 387. 37 p.
85. Shigo, A. L. 1976. Mineral stain. Northern Logger 24: 18-19.
86. Garrett, P. W., A. L. Shigo, and J. Carter. 1976. Variation in diameter of central columns of discoloration in six hybrid poplar clones. Can. J. For. Res. 6: 475-477.
87. Smith, D. E., A. L. Shigo, L. O. Safford, and R. Blanchard. 1976. Resistances to a pulsed electric current reveal differences between nonreleased, released, and released-fertilized paper birch trees. For. Sci. 22: 471-472.
88. Solomon, D. and A. L. Shigo. 1976. Discoloration and decay associated with pruning wounds on yellow birch. For. Sci. 22: 391-392.
89. Shigo, A. L. 1976. Communication of knowledge and needs between researcher and arboriculturist. J. Arboric. 2: 206-208.
90. Shigo, A. L. and C. L. Wilson. 1977. Wound dressings on red maple and American elm: Effectiveness after 5 years. J. Arboric. 3: 81-87.
91. Shigo, A. L. 1977. Injection wounds in elm. National Arborist Assoc. Symposium No. 1. The Current State of the Art of Dutch elm disease control. Washington, DC November 9-10. 1977.
92. Shigo, A. L., W. C. Shortle, and P. W. Garrett. 1977. Compartmentalization of discolored wood and decayed wood associated with injection-type wounds in hybrid poplar. J. Arboric. 3: 114-118.
93. Shigo, A. L., W. C. Shortle, and P. W. Garrett. 1977. Genetic control suggested in compartmentalization of discolored wood associated with tree wounds. For. Sci. 23: 179-182.
94. Shortle, W. C., A. L. Shigo, P. Berry, and J. Abusamra. 1977. Electrical resistance in tree cambium zone: Relationship to rates of growth and wound closure. For Sci. 23: 326-329.
95. Pottle, H. W., A. L. Shigo, and R. O. Blanchard. 1977. Biological control of wound hymenomycetes by Trichoderma harzianum. Plant Disease Reporter. 61: 687-690.
96. Shigo, A. L. 1977. Phialophora melinii: Effects of inoculations in wounded red maple. Phytopathology 67: 1333-1337.
97. Shigo, A. L. 1977. Superior tree production fights tree wound fatalities. Amer. Nurseryman 12: 10-11.
98. Shigo, A. L. 1977. A new look at tree care. Arboric. Jrnl. 3: 157-164.
99. Shigo, A. L., W. C. Shortle, and J. Ochrymowych. 1977. Shigometer method for detection of active decay at groundline in utility poles. Manual For. Serv. Gen. Tech. Rept. NE-35.
100. Shigo, A. L., N. Rogers, E. A. McGinnes, and D. Funk. 1978. Black walnut strip mine spoils: Some observations 25 years after pruning. USDA For. Serv. Res. Pap. NE-393. 14 p.
101. Shigo, A. L. and H. Marx. 1977. CODIT (Compartmentalization of decay in trees). Agric. Inf. Bull. 405. 73 p.
102. Shigo, A. L. 1977. Communication of knowledge and needs between forest researchers and practicing foresters. Northern Logger and Timber Processor 25: 7-8.

103. Shigo, A. L. and R. Campana. 1977. Discolored and decayed wood associated with injection wounds in American elm. J. Arboric. 3: 230-235.
104. Shigo, A. L. and W. C. Shortle. 1977. "New" ideas in tree care. J. Arboric. 3: 1-6.
105. Shigo, A. L., W. E. Money, and D. Dodds. 1977. Some internal effects of Mauget tree injections. J. Arboric. 3: 213-220.
106. Felix, R. and A. L. Shigo. 1977. Rots and rods. J. Arboric. 3: 187-190.
107. McGinnes, E. A., J. E. Phelps. P. S. Szopa, and A. L. Shigo. 1977. Wood anatomy after tree injury -A pictorial study. University of Missouri, Columbia Res. Bull. 1025. 35 p.
108. Blanchard, R., D. Smith, A. Shigo, and L. Safford. 1978. Effects of soil applied potassium on cation distribution around wounds in red maple. Can: J. For. Res. 8: 228-231.
109. Shigo, A. L. 1978. Tree decay: Time to expand the concept. IUFRO Proc. Kassell, Germany. 298-305.
110. Shortle, W. C., A. L. Shigo, and J. Ochrymowych. 1978. Patterns of resistance to a pulsed electric current in sound and decayed utility poles. For. Prod. Jrnl. 28: 48-51.
111. Walters, R. and A. L. Shigo. 1978. Discoloration and decay associated with paraformaldehyde treated tapholes in sugar maple. Can. J. For. Res. 8: 54-60.
112. Garrett, P. W. and A. L. Shigo. 1978. Selecting trees for their response to wounding. METRIA 1: 69-72.
113. Shortle, W. C. and A. L. Shigo. 1978. Effect of plastic wrap on wound closure and internal compartmentalization of discolored and decayed wood in red maple. Plant Disease Reporter. 62: 999-1002.
114. Collins, W. M., A. L. Shigo, and T. P. McGrail. 1978. RSV-induced tumors in chickens: resistance to a pulsed current in terminal and non-terminal types. Poultry Sci. 57: 1478-1481.
115. Shigo, A. L. 1978. Dealing with decay factors in our urban forests. Weeds, Trees, and Turf 17: 14-18.
116. Schmitt, D., P. Garrett, and A. Shigo. 1978. Decay resistant hardwoods? You bet! Northern Logger and Timber Processor 27: 20-21, 30-31.
117. Walters, R. S., and A. L. Shigo. 1978. Tapholes in sugar maples. What happens in a tree. For. Serv. Gen. Tech. Rept. NE-47. 12 p. illus.
118. Shigo, A. L., A. E. McGinnes, D. Funk, and N. Rogers. 1979. Internal defects associated with pruned and nonpruned branch stubs in black walnut. For. Serv. Res. Pap. NE-440. 27 p.
119. Shigo, A. L. 1979. Tree decay: An expanded concept. Agric. Bull. 419. 73 p.
120. Shigo, A. L. 1979. How to minimize the injury caused by injection wounds in trees. Proc. of Symp. on Systemic Chemical Treatments in tree culture. October 9-11, 1978. Michigan State Univ., East Lansing, MI.
121. Mulhern, J., W. Shortle, and A. L. Shigo. 1979. Barrier zones in red maple: An optical and scanning microscope examination. For. Sci. 25: 311-316.
122. Shigo, A. L. 1979. Decay resistant trees. Proc. of the 26th Northeastern Tree Improvement Conf. 64-72.
123. Garrett, P. W., W. K. Randall, A. L. Shigo, and W. C. Shortle. 1979. Inheritance of compartmentalization of wounds in sweetgum (Liquidambar styraciflua L.) and Eastern cottonwood (Populus deltoides Bartr.). For. Serv. Res. Pap. NE-443. 4 p.
124. Eckstein, D., W. Liese, and A. L. Shigo. 1979. Relationship of wood structure to compartmentalization of discolored wood in hybrid poplar. Can. J. For. Res. 9: 205-210.
125. Davis, W., A. L. Shigo, and R. Weyrick. 1979. Seasonal changes in electrical resistance of inner bark in red oak, red maple, and eastern white pine. For. Sci. 25: 282-286.
126. Shigo, A. L. and Walter C. Shortle. 1979. Compartmentalization of discolored wood in heartwood of red oak. Phytopathology 69: 710-711.
127. Shigo, A. L. 1979. Compartmentalization of decay associated with Heterobasidion annosum in roots of Pinus resinosa. Eur. J. For. Pathol. 9: 341-347.
128. Shigo, A. L. 1979. Science communication: Process and problems. Proc. Nat'l. Agric. Sci. Information Conf. Ames, IA October 22-26, 1979. 4-11.
129. Merrill, W. and A. L. Shigo. 1979. An expanded concept of tree decay. Phytopathology 69. 1158-1161.
130. Shigo, A. L. 1979. Patterns of discolored and decayed wood in black walnut. USDA For. Serv. Gen. Tech. Rept. NC-52. 88-93. Walnut insect and diseases. Workshop Proc.

131. Tippett, J. and A. L. Shigo. 1980. Barrier zone anatomy in red pine roots invaded by Heterobasidion annosum. Can. J. For. Res. 10: 224-232.

132. Shigo, A. L., R. Campana, F. Hyland, and J. Andersen. 1980. Anatomy of injected elms to control Dutch elm disease. J. Arboric. 6: 96-100.

133. Shigo, A. L. and F. G. Hawksworth. 1980. A dwarf mistletoe on red spruce in New Hampshire. For. Notes. Fall 1980.

134. Hawksworth, F. and A. L. Shigo. 1980. Dwarf mistletoe on red spruce in the White Mountains of New Hampshire. Plant Disease Reporter. 64: 880-882.

135. Shigo, A. L. 1980. Branches. J. Arboric. 6: 300-304.

136. Shigo, A. L. and R. Felix. 1980. Cabling and bracing. J. Arboric. 6: 5-9.

137. Bauch, J., A. L. Shigo, and M. Starck. 1980. Wound effects in the xylem of Acer and Betula species. Holzforschung 34: 153-160.

138. Owens, C. W., W. C. Shortle, and A. L. Shigo. 1980. Preliminary evaluation of Silicon Tetrachloride as a wood preservative. Holzforschung 34: 223-225.

139. Davis, W., W. C. Shortle, and A. L. Shigo. 1980. A potential hazard rating system for fir stands infested with budworm using cambial electrical resistance. Can. J. For. Res. 10: 541-544.

140. Shigo, A. L. 1981. To paint or not to paint. In: Handbook on Pruning. Brooklyn Botanical Gardens Plants and Gardens. Vol. 37: 20-22.

141. Shigo, A. L. 1981. Proper pruning of tree branches. In: The Garden. Vol. 106: 471-473.

142. Tippett, J. T. and A. L. Shigo. 1981. Barriers to decay in conifer roots. Eur. J. For. Pathol. 11: 51-59.

143. Mulhern, J. E., B. M. Stavish, S. L. Witkowski, W. C. Shortle, and A. L. Shigo. 1981. Voltage changes along geranium petioles after leaf blade excision. J. Experimental Bot. 22: 573-579.

144. Green, D., W. C. Shortle, and A. L. Shigo. 1981. Compartmentalization of discolored and decayed wood in red maple branch stubs. For. Sci. 27: 519-522.

145. Armstrong, J. E., A. L. Shigo, D. T. Funk, E. A. McGinnes, and D. E. Smith. 1981. A macroscopic and microscopic study of compartmentalization and wound closure after mechanical wounding of black walnut trees. Wood and Fiber 13: 275-291.

146. Shigo, A. L. and J. T. Tippett. 1981. Compartmemtalization of decayed wood associated with Armillaria mellea in several tree species. For. Serv. Res. Pap. NE-488. 20 p.

147. Ostrofsky, A. and A. L. Shigo. 1981. A myxomycete isolated from discolored wood of living red maple. Mycologia 73: 997-1000.

148. Butin, H. and A. L. Shigo. 1981. Radial shakes and "frost cracks" in living oak trees. For. Serv. Res. Pap. NE-478. 21 p.

149. Tippett, J. T. and A. L. Shigo. 1981. Barrier zone formation: A mechanism of tree defense against vascular pathogens. IAWA Bull. Vol.2: 163-168.

150. Leben, C., A. L. Shigo, and T. H. Hall. 1982. A method for evaluating tree wound treatment. Can. J. For. Res.12: 115-117.

151. Shigo, A. L. 1982. Tree health. J. Arboric. 8: 311-316.

152. Shigo, A. L. 1982. A pictorial primer for proper pruning. For. Notes. Spring issue. 18-21.

153. Shigo, A. L. 1982. Trees: How they build up and break down. In: Trees. 57-69. Published by Men of the Trees, Crawley, Sussex, England.

154. Shigo, A. L. Wood decay: In: Encyclopedia of Science and Technology. 5th Ed. New York. McGraw-Hill. 680-683.

155. Shigo, A. L. 1980. Trees resistant to spread of decay associated with wounds. In: Proc. of Third International Workshop on the Genetics of Host Parasite Interactions in Forestry; Wageningen, The Netherlands. September 14-21, 1980.

156. Shigo, A. L. and K. Dudzik. 1982. Chestnut blight: Defense reactions. Proc. of the USDA For. Serv. Am. Chestnut Cooperators Meeting. January 5-7, 1982. Morgantown, West Virginia.

157. Shigo, A. L. 1982. Tree decay in our urban forests: What can be done about it? Plant Disease 66: 763-768.

158. Shigo, A. L. and C. L. Wilson. 1982. Wounds in peach trees. Plant Disease 66: 895-897.

159. Shigo, A. L. 1982. Dutch elm disease: A CODIT perspective. Proc. Dutch elm disease Symp. and Workshop. October 5-9, 1981. Winnipeg, Manitoba, Canada. 151-168.

160. Shigo, A. L. 1982. Injections and injury. Proc. Dutch elm disease Symp. and Workshop. October 5-9, 1981. Winnipeg, Manitoba, Canada. 483-485.

161. Tippett, J. T., A. L. Bogle, and A. L. Shigo. 1983. Response to balsam fir and hemlock roots to injuries. Eur. J. For. Pathol. 2: 357-364.

162. Shigo, A. L. 1983. Targets for proper tree care. J. Arboric. 9: 285-294.

163. Shigo, A. L. and W. C. Shortle. 1983. Wound dressings: Results of studies over 13 years. J. Arboric. 9: 317-329.

164. Shigo, A. L. 1982. Tree decay. Proc. of Korea-USA Joint Seminar on Forest Diseases and Insect Pests. September 22-30, 1982. 188-203.

165. Shigo, A. L., D. Dorn, and H. C. Lee. 1983. Selections of maple and birch trees with high resistance to spread of decay associated with wounds. Proc. of NE Forest Tree Improvement Conf. July 7-9, 1983. University of New Hampshire. 110-117.

166. Shigo, A. L. and K. Roy. 1983. Violin woods: A new look. University of New Hampshire, Durham, NH. 67 p.

167. Shigo, A. L. 1983. The relationship between better trees and better wood products from spruce and fir. Proc. of Conference on utilization technology. August 17-19, 1983. Orono, Maine.

168. Shigo, A. L. 1983. Tree defects: A photo guide. USDA For. Service Gen. Tech. Report. NE-82. 167 p.

169. Shigo, A. L. 1984. Tree decay and pruning. Arboric. Jrnl. 8: 1-12.

170. Shigo, A. L. 1984. The right treatments for troubled trees. Amer. Forests, February issue. 13-16.

171. Rademacher, P., J. Bauch, and A. L. Shigo. 1984. Characteristics of xylem formed after wounding in Acer, Betula, and Fagus. IAWA Bull. n.s. 5(2): 141-151.

172. Ostrofsky, A. and A. L. Shigo. 1984. Relationship between canker size and wood starch in American chestnut. Eur. J. For. Pathol. 14: 65-68.

173. Shigo, A. L. 1984. Trees and discolored wood. In: Development and characteristics of discolored wood. Reprinted from IAWA Bull. 5(2):99. Edited by J. Bauch and P. Baas.

174. Shigo, A. L. 1984. Compartmentalization: A conceptual framework for understanding how trees grow and defend themselves. Ann. Rev. Phytopathology 22: 189-214.

175. Shigo, A. L. 1984. How to assess the defect status of a stand. Northern Journal of Applied Forestry 1(3): 41-49.

176. Peters, M., P. Ossenbruggen, and A. L. Shigo. 1984. Cracking and failure behavior models of defective balsam fir trees. Holzforschung 39: 125-135.

177. Shigo, A. L. 1984. Tree defects: Cluster effect. Northern Journal of Applied Forestry 1(3): 41-49.

178. Shigo, A. L. 1984. Tree survival after injury and infection. Eighth North American Forest Biology Workshop. July 30 - August 1, 1984. Utah State University, Logan, UT 11-24.

179. Shigo, A. L. 1984. Wood problems start in the living tree. Forest Notes, Fall:No. 158: 20-22.

180. Shigo, A. L. 1984. Root rots in trees. Proc. of the Sixth International Conf. on Root and Butt Rots of Forest Trees. G. A. Kile, ed. IUFRO Working Party, CSIRO, Melbourne, Australia. 305-312.

181. Andersen, J. L., R. J. Campana, A. L. Shigo, and W. C. Shortle. 1985. Wound response of Ulmus americana L. Results of chemical injection in attempts to control Dutch elm disease. J. Arboric. 11(5): 137-142.

182. DeGraaf, R. M. and A. L. Shigo. 1985. Managing cavity trees for wildlife in the Northeast. USDA For. Serv. Gen. Tech. Rep. NE-101. 21 p.

183. Ossenbruggen, P. J., M. Peters, and A. L. Shigo. 1985. Potential failure of a decayed tree under wind loading. Wood and Fiber 18 (1): 39-48.

184. Shigo, A. L. 1985. Stress and death of trees. Society of American Foresters Region VI Technical Conference. USDA For. Serv. Gen. Tech. Rep. NE-99: 31-38.

185. Shigo, A. L. 1985. Compartmentalization of decay in trees. Scientific American 252(4): 96-103.

186. Shigo, A. L. 1985. How tree branches are attached to trunks. Can. J. Bot. 63: 1391-1401.

187. Shigo, A. L. 1985. How trees survive after injury and infection. Proc. of the 1984 Stone Fruit Tree Decline Workshop. Appalachian Fruit Research Station, Kearneysville, WV.

188. Shigo, A. L. and K. R. Dudzik. 1985. Response of uninjured cambium to xylem injury. Wood Science and Technology 19: 6 p.

189. Shigo, A. L. and Walter C. Shortle. 1985. Shigometry — A Reference Guide. USDA, For. Serv. Agric. Handbook No. 646, 48 p.

190. Tower, L., A. L. Shigo, and E. Brennan. 1985. The short-term effect of simulated acidic rainfall on the formation of discolored wood in Acer rubrum. J. Arboric. 11(7): 197-199.

191. Shigo, A. L. 1985. Wounded forests, starving trees. J. Forestry 83: 668-673.

192. Shigo, A. L. 1986. Tree decay. Int. J. Tropical Plant diseases 4: 95-121.

193. Shigo, A. L. 1986. Journey to the center of a tree. American Forests 92: 18-22, 46-47.

194. Shigo, A., G. F. Gregory, R. J. Campana, K. R. Dudzik, and D. M. Zimel. 1986. Patterns of starch reserves in healthy and diseased American elms. Can. J. For. Res. 16: 204-210.

195. Shigo, A. L. 1986. A New Tree Biology. Shigo and Trees, Associates, Durham, New Hampshire. 595 p.

196. Shigo, A. L. 1986. A New Tree Biology Dictionary. Shigo and Trees, Associates, Durham, New Hampshire. 132 p.

197. Shigo, A. L., K. Vollbrecht, and N. Hvass. 1987. Tree Biology and Tree Care. SITAS - Skovvej 56, Ballerup, Denmark, (published also in German, Swedish, Danish, Dutch, French, and Italian).

198. Shigo, A. L. 1987. New tree health. Shigo and Trees, Associates, Durham, New Hampshire. 10 p. (Published in French, Italian, Dutch, and Spanish).

199. Shigo, A. L. 1988. A new tree biology. Annual Journal, Royal New Zealand Institute of Horticulture 15: 51-57.

200. Shigo, A. L. 1988. Branch failures: a closer look at crack drying. J. Arboric. 14: (in press).

INDEX

A New Tree Biology

Index

A New Tree Biology

TREE EDUCATIONAL MATERIALS
BY
Dr. Alex L. Shigo

ORDER
CODE   **BOOKS**

A.   **A NEW TREE BIOLOGY** — hard cover, 636 pages and **DICTIONARY** soft cover, 144 pages. (Sold only as a set).

C.   **TREE BASICS** —soft cover, 40 pages, what every person needs to know about trees.

H.   **TREE PRUNING** — hard cover, 127 full-color photos, 192 pages.

M   **MODERN ABORICULTURE** — hard cover, 311 diagrams, 16 photos, 440 pages.

F.   **ABORICULTURA MODERNA COMPENDIO** —Soft cover, 160 pages, Spanish.

R.   **100 TREE MYTHS** — soft cover, 80 pages, 100 myths, 26 near myths.

S.   **TREE ANATOMY** — Hard cover, 104 pages, micro views, 94 large full-color photos.

VIDEO

Q.   **A CLOSER LOOK AT TREES** — 2 hour video under a low power microscope.

SLIDE PACKAGES

J.   **TREE PRUNING slides** — 125 color slides from the book, with script.

N.   **MODERN ABORICULTURE slides** — 120 new color slides and script.

T.   **TREE ANATOMY, BELOW GROUND** — 80 color slides, script, and audio tape.

U.   **TREE ANATOMY, ABOVE GROUND** — 80 color slides, script, and audio tape.

BOOKLETS, BROCHURES, PAMPHLETS and POSTERS

D.   **NEW TREE HEALTH** — 12 page full color booklet.

L.   **CARING FOR YOUNG TREES** — 12 panel color brochure.

K.   **PRUNING TREES NEAR ELECTRIC UTILITY LINES** — a field pocket guide.

O.   **5 MINUTE TREE CARE** — 8 page booklet, red and green, diagrams.

E.   **TREE HAZARDS** — 10 panel fold-out brochure, 13 diagrams.

G.   **TOUCH TREES poster** — A fold-out green ball is the tree crown.

For Orders and Information, Contact:

SHIGO AND TREES, ASSOCIATES

P. O. BOX 769, DURHAM, NH 03824-0769 U.S.A.
PHONE 603-868-7459   FAX 603-868-1045